Mobilities

D1549161

Mobilities

John Urry

polity

First published in 2007 by Polity Press

Polity Press
65 Bridge Street
Cambridge CB2 1UR, UK.

Polity Press
350 Main Street
Malden, MA 02148, USA

ISBN-13: 978-07456-3418-0
ISBN-13: 978-07456-3419-7 (pb)

A catalogue record for this book is available from the British Library.

Typeset in 10.5 on 12 pt Times
by SNP Best-set Typesetter Ltd, Hong Kong
Printed and bound in Great Britain by MPG Books Ltd, Bodmin, Cornwall

The publisher has used its best endeavours to ensure that the URLs for external websites referred to in this book are correct and active at the time of going to press. However, the publisher has no responsibility for the websites and can make no guarantee that a site will remain live or that the content is or will remain appropriate.

Every effort has been made to trace all copyright holders, but if any have been inadvertently overlooked the publishers will be pleased to include any necessary credits in any subsequent reprint or edition.

For further information on Polity, visit our website: www.polity.co.uk

P. 17 excerpt from SELECTED PROSE 1909-1965, by Ezra Pound, copyright © 1973 by The Estate of Ezra Pound. Reprinted by permission of New Directions Publishing Corp; p. 112 excerpt from THE DIARY OF VIRGINIA WOOLF, Volume III: 1925-1930 by Virginia Woolf, copyright © 1980 by Quentin Bell and Angelica Garnett, reprinted by permission of Harcourt,Inc.; p. 211 John Guare *Six Degrees of Separation* 1999. Small Worlds. Princeton University Press; p. 271 excerpt from CRASH by J.G. Ballard. Copyright © 1973 by J.G. Ballard. Reprinted by permission of Farrar, Straus and Giroux, LLC.

Contents

Preface

I am very grateful for suggestions and discussions with many 'mobile' colleagues including Pete Adey, Alex Arellano, Matilde Córdoba Azcárate, François Ascher, Kay Axhausen, Jørgen-Ole Baerenholdt, Michael Bull, Peter Burns, Monika Buscher Javier Caletrio, Noel Cass, David Chalcraft, Anne Cronin, Tim Cresswell, Monica Degen, Saolo Cwerner, Tim Dant, Bülent Diken, Kingsley Dennis, Pennie Drinkall, Rosaleen Duffy, Mike Featherstone, Annemarie Fortier, Margaret Grieco, Michael Haldrup, Kevin Hannam, David Holley, Dave Horton, Michael Hulme, Ryuichi Kitamura, Juliet Jain, Caren Kaplan, Vincent Kaufmann, Sven Kesselring, Tomas Kvasnicka, Jonas Larsen, Scott Lash, Eric Laurier, John Law, Christian Licoppe, Glenn Lyons, Adrian Mackenzie, Will Medd, Pete Merriman, Jennie Germann Molz, Greg Noble, Peter Peters, Colin Pooley, Mary Rose, Andrew Sayer, Mimi Sheller, Elizabeth Shove, Bron Szerszynski, Nigel Thrift, John Trevitt, Amy Urry, Tom Urry, Soile Veijola, Ginette Verstraete, Sylvia Walby and Laura Watts.

Some material in this book is drawn from recent research grants. I am grateful to the funders and especially to the researchers/collaborators on these projects although none are responsible for the arguments expressed here. Some work presented here has or will appear in publications generated by these various projects. These grants include the EPSRC funding of the Travel Time Use in the Information Age Project conducted with the Transport and Society Centre at the University of the West of England; the Department for Transport funding of the CHIME and New Horizons Social Networks and Future Mobilities projects; the Department for Trade and Industry

Foresight Programme on Intelligent Information Systems and Transport; the Forestry Commission funding of the Growing Places Project with Jake Morris and Marcus Sangster; various funded research collaborations with colleagues in the Geography Dept at Roskilde University; and the COSMOBILITIES Network centred in Munich.

Lancaster

Still feel the need of physical location ?!

Part 1

Mobile Worlds

1

Mobilizing Social Life

For Move You Must! 'Tis now the rage, the law and fashion of our age

(Samuel Taylor Coleridge, quoted Buzard 1993: 84)

On the Move

It sometimes seems as if all the world is on the move (see Sheller, Urry 2006b; Hannam, Sheller, Urry 2006, for further elaboration). The early retired, international students, terrorists, members of diasporas, holidaymakers, business people, slaves, sports stars, asylum seekers, refugees, backpackers, commuters, young mobile professionals, prostitutes – these and many others – seem to find the contemporary world is their oyster or at least their destiny. Criss-crossing the globe are the routeways of these many groups intermittently encountering one another in transportation and communication hubs, searching out in real and electronic databases the next coach, message, plane, back of lorry, text, bus, lift, ferry, train, car, web site, wifi hot spot and so on.

The scale of this travelling is immense. It is predicted that by 2010 there will be at least one billion legal international arrivals each year (compared with 25 million in 1950); there are four million air passengers each day; at any one time 360,000 passengers are at any time in flight *above* the United States, equivalent to a substantial city; 31 million refugees roam the globe (Papastergiadis 2000: 10, 41, 54); and there were 552m cars in 1998 with a projected 730m in 2020, equivalent to one for every 8.6 people (Geffen, Dooley, Kim 2003). In 1800, people in the United States travelled on average 50 metres a day – they now travel 50 kilometres a day (Buchanan 2002: 121; Axhausen 2002; Root 2000). Today world citizens move 23 billion kilometres; by 2050 it is predicted that that figure will have increased fourfold to 106 billion (Schafer, Victor 2000: 171).

However, people do not spend more time traveling, since this appears to have remained more or less constant at around one hour or so per day, albeit with substantial variation within any society (Lyons, Urry 2005; but see Van Wee, Rietveld, Meurs 2006). People also do not necessarily seem to make more journeys; in the UK in recent years the number of domestic journeys per year remains at around 1,000 (DTLR 2001: Table 2.1; 3.1). But what is crucial is that people are travelling further and faster, if not more often or spending more time actually 'on the road' (see Pooley, Turnbull, Adams 2005, for the only detailed historical research on this). And given the spread of various communications such as the post, fax, the internet, fixed line phones, mobiles, mobile computing and so on, whose uses have all *increased* in recent decades, this book asks why do people physically travel, what are its uses, pleasures and pains and what social and physical ramifications does such movement possess.

Globally, travel and tourism constitute the largest industry in the world, worth $6.5 trillion and directly and indirectly accounting for 8.7 per cent of world employment and 10.3 per cent of world GDP (World Travel and Tourism Council 2006). And this mobility affects almost everywhere, with the World Tourism Organization publishing travel statistics for over 200 countries, with most sending and also receiving significant numbers of visitors (www.world-tourism.org/facts/metho.html: accessed 9.9.05).

Schivelbusch overall concludes that for: 'the twentieth-century tourist, the world has become one large department store of countrysides and cities', although of course most people in the world can only dream of voluntarily sampling that department store on a regular basis (1986: 197). This pattern of mainly but not entirely voluntary travelling is the largest ever-peaceful movement of people across borders. Such movement shows little sign of *substantially* abating in the longer term even with September 11th, SARS, Bali, Madrid and London bombings and other global catastrophes. Being physically mobile has become for both rich and even for some poor a 'way of life' across the globe. Pico Iyer identifies: 'an entirely new breed of people, a transcontinental tribe of wanderers . . . the transit loungers, forever heading to the departure gate' (undated: 6; and see 2000).

And materials too are on the move, often carried by these moving bodies whether openly, clandestinely, or inadvertently. Also the multinational sourcing of different components of manufactured products involves just-in-time delivery from around the world. The 'cosmopolitanization' of taste means that consumers in the 'north' expect fresh materials from around the world 'air-freighted' to their table, while consumers in the 'south' often find roundabout ways to access consumer goods from the north – carried by small-scale informal importers, packed into containers for relatives 'back home', or smuggled. And more generally there are massive flows of illegal if valuable materials, drugs, guns, cigarettes, alcohol, and counterfeit and pirated products. Mass media too has a materiality as videos, DVDs, radios, televisions, camcorders, and mobile phones get passed from hand to hand often across borders (Spitulnik 2002).

This movement of people and objects is hugely significant for the global environment with transport accounting for one-third of total carbon dioxide emissions (Geffen, Dooley, Kim 2003). Transport is the fastest growing source of greenhouse emissions, and with the predicted growth of car and lorry travel within China and elsewhere throughout the world, the rapid growth of air travel and transport, and the political movement especially in the United States critiquing the thesis of global climate change, there has been little likelihood of this growth abating (but see ch. 13 below). Many other 'environmental' consequences follow from the growth of mass mobilities: reduced air quality; increased noise, smell and visual intrusion; ozone depletion; social fragmentation; and many medical consequences of 'accidental' deaths and injuries, asthma and obesity (Whitelegg 1997; Whitelegg, Haq 2003).

The internet has simultaneously grown incredibly rapidly, faster than any previous technology and with huge impacts throughout much of the world. There are already one billion internet users (Castells 2001). Also, since 2001 there are world-wide more mobile phones than landlines (Katz, Aakhus 2002a). The overall volume of international telephone calls increased at least tenfold between 1982 and 2001 (Vertovec 2004: 223). Such virtual communications and mobile telephony is calling into being new ways of interacting and communicating within and across societies, especially with some less well-developed societies jumping directly to mobile rather than landline telephony and computing.

These converging mobile technologies appear to be transforming many aspects of economic and social life that are in some sense on the 'move' or away from 'home'. In a mobile world there are extensive and intricate connections between physical travel and modes of communication and these form new fluidities and are often difficult to stabilize. Physical changes appear to be 'de-materializing' connections, as people, machines, images, information, power, money, ideas and dangers are 'on the move', making and remaking connections at often rapid speed around the world.

Issues of movement, of too little movement for some or too much for others or of the wrong sort or at the wrong time, are it seems central to many people's lives and to the operations of many small and large public, private and non-governmental organizations. From SARS to plane crashes, from airport expansion controversies to SMS texting, from slave trading to global terrorism, from obesity caused by the 'school run' to oil wars in the Middle East, from global warming to slave trading, issues of what I term 'mobility' are centre-stage on many policy and academic agendas. There is we might say a 'mobility' structure of feeling in the air (Thrift 1996: 259), with Simmel and Benjamin, Deleuze and Lefebvre, de Certeau and Erving Goffman, proving important early guides to this mobile age. Virilio's 'dromology' (1997), Serres' 'angels' (1995), Bauman's 'liquid modernity' (2000), Thrift's 'movement-space' (2004b) and Hardt and Negri's 'smooth world of 'empire' (2000) are some recent manifestations of this structure of feeling (see my own Urry 2000; Sheller, Urry 2006b).

These theorists as well as more empirical analysts are mobilizing a 'mobility turn', a different way of thinking through the character of economic, social and political relationships. Such a turn is spreading in and through the social sciences, mobilizing analyses that have been historically static, fixed and concerned with predominantly a-spatial 'social structures'. Contributions from cultural studies, feminism, geography, migration studies, politics, science studies, sociology, transport and tourism studies and so on are hesitatingly transforming social science and especially invigorating the connections, overlaps and borrowings with both physical science and with literary and historical studies. The mobility turn is post-disciplinary.

This book brings together and systematizes the different contributions being made around the world to this mobility turn, a turn that emphasizes how all social entities, from a single household to large scale corporations, presuppose many different forms of actual and potential movement. The mobility turn connects the analysis of different forms of travel, transport and communications with the multiple ways in which economic and social life is performed and organized through time and across various spaces. Analyses of the complex ways that social relations are 'stretched' across the globe are generating theories, research findings and methods that 'mobilize' or assemble analyses of social ordering that are achieved in part on the move and contingently as processes of flow.

Part 1 of this book is concerned with theories, research findings and methods that 'mobilize' analyses within social science. I develop and establish a systematic elaboration of what I call the new mobilities paradigm that should come to re-order the contours of appropriate social science analysis. Subsequent parts of the book are concerned with applying this paradigm to re-thinking the nature of, and changes within, different modes of moving and communicating (in Part 2); and to re-thinking social science concerned with social inequality and exclusion, weak ties and meetings, networked relationships, the changing nature of places and complex systems, and global climate change (in Part 3). I try to show that most important social phenomena are only satisfactorily analysed if they are so 'mobilized'.

Part 1 then is mainly theoretical. The first chapter sets the scene by elaborating features of this mobile structure of feeling. I review various empirical and conceptual processes that seem to indicate shifts in how to understand and analyse diverse social processes. Some indications are provided of the wide array of substantive issues to be elaborated later. In chapter 2 I establish the heterodox theoretical and methodological resources that have to be assembled in order that this paradigm is established and stabilized out of many disparate elements. Chapter 3 sets out the paradigm's main features and discusses a handful of recent studies that exemplify the likely appeal and analytical strength of this emerging paradigm.

Different 'Mobilities'

In this section I detail some of the multiple aspects of mobility that are involved here. I begin by noting how there are four main senses of the term 'mobile' or 'mobility' (see Jain 2002; Kaufmann 2002). First, there is the use of mobile to mean something that moves or is *capable* of movement, as with the iconic mobile (portable) phone but also with the mobile person, home, hospital, kitchen, and so on. Mobile is a property of things and of people (as with the class designated the 'new mobility'; Makimoto, Manners 1997). Many technologies in the contemporary era appear to have set in motion new ways of people being temporarily mobile, including various physical prostheses that enable the 'disabled immobile' to acquire some means of movement. Mostly the term mobile here is a positive category, except in the various critiques of what has been termed 'hypermobility' (Adams 1999).

Second, there is the sense of mobile as a *mob*, a rabble or an unruly crowd. The mob is seen as disorderly precisely because it is mobile, not fully fixed within boundaries and therefore needs to be tracked and socially regulated. The contemporary world appears to be generating many new dangerous mobs or multitudes, including so-called smart mobs, which are less easily regulated and require for their governance, new and extensive physical and/or electronic systems of counting, regulation and fixing within known places or specified borders (Thrift 2004b).

Third, there is the sense of mobility deployed in mainstream sociology/ social science. This is upward or downward *social* mobility. Mobility is here vertical. It is presumed that there is relatively clear cut vertical hierarchy of positions and that individuals can be located by comparison with their parent's position or with their own starting position within such hierarchies. There is debate as to whether or not contemporary societies have increased the circulation of people up and down such hierarchies, making the modern world more or less mobile. Some argue that extra circulation only results from changes in the number of top positions and not in increased movement between them (Goldthorpe 1980). There are complex relations between elements of physical movement and social mobility as I examine especially in chapter 9.

Fourth, there is mobility in the longer term sense of migration or other kinds of semi-permanent geographical movement. This is a horizontal sense of being 'on the move', and refers especially to moving country or continent often in search of a 'better life' or to escape from drought, persecution, war, starvation and so on. Although it is thought that contemporary societies entail much mobility in this sense, previous cultures often presupposed considerable movement such as from Europe to the dominated countries of their various Empires or later to North America.

This book investigates all these 'mobilities'. Such a generic 'mobilities' includes various kinds and temporalities of physical movement, ranging from standing, lounging, walking, climbing, dancing, to those enhanced by technologies, of bikes, buses, cars, trains, ships, planes, wheelchairs, crutches (see Thomsen, Nielsen, Gudmundsson 2005; Cresswell 2006; and Kellerman 2006, for related recent book-length treatments). Movements examined range from the daily, weekly, yearly and over people's lifetimes. Also included are the movement of images and information on multiple media, as well as virtual movement as communications are effected one-to-one, one-to-many and many-to-many through networked and embedded computers. A mobilities turn also involves examining how the transporting of people and the communicating of messages, information and images may overlap, coincide and converge through digitized flows. And the ways in which physical movement pertains to upward and downward social mobility is also central to a mobilities analysis. Moving between places physically or virtually can be a source of status and power, an expression of the rights to movement either temporarily or permanently. And where movement is coerced it may generate social deprivation and exclusion.

In some ways this current book is an extension of *Sociology Beyond Societies* where I asserted and developed some new mobile rules for sociological method (2000). These were set out as follows:

- to develop through appropriate metaphors a sociology which focuses upon movement, mobility and contingent ordering, rather than upon stasis, structure and social order
- to examine the extent, range and diverse effects of the corporeal, imagined and virtual mobilities of people, for work, for pleasure, to escape torture, to sustain diasporas and so on   × 3
- to consider things as social facts – and to see agency as stemming from the mutual intersections of objects and peoples
- to embody one's analysis through investigating the sensuous constitution of humans and objects
- to investigate the respective and uneven reach of diverse networks and flows as they move within and across societal borders and of how they spatially and temporally interconnect
- to examine how class, gender, ethnicity and nationhood are constituted through powerful and intersecting temporal regimes and modes of dwelling and travelling
- to describe the different bases of people's sense of dwelling, including their dependence upon various mobilities of people, presents, photographs, images, information, risks and so on
- to comprehend the changing character of citizenship as rights and duties are increasingly owed to, and derive from, entities whose topologies criss-cross those of society
- to illuminate the increased mediatization of social life as images circulate increasingly fast and with added reach so as to form and reform various imagined communities
- to appreciate the increasing interdependencies of 'domestic' and 'foreign' issues and the reduced significance of the means of physical coercion to the determination of the powers of states
- to explain changes within states towards an emphasis upon 'regulating' mobilities and their often unpredictable and chaotic consequences

- to interpret how chaotic, unintended and non-linear social consequences can be generated which are distant in time and/or space from where they originate and which are of a quite different and unpredictable scale
- to consider whether an emergent level of the 'global' is developing which can be viewed as recursively self-producing, that is, its outputs constitute inputs into an autopoietic circular system of 'global' objects, identities, institutions and social practices

I tried to deal with all those topics in that earlier book. However, in that book I never really developed a detailed analysis of just how and why mobilities make such a difference to social relations. And it did not sufficiently distinguish between different kinds of mobility systems and movement, tending to treat them all as rather similar to each other. I will thus seek to complete the project of that book by developing much more developed analysis of different mobilities and what I now call mobility-systems. These will be shown to be utterly significant in their own right and needing to be understood in terms of the social relations that surround and implicate them. And I will try to use these analyses to engage with and promote new analyses of a range of social science topics through various novel concepts, especially network capital, meetingness, interspace, the post car and various scenarios of the future. I also will seek to interrogate how rather different mobilities intersect. And I will not assume the movement of bodies is necessarily more rapid and extensive than other global processes. Hirst and Thompson remind us that: 'people are less mobile than money, goods or ideas, and in a sense they remain "nationalized", dependent upon passports, visas, residence and labour qualifications' (1999: 257).

In order to develop my argument I suggest that there are twelve main mobility forms in the contemporary world. Some of these are highly dependent upon passports, visas, residence and labour qualifications although others are much less so (see Williams 2006, on many of these). There are also various ways in which these forms overlap and impinge upon each other. These forms are:

- asylum, refugee and homeless travel and migration (Marfleet 2006; Cloke, Milbourne, Widdowfield 2003)
- business and professional travel (Davidson, Cope 2003)
- discovery travel of students, au pairs and other young people on their 'overseas experience', where this can constitute a 'rite of passage' and which typically involves going overseas to civilizational centres (Tully 2002; Williams 2006)
- medical travel to spas, hospitals, dentists, opticians and so on (Blackbourn 2002)

- military mobility of armies, tanks, helicopters, aircraft, rockets, spyplanes, satellites and so on which have many spinoffs into civilian uses (Kaplan 2006)
- post-employment travel and the forming of transnational lifestyles within retirement (Gustafson 2001; O'Reilly 2003)
- 'trailing travel' of children, partners, other relatives and domestic servants (Kofman 2004)
- travel and migration across the key nodes within a given diaspora such as that of overseas Chinese (Cohen 1997; Ong 1999)
- travel of service workers around the world and especially to global cities (Sassen 2000) including the contemporary flows of slaves (estimated by Bales at 27 m: 1999: 8)
- tourist travel to visit places and events and in relationship to various senses including especially through the 'tourist gaze' (Urry 2002c)
- visiting friends and relatives but where those friendship networks may also be on the move (Conradson, Latham 2005; Larsen, Urry, Axhausen 2006)
- work-related travel including commuting (Grabher 2004; Kesselring 2006a)

Analysing these various mobilities involves examining many consequences for different peoples and places that can said to be in the fast and slow lanes of social life. There is the proliferation of places, technologies and 'gates' that enhance the mobilities of some while reinforcing the immobilities of others (Graham, Marvin 2001). And mobilities are often also about duties, about the obligation to see the other, to return the call, to visit the ageing relative. These networks of often reciprocal obligations between people are the stuff of life, of how organizations, friendship networks, families, work groups, political organizations perform themselves as such across space and over time.

Moreover, the time spent traveling is not necessarily unproductive and wasted dead time that people always wish to minimize. Movement often involves an embodied experience of the material and sociable modes of dwelling-in-motion, places of and for activities in their own right, to climb a mountain, to do a good walk, to take a nice train journey. There are activities conducted at the destination; activities conducted while traveling including the 'anti-activity' of relaxing, thinking, shifting gears; and the pleasures of travelling itself, including the sensation of speed, of movement through and exposure to the environment, the beauty of a route and so on.

Furthermore, various technologies (beginning with the humble book in the mid nineteenth century) develop which are also 'mobile' and provide new affordances enabling 'activities' to those on the move. And we will see how new social routines are engendering spaces that are 'in-between' home, work and social life, forming 'interspaces'. These are places of intermittent movement where groups come together, involving the use of phones, mobiles, laptops, SMS messaging, wireless communications and so on, often to make arrangements 'on the move'.

Mobilities at the same time though entail risks, accidents, diseases, trafficking, terrorism, surveillance and especially global environmental damage. The contemporary mobile world seems to be characterized by awesome new dangers and restrictions for people, places and environments, as well as by new opportunities for mobile risky lives.

This book then is about this thesis of a mobile world: what makes a person or sign or communication mobile, what are the characteristics of mobility within different kinds of society, how should such mobilities be investigated in terms of theory and research? How much does a mobilities turn make social phenomena across the world comprehensible when they were previously opaque? Is it good to be mobile?

Overall mobilities have been a black box for the social sciences, generally regarded as a neutral set of processes permitting forms of economic, social and political life that are explicable by other more causally powerful processes. To the extent to which transport and communication are studied they are placed in separate categories with little interchange with the rest of social science. Holidaymaking, walking, car driving, phoning, flying and so on are mainly ignored by the social sciences although they are manifestly significant within people's everyday lives. Further there is a minimization of the significance of such movement *for* the nature of work relations, family life, leisure, politics and protest. These all involve movement or potential movement and affect the form taken by such social relations. Moreover, the social sciences overly concentrate upon subjects interacting together and ignore the enduring systems that provide what we might call the infrastructures of social life. Such systems *enable* the movement of people, ideas and information from place to place, person-to-person, event to event, and yet their economic, political and social implications are mostly unexamined in social science.

Systems

In this book I particularly examine such systems. Each intersecting 'mobility' presupposes a 'system' (in fact many such systems). These systems make possible movement: they provide 'spaces of anticipation' that the journey can be made, that the message will get through, that the parcel will arrive. Systems permit predictable and relatively risk-free repetition of the movement in question. Systems enable repetition. In the contemporary world these systems include ticketing, oil supply, addresses, safety, protocols, station interchanges, web sites, docks, money transfer, inclusive tours, luggage storage, air traffic control, barcodes, bridges, timetables, surveillance and so on. The history of these repetitive systems is in effect the history of those processes by which the natural world has been 'mastered' and made secure, regulated and relatively risk free. For people to be able to 'move', and for them in turn to move objects, texts, money, water, images, is to establish how it is that nature has been subdued. As Marx wrote: 'n[Nature] builds no machines, no locomotives, railways, electric telegraphs, self-acting mules, etc. These are products of human history . . . of human participation in nature' (1973: 706). In that human participation *in* nature, the production of ever more extensive systems of circulation is centrally significant as both a set of processes and as novel kinds of discourse.

This significance of ideas of movement and circulation especially followed Harvey's discovery of how blood circulates within the human body and Galileo's notion that a natural state is to be in motion and not at rest. Circulation is a powerful notion here that had many impacts upon the social world, especially in the development of Hobbesian political philosophy (Cresswell 2006: chap 1). More precisely with regard to the city: 'Enlightened planners wanted the city in its very design to function like a healthy body, freely flowing. . . . the Enlightenment planner made motion an end in itself' (Sennett 1994: 263–4). Systems increasingly develop in which there is an obligation to be circulating, and this is true of water, sewage, people, money, ideas (Virilio 1986). There is in the modern world an accumulation of movement that is analogous to the accumulation of capital – repetitive movement or circulation made possible by diverse, interdependent mobility-systems.

Some pre-industrial mobility-systems included walking, horse-riding, sedan chairs, coach travel, inland waterways, sea shipping and so on. But many of the mobility-systems which are now significant date from England and France in the 1840s and 1850s. Their interdependent development defines the contours of the modern mobilized world that brings about an awesome 'mastery' of the physical world (generally known as the 'industrial revolution'). Nature gets dramatically and systematically 'mobilized' in mid nineteenth-century Europe. Systems dating from that exceptional moment include a national post system in 1840 (Rowland Hill's Penny Post in Britain based upon the simple invention of the prepaid stamp), the first commercial electrical telegram in 1839 (constructed by Sir Charles Wheatstone and Sir William Fothergill Cooke for use on the Great Western Railway), the invention of photography and its use within guide books and advertising more generally (Daguerre in France in 1839, Fox Talbot in England in 1840), the first Baedeker guide (about the Rhine), the first railway age and the first ever national railway timetable in 1839 (Bradshaws), the first city built for the tourist gaze (Paris), the first inclusive or 'package' tour in 1841 (organized by Thomas Cook between Leicester and Loughborough in Britain), the first scheduled ocean steamship service (Cunard), the first railway hotel (York), the early department stores (first in Paris in 1843: Benjamin 1999: 42), the first system for the separate circulation of water and sewage (Chadwick in Britain) and so on. In 1854 Thomas Cook declared as the slogan for such a period: 'To remain stationary in these times of change, when all the world is on the move, would be a crime. Hurrah for the Trip – the cheap, cheap Trip' (quoted Brendon 1991: 65).

The twentieth century then saw a huge array of other 'mobility-systems' develop, including the car-system, national telephone system, air power, high speed trains, modern urban systems, budget air travel, mobile phones, networked computers (these are examined in Part 2 below).

As we move into the twenty first century these 'mobility systems' are developing further novel characteristics. First, systems are getting even more complicated, made up of many elements and based upon an array of specialized and arcane forms of expertise. Mobilities have always involved expert systems but these are now highly specific, many are based upon entire university degree programmes and there is the development of highly specialized companies. Second, such systems are much more interdependent with each other so that individual journeys or pieces of communication depend upon multiple systems, all needing to function and interface effectively with each other. Third, since the 1970s onwards, systems are much more dependent upon computers and software (Thrift, French 2002). There has been a large-scale generation of specific software systems that need to speak to each other in order that particular mobilities take place. Fourth, these systems have become especially vulnerable to 'normal accidents', accidents that are almost certain to occur from time to time, given the tightly locked-in and mobile nature of many such interdependent systems.

So what is the point of such increasingly complex, computerized and risky systems? As daily and weekly time–space patterns in the richer parts of the world are desynchronized from historical communities and place, so systems provide the means by which work and social life can get scheduled and rescheduled. Organizing 'co-presence' with key others (workmates, family, significant others, friends) within each day, week, year and so on becomes more demanding with this loss of collective co-ordination. As we will see the greater the personalization of networks, the more important are systems to facilitate that personalization.

Human beings are being reconfigured as bits of scattered information distributed across various 'systems' of which most are unaware. Individuals thus exist beyond their private bodies, leaving traces of their selves in space. In particular as vast numbers of people are on the move so these traces enable them to be subject to systems of intrusive regulation. In what has been called the 'frisk society', places are increasingly like airports using novel systems of monitoring, surveillance and regulation to control those mobile bodies.

In subsequent chapters I consider in what sense we might say that this mobile life is a good life. Is it good to move, how often should this happen, would a good society be a more or less mobile society? If mobilities entail systems of massive regulation and monitoring would a less mobile society be preferable? And is this mobility now inevitable, an irreversible trend that short of a nuclear winter or global warming that tips the global order into mass flooding (New Orleans as a forerunner), 'feeds' upon itself and inexorably expands?

And in examining these issues, which hold the whole earth's future in their hands, there are new configurations of what Latour terms 'circulating entities' (1999). Circulating entities for this coming century are complex, arcane and risky systems that facilitate the speeded up circulation of people, goods and information. These systems produce *and* presuppose personalized networking and 'do-it-yourself' scheduling through machines that are individualized, smart and corporeal. Circulating entities we might say are increasingly productive of circulation itself.

So while it is true that all societies have involved multiple mobilities, I explore how the twenty-first century places interdependent digitized *systems* of mobility at its very core. This is why their study cannot but be central to deciphering the principal contours of life in a world that combines exceptional freedom (at least for some on some occasions) and exceptional system dependence. We might say that we can go wherever we want to go but only because Big Brother got there first and knows (if the systems have not crashed) where we are choosing to go, with whom we are going, where we have been and where we are likely to go next.

These changes involve novel, extensive and 'flickering' combinations of the presence *and* absence of peoples, enemies, friends and risks that new mobilities are bringing about as the new century unfolds. Methods and theories thus need to be ever on the move to keep up with new forms of mobility, new systems of scheduling and monitoring, novel modes of mobilized inclusion and exclusion and extraordinary system dangers and risks.

2

'Mobile' Theories and Methods

Transportation is civilisation

(Ezra Pound [1917] 1973: 169)

The Mobilities Paradigm

In part this book develops a wide-ranging analysis of the role that the *movement* of people, ideas, objects and information plays in social life. I draw upon many examples from various places to show different ways that movements are located within and help to constitute different kinds of 'society', especially within the current global epoch.

I thus seek to bring into vision how social life presupposes many issues of movement and non-movement, of forced movement and of chosen fixity, of people, images, ideas and objects. It is an empirical question as to how important such movement is within different societies or types of society. It seems likely that contemporary societies demonstrate more movement for more people across longer distances albeit occurring for shorter time periods (although see discussion of Simmel below for a counter-argument). It also seems that there are more diverse forms of such movement. I have noted how new technologies of both transport and communications characterize modern societies, although one consequence of new communications means that physical movement may on occasions be less necessary. It is also clear that movement is increasingly deemed something of a right in such societies, as in the UN Declaration of Universal Rights or in the constitution of the European Union. And those who for whatever reason are denied such movement suffer multiple forms of exclusion. There is an ideology of movement.

But also as noted above I seek to I establish and stabilize a new cross or post-disciplinary *mobilities paradigm*. It is argued that thinking through a mobilities 'lens' provides a distinctive social science that is productive of different theories, methods, questions and solutions. The term paradigm is derived from Kuhn's exemplary analysis of normal science, scientific exemplars and what constitutes scientific revolution (1970).

It will be argued that a mobilities paradigm is not just substantively different, in that it remedies the neglect and omissions of various movements of people, ideas and so on. But it is transformative of social science, authorizing an alternative theoretical and methodological landscape as I detail. It enables the 'social world' to be theorized as a wide array of economic, social and political practices, infrastructures and ideologies that all involve, entail or curtail various kinds of movement of people, or ideas, or information or objects. And in so doing this paradigm brings to the fore theories, methods and exemplars of research that have been mostly subterranean, out of sight. So I use the term mobilities to refer to the broader project of establishing a movement-driven social science.

And in making the subterranean visible it redraws many ways in which social science has been practised, especially as organized within distinct 'regions' or 'fortresses' of policed, bounded and antagonistic 'disciplines'. I use the term subterranean to indicate how this paradigm is not being generated *de novo*. There are various paradigmatic fragments found in multiple archives that rest uneasily within their current disciplinary fortresses (see *inter alia* Serres 1995; Virilio 1997; Urry 2000; Riles 2001; Graham, Marvin 2001; Solnit 2001; Verstraete, Cresswell 2002; Amin, Thrift 2002; Rheingold 2002; Coleman, Crang 2002; Sheller 2003; Cresswell 2006; Sheller, Urry 2006b; Kellerman 2006). The new paradigm will seek to release these fragments from their cage and enable them to fly, confronting and engaging with other 'angels' in flight, as Michel Serres might fancifully express it (1995). And there are plenty of other sites where the mobilities paradigm is being set loose (such as the European research network 'Cosmobilities').

So the aim here is both to make the substantive claim that there are multiple kinds of movement and that much social science has inadequately examined them, *and* that there is a putative new paradigm which involves a post-disciplinary, productive way of doing social science, especially in the new century where mobility issues would seem to be evidently centre-stage.

In the previous chapter it was noted that much social science has been 'a-mobile'. This can be seen in three different ways. First, there has been *neglect* of movement and communications and the forms in which they are economically, politically and socially organized. Thus although such activities are often personally and culturally significant within people's lives (such as holidaymaking, walking, car driving, phoning, flying), they are mostly ignored by social science. Along with others I have sought to draw such topics into the view-finder of social science, especially the topics of holidaymaking, leisurely travel and the experiences of different forms of movement (Urry 2002c).

Second, there has been the *minimization* of the significance of these forms of movement for the very nature of work, schooling, family life, politics and protest, that is, within crucially important social institutions. And yet for example families depend upon patterns of regular visiting, schools are chosen in terms of catchment areas, work patterns depends on the way congestion structures commuting flows, new industries depend upon new migrants, protest movements depend upon marches and co-present demonstrations. These patterns of movement structure how these social institutions and activities develop and change, something often minimized in conventional 'structural' analyses.

Third, social science mostly focuses upon the patterns in which human subjects directly interact together and ignores the underlying physical or material infrastructures that orchestrate and underlie such economic, political and social patterns. Almost all mobilities presuppose large-scale immobile infrastructures that make possible the socialities of everyday life. These immobile infrastructures include paths, railway tracks, public roads, telegraph lines, water pipes, telephone exchanges, pylons, sewerage systems, gas pipes, airports, radio and TV aerials, mobile phone masts, satellites, underground cables and so on (Graham, Marvin 2001; Sheller, Urry 2006a). Intersecting with these infrastructures are the social solidarities of class, gender, ethnicity, nation and age orchestrating diverse mobilities, including both enforced fixity as well as coerced movement (see Ray 2002).

To the extent to which transport and communication systems are researched, this mainly takes place in separate disciplinary fortresses with little interchange with the rest of social science. The study of transport mostly concentrates upon the changing nature of transport systems and has deployed something of a technological determinism. It little examines the complex social processes that underlie and orchestrate the uses of such transports. There is we might say too much transport in the study of travel and not enough society and certainly not enough thinking through their complex intersecting processes (but see Kaufmann 2002; and Ashgate's *Transport and Society* book series). In examining those connections over time it is necessary to avoid what we might describe as either a 'society first' or a 'transport technology first' approach and develop formulations of a new mobilities paradigm that will transcend such a divide.

In the next section I turn to Georg Simmel, the author within social science who did most to think about the organization and consequences of mobilities within social life more generally. Simmel was the first to attempt the development of a mobilities paradigm, developing analyses of proximity, distance and movement in the modern city (Jensen 2006: 146).

Simmel and Mobilities

Simmel provides a somewhat Heidegger-ian interpretation of the significance of mobility infrastructures. Simmel notes the exceptional human achievement that is involved in creating a 'path' that links two particular places. No matter how often people have gone backwards and forwards between the places and 'subjectively' connected them in their mind, it is he says: 'only in visibly *impressing* the path into the surface of the earth that the places were objectively connected' (Simmel 1997: 171; ital added). Such visible impressions of path-building create a permanent 'connection' between such places. This human achievement is derived from the 'will to connection' as he expresses it. This will to connection is a shaper of things and of relations. Animals by contrast cannot accomplish such a 'miracle of the road', that is an even more developed 'impressing . . . into the surface of the earth' having the effect, Simmel maintains, of 'freezing movement in a solid structure' (1997: 171). We see later many other examples of how 'movement' is 'frozen' into a solid structure and more generally the consequences of a Nietzschean 'will to connection'.

And this freezing, this achievement of connection through a new 'movement-space' (Thrift 2004b), reaches its zenith with a bridge that 'symbolizes the extension of our volitional sphere over space' (Simmel 1997: 171). Only for humans are the banks of the river not just apart but separated and thus potentially bridge-able. And like Marx's analysis of the 'architect' (as opposed to the bee) humans are able to 'see' these connections in their mind's eye as separated *and* as therefore

needing connection. Simmel summarizes the power of human imagination, of 'conception': 'if we did not first connect them in our practical thoughts, in our needs and in our fantasy, then the concept of
separation would have no meaning' (1997: 171).

Such a bridge moreover can often become part of 'nature', picturesque, as it accomplishes the connection between the places. For the
eye the bridge stands in a close and fortuitous relationship to the
banks. Such a freezing of movement can seem like a natural 'unity',
with high aesthetic value, as almost an improvement upon 'nature'
since it appears 'naturally' to connect the banks.

So what of movement itself? Simmel distinguishes between various
socio-spatial patterns of mobility. These include nomadism, wandering, a royal tour of the kingdom, diasporic travel, the Court's travel,
migration, and adventure and leisure travel. In each case what is
distinct is its social form, the 'form of sociation . . . in the case of a
wandering group in contrast to a spatially fixed one' (Simmel 1997:
160). And this contrast stems from the 'temporal duration' implicated
in the period 'away'. Time structures the 'nuancing of the course of
a gathering' – but this is no simple and direct relationship. Sometimes
a short time encounter can lead to the conveying of secrets through
the role of the temporary 'stranger'; while on other occasions spending a long time together is necessary for mutual adaptation to occur
so as to develop the trust of all involved.

Simmel also emphasizes how physical or bodily travel is interconnected with other mobilities. He hypotheses (incorrectly) that there
was more travel by scholars and merchants in the Middle Ages than
there was travel at the beginning of the twentieth century. This is
because in the latter period there are: 'letters and books, bank
accounts and branch offices, through mechanical reproduction of the
same model and through photography' (Simmel 1997: 165). In the
Middle Ages all this information 'had to be brought about through
people traveling' from place to place since there were few other
'systems' to move ideas, information and especially money (Simmel
1997: 167). And yet that travelling was almost always full of 'dangers
and difficulties', especially since there were relatively few 'expert
systems' that would mitigate the risks of such physical travel (Simmel
1997: 167).

Indeed there were also many itinerant poor, the vagabonds, whose
lives were based upon a 'restlessness and mobility' which generated
various 'fluid associations' such as bands of 'wandering minstrels'
characterized by the 'impulse for a continuous change of scene, the
ability and desire to "disappear"' (Simmel 1997: 168). His schematic
account of the Middle Ages is interesting for its emphases upon

movement and fluidity, and for the ways that travel was deemed obligatory for many to exchange information, money and objects, a need partly *reduced* in the modern age through the replacement of physical travel by systems that enable the large-scale movement of letters, books, money and photographs. These complex intersections between different mobility systems are returned to at many places in this book.

But Simmel has also much to say about the contemporary city where new modes of movement and restlessness are widespread. He famously writes in 'Metropolis and the City' that the metropolitan type of personality consists in 'the *intensification of nervous stimulation* which results from the swift and uninterrupted change of outer and inner stimuli' (Simmel 1997: 175). The modern city involves the 'unexpectedness of onrushing impressions ... With each crossing of the street, with the tempo and multiplicity of economic, occupational and social life', he says that the city sets up a 'deep contrast with small town and rural life with reference to the sensory foundations of psychic life' (Simmel 1997: 175; and see Simmel 1990).

And because of the richness and diverse sets of onrushing stimuli in the metropolis people are forced to develop an attitude of reserve and insensitivity to feeling. Without the development of such an attitude most would not be able to cope with such overwhelming experiences caused by a high density of population and its movement. The urban personality is thus reserved, detached and blasé. The unrushing stimulations create a new psychic and sensory configuration, the blasé attitude, the incapacity to react to new sensations with appropriate energy. The movement of the city, as well as the rapid movement of money, generates reserve and indifference (Jensen 2006: 148–9).

Thus Simmel does not explain urban life in terms of the spatial form of the city. It is more an early examination, paralleling Marx and Engels from the mid nineteenth century as set out in the modernist *The Manifesto of the Communist Party*, of the effects of 'modern' patterns of mobility upon social life wherever it is found (Marx and Engels 1952; Berman 1983). Simmel analyses the fragmentation and diversity of modern life and shows that motion, the diversity of stimuli and the visual appropriations of place are centrally important features of that new modern urban experience.

Moreover, because of the effect of money with 'all its colourlessness and indifference' (Simmel 1997: 178; and see 1990), but also because of its twin, the modern city, a new precision comes to be necessary in social life. Agreements and arrangements need to demonstrate unambiguousness in timing and location. Life in the mobile onrushing city presupposes punctuality and this is reflected according to Simmel by the 'universal diffusion of pocket watches' (1997: 177). The watch a century ago was as striking and symbolic of the 'modern' as the ubiquitous mobile phone is today. Simmel argues that the 'relationships and affairs of the typical metropolitan usually are so varied and complex that without the strictest punctuality in promises and services the whole structure would break down into an inextricable chaos' (1997: 177). This necessity for punctuality: 'is brought about by the aggregation of so many people with such differentiated interests who must integrate their relations and activities into a highly complex organism' (Simmel 1997: 177).

So the forming of a complex system of relationships means that meetings and activities have to be punctual, timetabled, rational, a system or 'structure of the highest impersonality' often involving much distance-keeping politeness (Simmel 1997: 178; Toiskallio 2002: 171). This 'system-ness' of mobility is crucial here and results in the individual becoming 'a mere cog in an enormous organization of things and powers'; as a result 'life is made infinitely easy for the personality in that stimulations, interests, uses of time and consciousness are offered to it from all sides' (Simmel 1997: 184). Simmel tellingly notes how as a consequence: 't[T]hey carry the person as if in a stream, and one needs hardly to swim for oneself' (Simmel 1997: 184).

But simultaneously modern city life produces people each with a 'highly personal subjectivity', a tendency to be 'different', of standing out in a striking manner and thereby seeking attention (Simmel 1997: 178). Urban life produces what we now call a pronounced 'culture of narcissism' (Lasch 1980). Simmel argues that people gain self-esteem through being aware of how they are specifically perceived by others. But because of the scale of mobility in the metropolis there is a 'brevity and scarcity of inter-human contacts' (Simmel 1997: 183). Compared with the small-scale community, the modern city gives room to the individual and to the peculiarities of their inner and outer development. It is the spatial form of modern urban life that permits the unique development of individuals who socially interact with an exceptionally wide range of contacts. People seek to distinguish themselves; they try to be different through adornment and fashion encountering each other in brief moments of proximity. So metropolitan life, its rush and fragmentation, generates both powerful objective systems partly concerned with maintaining rules of distance and formality, *and* very varied personal subjectivities, a perverse combination examined below in the context of the novel multiple mobilities of the twenty-first century.

In his analysis of moments of co-presence, Simmel develops a general sociology of the senses and the respective significance of sight, hearing and smell. He places particular emphasis upon the eye as a 'unique sociological achievement' (Simmel 1997: 111). It effects the connection and interaction of individuals, it is the 'most direct and purest interaction that exists' (Simmel 1997: 111). People cannot avoid taking through the eye without at the same time giving. The eye produces 'the most complete reciprocity' of person to person, face to face (Simmel 1997: 112). Later I show how face-to-face co-presence is key to the obligations to, and consequences of, travel. Boden and Molotch summarize how: 'Copresent interaction remains, just as Georg Simmel long ago observed, the fundamental mode of human intercourse and socialization, a "primordial site for sociality"' (1994: 258).

For Simmel the expressive meaning of the face provides a special kind of knowing. Unlike other parts of the body, the face does not act but it is especially revealing. We see how the face of the other person 'is' and therefore how that person 'is' and indeed has been. Simmel talks of the 'timeless dowry of nature . . . revealed in their face' (1997: 115). The face tells others about the person's life, revealing that which has been deposited upon it or even within it over the course of each person's lifetime or through our inevitable movement until death.

Simmel makes two further important points about travel. First, he argues that not only are people attracted to each other because of ulterior reasons but also for the pleasures of 'free-playing sociability', for forms of social interaction that are freed from content, substance and ulterior end. Co-present conversations happen in and for themselves, a kind of 'pure interaction' that can be an end in itself (Simmel 1997: 9–10). Much of social life and hence the perceived need or obligation to travel stems from the pleasures and attractions of talk face-to-face, and sometimes body-to-body.

Second, Simmel describes the 'socialistic wholesale opening-up and enjoyment of nature' that stemmed from building railways into the Alps (Simmel 1997: 219). Such railways engendered new mass travel into and through nature. He does not see this as undesirable but doubts whether such traveling has 'educative value' for most visitors. Although there is a 'momentary rapture' this is quickly followed by a 'return to the mundane' (Simmel 1997: 220). Simmel especially critiques those who believe that surmounting life-endangering difficulties is morally commendable. He questions the egoistic enjoyment of alpine sports: 'playing with danger and the emotion of the panoramic view' (Simmel 1997: 220). Simmel also, though, examines the attractions of the 'adventure' in shaping the desire to be elsewhere; such an 'adventure' occurs 'outside the usual continuity of this life' (Simmel 1997: 222). The adventure he says is in the present, not determined by the past and where there is no future. Because life has become 'easy' in the city, so it is outside, in places of adventure, where the body might come *to* life, it is a 'body in motion' that finds its way, being natural, knowing nature, saving oneself 'naturally'. The adventure thus enables the body to escape the blasé attitude, to be rejuvenated during moments of bodily arousal in motion. Simmel summarizes how 'we are adventurers of the earth'; but adventure only occurs when tensions 'have become so violent that they gain mastery over the material through which they realise themselves' (1997: 232).

More generally Simmel presents an early approach to what we would now call complexity theory. He sets himself against analyses that seek to explain social phenomena in terms of individual acts. Important social phenomena are not the consequence of combinations of a lower order. He is anti-reductionist, being concerned with an array of emergent social forms, the elementary substance of social life according to Lash (2005: 11). Simmel's approach speaks of a language of autopoiesis. He talks of how 'things find their meaning in relation to each other, and the mutuality of the relationships in which they are involved constitutes what and how they are' (1990: 128–9; Staubmann 1997; see Lash 2005, on Simmel's vitalism).

Specifically Simmel views money in his magnum opus on *The Philosophy of Money* as a medium of self-organization of economic exchange and that economic exchange generates emergent effects that are non-reducible to individual acts of exchange (1990). It is he says possible to examine 'reciprocal causality' or what now is referred as co-evolution and adaptation. Lash has recently suggested that the media and communication are similar self-organizing forms of life that change and threaten the power of the social (2005: 8–10). Analogously I suggest below that 'mobility' or 'circulation' should be seen as similar to money, as another medium of exchange that is self-organizing and irreducible to individual patterns or preferences.

Further it has been recently argued that Simmel elaborates the nature of flux not flow and this corrects a conceptualization of mobilities as simple flows (Lash 2005). Flux involves tension, struggle and conflict, a dialectic of technology and social life or as I develop below the complex intersections of immobilities and mobilities. There is no simple or pure flow according to Simmel but more a vitalist flux.

I suggest that it is the *complex* (rather than *vitalist*) character of social life stems from this flux-like dialectic of immobility and mobility, and in particular from the Simmelian inspired-account of the dialectic of systematization and personalization. Overall Simmel provides the framework for this book by referring to most issues and topics to be examined. I essay a series of chapters that provide elaborations and developments of his writings that one hundred or so years ago was the basis of a process or vitalist or complexity social science concerned with multiple flux-like mobilities.

Some elements of Simmel's ideas were developed within the Chicago School which in the first half of this century provided a range of post-Simmelian mobility studies especially concerned with the itinerant lives of hoboes, gangs, prostitutes, migrants and so on (see Park 1970, for example). However, this development was really cut short in its tracks as a range of structural or static theories took over within sociology, including structural functionalism, positivist analysis of 'variables', structural Marxism and so on. Meanwhile the study of mobilities turned into the professional examination of 'transport' and to a lesser extent of 'tourism', that were taken to be differentiated and specific domains to be researched far away from the provocative promptings of Simmel's essays and analyses.

In the next sections I draw upon an eclectic range of more recent theories and programmes of research to elaborate and develop Simmel's brief sketch of a mobilities paradigm. This paradigm has we might say waited one hundred years to get out of the garage since Simmel first sketched the prototype nearly a century ago. I begin with complexity and then in the next section consider a wide array of other theories.

Complexity

Leading physicists Laughlin and Pines summarize how, while physics once studied fundamental laws to which everything could be reduced, it now studies multiple forms of emergent organization:

> The central task . . . is no longer to write down the ultimate equations but rather to catalogue and understand emergent behaviour . . . We call this . . . the study of complex adaptive matter . . . We are witnessing a transition from . . . reductionism, to the study of complex adaptive matter (cited Buchanan 2002: 207).

While the *Gulbenkian Commission on the Restructuring of the Social Sciences* argues that we should dissolve the boundaries between 'natural' and 'social' science through seeing both characterized by 'complexity' (the Commission included non-linear Nobel prize-winning scientist Ilya Prigogine). Analysis 'based on the dynamics of non-equilibria, with its emphasis on multiple futures, bifurcation and choice, historical dependence, and . . . intrinsic and inherent uncertainty' should be the 'model for *all* the sciences' (Wallerstein 1996: 61).

An emergent complexity 'structure of feeling' is in the air according to Thrift (1999; Byrne 1998; Capra 2002; Urry 2004, 2005). Such an emergent structure of feeling derives from a series of processes that are bringing notions of complex adaptive systems into the analysis of mobilities such that there is an increasingly elective affinity between the two. Some processes that have put complexity notions onto this intellectual map include:

1. the awareness of rapid and unexpected movements of money, images, people, capital and information around the globe (see Harvey 1989, on time–space compression) – so making order contingent and something to be achieved, and producing neither simply chaos or order but what physicists call metastability (Ball 2004)
2. the growth of micro-electronics based communications technologies that shifts dominant modes of organization from hierarchy to computerized networks that autopoietically self-reproduce themselves across the globe (Castells 1996, 2001), including the phenomenon of 'smart mobs' (Rheingold 2002)
3. the emergence of 'global microstructures' such as anti-globalization movements, financial markets or terrorist networks, of 'forms of connectivity and co-ordination that combine global reach with microstructural mechanisms that instantiate self-organizing principles and patterns' (Knorr Cetina 2005)
4. the increase in the hyper-complexity of products and technologies: the Eli Whitney musket of 1800 had 51 components while the space shuttle contained 10 million. As late as 1970 most products in world trade were simple products produced by simple processes, but a quarter-of-a-century later, two-thirds of the most valuable products are complex processes *and* complex products involving vast numbers of components, cybernetic architectures and sociotechnical hybrid systems (Rycroft, Nash 1999)
5. the more general significance of hybrid systems, of social relations and physical objects such as health, terrorism, global warming and so on that presuppose and generate overlaps and parallels between the physical, biological *and* social worlds.

Capra advocates a unified conceptual framework for the understanding of such material-and-social structures (2002)
6. the sheer unpredictability of events and outcomes in time–space
    and especially the complex ways in which events return to haunt
    those apparently initiating such processes, demonstrating a
    'boomerang' effect with the boomerang paradoxically returning
    to slice off the head of those from where the process started
    (Beck 2001)
7. the diverse non-linear changes in relationships, households and
    societies taking place across the globe in which there seem to
    be no clear relationships between 'causes' and 'effect'; that
    things happen which involve unexpected disproportionalities
    that cannot be predicted and let alone controlled (Nicolis
    1995)
8. the significance of points of bifurcation, such as the almost
    overnight collapse of the Soviet Empire, the spread of the
    internet from almost no users to one billion in a decade or
    the take up of SMS texting which went from almost no adopters
    to almost 100 per cent adoption in certain cultures (Gladwell
    2000)
9. the increasing plausibility of seeing the coupling together of all
    the organisms and the material environment of the earth as a
    single, self-regulating system or what Lovelock has for decades
    termed Gaia (2006: 23–5). His recent examination of 'global
    heating' brings out a set of possibly irreversible processes that
    are transformative of this single once self-regulating system
10. the increasing organization of science itself on a global basis in
    which its patterns of growth, commercialization and systems of
    funding and support involves sets of self-organizing networks
    that do not provide a reductionist mirror of nature, indeed the
    growth of scientific networks takes various domains further
    away from equilibria (Wynne 2005)

Twentieth-century science had dismantled elements of Newtonian
science and this prepared the way for the complexity turn (see Urry
2003; and the 2005 *Theory, Culture and Society* collection for more
detail). Pre-twentieth-century science operated with a view of time
as Newtonian: invariant, divisible into space-like units, measurable
in length, expressible as a number and reversible. It is time seen as
Cartesian space comprising invariant measurable lengths to be moved
along, forwards *and* backwards. Twentieth-century sciences dismantled such a notion (Capra 1996). Einstein showed that there is no
fixed or absolute time independent of the system to which it is refers.

Time is a local, internal feature of any system of observation and measurement. Time and space are not separate from each other but are fused into a four-dimensional time–space curved under the influence of mass. Thus time and space are 'internal' to the processes by which the physical and social worlds themselves operate, helping to constitute their powers (Coveney, Highfield 1990). Indeed the beginning of the universe occurred without a pre-existing cause, and its very happening created in that moment both space and time. Space and time have been spontaneously created, part of the systemic nature of the universe (Davies 2001). Moreover, quantum theory describes a virtual state in which electrons try out instantaneously all possible futures before settling into particular patterns (Zohar, Marshall 1994). Quantum behaviour is instantaneous, simultaneous and unpredictable. The interactions between the parts are far more fundamental than the parts themselves. Thermodynamics showed that there is an irreversible flow of time. An arrow of time results in loss of organization and an increase in randomness or disorder over time within open systems. This accumulation of disorder or positive entropy results from the Second Law of Thermodynamics. However, there is not a simple growth of disorder. Prigogine shows how new order arises but is far from equilibrium. There are dissipative structures, islands of new order within a sea of disorder, maintaining or even increasing their order at the expense of greater overall entropy (Prigogine 1997). While the irreversibility of time can be seen in the expansion of the universe following the singular event of the 'big bang' fifteen billion or so years ago. The arrow or flow of time results in futures that are unstable, relatively unpredictable and characterized by various possibilities. Time is both multiple and unpredictable. Prigogine talks of the 'end of certainty' as the complexity sciences overcome what he calls the alienating images of a deterministic world and an arbitrary world of pure chance. Order and chaos are in a kind of balance where the components are neither fully locked into place but yet do not fully dissolve into anarchy.

Central to such dynamic systems is the idea of emergence, there are system effects that are different from their parts (Nicolis 1995). Complexity examines how components of a system through their interaction 'spontaneously' develop collective properties or patterns, even simple properties such as colour, that do not seem implicit within, or at least not implicit in the same way, within individual components. Such large-scale patterns or characteristics emerge from, but are not reducible to, the micro-dynamics of the phenomenon in question. Thus gases are not uniform entities but comprise a seething confusion of atoms obeying the laws of quantum mechanics.

The laws governing gases derive not from the behaviour of each individual atom but from their statistical patterning. Moreover, once a system passes a particular threshold with minor changes in the controlling variables, switches occur such that a liquid turns into a gas or small increases in the earth's temperature result in massive and uncontrollable global heating (Lovelock 2006). Such 'tipping points' can give rise to unexpected structures and events whose properties are quite different from those of the underlying elementary laws (Gladwell 2000).

Thus complexity investigates of multiple hybrid systems adapt and evolve as they self-organize over time and within a fitness landscape structured by each (see Mitleton-Kelly 2003). Such complex interactions of systems are like walking through a maze whose walls rearrange themselves as one walks. New steps have then to be taken in order to adjust to the walls of the maze that are adapting to one's movement through the maze (Gleick 1988: 24). Complexity thus investigates emergent, dynamic, self-organizing and interdependent systems that interact in ways that influence later probabilities (Prigogine 1997: 35).

Such systems are seen as developing in and through time so that agents are locked into apparently stable 'path dependent' practices resulting from some relatively small-scale early events (such as those initiating the steel-and-petroleum car; see ch. 6). But systems can occasionally change very rapidly through reaching a 'tipping point' (Gladwell 2002). A recent example of such a tipping point is how communications between offices during the 1990s all suddenly required a fax machine – without a fax machine an office was really not an 'office' because it could not communicate with other 'offices'. This complex systems world is then a world of avalanches, founder effects, self-restoring patterns, apparently stable regimes that suddenly collapse, punctuated equilibria, 'butterfly effects', and thresholds as systems suddenly tip from one state to another (Axelrod, Cohen 1999).

Especially significant in these analyses are non-linear, *positive* feedback loops. These are viewed as exacerbating initial stresses in the system, so rendering it unable to absorb shocks and re-establishing the original equilibrium, as Lovelock recently examines in the case of the 'global heating' of the earth system (2006: 33–5). Positive feedback occurs when a change tendency is reinforced rather than dampened down as occurs with the negative feedback. Such positive feedback is involved in analyses of the increasing returns that generate path dependence found in the history of various economic-technological systems (such as VHS video system replacing the technologically superior Betamax). Such irreversible path dependence occurs when contingent events set into motion institutional patterns or event chains over time that then have deterministic properties through what Arthur terms 'lock-ins' (1994a, 1994b; Waldrop 1994).

Other Theoretical Resources

Sedentarism

This locates bounded and authentic places or regions or nations as the fundamental basis of human experience (Cresswell 2002: 12–15; 2006; Relph 1976). Such sedentarist thinking is often derived from Heideggerian notions. For Heidegger dwelling means to reside or to stay, to dwell at peace, to be content or at home within a place. To build (*bauen*) involved cherishing and protecting, tilling soil and cultivating vines. Such building involved care and was habitual. Heidegger wants to ensure how building and dwelling can be combined once again, calling this 'letting dwell' (Heidegger 1993: 361; Zimmerman 1990: 151).

Such dwelling involves a staying *with* things which are bodily ready-to-hand. Thus Heidegger argues against the separation of man [*sic*] and space, as though they stand on opposite sides. Rather to speak of men [*sic*] is to speak of those who already dwell through moving through space: 'To say that mortals *are* is to say that *in dwelling* they persist through spaces by virtue of their stay among things and locales. And only because mortals pervade, persist through, spaces by their very essence are they able to go through spaces' (Heidegger 1993: 359). But people only go through spaces in ways which sustain them through the relationships which are established 'with near and remote locales and things' (Heidegger 1993: 359). When one goes to open the door of a room one is already part of that room. A person is not a separate 'encapsulated body' since such a person already pervades the space of the room they are about to enter. Only because of the form of dwelling is it possible to go through that particular door. To dwell we might say is always to be moving and sensing, both within and beyond.

Heidegger like Simmel discusses the significance of bridges. They do not connect banks that are in a sense already 'there'. The banks only emerge as a consequence of a bridge that now crosses the stream. A bridge causes the banks to lie across from each other. This has the effect that surrounding land on either side of the stream is brought into closer juxtaposition. Heidegger argues that the bridge functions as what we would now call an actant; it: 'brings stream and bank and land into each other's neighbourhood. The bridge *gathers* the earth as landscape around the stream' (1993: 354).

Furthermore, a new bridge reorganizes how people dwell/move within that area. Bridges initiate new social patterns, forming a locale or connecting different parts of a town, or the town with the country, or the town with 'the network of long-distance traffic, paced and calculated for maximum yield' (Heidegger 1993: 354). A bridge is ready on call, waiting for slow movement across it, the 'lingering' ways of people to and fro across the bridge, moving from bank to bank. Tourist places are waiting also, on call for inspection by a tourist group ordered there by the vacation industry (Heidegger 1993).

More recently, Ingold somewhat similarly writes how: 'landscape is constituted as an enduring record of – and testimony to – the lives and works of past generations who have dwelt within it, and in so doing, have left there something of themselves' (1993: 152). Landscape is thus neither nature nor culture, neither mind nor matter. It is the world as known to those who have dwelt in that place, those who currently dwell there, those who will dwell there, and those whose practical activities take them though its many sites and journey along its multiple paths. It is, Ingold argues, the 'taskscape' of any environment that produces the social character of a landscape.

Paths moreover demonstrate the accumulated imprint of the countless journeys made as people go about their everyday business. The network of paths shows the sedimented activity of a community stretching over generations; it is the taskscape made visible (Ingold 1993: 167). People imagine themselves treading the same paths as earlier generations as the path gets impressed into the ground. And thus the redirection of a path, or its elimination with a new road, will often be viewed as vandalism against that community and its collective memories and forms of dwelling/moving in and through a given place.

Fluidity and nomadism

An alternative source of ideas about mobility is provided by metaphors and theories of fluidity and nomadism (Cresswell 2002: 15–18; Urry 2000: ch. 2; Bauman 2000). Many writers have developed metaphors of sea, river, flux, waves, liquidity, the vagabond, the pilgrim and nomadism. Such metaphors often draw upon Derrida who says: '*Différance* is incompatible with the static, synchronic, taxonomic, ahistoric motifs in the concept of *structure*' (1987: 27).

Deleuze and Guattari elaborate on the implications of nomads, external to each state (1986: 49–53). Nomads characterize societies of de-territorialization, constituted by lines of flight rather than by points or nodes. They maintain that: 'the nomad has no points, paths or land . . . If the nomad can be called the Deterritorialized *par excellence*, it is precisely because there is no reterritorialization *afterwards* as with the migrant' (1986: 52). More generally here, this neo-vitalism emphasizes process and change, as the core of social life (see Lash 2005). There is no stasis, only processes of creation and transformation. There is nothing before movement; movement expresses how things are.

Other mobile metaphors are those of the vagabond and the tourist (Bauman 1993). The vagabond is a pilgrim without a destination, a nomad without an itinerary; while the tourist 'pay[s] for their freedom; the right to disregard native concerns and feelings, the right to spin their own web of meanings . . . The world is the tourist's oyster . . . to be lived pleasurably – and thus given meaning' (Bauman 1993: 241). Both vagabonds and tourists move through other people's spaces, they involve the separation of physical closeness from any sense of moral proximity and they set standards for happiness (Bauman 1993: 243). More generally, Bauman argues that there is a shift from modernity as heavy and solid to one that is light and liquid and where speed of movement of people, money, images and information is paramount (2000; the strange death of Concorde partly showing the limits of this claim).

A further nomadic metaphor is that of the 'motel' (Morris 1988). The motel has no real lobby, it is tied into the network of highways, it functions to relay people rather than to provide settings for coherent human subjects, it is consecrated to circulation and movement, and it demolishes the sense of place and locale. Motels 'memorialize only movement, speed, and perpetual circulation' (Morris 1988: 3); they 'can never be a true *place*' and one is only distinguished from another in 'a high-speed, *empiricist* flash' (Morris 1988: 5). The motel, like the airport transit lounge, represents neither arrival nor departure but the 'pause' (Morris 1988: 41; Augé 1995).

Wolff and others criticize the masculinist character of many of these nomadic and travel metaphors since they suggest that there is ungrounded and unbounded movement (1993; Skeggs 2004). But clearly different social categories have very different access to being 'on the road' both literally and metaphorically. Jokinen and Veijola show that certain male metaphors can be re-written or coded differently (1997). If these male metaphors are so re-written, as say, paparazzi, homeless drunk, sex-tourist and womanizer, then they lose such positive valuation. Jokinen and Veijola also propose female metaphors of movement, including those of the prostitute, the babysitter and the *au pair* (1997).

Materials on the move

In the 1980s there was a 'spatial turn' in the social sciences. This involved theory and research that demonstrated that social relations are spatially organized and such spatial structuring makes a significant difference to social relations (see Gregory, Urry 1995). Massey proclaimed that 'space matters' to social life (1994b). Now space is increasingly viewed as made up of moving elements involving various 'power-geometries'. Most relevant here is the way that spaces are viewed as comprised of various materials, of objects and environments, that are intermittently in motion. These materials are assembled and reassembled in changing configurations and rearticulated meanings (Cresswell 2001; Verstraete, Cresswell 2002; Cresswell 2002).

Studies of travel, migration and belonging show how cultural objects are variably on the move and how they may hold their meaning as they move and are moved around. There are different kinds of objects and they variably hold or lose their value as they move from place to place. Objects variably mobilize place and they are involved in the reconstitution of belonging and memory (Lury 1997; Fortier 2000; Molotch 2003).

Many analyses here draw upon science and technology studies which are often concerned with 'transport', with how the laws of science sometimes but contingently work similarly across the globe through the effective movement of scientific procedures, methods and findings. It is essential to understand how it is that machines and machinations travel (Law, Mol 2001: 611). Science and technology studies show how humans are intricately networked *with* machines, and also with software, texts, objects, databases and so on. Law thus goes on to argue much more generally that: 'the notion that social ordering is, indeed simply social disappears. . . . what we call the social is materially heterogeneous: talk, bodies, texts, machines, architectures, all of these and many more are implicated in and perform the social' (1994: 2). Such hybrids are on occasions tightly coupled with complex, enduring and predictable connections between peoples, objects and technologies, and these may move scientific findings across multiple and distant spaces and times (Law 1994: 24).

A particular scientific theory and set of findings may constitute an 'immutable mobile' where relative distance is a function of the relations between the heterogeneous components comprising that actor-network (Law, Hassard 1999). The invariant outcome of a network may be delivered so as to overcome regional boundaries. Things can be made *close* through networked relations.

Mobilities involve heterogeneous 'hybrid geographies' of humans-and-machines that contingently enable people and materials to move and to hold their shape as they move across various networks (Whatmore 2002). Dant develops the hybrid of the 'driver-car' that is neither the car nor the driver but the specific hybrid or intermittently moving combination of the two (2004). There are many other mobile hybrids that are encountered below, including the 'leisure-walker', the 'train-passenger', the 'cycle-rider' and so on.

Migrations and diasporas

Multiple mobilities have been central to much historical development and are not simply 'new'. Thus over many centuries there were complex trading and travel routes that constituted what we now call the Mediterranean world (Braudel 1992). The ships, sea routes, and interconnectivity of the slave and post-slave trade engendered what Gilroy terms the 'Black Atlantic' (1993). And the complex mobilities of diasporas and transnational migrants are key to examining many contemporary post-colonial relationships. There is a 'diasporization' of communities in the contemporary era (Cohen 1997; Paperstergiadis 2000: 89).

But although these are not new the mobile character of such processes is now much more evident. Analyses of migration, diasporas and more fluid citizenships are central to critiques of the bounded and static categories of nation, ethnicity, community and state present in much social science (Brah 1996; Joseph 1999; Ong 1999; Ong and Nonini 1997; Van der Veer 1995). Various works theorize the multiple, overlapping and turbulent processes of migration, dislocation, displacement, disjuncture, and dialogism. These massive contemporary migrations, often with oscillatory flows between unexpected locations, have been described as a series of turbulent waves, with a hierarchy of eddies and vortices, with globalism being a virus that stimulates resistance, and with the migration system's 'cascading' moves away from any state of equilibrium (Papastergiadis 2000: 102–4, 121).

For example, the fluid diaspora of the 32 m or so Latinos now living in the United States is the largest ethnic group in Los Angeles, forming a city within a city, and they will soon outnumber whites living in California (Davis 2000). There are wide-ranging processes of 'cultural syncretism that may become a transformative template for the whole society' as the United States becomes Latinized (Davis 2000: 15). Much of this syncretism stems from such 'transnationalized communities' moving between especially Mexico, now very much a 'nomadic' country, and the United States 'like quantum particles in two places at once' (Davis 2000: 77).

In such studies of such turbulence around the world, analyses of the global level are intertwined both with more 'local' concerns about everyday transportation and material cultures, as well as with the 'technologies' of information and communication technologies and the emerging infrastructures of mobility and surveillance (see Clifford 1997; Miller, Slater 2000; Sheller 2003). These studies of far-flung communities also bring out why and how members of such diasporic communities, although increasingly using the internet and mobile telephony, do meet on occasions face-to-face, in other words with the necessity of travel and meetings to reconstitute friendship or business networks or a family life lived at a distance.

And also increasingly significant within the contemporary world are multiple forms of forced migration (see Marfleet 2006). Such migrants originate in zones of economic and political crisis in the most vulnerable parts of the developing world. Their mobility is engendered by the instability of economic, social and environmental structures and especially the weakness of local states. Migrants mainly originate from 'wild zones' that the globalizing world engenders and especially from a 'culture of terror'. As Ascherson writes: 't[T]he subjects of history, once the settled farmer and citizens, have now become the migrants, the refugees, the *Gastarbeiter*, the asylum seekers, the urban homeless' (cited Paperstergiadis 2000: 1). And once people are forced to migrate, they then encounter the legal and social systems of the developed world which sets up many restrictions and limitations upon their migration and upon their capacity to stay. And their journeys are often extraordinarily long and complex, involving multiple relationships often of an exploitative character, various transit points especially in major cities and different modes of transport, some of which are notoriously unsafe (Marfleet 2006: ch. 10 on 'circuits of migration').

Pleasures

But travelling can also entail various kinds of pleasure resulting from non-cognitive processes. Patterns of movement involve an intermittent face-to-face relationship with other people (friends, kin, workmates, colleagues, networks), with other places (beaches, cities, river valleys, mountains, lakes) and with events (conferences, meetings, Olympics, festivals, exhibitions: Urry 2002b, 2003b). These face-to-face proximities produce a strong obligation to travel in order to experience the person, place or event and to be in their presence (but see De Botton 2002, on the contrary delights of armchair travel).

Especially significant are analyses of occasioned, intermittent face-to-face conversations and meetings that 'have' to occur within certain places at certain moments. Such intermittently occurring meetings seem obligatory for the sustaining of family, friendship, workgroups, businesses and leisure organizations (Goffman 1963, 1971a, 1971b, 1972; Amin, Thrift 2002; Urry 2003b). At the same time there are periods of distance and solitude in between these intermittent moments of co-presence.

Such mobilities often also entail distinct social spaces or nodes where these face-to-face encounters take place, such as stations, hotels, motorways, resorts, airports, corners, malls, subway stations, buses, public squares, leisure complexes, cosmopolitan cities, beaches, galleries, roadside parks and so on (Hajer, Reijndorp 2002). These are places of intermittent movement where specific groups come together, normally now involving the use of phones, mobiles, laptops, SMS messaging, wireless communications and so on, often to make arrangements 'on the move'. Some of these 'meetings' consist of 'underground' social gatherings or 'smart mobs' (Rheingold 2002). While other groups involve moving through relatively smooth corridors linking different nodes, as with business class air travel, fast lanes, express checkouts, business lounges and so on (see Lassen 2006, on the smooth corridors of aeromobility).

In particular, places are also experienced through diverse senses (see Urry 2000). Various theories of romanticism, the sublime, the picturesque and the performative are necessary to account for why certain groups feel a burning desire to be by a given lake, up a mountain, on that beach. These are distinctly visceral desires and they mobilize huge numbers of people regularly to travel and then to move around particular sites (Urry 2002c; Toiskallio 2002).

Moreover, different modes of travel involve different embodied performances, they are forms of material and sociable dwelling-in-motion, places of and for various occasioned activities. Different means of transport provides contrasting experiences, performances and affordances (Gibson 1986). Thus the railway in the late nineteenth century provided new ways of moving, socializing and seeing the swiftly passing landscape (Schivelbusch 1986). Recent analyses show how the car is 'dwelt in' or corporeally inhabited and experienced through a combination of senses (Featherstone, Thrift, Urry 2004). These sensuous geographies of the car are not so much located within individual bodies but extend to familial spaces, neighbourhoods, regions, and national cultures through various sensuous dispositions (Sheller 2004a; Bijsterveld 2001).

Various technologies are organized around and are part of movement. The iconic Sony Walkman was described as virtually an extension of the skin, moulded like much else in modern consumer culture to the body and designed for movement (Du Gay et al. 1997: 23–4). Indeed there are many activities possible while on the move some of which presuppose new mobile technologies. These include talking face-to-face and on mobile phones, glancing at the scenery, texting, working, listening to music (Walkman/iPod), using computers, information-gathering and being connected through maintaining a moving presence with others also on the move (Lyons, Jain, Holley 2007). Many of these entail pre-cognitive skills that are taken-for-granted, that are in the background and only partially articulated (Thrift 2004c). People know how to behave 'on the move' even if actually how the behaving is to be performed is hard to articulate. The technologies that are components of that life on the move can be 'ready-to-hand'.

Motility

Kaufmann especially argues against theories that emphasize fluidity and nomadism, maintaining that physical movement is something of an empty category (2002). It needs to be deconstructed so that the increasing speed of transport systems is not confused with a heightened significance of movement in social life. Furthermore, it is necessary to separate out actual movement from the potential for movement. The latter, motility, which can be defined as: 'the way in which an individual appropriates what is possible in the domain of mobility and puts this potential to use for his or her activities' (Kaufmann 2002: 37; all emphasized in original). Motility determinants include physical aptitude, aspirations, accessibility to transportation and communications, space-time constraints, knowledge, licenses and so on. These determinants of motility can be categorized in terms of 'access', 'skills' and 'appropriation', structured in terms of various system logics.

Mobility by contrast consists of observable movement, but Kaufmann notes that this takes various forms: residential movement, migration, travel and daily mobility and that it is necessary to distinguish between them. However, various motility determinants in certain parts of some societies are now producing certain hybrid forms lying in-between these four forms, of dual residence, very long-distance commuting combined with some working from home, households with separate homes, and short term tourism (Kaufmann 2002: 40–2). He shows empirically that simply because people can travel faster and further they are not necessarily more mobile; and that increased freedom does not necessarily result from all this motility potential.

Kaufmann also goes on to argue that there is a new important form of capital in some contemporary societies, namely motility capital that can be regarded as relatively autonomous from economic, social and cultural capital. Overall contemporary societies involve extensive temporal-spatial constraints. The degree of motility capital then constitutes 'an indispensable resource to enable people to get around the many spatial constraints that bind them. Quality of life often depends on the ingeniousness of the solutions invented and applied' (Kaufmann 2002: 103). A high degree of motility capital can then be necessary in order to compensate for capital deprivation elsewhere; alternatively high motility capital can augment other forms of capital. I will develop this notion of motility capital through a related notion of 'network capital' in order to connect the mobilities paradigm to issues of socio-spatial inequalities.

I have thus briefly set out an eclectic range of theoretical resources that will be drawn upon and developed in different chapters as I move through the ways in which various mobilities are part of and help to constitute local, national and global social relations.

Mobile Methods

In this section I examine how the mobilities paradigm involves new kinds of methods and new exemplars of what is appropriate research (again loosely following Kuhn's account of paradigm change: 1970). What I establish here is that research methods also need to be 'on the move', in effect to simulate in various ways the many and interdependent forms of intermittent movement of people, images, information and objects (see Bærenholdt, Haldrup, Larsen, Urry 2004; Sheller, Urry 2006b, for other versions). These varied 'mobile methods' are briefly introduced here – later examples of each are encountered and developed in the context of specific studies.

First, there is the 'observation' of people's movement, of bodies strolling, driving, leaning, running, climbing, lying on the ground, photographing and so on (a method Goffman especially undertook) This involves directly observing mobile bodies or observing them in digitally enhanced forms. Such bodies are observed undergoing various performances of travel, work, and play (Bærenholdt, Haldrup, Larsen, Urry 2004). Especially significant is the observing how people effect face-to-face relationships with places, with events and with people. Mobility involves occasioned, intermittent face-to-face conversations and meetings within certain places at certain moments that seem obligatory to some or all of the participants. Direct observation can be augmented by interactional, conversational and biological studies of how it is that people read and interpret the face of the other, as well as the body more generally (Hutchby 2001).

Second, there are several forms of participation in patterns of movement while simultaneously conducting ethnographic research. This can, for example, involve 'walking with', or travelling with people, as a form of sustained engagement within their worldview (see Morris 2004, on the research method of 'walking with' farmers in Peru and the Yorkshire Dales; Cass, Shove, Urry 2003). Through such 'co-present immersion' the researcher moves within modes of movement and employs a range of observation and recording techniques (Laurier 2002). It can also involve 'participation-while-interviewing' (Bærenholdt, Haldrup, Larsen, Urry 2004), in which the ethnographer first participates in patterns of movement, and then interviews people, individually or in focus groups, as to how their diverse mobilities constitute their patterning of everyday life.

A further method is keeping time–space diaries in which respondents record what they are doing and where, how they move during those periods and the modes of movement (Kenyon 2006). Such a diary enables researchers to plot for example how the household, and indeed different household members, move through time–space and perform activities that are intermittently on the move (see Bærenholdt, Haldrup, Larsen, Urry 2004: ch. 4). The diary can be textual, pictorial or digital or some combination. In a reflexive move the researcher's own trajectories of travel and affordances may also be interrogated in order to examine how it is generated on the move (Watts 2006).

Then there are varied methods that explore the imaginative and virtual mobilities of people through analysing texting, web-sites, multi-user discussion groups, blogs, emails and listserves (Wellman, Haythornthwaite 2002). Molz explores the interplay between round-the-world travellers' web-sites and blogs *and* the corporeal travel of round-the-world-travellers. This research involves web-surfing, in-person and email interviewing, and interaction in interactive sites and discussion groups (Molz 2006).

Much movement involves experiencing or anticipating in one's imagination the 'authentic atmosphere' of another place of places. But atmosphere is not reducible to material infrastructures nor to discourses of representation. Re-creating the nature of a place's atmosphere and its appeal or repulsion to imaginative travel necessitates the use of multiple qualitative methods including especially literary, artistic and imaginative research (De Botton 2002; Halgreen 2004; Bærenholdt, Haldrup, Larsen, Urry 2004). Comprehending the atmosphere or 'feeling' of particular kinds of movement often features in the imaginative travel (often through poetry and literature) of migration, exile and displacement across substantial geographical boundaries.

Much mobility involves the active development and performances of 'memory' of other people, places and especially meetings. Recovering such memories necessitates methods that qualitatively recreate how photographs, letters, images, souvenirs and objects are deployed within large social groupings or within family and friendship groups (Larsen 2005). This can involve researching the pictures and objects that people carry with them and which can then used to reassemble memories, practices and even landscapes in their varied sites of dwelling. However, as much of this is familial or private there is a major challenge to get inside such private worlds and to excavate those 'family secrets' especially about places of loss or desire.

Methods need to be able to follow around objects. This is because objects move as part of world trade which increasingly involves complex products; objects move in order to be combined into other objects (such as the components of a computer that travel the equivalent of journey to the moon); some objects travel and lose their value (cheap souvenirs) while other enhance their value through movement (an 'old master': Lury 1997); and as objects travel their cultural significance can grow as they accrete material and symbolic elements. Lash, Lury, Boden describe the appropriate methodology as establishing a cultural biography of objects (2006). Also the geographical flows of messages and of people can be tracked through the use of GPS and other technologies involved in contemporary communications (Licoppe 2004). Social positioning methods are likely to develop over the next few years which will enable the digital mapping and measuring of people's space-time movements through streets, buildings and neighbourhoods, part of what in chapter 13 I characterize as a 'digital panopticon' (Ahas, Mark 2005).

Further places themselves are not so fixed but implicated within complex networks that need to be examined (as researched in Bærenholdt, Haldrup, Larsen, Urry 2004). They can be dynamic – 'places of movement' (Hetherington 1997; see Wong 2006, on nineteenth-century Singapore). Places we might then say are like ships that move around and do not fixed within one location. Places thus travel, slow or fast, greater or shorter distances, within networks of human and non-human agents. Such hybrid systems that contingently produce distinct places need examination through methods that plot, document, monitor and juxtapose places on the go (see Sheller, Urry 2004, for various examples of such 'moving places').

Finally, research can examine how multiple tracks of people pass through various 'transfer points', places of in-between-ness. This is where 'populations' who are mobile can be monitored by various agencies charged with policing that territory; and simultaneously can be researched since they are temporarily immobilized – within lounges, waiting rooms, cafés, amusement arcades, parks, hotels, airports, stations, motels, harbours and so on. These transfer points necessitate a significant immobile network that is partly concerned to effect surveillance of intermittently moving populations. Material objects too move through such transfer points and they too can be tracked (and researched) as they move through such nodes especially as they often slow down as populations are also slowed down (Kesselring 2006b).

Conclusion

In this chapter I set out a range of resources of what I have termed the new mobilities paradigm. Especially significant are the varied writings of Simmel who did much to establish the contours of this paradigm. However, there was little further development during much of the twentieth century. But in the past decade or so an array of new initiatives in both theory and methods has begun to make possible the mobilities paradigm. I have especially noted the theoretical significance of various theoretical innovations, including complexity, sedentarism, fluidity and nomadism, moving materials, migration and diasporas, the pleasures of movement, social network analysis, and motility. I have also outlined various methodological innovations that in different ways simulate the movement of people, transport, objects, information and images.

The mobilities paradigm, as I detail in the next chapter, is not just substantively different, in that it remedies the academic neglect of

SuM
↓

various movements of people, object, information and ideas. It is transformative of social science, authorizing an alternative theoretical and methodological landscape. It enables the 'social world' to be theorized as a wide array of economic, social and political practices, infrastructures and ideologies that all involve, entail or curtail various kinds of movement of people, or ideas, or information or objects. And in so doing this paradigm brings to the fore theories, methods and exemplars of research that so far have been mostly out of sight. The term 'mobilities' refers to this broad project of establishing a 'movement-driven' social science in which movement, potential movement and blocked movement are all conceptualized as constitutive of economic, social and political relations.

3

The Mobilities Paradigm

> No changing of place at a hundred miles an hour will make us
> one whit stronger, happier or wiser . . . the really precious things
> are thought and sight, not pace
>   (John Ruskin, quoted de Botton 2002: 222)

I have elaborated some distinct theoretical and methodological
resources for the development of a mobilities paradigm within the
social sciences. An eclectic array of theories and methods has been
outlined. In this chapter I develop the main claims of this book that
are elaborated in later chapters. The starting point is that the analysis
of mobilities transforms social science. Mobilities make it different.
They are not merely to be added to static or structural analysis. They
require a wholesale revision of the ways in which social phenomena
have been historically examined. As we have seen all social science
needs to reflect, capture, simulate and interrogate movements across
variable distances that are how social relations are performed, organized and mobilized. They overcome diverse 'frictions of distance'
at local, national and global levels, although newly visible global
processes have brought such topics much more to the forefront of
current analysis.

Before that, however, I examine briefly the implications of my
claims for some debates currently sweeping through the social sciences relating to the notion of the 'post-human' (see Hayles 1999).
In a simple sense the analysis of mobilities and especially of multiple
and intersecting mobility systems, where each is an adaptive and
evolving relationship with each other, is an example of post-human
analysis. However, arguing that there is a substantive shift from
the human to the post-human presupposes that there was really

a previous era where the world was 'human' and principally constituted through disembodied and de-materialized cognition. This is the Enlightenment view which presumes a primacy of head over heels, mind over body and of humans separate from and productive of society and culture (Ingold 2004).

In that sense a mobilities turn is part of the critique of such a humanism that posits a disembodied cogito and especially human subjects able to think and act in some ways independent of their material worlds (Latour 1993; 2004). This book presumes the powers of 'humans' are always augmented by various material worlds, of clothing, tools, objects, paths, buildings and so on.

Thus we have never been simply 'human', let alone purely social (Latour 1993). Human life we might say is never just human. Indeed following Marx there are not only the relations of life but also the forces of life, those multiple objects that are 'ready-to-hand', as opposed to being merely 'present-at-hand'. Things are ready-to-hand, according to Heidegger, because we are doing things with them with a view to achieving something (1962). A hammer is ready-to-hand, it is used without theorizing. Only when it breaks or something goes wrong do we see the hammer as present-at-hand, just lying there inert. And what the mobilities paradigm emphasizes is that the objects that are ready to hand are highly varied, providing different affordances, especially many variably enabling or presupposing movement.

Objects can thus be distinguished in terms of whether they are *fixed* in place (railway track, hotel), temporarily *stationary* (car in garage, engine in engine shed), *portable* (book, car transporter), *corporeally interwoven* (Walkman, watch), *prosthetic* (heart pacemaker, mobile phone), *constitutive* of a mobility system (car, plane) or consist of *code* (washing machine, spreadsheets). Such a classification of 'objects' brings out huge variations in their ready-to-handedness but in all cases humans are nothing without such objects organized into various systems. The systems I argue below come first and serve to augment the otherwise rather puny powers of individual human subjects. Those subjects are brought together and serve to develop extraordinary powers only because of the systems that implicate them, and especially of those systems that move them, or their ideas, or their information or various objects.

Thus I seek in this book to examine a wide array of what Thrift terms 'movement-spaces', that is: 'the utterly mundane frameworks that move "subjects" and "objects" about' (2004b: 583). This book seeks to examine many such mundane frameworks that deal with various movement-spaces and not just the current processes of 'qualculation' engendered by new software. And I also seek to convey something of the dramatic changes involved in shifts from one mundane framework to another, and I try to examine such shifts through the language of complex adaptive systems. These movement spaces though increasingly depend upon what Thrift refers to as a kind of technological unconscious which bends and organizes bodies-with-environments, so generating some actions that are without cognitive input (Thrift 2004b: 585). Things simply get done that way and much of the time there is no thought given.

But what is also striking about the contemporary world is the notion of human perfectibility. Knorr Cetina argues that the biological sciences are encouraging the move away from the ideals of the Enlightenment towards an idea of individual perfectibility and enhancement, a shift from humans to a perfect life (2005). But life is not just a question of looking good through such enhancement but also being smart, sociable, full of integrity, pleasure seeking and especially mobile. And mobile communications both now and as they are rapidly morphing into is most emblematic of such changes. These small machines (or 'handies' as mobiles are known in various European countries) carry one's life in one's hand. Thus one's life is we might thus say 'ready-to-hand' with personalized information, address book, diary, telephone, message centre, photos, and one's personal network. Life is 'handy' and that is most definitely a new configuration. And that 'ready-to-handedness' travels with one as long as the batteries last, the system does not go down and the machine is not stolen (that is, it is too mobile!). And that handy is itself dependent upon its environment which is full of information, messages and increasingly senses (Thrift 2004b: 591).

Given these emphases I now set out the central features of a mobilities paradigm (this is derived from Sheller, Urry 2006b).

The New Paradigm

First, all social relationships should be seen as involving diverse 'connections' that are more or less 'at a distance', more or less fast, more or less intense and more or less involving physical movement. Social relations are never only fixed or located in place but are to very varying degrees constituted through 'circulating entities' (Latour 1987, 1993, 1999). There are many such circulating entities that bring about relationality within and between societies at multiple and varied distances.

Historically, the social sciences have overly focused upon ongoing geographically propinquitous communities based on more or less face-to-face social interactions with those present. Social science presumes a 'metaphysics of presence', that it is the immediate presence with others that is the basis of social existence. This metaphysics generates analyses that focus upon patterns of more or less direct co-present social interactions (as shown in Chayko 2002: 5).

But many connections with peoples and social groupings are not based upon propinquity. There are multiple forms of 'imagined presence' occurring through objects, people, information and images travelling, carrying connections across, and into, multiple other social spaces (Chayko 2002). Social life involves continual processes of shifting between being present with others (at work, home, leisure and so on) and being distant from others. And yet when there is absence there may be an imagined presence depending upon the multiple connections between people and places. All social life, of work, family, education and politics, presume relationships of intermittent presence and modes of absence depending in part upon the multiple technologies of travel and communications that move objects, people, ideas, images across varying distances. Presence is thus intermittent, achieved, performed and always interdependent with other processes of connection and communication. All societies deal with distance but they do so through different sets of interdependent processes and these include various discourses of movement.

Second, these processes stem from five interdependent 'mobilities' that produce social life organized across distance and which form (and re-form) its contours. These mobilities are:

- The *corporeal* travel of people for work, leisure, family life, pleasure, migration and escape, organized in terms of contrasting time–space modalities (from daily commuting to once-in-a-lifetime exile)
- The physical movement of *objects* to producers, consumers and retailers; as well as the sending and receiving of presents and souvenirs
- The *imaginative* travel effected through the images of places and peoples appearing on and moving across multiple print and visual media
- *Virtual* travel often in real time thus transcending geographical and social distance
- The *communicative* travel through person-to-person messages via messages, texts, letters, telegraph, telephone, fax and mobile

Social research typically focuses upon one of these separate mobilities and its underlying infrastructures and then generalizes from its particular characteristics. This new paradigm by contrast emphasizes the complex assemblage between these different mobilities that may make and contingently maintain social connections across varied and multiple distances (Urry 2004a). It focuses upon the interconnections between these five mobilities, as well as the discourses that may prioritize one or other such mobility (such as the belief that business has to be done 'face-to-face'). Weak ties based on intermittent corporeal travel connect people to the outside world, providing a bridge other than densely-knit 'clumps' of close friends and family. These extensive weak ties generate social networks that are sustained through intermittent meetings and communications. Such networks are increasingly spread across the globe and therefore depend upon multiple mobilities for their reproduction.

Third, physical travel involves lumpy, fragile, aged, gendered, racialized bodies. Such bodies encounter other bodies, objects and the physical world multi-sensuously. Travel always involves *corporeal movement* and forms of pleasure and pain. Such bodies perform themselves in-between direct sensation of the 'other' and various sensescapes. Bodies are not fixed and given but involves performances especially to fold notions of movement, nature, taste and desire, into and through the body. Bodies navigate backwards and forwards between directly sensing the external world as they move bodily in and through it, and discursively mediated sensescapes that signify social taste and distinction, ideology and meaning. The body especially senses as it *moves*. It is endowed with kinaesthetics, the sixth sense that informs one what the body is doing in space through the sensations of movement registered in its joints, muscles, tendons and so on. Especially important in that sense of movement, the 'mechanics of space', is that of touch, of the feet on the pavement or the mountain path, the hands on a rock-face or the steering wheel. Various objects and mundane technologies facilitate this kinaesthetic sense as they sensuously extend human capacities into and across the external world. There are thus various assemblages of humans, objects, technologies and scripts that contingently produce durability and stability of mobility. Such hybrid assemblages can roam countrysides and cities, remaking landscapes and townscapes through their movement. One effect is to change the nature of vision. The 'static' forms of the gaze of visitors, such as that from 'the balcony vantage point', focuses on the two-dimensional shape, colours and details of the view that is laid out before one and can be moved around with one's eyes (Pratt 1992: 222). Such a static gaze is paradigmatically captured through the still camera. There are emerging in the modern world various ways of capturing sights in passing, from a railway carriage, through the car windscreen, the steamship porthole, the camcorder viewfinder, or the mobile phone (Urry 2002c).

Fourth, on occasions and for specific periods, face-to-face connections are made through often extensive movement, and this was true in the past as it is now (as Simmel argued: see ch. 2). People travel on occasions to connect face-to-face but this face-to-faceness itself needs explanation. As well as various discourses there are five processes that generate face-to-face meetings (Urry 2003b). These are legal, economic and familial obligations to attend a relatively formal meeting; social obligations to meet and to converse often involving strong expectations of presence and attention of the participants; obligations to be co-present with others to sign contracts, to work on or with objects, written or visual texts; obligations to be in and experience a place 'directly' on occasions through movement through it and touch; and obligations to experience a 'live' event that happens at a specific moment and place. These obligations can be very powerful and generate what Durkheim termed 'effervescence' (1915). Chayko describes this as a 'powerful force or "rush of energy" that people sometimes feel within them in circumstances of togetherness' (2002: 69–70). Such feelings of intense affect can generate a compulsion to travel, often at specific times along particular routeways. This significance of intermittent face-to-faceness will be central to my analysis below of what is necessary for enduring forms of social life that much of the time are conducted at distance from the other(s).

Fifth, the facts of distance raise massive problems for the sovereignty of modern states that from the eighteenth century onwards seek to effect 'governmentality' over their populations. The targets of power, Foucault shows, are 'territory' and 'subjects' and their relationship. State sovereignty is exercised upon territories, populations and, we may add, the movement of populations around that territory. The central notion is that of disciplining the 'ensemble of a population' (Foucault, cited Gordon 1991: 20). That modern societies conceive of 'population' as a thinkable entity is key to their effective governmentality. Governing according to Foucault involves: 'a form of surveillance and control as attentive as that of the head of a family over his [*sic*] household and his goods' (1991: 92). And from the early nineteenth century onwards governmentality involves not just a territory with fixed populations but mobile populations moving in, across and beyond 'territory'. The 'apparatuses of security' involve dealing with the 'population' but any such population is at a distance, on the move and needing to be statistically measured, plotted and trackable, that is what Deleuze terms societies of control with power being more fluid and de-centred (1995). Such a 'mobile population' is immensely hard to monitor and to govern. The security of states increasingly involves complex control systems of recording, measuring and assessing populations that are intermittently moving, beginning in the 'west' with the system of the humble passport (Torpey 2000) but now involving many elements of a 'digital order' (Deleuze 1995). Imposing systems of reason upon the rapidly moving, the restless and the furtive is hugely problematic especially as discourses of movement carry much weight in the contemporary historical moment (see Law, Urry 2004).

Sixth, while social science typically treats social life as purified, as a social realm independent of the worlds of 'nature' and 'objects', this viewpoint is challenged here, as it is by Foucault who emphasizes how 'men' and 'things' are involved in governmentality. Studies in science and technology show that this purified *social* formulation is a misleading vision for social science (Latour 1993). What constitutes social life is fundamentally heterogeneous and part of that heterogeneity is are various material objects (including 'nature' and 'technologies') that directly or indirectly move or block the movement of objects, people and information. In order to concretize the social science turn toward incorporating the object world, it is necessary to examine the many ways in which objects and people are assembled and reassembled through time–space. Objects themselves travel across distance; there are objects that enable people to travel forming complex hybrids; there are objects that move other objects; there are objects that move that may mean that people do not move; there are objects and people that move together; there are objects can be reminders of past movement; and there are objects that possess value that people travel often great distances to see for themselves. So the entities that combine together to produce and perform social practices are highly heterogeneous. As they intermittently move they may resist or afford movement of other entities with which they are tightly or loosely coupled.

Seventh, crucial to analysing these relationships is the concept of 'affordance'. People do not encounter a set of objective 'things' in the environment that may or may not be visually perceived (Gibson 1986: ch. 8). Rather different surfaces and different objects, relative to the particular human organism and its technologies, provide affordances. These are objective *and* subjective, both part of the environment and of the organism. Affordances stem from their reciprocity through people's kinaesthetic movement within their particular world. Affordances constrain behaviour along certain possibilities:

'there are a range of options . . . implicit within a physical milieu and this implicitness is directly connected to the bodily capacities and limits of the [human] organism' (Michael 1996: 149). Given certain past and present social relations then particular 'objects' in the environment affords possibilities and resistances, given that humans are sensuous, corporeal, technologically extended and *mobile* beings. Examples of such affordances are a path that draws people to walk along it, a beach that invites one's skin to be tanned, a mountain that reveals a clear way of climbing it, a wood that is a repository of childhood adventures, and a museum that facilitates 'touching' the displays by the visually impaired moving through it.

Eighth, the focus upon objects combining with humans into various coupled relationships also implies the significance of systems that distribute people, activities and objects in and through time–space and are key in the metabolic relationship of human societies with nature. The human 'mastery' of nature has been most effectively achieved through movement over, under and across it. In the modern world automobility is by far the most powerful of such mobility-systems, while other such systems include the pedestrian-system, the rail-system and aeromobility. Historically earlier systems include the road system of the Roman Empire, the mediaeval horse-system after the invention of the stirrup, and the cycle-system in twentieth-century China. Historically most societies have been characterized by one major mobility-system that is in an evolving and adaptive relationship with that society's economy, through the production and consumption of goods and services and the attraction and circulation of the labour force and consumers. Such mobility-systems are also in adaptive and co-evolving relationships with each other, so that some such systems expand and multiply while others may over time shrink in terms of their range and impact. Such systems provide the environment within which each other system autopoietically functions.

Further, the richer the society, the greater the range of mobility-systems that will be present, and the more complex the intersections between such systems. These mobility-systems have the effect of producing substantial inequalities between places and between people in terms of their location and access to these mobility-systems. All societies presuppose multiple mobilities for people to be effective participants. Such access is unequally distributed but the structuring of this inequality depends *inter alia* on the economics of production and consumption of the objects relevant to mobility, the nature of civil society, the geographical distribution of people and activities, and the particular mobility-systems in play and their forms of interdependence. We might say that unforced 'movement' is power, that is, to be able to move (or to be able voluntarily to stay still) is for individuals and groups a major source of advantage and conceptually independent of economic and cultural advantage. High access to mobility depends upon access to more powerful mobility-systems and where there is not confinement to mobility-systems reducing in scale and significance.

Tenth, mobility-systems are organized around the processes that circulate people, objects and information at various spatial ranges and speeds. In any society there will tend to be a dominant process of circulation. The key issue is not the objects that are involved in movement (such as vehicles or telephones or computers) but the structured routeways through which people, objects and information are circulated. Such routeways in a society include the networks of bridleways, of footpaths, of cycle tracks, of railways, of telephone lines, of public roads, of networked computers, of hub airports (Graham, Marvin 2001). These routeways entail different modes of circulation and different forms of mobility-capital. And the more that a society is organized around the value of 'circulation', the greater the significance of network capital within the range of capitals available within a society. Although modern societies value circulation they are not equivalent in this valuation. Some societies are more organized for circulation, such as Singapore, with multiple overlapping modes of circulation (see Hanley 2004). Other societies especially in sub-Saharan Africa are characterized by a paucity of circulation modes. Societies further vary as to the degree to which their modes of circulation are localized, nationalized or internationalized.

Moreover, the range, complexity and choices between routeways generate the potential for movement or motility. High motility provides opportunities for circulation, enhancing the capital for those with high motility and worsening it for others. Motility also structures obligations. Opportunities entail obligations to make a call, to undertake a visit, to go to a conference, to reply to the email and so on. The opposite side of motility is the burden of mobility (Shove 2002). The larger the scale and impact of circulation, the greater will be the importance of network capital, as well as the plentiful burdens of mobility and the likelihood of various kinds of forced movement.

Eleventh, these various mobility-systems and routeways linger over time. There can be a powerful spatial fixity of such systems. New systems have to find their place physically, socially, economically and discursively within a fitness landscape in which there are already physical structures, social practices and economic entities that overcome distance and structure mobility in sedimented or locked in forms. Some of these sedimented systems are organized over very large spatial scales; their spatial fixing will be national or international. Systems are organized through time and this entails a path-dependency or lock-in of such systems (Arthur 1994a, 1994b). The last decade or so has seen the establishment of two new mobility-systems, 'networked computers' and 'mobile telephony'. These are ushering in new environments, social practices, economic entities and discourses that are laying down path-dependent patterns whose consequences will change mobility and motility patterns for much of this century.

Twelfth, mobility systems are based on increasingly expert forms of knowledge. This can be seen in the shifts in corporeal movement from slow modes such as walking and cycling to fast modes based on arcane technologies that require exceptional technical expertise. Such mobility systems tend to be based upon computer software that increasingly drive, monitor, regulate and in cases repair the system in question. The way that computers have entered the car is a good example of a progressive 'expert-ization' of systems which makes cars less easy to understand, let alone repair by the mere driver except in many developing societies where cars remain repairable with a complex recycling of parts (Miller 2000a, 2000b). The user is alienated from the system and yet simultaneously is more dependent upon such systems. If the systems go wrong, which of course they do, they are mostly unrepair-able. And at the minimum they require re-programming. These systems are moreover interdependent so that failures in one typically impact upon others especially where they are closely coupled. And yet in societies with high levels of mobility, social and economic practices increasingly depend upon such systems working out, being up-and-running so that personal, flexible and timetabled arrangements work out. People require systems being 'ready-to-hand' but such systems intermittently break down as well as being alienating.

Moreover, as people move around developing their individual life projects, especially in the 'north', so they extend their personal networks and appear to exert increased 'agency'. But as they exert such 'agency' so much about them gets left behind in traces on computers central to almost all mobility-systems. These reconfigure humans as bits of scattered informational traces resulting from various 'systems' of which most are unaware. Thus individuals increasingly exist beyond their private bodies and leave traces in informational space. The self come to be spread out or made mobile as a series of traces.

Finally, interdependent systems of 'immobile' material worlds, and especially exceptionally immobile platforms (transmitters, roads, garages, stations, aerials, airports, docks) structure mobility experiences. The *complex* character of such systems stems from the multiple fixities or moorings often on a substantial physical scale. Thus 'mobile machines', such as mobile phones, cars, aircraft, trains, and computer connections, all presume overlapping and varied time–space immobilities (Graham, Marvin 2001; Adey 2006b). There is no linear increase in fluidity without extensive systems of immobility. The latter include wire and co-axial cable systems, the distribution of satellites for radio and television, the fibre-optic cabling carrying telephone, television and computer signals, the mobile phone masts that enable micro-wave channels to carry mobile phone messages and the massive infrastructures that organize the physical movement of people and goods. The aeroplane central to contemporary global experiences requires the largest and most extensive immobility, the airport-city with tens of thousands of workers, helping to orchestrate millions of daily journeys by air.

There are several of these systems, co-evolving and interdependent, that extend and reorganize mobilities in the contemporary era. This involves the bending of time and space and generating dynamic system characteristics. Systems of material worlds produce *new* moments of unintended co-presence. The 'gates' designed to prevent networks from colliding are less sustainable, eliminating invisibilities that kept networks apart. Some of these new material worlds produce increasingly exciting *and* equally dangerous flows across otherwise impenetrable distances.

Dealing with Distance

I have set out the main features of the new paradigm. This paradigm examines how social relations necessitate the intermittent and intersecting movements of people, objects, information and images across distance. It has been shown how social science needs to reflect, capture, simulate and interrogate such movement across variable distances. This paradigm forces us to attend to this economic, social and cultural organization of distance, and not just to the physical aspects of movement. Most social science has not seen distance as a problem or even as particularly interesting (except for transport studies and transport geography). This mobilities paradigm though treats distance as hugely significant, as almost the key issue with which social life involving a complex mix of presence and absence has to treat. To illustrate these points and to conclude here I summarize some recent studies that demonstrate different elements of this emergent paradigm, studies that are helping to form the theories, methods and exemplars that are bringing such a paradigm into being.

I begin with 'traffic' and surprisingly with Karl Marx who described the body of the industrial worker who undertook repetitive operations. Such industrial work, he says: 'converts his whole body into the automatic, specialised implement of that operation' (Marx 1965: 339). Through such work the labourer is converted into a 'crippled monstrosity' as a result of becoming 'the automatic motor [*sic*] of a fractional operation' (Marx 1965: 360). And the contemporary city is similarly organized around: 'the objective architectonic of motion' and it produces bodies in thrall to traffic (Scanlan 2004). Traffic is patterned, embodied and mostly effective movement. The moving body in such traffic, a crippled monstrosity, is mostly able to find how to get around with the minimum of disorder (at least in some legible cities). Difficulties are temporary. The familiarity of a city can be found in multiple forms of dispersed knowledge, with taxi drivers, by-passers, street maps, signage and so on. Scanlan discusses Harry Beck's London Transport map of 1933 that conveyed a rational order of modern movement involving right angles and straight lines. Such way-finding in traffic occurs without reflection except when the systems break down. There are innumerable systems that enable: 'an ease of motion unknown to any prior urban civilization . . . we take unrestricted motion of the individual to be an absolute right. The private motorcar is the logical instrument for exercising that right, and the effect on public space, especially the space of the urban street, is that the space becomes meaningless . . . unless it can be subordinated to free movement' (Sennett 1977: 14).

Traffic moreover requires 'publics' based on trust, in which mutual strangers are able to follow shared rules, communicate through common sets of visual and aural signals, and interact even without eye-contact in a kind of thirdspace available to all 'citizens of the road' (Lynch 1993). The driver's body in traffic is fragmented and disciplined to the machine, with eyes, ears, hands, and feet, all trained to respond instantaneously, with the desire to stretch, to change position, or to look around being suppressed. The car becomes an extension of the driver's body, creating new urban subjectivities (Freund 1993). I examine in chapter 6 how the car is the 'iron cage' of modernity, motorized, moving and privatized since traffic is everywhere. And that traffic relentlessly moves, mostly finds it way, mostly moved through and by a system world that only reveals itself when it shuts down through congestion.

Second, in this examination of various analyses of mobility and distance, I turn to children and their protection (but not here from traffic which is a major killer of children). Ferguson argues that child protection is: 'pervasively an experience of mobility, of acting at speed to reach children, of the emotions and senses and intimate engagement with the sights, sounds and smells of other's lives and homes' (2004: 1). The development of child protection is a quintessentially modern phenomenon since it involves forceful interventions within other's homes and lives in order to protect a specific class of person. This is achieved through various practices conducted 'on the run'. Without movement there can be no child protection, with even the humble bicycle in the 1890s transforming the work of NSPCC officers since it enabled children to be seen directly and quickly (Ferguson 2004: 54–5). This led to the wider view that no one could and should escape the gaze of such child protection processes.

Later mobility developments, of the motorbike from the 1940s, the car from the 1950s and then the telephone, the computer and the mobile phone, added to the increased visibility of the endangered child located within the family home but away from the office. These all bring about a heightened instantaneity of time for child protection workers. At the same time the car provides a sanctuary for caseworkers away from the office and away from threatening clients (Ferguson 2004: 187). Overall child protection is a form of 'dwelling in mobility', getting to work, going to the client's home, meeting up for case conferences, gathering information through ICTs, phones, mobiles, and being out of the office.

It should also be noted that certain categories of 'children' are seen as problematic and maybe needing 'protection'. These are children who are standing still, loitering especially these days as captured on CCTV cameras. Here what indicates suspicion is that the children are suspiciously immobile (Neyland 2005).

The third illustrative case of the new mobilities paradigm concerns the varieties of performance that are involved in the potential purchase of a jug (Zukin 2003; actually a chicken-pitcher). The simple 'purchase' is performed in very different ways with distinct performances involving different 'mobilities'. It is the various mobilites that enable us to distinguish the different kinds of 'purchase' involved. Only by examining these different mobilities can we begin to see the different meanings involved in apparently the same consumption process. First, in Manhattan Zukin goes strolling around an area of high quality 'European' shops and sees a particular jug that she appreciates. Her mode of mobility here is that of *flâneurie* in an area that signifies quality. She visually consumes a particular style of jug although she does not actually purchase one. A little later she goes to Tuscany and encounters dozens of this 'same' jug but this time they are for her tourist kitsch. Her mobility here is again that of walking but she is carrying out the performance of a *tourist* consumer looking for souvenirs of a memorable visit. She buys one of these jugs. Later Zukin comes to develop expertise in this style of jug so she begins to practise the performance of a *connoisseur* enjoying the thrill of travel, search and acquisition of particular objects. She is able to compare and contrast different forms of this particular style of jug. She buys two or three while walking around various destinations.

And fourth Zukin goes virtually travelling to eBay and, as she develops into an accomplished user of eBay, she becomes a *commercial* buyer and seller of these jugs. They no longer signify taste, nor are souvenirs of a memorable visit, nor are collected qua connoisseur. They are objects of monetary gain. Thus the apparently simple task of buying a jug is performed and perform-able in strikingly different ways, through four modes of 'mobility', of *flâneurie*, tourist consumerism, connoisseurship and virtual commercial travelling. Only the different modes of mobility reveal the various meanings involved here.

The fourth illustrative example concerns the 'Caribbean' where multiple mobilities are involved in these apparent unchanging places of paradise (Sheller 2003; 2004b). The Caribbean has come to be generated out of massive flows of plants, people, ships, material resources, foodstuffs, technologies, know-how, and venture capital occurring over centuries. Early tropical travel to the Caribbean involved visitors from Europe being able to taste new fruits, to smell the flowers, to feel the heat of the sun, to immerse one's body in the moist greenery of the rainforest, as well as to see new sights (see Sheller 2003, 2004b).

The modern Caribbean, defined by its turquoise-blue sea and loosely tied together by shipping routes, airline networks, and radio, cable and satellite infrastructures, is the result of multiple, intersecting mobilities. Indeed it has been more deeply and continuously affected by migration than any other world region; the essence of Caribbean life is movement. Even 'local' populations in a place are never entirely immobilized, and have their own routes, migrations, and internet sites. Places to travel are thus places of habitation that reflect patterns of slavery, labour migration and transnational dwelling (Miller, Slater 2000).

Moreover, Sheller shows that not only does each Caribbean society embody and encompass a rich mixture of genealogies, linguistic innovations, syncretistic religions, complex cuisine and musical cultures, but these islands export their dynamic multi-cultures abroad where they recombine and generated new diasporic forms and places. The notion of the 'Caribbean' is not fixed and given but is on the move, travelling the world via the media, the internet and the World-Wide Web, or packed away in the suitcases of informal commercial importers, music pirates and drug dealers. There is no given original paradise on these paradise islands. The Caribbean is only comprehensible through multiple, overlapping and massively complex mobilities.

The final example of new mobility analysis concerns not beaches of paradise but rotting carcases of pigs and sheep. A multiplicity of movement forms was seen in the 2001 UK outbreak of foot and mouth disease (FMD) that occurred in pigs, sheep and cattle (Law 2006). The particular strain of FMD first appeared in central India in 1990; by 1995 it spread across much of India, and by 1998 it inserted itself into the international trade in animal products and was moving more rapidly. It appeared in Malaysia, in various impoverished countries of East Africa, and in Iran, Iraq and Turkey. By 2001 it appeared in countries that had been free of foot and mouth, including South Korea, Japan, and the UK. FMD can move so quickly across space because of the movements of infected animals, the movement brought about by direct contacts between animals, the movement of meat or meat products that circulate through trade, and the movement effected by human contact when people are in close proximity with infected animals.

The organization OIE (Organization International des Épizooties) classifies countries across the world in of three categories with regard to FMD: disease free without (routine) vaccination; disease free with vaccination; and disease endemic. This classification has major consequences since it serves to regulate trade, the flows of animals and of meat products. Countries that are disease free without routine vaccination may export their animals anywhere. The OIE/WTO rules of trade act like a dike around these privileged areas. The EU moved to a vaccination-free policy and this brought significant benefits but it also increased the likelihood that once the dikes were breached then the virus would pour into European space.

And this is what happened, spreading especially within the UK because three further processes heightened the scale of livestock movement. First, much foodstuff is imported into the UK, especially within the 2.5m containers that arrive each year, with most being unexamined. Second, since the BSE outbreak in the 1980s around four-fifths of UK abattoirs have been closed, partly because each abattoir now needs a resident vet. As a result the livestock has to travel further in order that it can be slaughtered within an approved abattoir. Third, the Common Agricultural Policy works through an annual payment per animal. Farmers, who do not reach their quota on the due date, are penalized. In January and February 2001 two million sheep were traded in the UK, as farmers sought to top up their quotas so as to receive appropriate EU payment. These exceptional movements had the effect of rapidly carrying the foot and mouth virus once it had 'landed' within UK borders (Law 2006).

Further, the social science analysis of 'normal accidents' shows that when things go wrong in systems where the flows of materials are quick and complex, then the consequences can be unpredictable, difficult to control, and likely to ramify unpredictably throughout the system (Perrow 1999; Law 2006). When something goes wrong it goes wrong very quickly. In a complex system with such rapid flows, normal accidents are always waiting to happen, and happen they did in this case with beasts, micro-organisms, people, money, trucks and feed moving around in ways that are complex and often too fast for intervention. The barriers holding the flows apart were unreliable. In 2001, the virus spread around much of England before anyone knew that it had even arrived. That we might say is fast mobility, a normal accident.

Conclusion

So in Part 1, I have established the lineaments of a mobilities paradigm. I outlined some of the substantive phenomena that helped to provide the preconditions for a mobility structure of feeling. I set out some theoretical and methodological resources for the paradigm. And finally I briefly discussed five different examples which show the power of such a paradigm to reveal what an a-mobile social science would leave buried.

In Part 2, I go on to analyse five different modes of moving about, corporeally and through virtual and communicative travel (see Cresswell 2006, for various other movement-forms including dance that I do not consider here). I show how each case of movement is socially and materially organized and only rarely and exceptionally is it merely a way of getting from A and B as fast as possible. I also show such movement is intertwined with social practices which have powerful time and space dependent consequences. Also and relatedly these forms of movement are important ways in which the world beyond the self is sensed and experienced, with in a way how the world comes to be seen, felt, experienced and known about, how it is made an object of 'affect'. Mobilities are thus in significant ways ontological and epistemological. Moreover, much of that knowing occurs through various objects with which that form of movement is intertwined. I begin in the first chapter of Part 2 with walking and the affordances provided by the crucially important objects of pavements and paths (as well as footwear, clothing, maps and so on) without which the modern world would have been a very different kind of world.

AND ANCIENT ?

Part 2

Moving and Communicating

4

Pavements and Paths

Take only photographs, leave only footprints
(Sierra Club dictum)

Walking and the Social World

In a way all movement involves intermittent walking. Pedestrianism is everywhere, even when using those big mobility machines encountered in later chapters. In terms of the history of movement, walking is easily its most significant form, and it is still a component of almost all other modes of movement. This chapter thus discusses the form of movement underpinning most mobilities.

Walking was encountered a number of times in Part 1. I noted Simmel's account of how walking impresses into the surface of the earth and that over time this movement is frozen into the solid structure of a path (1997: 171). Paths demonstrate the accumulated imprint of journeys made as people go about their everyday business. Ingold describes how the network of paths shows the sedimented activity of a community stretching back over generations (1993: 167). People can imagine themselves treading the same paths as earlier generations as a given path comes to be iteratively impressed into the ground.

I also noted how one source of the term 'mobile' is 'mob' and its connections with 'governmentality'. Before the late eighteenth century in Europe, walkers were the dangerous 'other', as vagrants or a potential mob. There were laws and systems designed to outlaw those who were walking about. Walkers were 'other' unless part of an army. No one would go walking unless they could not avoid doing so. And many of those walking were forbidden to go into many places (such as Beijing's Forbidden City). There were often draconian laws against trespassing. There were few rights to roam although customary routes did exist where footpaths had been established and maintained through regular use.

Also I noted how different societies are characterized by the domination of one or other mobility-system. Thus footpower's 'long slide towards obsolescence' symbolically begins in 1830 with a million Britons watching the iconic opening of the Liverpool and Manchester railway, the first large-scale passenger railway (Solnit 2000: 256). Footpower came to be further challenged by the mobility systems of cycling and automobility, systems unequally distributed in terms of class, gender, ethnicity, age and dis/ability relations.

This chapter thus examines various moments in this history of walking, moments that reveal four characteristics. First, there are many different ways in which the walking body produces and reproduces social life. Those rhythms of the body, treading and re-treading its footsteps, engender an astonishing array of biosocial practices. As Solnit maintains: 'Walking has created paths, roads, trade routes; generated local and cross-continental senses of place; shaped cites, parks; generated maps, guidebooks, gear, and, further afield, a vast library of walking stories and poems, of pilgrimages, mountaineering expeditions, meanders and summer picnics' (2000: 4). Walking may be slow but it is the commonest means of overcoming the friction of distance and it is therefore part and parcel of multiple socialities, in countrysides, suburbs and cities. Up to the development of the 'sitting society' over the past two or three centuries, the principal features of life were experienced through walking and squatting (Ingold 2004: 323).

Second, although pedestrianism may underpin other mobilities and its form distinguishes humans from all other species, there is nothing 'natural' about walking (Ingold 2004). Mauss shows that walking involves specific and societally variable techniques of the body (1979). Walking varies greatly, within and across different societies. According to Mauss this results from the 'social nature of the "habitus"' (1979: 101). There are various styles, different ways of moving upright through varied environments. We might say there are different walking bodies, such as Japanese and European walking bodies (Kawada 1996). Each kind of walking involves a set of bodily techniques, each dependent upon different pre-cognitive ways of anticipating how to be in the world that surrounds and constructs each person.

Third, there are thus many ways to walk, sometimes walking is mundane (to shop), sometimes the basis of unutterable suffering (to go on a forced march) and sometimes an activity of joyous fulfilment (to climb a much-loved hill). Each contests the general dominance of 'head over heels', of cognition over groundedness, in the long history of western thought (Ingold 2004). Rather we should reinsert the epistemological and ontological significance of walking. It is everywhere and combined with hands, it is how people are embedded or inserted into their physical and social worlds. Through locomotion the environment is perceived, known about, lived within. And in locomotion one particularly strange 'modern' form is walking for its own sake, freely chosen, sending the bare body off into environments sometimes of danger and foreboding. Such peak moments, pushing the body to extremes, provide: 'a means to contact the Earth, to be at one with "nature", even to be deemed therapeutic. It becomes a means of gathering stillness' (Thrift 2001: 46).

Finally, walking is interdependent with multiple technologies that afford different possibilities for walking, and especially walking for its own sake. The walker combines with an array of both general and specific technologies that enable walking to different places, at different speeds, in different styles. These technologies include footwear, other clothing, places of rest, paving and pathways, other means of movement, places to walk to, rules and regulations about movement and access, signage and so on. Such technologies intersect with the capacities of human bodies, of strength, height, weight, vision, balance, touch and so on. In combination they produce different capacities to 'walk the walk', to touch the world, to know how places are and might be, to produce different walking bodies (Ingold 2004; see Shilling 2005, generally on bodies and technologies).

In the next section I examine some features of walking the streets of modern cities, a practice intertwined with notions of rambling and *flâneurie*, strategy and tactics. The third section analyses the development of leisurely walking in the countryside showing its connections with other technologies of movement, its hybridized character and its capacity to produce different 'countrysides'. In the conclusion the changing connections of walking with social life, networks and social relations lived at-a-distance are briefly elaborated, connections that reveal the emergence of walking as a site of leisure and bodily pleasure.

Walking Streets

City streets were not so much paved with gold but increasingly they were paved, and paving transforms the bodily techniques of walking. Beginning with London in the mid eighteenth century modern societies learned to pave their routeways, turning urban spaces into something closer to a parade ground. This produced a major transformation in the nature of walking, since previously walkers had had to pick their way: 'along pot-marked, cobbled or rutted thoroughfares, littered with the accumulated filth and excrement of the countless households and trades whose businesses lay along them' (Ingold 2004: 326).

Walkers were from all classes, the only exception being elite groups able to get other walkers to carry them through those pot-marked, cobbled or rutted thoroughfares. In China, during the Han dynasty, the elite travelled in light bamboo seats supported on a carrier's back, while in later dynasties wooden carriages on poles are documented on various scrolls. Elderly and women members of the elite were particularly likely to ride in what in the west came to be known as sedan chairs. These seem to have been widespread in the sixteenth to eighteenth centuries, in London and Bath. The chairs often stood in the hallways of great houses, so enabling 'ladies' to be transported to their destination without setting foot on the filth and excrement of the typical street. By the mid seventeenth century sedans for commercial hire had become common in London, partly popular because they took up less road space than horse-drawn carriages. Other examples of walkers as 'transporters' were found in Scotland, Latin America and North America (www.calsky.com/lexikon/en/txt/s/se/sedan_chair.php: accessed 28.11.04).

However, walking was afforded new possibilities followed legislation in 1761 to ensure that London street surfaces in richer neighbourhoods should be smooth and uniform, intermittently cleaned, free from sewage and rubbish, lit at night and open and straighter, so providing the capacity to see and to be seen (Rendell 1998: 78–9). This can be seen as a pivotal moment, involving what Ingold calls the increasing groundlessness of modern society, a 'reduction of pedestrian experience to the operation of a stepping machine' (2004: 329). And stepping machines were increasingly everywhere, leaving no mark on the surface of the pavement and affording new kinds of speedier and distant walking to many. This we might see as a moment in Elias' analysis of the 'civilizing process' where there is long term demise of the sense of touch achieved through hands and feet (1978;

see Lewis 2001: 67). We leave no footprints – but only because the paths have already been paved.

But while paving afforded new affordances to all 'pedestrians', they were profoundly marked by distinctions of class, gender, age and ethnicity. From an early stage these paved streets of London became sites of urban male rambling (see Rendell 1998). For single, upper-class, heterosexual, young men, rambling involved walking without a definite route, distracted and concerned with adventure, entertainment and sexual pleasure. Rambling converts the city into a space of flows with women on the streets being made visible, on display, waiting to be 'consumed'. The proliferation of clubs, opera houses, theatres and arcades provided a series of linked places for the male rambler to move between while on a 'promiscuous ramble', often taking in places of the 'other' in London's East End (Rendell 1998: 85). More generally, the experiences of the solitary male walker came to define the presumed qualities of the streets of the emergent modern cities (in London, especially through the literature of Blake, Wordsworth, de Quincey, Dickens: Solnit 2000: 183–5). In the early decades of the nineteenth century, Nash's plans for the area around Piccadilly involved establishing an upper-class shopping and entertainment zone, a zone that opened up vistas marking out a 'city as spectacle' for those walking in and through that area.

Such a spectacle was though emulated within mid-nineteenth-century Paris with Haussmann's rebuilding. A large network of new boulevards was blasted through the heart of the old mediaeval city. This rebuilding displaced 350,000 people; by 1870 one-fifth of the streets of central Paris were Haussmann's creation; and at the height of the reconstruction one in five of Parisian workers worked in construction (Berman 1983: ch. 3; Clark 1984: 37; Edholm 1993).

Paris was the first city to afford long range vistas for the peripatetic local and for visitors. Paris came to be possessed by those who were able to consume as they walked along the new paved boulevards and passed by, and into, the brightly lit arcades, shops, department stores and cafés. The Marquis de Salvo described the capital in 1846: 'tumult, a mass of objects which every day reproduce the sensations of the day before: the sight of beautiful shops, richly decorated cafes, elegant carriages, lovely costumes, lovely women . . . and all this kaleidoscope which changes, stirs, bemuses' (quoted Green 1990: 75; Berman 1983; Benjamin 1999).

The paved boulevards were central to this planned reconstruction, being like arteries in a massive circulatory system and functional also for rapid troop movement (as Benjamin 1999, argues). However, they also restructured what could be seen or gazed upon by those out walking the city. Haussmann's plan entailed the building of markets, bridges, parks, the Opera and other cultural palaces, many being located at the end of the boulevards. For the first time in a major city people could see well into the distance, their eyes were seduced by the sights in question, and they could envisage where they were going to and where they had come from. Great sweeping vistas were afforded, so that walks along these boulevards led up to a dramatic climax. As Berman says: 'All these qualities helped to make Paris a uniquely enticing spectacle, a visual and sensual feast . . . after centuries of life as a cluster of isolated cells, Paris was becoming a unified physical and human space' (1983: 151).

These boulevards brought enormous numbers of people to encounter each other in novel ways. Berman talks of how the boulevards and cafés created a new kinds of space, especially one where friends and lovers could be 'private in public', intimately together without being physically alone (1983: 152). Lovers caught up in the movement of modern Paris in the 1860s and 1870s could intensely experience their emotional commitment. It was the traffic of people and also horses that transformed social experience in this modern urban area. Urban life for the prosperous was exceptionally rich and full of possibilities, and at the same time dangerous and frightening. Baudelaire wrote: 'I was crossing the boulevard, in a great hurry, in the midst of a moving chaos, with death galloping at me from every side' (quoted Berman 1983: 159). New systems of circulation brought many more horses as well as pedestrians moving faster along these new Parisian streets, the first modern city 'concretizing' pedestrianism (at least for the rich). The city came to belong to those who could consume it through their pedestrianism (Edholm 1993: 149).

To be private in the midst of danger and chaos created the perfect romantic setting of modern times; and millions of visitors re-experience that quality while moving along and into the boulevards and cafés. Part of the experience of the new modern city was the multitude of other walkers passing by, who enhanced the lovers' vision of themselves and who in turn provide an endlessly fascinating source of curiosity. The more each saw of others and showed themselves to others – the more that people participated in the extended 'family of eyes' – the richer became their vision of themselves (Berman 1983: 152).

Paris was said to be increasingly a city of vice, display, fashion and consumption (see Clark 1984: 46–7). In particular it was the city of the new urban type, a modern hero, the *flâneur* (Frisby 1994). It is fascinating to note that it was a category of walker that has been seen as emblematic of a society in which 'all that is solid melts into air' (subsequently of course much else has melted into air; Berman 1983). The anonymity of the crowd provided asylum for those on the margins of society who could walk about unnoticed, observing and being observed, but never really interacting with those encountered. The *flâneur* was the modern hero, able to travel, to arrive, to gaze, to move on, to be anonymous, to be in a liminal zone; in other words to be out in public and moving about in the city's paved, public spaces among strangers (Tester 1994a: 5, 1994b; Benjamin 1999).

Paris thus gave rise to a new urban type, an urban myth, presumed to be an observant and solitary man strolling around the city and partly able to be lost in the crowds of other walkers at the same time that he explored them. The *flâneur* strolled, afforded new opportunities by the pavements and boulevards, and viewed by others and yet hidden from view because of the crowds of others also able to walk about (Benjamin 1999: 420). Benjamin specifically links this to the new form taken by the surface that is walked along. He describes the 'gaze of the *flâneur* . . . who seeks refuge in the crowd' as he goes 'botanising on the asphalt' (Benjamin 1999: 21). The *flâneur* seeks the essence of a place while at the same time becoming a consumer of it especially as later new department stores 'put flâneurie to work for profit' (Benjamin 1999: 21). Such walking involved visual pleasure (a 'phantasmagoria'), the immersion in the crowd, the consuming of new goods and services and the general development of leisureliness. This way of walking, as though one had 'all the time in the world' meant 'scrutinising, detective work, and dreaming [that] set the *flâneur* apart from the rush-hour crowd' (Game 1991: 150). This specific type of 'walker', the *flâneur*, is a character in much literature of the period especially in Baudelaire and Balzac (and later Musil and Sartre: Tester 1994a: 8–12).

But walking varies for different social groups. The *flâneur* was rich and male. Yet their visibility was at the expense of restricting 'respectable' women to the domestic sphere through what has been conceptualized as 'private patriarchy' (Walby 1990). At the same time such women were colonizing other emerging public spheres in the nineteenth century, especially the department store, one place at least that was not out of bounds to the *flâneuse* (Wolff 1993). Power relations determined where and when, different social groups were able to walk, these nineteenth-century metropolises revealing the politics of walking, especially significant when walking was the dominant mobility-system.

For working-class women walking in the crowd in the nineteenth-century space of Paris was full of risks, especially from the gaze of male *flâneurs*. Such women lived on the streets and were presumed to be sexually available as prostitutes, for sexual consumerism. And there were indeed huge numbers of prostitutes in nineteenth-century Paris, a city overwhelming in its size and grandeur for those only able to walk around on foot (Palmer 2000: 149; Edholm 1993).

Overall, though, the arcades, the new boulevards built for movement, the wide pavements, the use of gas lighting, the new monuments, the cafes and shops to visit and the emerging department stores provided an array of new affordances for prosperous male walkers. The young Baudelaire was said to have strolled about all evening on the boulevards and in the Tuileries (Solnit 2000: 201). Paris became a city for pedestrianism, a city dominated by the mobility system of walking, a pattern that in part survived for almost a century (see Solnit 2000: 211, on the dominance of the car-system by the 1970s). In Paris, walking continued to be stimulated by a plethora of desires and goals stemming from the interrelations between bodily movement, fantasy, memory and the texture of urban life. It was a place that invited strolling around and possessing it. People were invited into its nooks and crannies, at the same time that their eyes were afforded grand vistas stretching into the far distance.

Research on nineteenth-century Vienna shows something similar. It is argued that various improvements in its infrastructure, new forms of social control and new kinds of sight-seeing travel had the effect of generating a 'linear' perception of nineteenth-century Vienna (Spring 2006). Earlier guidebooks had not indicated how to move from sight to sight; but as the nineteenth century progressed, so guidebooks began to trace continuous lines and narratives of the city, a feature related to the efforts made to open up Vienna for traffic and for its increasingly rapid and extensive movement. A linear notion of the city of Vienna came into being and this included walking tours for visitors as a key element.

Indeed the strolling *flâneur* was a forerunner of the twentieth-century tourist more generally, and of the activity emblematic of tourists, the taking of photographs while walking about more or less every other city and countryside across the globe (Urry 2002c). Sontag describes how the strolling photographer, looking but not possessing:

> first comes into its own as an extension of the eye of the middle-class *flâneur* . . . The photographer is an armed version of the solitary walker reconnoitring, stalking, cruising the urban inferno, the voyeuristic stroller who discovers the city as a landscape of voluptuous extremes. Adept of the joys of watching, connoisseur of empathy, the *flâneur* finds the world 'picturesque' (1979: 55).

Strolling around, being seen and recorded, and of seeing others and recording them, presumes a distinct hybrid, the strolling 'walker-photographer'. Such a hybrid has been enormously significant in making notable whatever is photographed. The objects then of cameras and films serve to constitute how to walk the city as a leisured 'visitor', they have constructed a twentieth-century sense of what is worth walking to in order to 'sight-see'. For the hybrid 'walker-photographer' walking involves strolling from one 'good view' to a series of others (the linear city mentioned above) and being on the lookout, ready to detect and capture each unmissable view (Tester 1994b, on the *flâneur* as detective).

So far I have described walking in fairly general terms. I now consider some more specific formulations about the organized character of walking the contemporary city, a topic that has concerned diverse analysts including Situationists, symbolic interactionists, ethnomethodologists, urban ethnographers, and campaigners for the 'disabled'.

Debord and de Certeau both developed the idea of walking as a politics of resistance. Debord developed a theory of the *dérive* or drifting. He argued that walkers in the city should drop their usual reasons and bases of movement or action and let themselves be spontaneously drawn to the attractions of the terrain and to any social encounters that they might experience (Debord 1981: 5). Such a Situationist take on walking believed that it could involve a revolutionary contestation of the patterning of the city, establishing an imaginary city rather than that specified by the routine practices of ordinary life.

This *dérive* has echoes in de Certeau's analysis of the acts of walking as constituting the city, analogous to the ways in which individual speech acts constitute language (1984). His analysis of this ironically begins by looking down from the roof of New York's former World Trade Center. De Certeau contrasts the strategies with the tactics of walking. The former involves the victory of space over time. Strategies involve disciplining and regimentation, based upon notions of what are proper activities and ways of walking within and through particular spaces. Tactics by contrast consist of the inventive seizing of opportunities within the city that happen to occur. They serve to constitute lived space and are improvisational and unpredictable, able to bring out feelings and relationships that are repressed and hidden away. Walkers and walking can give shape to how places are and should be dwelt in and used. For de Certeau, while a place, such as a street, is ordered and stable, spaces only exist through movements, velocities, activated by the ensemble of

everyday movements occurring within it. Such performances generally involve conflictual tactics and contestation over the uses of space
by social groups improvising in time. De Certeau articulates here a
romanticism of the mundane and everydayness of the walker. Walking
is potentially creative, contestatory, developing meaningful encounters, extending social relations and sometimes impressing a new path
into the urban fabric (Thrift 2004a, on a de Certeau-influenced
analysis of 'driving the city').

Such a conceptualization of walking enables one to analyse how
the same space can harbour very different walking practices. At the
iconic world site of the Taj Mahal, Edensor describes how in 'enclavic
tourist spaces' walking is smooth and ordered with rapid movement
and clear functions of the different zones (1998). Various personnel
regulate the walking of package holiday visitors who often internalize
modes of *appropriate* walking. Space dominates time and there is
little fantasy, memory and desire to effect tactical subversion and
innovation.

By contrast backpackers in 'disorganized tourist spaces' walk in a
less programmed manner, they are improvizational with vivid encounters with diverse and disruptive elements. Local people will often
seek to interrupt movement through particular spaces and it will be
difficult to avoid touching 'others'. Contacts with vehicles and animals
are also unavoidable. The trajectories of visitors will co-exist with,
and criss-cross, local pathways. This engenders less rigid bodily pos-
tures and a more casual wandering and lounging, even the deliberate
seeking out of risky environments that enhance the possibilities of
getting lost, developing *dérive* or drifting à la Debord. In such streets
of everyday confusion there are many tactical possibilities as there
are in Calcutta where walking is a 'zigzag, serpentine, stop-and-start,
crab affair' (Hutnyk 1996: 135). Footpaths are uneven, full of rubble,
often flooded, overflowing with hawkers and families on the streets.
Indeed these are fewer places for pedestrianism and more for dwelling and so tourist walking is often practised on the road side, just off
the overwhelming bustle, noise, activity along the unpaved sidewalks.
However, for all the 'chaos' of Indian streets there are plenty of
rules and conventions, a kind of order out of chaos (Hutnyk 1996:
135–6).

Some of these rules relate very directly to issues of bodily security
that are of major significance for diverse social groups in affording
the kinds of walking possible within different environments. Generally, it is presumed that the more there are other people also visibly
walking about, the greater the bodily security afforded by that place.
If there are what Jane Jacobs calls 'eyes on the street' then normally

the environment will afford relatively safety for people to be bodily present within it, to be co-present with unknown strangers (1961). It is those unknown others, and especially a wide mixture of such others, that give places the kind of 'atmosphere' conducive to walking, an invitation to stroll, linger, pause, move on again, bearing in mind of course that such other bodies are always marked by gender, class, age, ethnicity, place, dis/ability and so on.

Such atmospheres stem from how people are 'attuned' to particular places (Heidegger 1962). For example on the island of Bornholm research shows how an apparently unspectacular fishing village invites 'strolling, drifting, hanging around, shopping, eating and chatting around a "non-sight" site' (Bærenholdt, Haldrup, Larsen, Urry 2004: 45). This particular place, like many others, has the kind of atmosphere such that pleasures and bodily security are afforded to those able to walk about. Atmosphere is in the relationship of peoples and objects. It is something sensed often through movement and experienced in a tactile kind of way, what Thrift terms 'non-representational' practices (1996).

One set of places with a very different atmosphere, which appears not to afford the possibilities of walking about for many, are 1960s/1970s public housing estates found in many cities across the world. These are characterized by dense apartment living within a modernist environment and where very few people are typically out and about in the public spaces. Such estates are places of absence. Halgreen evocatively describes their virtual emptiness; how on 'the large lawns made for playing, on the wide pavement make for walking, and on the great plazas created for the gathering of people, emptiness reigns . . . The lack of people evokes an intangible, uneasy feeling that something is wrong', there is an enigmatic void that exudes danger and insecurity (2004: 150). One visitor describes such a forbidding atmosphere: 'There was nothing but cold, brutal concrete – not a single person in sight. It really touched me being able to walk between these huge buildings and there was no life whatsoever. I imagined that if any life did appear, it would be a violent sort of life' (quoted Halgreen 2004: 151).

Visitors deploy various de Certeau-type tactics to get by in moving around empty spaces providing so few affordances to the leisurely walker (no maps, routeways, sights, refreshments for those 'visiting'). First, one can walk as though one is a local, moving fast and seeking to get through the concrete desert speedily, not looking around and certainly not photographing anything. Second, one can imagine that one is local and play at appreciating the atmosphere of modernist utopian buildings, trying out its exciting new features for the period such as the lifts. And third, one can be a tourist (or better a post-tourist). Here one walks through the lonely concrete desert, carrying a camera, stopping, and looking around with feigned curiosity, even if no inviting teashop ever looms into view (see Halgreen 2004: 152–3, on these tactics).

These places of absence thus bring out how the co-presence of others seems crucial to producing bodily security, to be able to walk with ease and to avoid the 'interactional vandalism' that can be directed at women, ethnic groups, older people, depending upon the kinds of places in which one is walking. Roughly speaking the more diverse the others walking about, the safer the environment. Overall it seems that what is important is the complexity of place, heterogeneity makes the environment interesting and safe for those doing walking in the presence of strangers.

Places thus provide greater affordances for (able-bodied) walkers when people walk slowly, finding clutter and complexity. While the more the environment is designed to be walked through fast or driven through, the worse the affordances for other able-bodied walkers. And the more the environment is good for slow walking, the worse it then is for car drivers (Demerath, Levinger 2003: 223). Overall the greater the diversity of activity on the street the more likely are potential forms of interaction, interactions being very varied in content and significance (hence the problem of 'unwanted attention'). Seats, benches, entertainers, street hawkers, vendors, cafes, open air markets, shops, other pedestrians all afford greater possibilities of pausing and conversing through finding common topics to begin talk (Demerath, Levinger 2003: 221–2). A key notion here is that of 'pausability', the ease of interrupting the activity of walking and then of resuming it again, something not effectively afforded through modernist estates except for teenage walkers who may well find it full of relevant affordances (Demerath, Levinger 2003: 230).

Research on the 1995 Chicago heatwave shows the importance of the possibilities of walking, pausing and conversing (Klinenberg 2002). Thousands of people died prematurely in this heatwave but what was striking was how similar poverty-stricken areas demonstrated very different patterns of death. In areas that afforded opportunities for people to get out and about, to visit shops and local services, where there was an atmosphere encouraging diverse opportunities for social interaction, the death rate from the heatwave was much lower. The connectedness of houses with habitable streets, accessible parks, shops, cafes, neighbours and so on provided affordances for everyday walking. Where these affordances were rich and diverse then people would go out and about even in very high temperatures. In such areas where people were walking and talking they survived the heatwave. But in the opposite case, where there were poor affordances within people's neighbourhoods for walking and talking, then people died in larger numbers.

It should also be noted that the affordances of walking include many aspects of the material layout and current condition of streets, pavements, ramps, kerbs, signs and potential shelter, and their relationship to people's varied bodily capacities (see Hodgson 2002). For the up to 1 m blind and partially sighted people in the UK, the urban environment, its streets, pavements, ramps, kerbs, signs and shelter, can all resist their routine walking and thus afford less movement and activity in time–space. This is so even when assisted by canes, guide dogs, ramps and street indicators. Recently, a few rich cities are developing various technologically advanced 'wayfinding' technologies deploying radio frequency beacons and these provide information to the visually impaired so as to counter the many resistances of place (Hine, Swan, Scott, Binnie, Sharp 2000). More generally we must note the specificity of walking and problematize the claim that it is simply 'good to walk' (Oliver 1996).

For the visually unimpaired, walking is often highly organized through time–space. Engels describes how in nineteenth-century London: 'hundreds of thousands of all classes and ranks [are] crowding past each other . . . as though they had nothing in common' (cited Benjamin 1999: 427). The only agreement of each person within the crowd was, according to Engels, the tacit one: 'that each keep to his own side of the pavement, so as not to delay the opposing streams of the crowd – while no man thinks to honor another with so much as a glance' (cited Benjamin 1999: 427–8).

Goffman developed this argument by describing various techniques that pedestrians employ to avoid bumping into each other, what he calls 'pedestrian routing practices' (Goffman 1971: 13). In particular, people use an overall body gesture to indicate features of their situation. The walker performs himself or herself as someone whom it is possible to interpret as they are approached. And at the same time people scan those coming towards them in order to avoid them, only at the last minute and not always with any brief face engagement. Thus, walking in the crowd in a paved street is so sociospatially organized that people rarely bump into each other, although they pass in close proximity. This avoidance of collision is a particularly strong marker of how there is often no honouring through so much as a glance at the other because of the necessity to maintain what Goffman terms the 'civil inattention' to others moving about in crowded corporeal proximity within large urban centres (1971: 322).

Whyte's extensive research reported in *City* showed this organization of walking; how crowds of people make a huge number of small subtle adjustments to pace, stride and direction as they are walking and these produce the well-co-ordinated crowd able to move relatively smoothly, efficiently and quickly (1988; Surowiecki 2004: 84–5). This has been characterized in ethnomethodological terms as 'doing walking, as the concerted accomplishment of members of a community' so as to avoid collisions (Ryave, Schenkein 1974: 265).

Indeed, these practices presuppose accessing various senses in order that such pedestrians are able to move at similar speed to each other. These observations, though, mainly refer to fit, visually unimpaired and able-bodied people moving around during the daytime. But much walking about now occurs at night with people going out together, partly as a consequence of the growth of street lighting and of the very idea of a 'night life' (see Thrift 1996: 267–70). There can be tactile pleasures from walking *in* a crowd, with each moving body co-ordinated with the moving mass of other walking bodies moving up or down a particular street (see Shields 1997: 25, on Rodeo St, Seoul). Urban nightscapes present a distinct collective, hedonistic and youthful domination of many streets in city centres with different categories of young people out on a night out and organized through time–space itineraries that exclude other categories of potential walkers (Chatterton, Hollands 2003).

During the twentieth century, the pedestrian system with its inequalities of access and movement has been up against a ferocious enemy, the car system. This irreversibly transforms the possibilities of city walking that are now often only possible in malls and other pedestrianized enclaves or camps. Two central figures in the contestation between these mobility systems were Jane Jacobs and Le Corbusier. The former detailed the rhythms of pedestrian, everyday life in Greenwich Village, something made possible by the street as multi-functional, full of diverse activities, busy and affording safety (Jacobs 1961; Berman 1983: 170–2). Intricate minglings of movement, use and activities are not chaotic but 'represent a complex and highly developed form of order' (Jacobs 1961: 222). She especially railed against the single function expressways advocated by Corbusier, and later Robert Moses in New York. Corbusier envisaged a new kind of street – a 'machine for traffic' that would kill the 'street' as it had been known (quoted Berman 1983: 167, 317). No longer would streets be for people but for cars. Corbusier argued that: 'Cafés and places of recreation will no longer be the fungus that eats up the pavements of Paris' (quoted Berman 1983: 167).

Such streets of movement were especially found in the modernist Brasilia of 1960; a city we might say that literally 'concretized' the dominance of car system, ending the 'street corner society' and the pedestrian crowds and proximities of nineteenth-century cities that Jacobs championed (Fyfe 1998: 3)

There are also other technologies and objects, such as the Sony Walkman, the iPod and the mobile phone, that produce a new solitary 'cool walker' who especially reorganizes the soundscapes of city-life (du Gay et al. 1997; Bull 2005). Bull describes how iPod users reorganize the sounds of the city to his or her desires. Akin to how mobile telephony enables people to personalize their social networks, so iPods (and other MP3 players) empower the ears of the city dweller through personalizing the sounds of the city. No longer is the ear a defenceless sense. Now the 'city becomes a personalized audio visual environment . . . making the iPod user happier as they move, empowered through the street' (Bull 2005: 352).

In the next section, I turn to walking in rural areas, places originally away from that 'free movement' but which have also been transformed by fast-moving iron cages that now deposit leisure walkers onto far-flung rural paths, a kind of rural pavement we might say.

Leisure Walking in the Countryside

Being a leisurely walker in the so-called countryside is historically unusual behaviour. There were it seems some eccentric Englishmen who from the fourteenth century onwards were enthusastic 'pedestrianizing animals' and even wrote rudimentary guide books (Marples 1949: ch. 1). But in general almost all societies have seen rural areas as sites of back-breaking work, grinding poverty and forced movement – so as to walk to market, to work or to escape imprisonment, slavery or serfdom.

Moreover, walkers in rural areas have been seen as up to no good, often dangerous, often excluded. Thus when King Lear leaves court to wander on the heath: 'he does not meet bobble-hatted hikers in sensible boots enjoying a refreshing tramp across the moors. He is among the naked, the starving and the mad, the excluded of society in this hostile wilderness' (Hewison 1993). Those out walking in the countryside have been mostly regarded as poor, mad or criminal (hence the term 'footpad'; Jarvis 1997: 22–4).

This section is then a reflection on how it came to be believed that walking in rural areas could be a sign, not of poverty, compulsion, danger and madness but of culture, leisure, taste and sanity. How was it that first in northern Europe and then in North America 'bobble-hatted hikers in sensible boots' were thought of as the epitome of sanity, culture and taste? What kinds of objects, of hats and boots and other items, and what kinds of environments, came to constitute the hybrid of the leisurely walker moving unproblematically and with taste through the fields, woods, moors and farms of rural areas?

I begin this account with the British countryside, almost certainly the first site of an extensive middle-class struggle to gain 'access' over land owned and controlled by the landed upper class (although not the first in which long-distance leisure walking was to be found: Marples 1949: chs. 1, 2). From the eighteenth century onwards there was a continuing struggle by the growing middle class to acquire rights of access so as to be able to walk over landlord-dominated rural areas, areas in part the site of upper-class leisure in the form of hunting, fishing and other field sports (Macnaghten, Urry 1998: ch. 6). This can be seen as a class struggle centred upon the rights to walk. The middle class struggled against the landlord class who sought to sustain their rights to land in general and their specific rights to ride, shoot, fish, quarry, grow timber and farm. This intense class struggle emerged in the later eighteenth century when notions of 'leisure walking' and 'scenic tourism' developed within the mainly male middle class (Ousby 1990; Marples 1949 ch. 3). The interests of this middle class had been worsened by the landlord class closing various traditional rights of way following an Act of Parliament in 1815 (Solnit 2000: 161).

There were various key elements involved in this 'class struggle' between landowners and middle-class walkers (see Marples 1949, for detail). There had been the eighteenth-century shift in the nature of travel that moved from scientific exploration to more of a visual consumption of place (Adler 1989; Urry 2002). Ruins and landscapes were 'discovered' by walkers who increasingly appreciated them as 'picturesque' (Ousby 1990). The emergence of the Romantic movement led to the reassessment of previously inhospitable scenery as being suitable for walking around, as no longer the 'wildest, most barren and frightful' of landscapes (as Defoe described the Lake District, quoted Nicholson 1978: 25). Elsewhere in Europe other places of inhospitality, the Scottish highlands, the volcanoes of Etna and Vesuvius, and the Alps were all transformed into symbols of nature's power and well worth walking and climbing, being places to rejuvenate both body and mind (Ring 2000). The discourse of walking in the 'open air' was a powerful stimulant for those otherwise confined to the 'unnatural' industrial cities that were seen as invading every orifice, places unnaturally smelly with odours of death, madness and poverty (Classen et al. 1994; see Elizabeth Gaskell's *North and South*: 1998).

Railways in the mid nineteenth century opened up a newly imagined 'countryside' to visitors from the towns. It also meant that walking was not bound up with notions of necessity, poverty and vagrancy. Since ordinary people no longer always had to walk, so those walking were not necessarily stigmatized as poor or disreputable (Wallace 1993; Jarvis 1997). Further, the diversity of modes of transport enabled people to compare and contrast different forms of mobility and to begin to see the virtues of slower ways of overcoming the 'friction of distance'. Pursuing the 'freedom' of the road and path also constituted acts of rebellion against social hierarchy and the power of the landed class (Jarvis 1997: chs. 1 and 2 on 'radical walking'). This was illustrated by Wordsworth's prodigious walk from England to Switzerland and northern Italy in 1790 at the very time that he should have been taking his university exams. Travelling on foot was the act of a political radical, expressing unconventionality and showing identification with the poor who were encountered *having* to walk along paths and roads (Solnit 2000: 107–9).

Over the course then of the nineteenth century, walking and then climbing emerge as appropriate and desired forms of leisurely activity for the male middle class (see Urry 1995). Especially important in this class struggle and rebellion against social hierarchy were the world's first conservation organizations, the Association for the Protection of Ancient Footpaths (1824), the Scottish Rights of Way Society (1845) and the Commons, Open Spaces and Footpaths Preservation Society (1865; this developed into the National Trust in 1895; Solnit 2000: 161–2). These organizations were especially concerned with the sustaining of footpaths, those rights of access and movement across land that was owned and regulated by the landlord class. Over many decades a class compromise was arrived at with the countryside coming to be regarded as suitable for 'quiet recreation' and especially for walking (see Bunce 1994, on the history of the concept of 'countryside'). The middle class obtained access to land in order to move across it but on terms fundamentally structured by existing land ownership rights (Solnit 2000: 115).

The emergent (male) professional and managerial class thus began to walk (and later to climb: Milner 1984) along paths impressed into the land. Walking became a way of being and not simply a means of travel. Wordsworth, Coleridge and Southey regularly walked the twelve to thirteen miles between their Lake District homes in

Grasmere and Keswick, moving along unmade, unlit roads and wearing clogs (Jones 1997; Solnit 2000: ch. 7). According to De Quincey, Wordsworth must have walked at least 175,000 miles in his lifetime (Solnit 2000: 104). Their example stimulated pedestrian activity by their contemporaries and then by many other affluent men (on the gendering of this walking, see Jones 1997). William Hazlitt claimed to walk forty or fifty miles a day; De Quincey walked seventy to one hundred miles a week; and Keats apparently covered 642 miles during his 1818 tour of the Lakes and Scotland (Wallace 1993: 166–7). At the time, poetry and pedestrianism seemed to have gone hand in hand, according to Marples (1949: 67).

By the middle of the century 'the very highest echelon of English society regarded pedestrian touring as a valuable educational experience' and it became fashionable for many to walk very significant distances and especially to go off on walking tours (Wallace 1993: 168). And almost certainly walking came to be viewed by young middle-class women also as a desirable leisure activity, following in part the example provided by Dorothy Wordsworth, who walked exceptional distances on her own or with her brother or Coleridge (Marples 1949: chs. 8, 9; Jones 1997). Female as well as male characters in Jane Austen's novels are always walking. Walks are: 'everywhere in *Pride and Prejudice*. The heroine walks on every possible occasion and in every location, and many of the crucial encounters and conversations . . . take place while two characters are walking together . . . walking provided a shared seclusion for crucial conversations' (Solnit 2000: 97, 99). And such female characters often met opposition from friends and relatives and challenged such comments by insisting on their right to walk (Wordsworth wrote a poem entitled 'To a Young Lady who has been Reproached for taking Long Walks in the Country').

Complex discourses developed around the nature of these 'leisured' walking practices, justifying what Marples describes as: 'something of an adventure to go pedestrianizing' (1949: 43). Wallace describes the development of a 'peripatetic theory' that showed how walking would recreate pedestrians with nature. Wordsworth referred to the disciplined nature of such 'walking tours' (Wallace 1993: ch. 3). The walker it is said should not wander aimlessly or in a socially disruptive fashion. The wanderer should return along paths that have already been walked. Since there is a clear intention to return and not to wander aimlessly without direction, this would ensure connection and stability with nature.

Some key texts in this peripatetic theory developed include Hazlitt's *On Going on a Journey* in 1821; Coleridge's various walking diaries; Thoreau's *Walking* in 1862; Robert Louis Stevensons's *Walking Tours* in 1881; Leslie Stephen's *In Praise of Walking* in 1901; and G. M. Trevelyan's *Walking* in 1913 (Marples 1949: chs. 4, 14, 17; Wallace 1993: 172–3; Jarvis 1997). Most of these texts explore Wordsworth's justification for walking. They differ though as to whether 'the peripatetic' is seen as connecting people back to local communities or whether walking is more of a private emotional activity.

It is important to note the very class (and gender) specific nature of this leisurely activity; two social classes are absent in this account of nineteenth-century walking through the countryside. First, at the time by far the largest class statistically were agricultural workers and their families, who had little or no choice but to walk and to walk, unless they could get a ride on an ox cart. They benefited from no discourse of walking; they walked from sheer necessity as revealed in the many heart-wrenching journeys made through rural areas as described in Thomas Hardy's novels of rural hardship.

Second, by the end of the century the urban working class had become the largest social class in Britain. Because of limited means of access, this class had been mostly absent from the countryside as a site for embodied leisure. However, an increasingly key element in working-class struggle was over entitlements to holidays (holidays with pay being granted in the UK via an act in 1938), and over access to the areas surrounding northern industrial towns especially directed against landowners who historically prevented access. The late nineteenth century onwards saw a wide array of organizations develop, seeking to gain access to, and organization of, travel within wild upland countryside for walking, rambling and cycling. This became a powerful social movement, with 'mass trespassing' as a subsequent key tactic (Solnit 2000: 164). In the UK the most famous trespass took place some time later in 1932 at Kinder Scout in the Peak District (located between Manchester and Sheffield). This trespass followed action during the nineteenth century by landowners taking away ancient rights of access, thereby making the overall area and some impressed paths 'forbidden territory'.

The more general mass enthusiasm for inter-war cycling and hiking revolved around the notion of 'open air' thought to make people better, as they experience open, panoramic, uninhibited scenery and very lengthy walks (with little or no specialist clothing). Walking holidays were not so much for relaxation but a way of strengthening body and soul, especially when the weather was hostile. For the young ramblers of the north: 'the countryside was seen as an energizer: their intention was not so much to see the landscape as to experience it physically, to walk it, climb it or to cycle through it' (Samuel 1998: 146). Villages in this period were generally not regarded as visual enticements; they were 'rural slums, with rising damp, leaky roofs, tiny windows, and squalid interiors' (Samuel 1998: 146). The practices of rambling, climbing, cycling, camping and so on mostly ignored the lives and habitats of those dwelling in that countryside, for whom obligatory walking continued to be the main means of movement.

One significant late nineteenth-century phenomenon in Europe was how walkers choosing to walk in the countryside were increasingly pitied rather than regarded as mad or dangerous. Beginning in France, such travellers were thought to be suffering from a new mental illness, identified as 'fugue' or the compulsion to walk and travel (Hacking 1998; O'Dell 2004). In 1886 Albert Dadas from Bordeaux was the first person who was thought to be suffering from fugue. Dadas would set off and would walk seventy or so kilometres each day after several days of headaches, insomnia and mounting anxiety. He was *driven* to walk and travel; it was an unhealthy compulsion. And he was not alone. An epidemic of fugue behaviour occurred throughout Europe. This was so significant an affliction that various medical conferences were held on the topic before fugue was thought to have finally dissipated.

This fugue epidemic seems connected with harsh anti-vagrancy laws introduced in France in 1885, the presence of military conscription with the resulting concern with identifying and capturing 'deserters' walking the countryside, the growth of middle-class tourism infrastructures across Europe, and the development of experts supposedly able to distinguish between mentally ill fuguers and mentally well tourists (O'Dell 2004: 5). French society in particular increasingly distinguished between people deemed as mentally ill and unsuitable walkers, from those thought to be appropriate walkers. One leading psychiatrist judged Dadas to be suffering from 'pathological tourism'; this of course being an era of much tourism and leisure developments as well as the popularization of various fantasies of travel such as Jules Verne's *Around the World in Eighty Days* (see Hacking 1998: 27). By the twentieth century it is those without the desire for travel who came to be pathologized and treated as lacking sufficient mobile desires.

In North America, walking was something to be undertaken within national parks, publicly owned areas of wilderness and where other economic activities are forbidden. They are places of 'wilderness', 'gated wilderness' we might now say. These parks of North America are highly distinct spaces, entirely devoted to leisurely walking and climbing in bounded and 'untouched' environments. They are wilderness 'camps' (Diken, Laustsen 2005). The Sierra Club was especially significant in their development. This Club was formed in 1892 by John Muir and others who sought to defend Yosemite National Park from potential developers (Solnit 2000: 148–55). The Sierra Club was a distinct hybrid – of a walking/ mountaineering organization *and* a conservation society. The first major trip through Yosemite occurred in 1901. The Club was open to both men and women and can claim to be the first environmental organization in the world but one which advocated certain forms of bodily presence *within* specified and bounded 'wilderness' areas. The Sierra Club came to justify walking and climbing in and through the Park as an ideal way of being in the world, one that supposedly left only footprints, one that helps to conserve 'nature'.

But places of leisurely walking are never just this. Also implicated are the technologies of transport, accommodation, clothing, entertainment and retailing that serve to realize the place as appropriate for leisured activities such as walking. Indeed it is interesting to return to Wordsworth and his friends two centuries ago to realize just how little of what we now refer to as the leisure industries were then present to provide appropriate affordances to the walker. There was more or less no 'leisure industry' and hence the prodigious feats of walking were achieved almost without maps, guidebooks (Wordsworth of course produced his own), signposts, boots, lightweight materials, packaged food/drink and so on. Wordsworth and friends were not what we would later call 'leisure walkers'; they were yet to be hybridized with the specifically 'leisured' objects, technologies and transformations of roads and paths that constitute the leisure walker of the twentieth, let alone the twenty-first century (but see Marples 1959, on the early use of guidebooks).

One important absence from Wordsworth's possessions was that of maps that travel along with the walker. Maps had originally developed as practical tools for merchants, state officials and especially armies (Harley 1992). They involve taking an imaginary bird's eye view of the world rather than that of a human subject walking or wayfinding within the landscape. Maps do not realize an exact or realist reproduction of the landscape, being highly symbolic, with the use of apparently arbitrary signifiers, of figures, lines, shapes, shadings and so on.

But gradually such maps became available for laypersons, they became 'democratized' so that walkers and climbers and indeed anyone could carry them on their leisurely expeditions. They became part of the ready-to-hand equipment in the background and little remarked upon at least within various societies of the rich 'north'. New technologies of printing and packaging converted them into portable accompaniments for leisurely walkers and climbers (Rodaway 1994: 133–4; Pinkney 1991: 43–5; GPS and digitization has carried this even further). Moreover, the seeing of landscapes through printed and carried maps allowed people to think of them as 'something laid out before their eyes' and potentially to be possessed as they are moved along and especially as walkers gain access to ridges, hill tops and viewing points (Ong 1982: 73). Within twentieth-century Britain there has been considerable contestation over rights of way across land still being used for other purposes and this crucially involves their mapping, institutionalizing access and new legislation.

More generally, in the twentieth century leisurely walking has become intertwined with many other products such as boots, maps, socks, anoraks, shorts, hats, compasses, cars/vans and so on. Samuel describes how in 1930s and 1940s leisure walking in Britain 'required stamina and strength, "practical" clothing and "sensible" shoes' (1998: 133). No longer did walkers necessarily wear work clothes. Such a 'uniform' obliterated some differences between men and women since they were equally 'hikers' and constituted through these uniform products although mostly these develop in the post-war period with the emergence from enthusiasts of new kinds of leisure industry companies.

So walking gets performed and practised in many different ways depending especially upon a range of material and discursive connections which will now be briefly summarized. First, in the post-second world war period various 'mundane technologies' became much more widespread and they spread to and emerge from many societies and in part from groups of enthusiasts. A whole new set of industries develop, producing and marketing specialist leisure products. Such novel products served to constitute the hybrid of 'the [leisurely] walker' (see Michael 2001, on the mountain boot and its related affordances). Such technologies are subject to rapid technological change that transforms the affordances they offer to the regular walker.

There are indeed *cascades* of affordances, as a new kind of sock material transforms what a particular walking boot affords, which in turn affects some other set of objects and so on (Michael 2001: 112). The huge increase in those now able to walk and climb parts of the Everest range stems from a transformed cascade of affordances provided by technological innovations that enable those seeking what in other decades would have been unrealizable corporeal ambitions.

What is striking about many such innovations is that they can be 'invisible' or 'mundane', so rendering one's contact with the ground as unproblematic (even while on Everest according to Parsons and Rose 2003). Sometimes, though, various objects are anything but 'invisible' – they then become parasitical interventions causing pain, inconvenience, being lost, terror and so on.

Narratives of the heroic overcoming of the pain, inconvenience and trauma of the journey can offset such visibilities. The practice of walking (and climbing, rock climbing, cycling and so on) often involves strenuous physical effort. Sennett argues: 'the body comes to life when coping with difficulty' (1994: 310; note how travel comes from *travail*, to work, Buzard 1993). Only if real exertion and pain is involved to get to some peak or ridge or hill top is it to be properly appreciated, as shown in recent research on the notion of 'Munro-bagging' in Scotland (Lorimer, Ingold 2004).

The importance of bodily effort is elaborated in Barthes' analysis of the *Guide Bleu* where he shows that it combines the cult of nature, puritanism and individualistic ideology. Morality is associated with significant bodily effort. Leisure practices are only appropriate to get to 'know' nature when they entail physical achievement, in order to overcome uneven ground, to ascend a mountain, to cross a gorge, to pass over a torrent and so on. The *Guide* emphasizes 'regeneration through clean air, moral ideas at the sight of mountain tops, summit climbing as civic virtue, etc.' (Barthes 1972: 74). In order to know nature, it is presumed that the individual must move corporeally within and across particular terrain and where the affordances cannot be so complete that there is no space left for human effort. Walking has to be lengthy, often very slow and where there are gaps – and it is the gaps that provide the achievement (see Spufford on Scott's slow 'walk' to the North Pole: 1996). Lewis provides analysis of how the gaps involved in adventure rock climbing is deemed by its practitioners in Britain as far superior to sports climbing which involves the intrusive use of bolts and other equipment that in effect fill the gaps (2001).

These various hybrids fit certain places for leisure, while elsewhere they can be strangely 'out-of-place' (although some specific technologies then become mainstreamed and can become part of normal leisure wear). Just outside one such specific site, the English Lake District, are various former industrial towns where leisurely 'walking' and its equipment are less appropriate. One researcher describes walking into one of these former industrial towns, Cleator Moor, wearing the clothing much more appropriate for walking in the Lake District, with breeches, boots, brightly coloured socks, orange waterproofs and a rucksack (Chapman 1993). But instead of feeling intrepid, the researcher felt acutely out of place since he was wearing what was in effect fancy-dress along the rough streets of Cleator Moor. He had walked beyond the Lake District with its practices of leisurely rural walking and the hybrid of 'the [leisure] walker'.

Finally, here we should note just how there are many modes of the doing of walking as Ryave and Schenkein put it in their classic ethnomethodological account (1974; see Edensor 2001). There are four important features to separate out: whether walking is an adventure, whether it is undertaken in solitary fashion, whether it is interconnected with specific notions of health and fitness, and whether it involves practices that transform the material conditions under which it is itself undertaken.

First, then, some walking constitutes an 'adventure', islands of life resulting from bodies that are kinaesthetically in motion and finding ways through time and space (Simmel 1997; Lewis 2001; and see ch. 2 above). Adventure involves the body as spatially situated, experiencing and knowing the world through being in and moving around it. This is 'wayfinding', moving around *within* a world, a process of constant engagement and readjustment in relation to the environment – rather than 'map-reading' that is moving across a surface as imagined from above (Ingold 2000: 227; Szerszynski, Urry 2006). A classic account is found in Coleridge's walking diaries penned during his twenties (Lewis 2001: 69; Marples 1949: ch. 4). The opposite of this is the kind of walking through spaces that are signposted, organized, and highly predictable, or McDonaldized as Ritzer and Liska generally describe (1997). An example of this is the walking practised by package tourists within the Taj Mahal (Edensor 1998: 2004). In such 'enclavic tourist spaces' walking is smooth and ordered with rapid movement and clear functions of the different zones. 'Guides' and on occasions 'guidebooks' regulate the walking of visitors who internalize modes of the *appropriate* ways to walk. Walking without adventure normally takes place within specific locations or 'camps' such as promenades, piers, parks, themed environments, national parks and so on (Diken, Lautsten 2005).

A further distinction surrounds whether walking should or should not be performed on one's own. Some emphasize the virtues of private solitary walking, being alone and individually reflexive (at home with one's thoughts) so that there is 'no cackle of voices at your elbow' as Robert Louis Stevenson expressed it (cited Marples 1949: 151, see ch. 4; Solnit 2000: 107). Others emphasize how walking should entail sociability as a result of being with others and indeed bonding through the shared achievement of covering a certain 'walk' or getting to a particular viewing point. This collective notion lay behind the development of walking clubs and ramblers (Edensor 2001: 90–1).

A third distinction is around the relationship between walking and personal fitness. On one hand, walking can be unrelated to notions of health and fitness, as in the Romantic movement where walking was not viewed through, or justified by, discourses of health (in fact sometimes it was deemed to have the opposite effect). And on the other hand, walking is intertwined with discourses of health and fitness. The recent development of Nordic or fitness walking is a good example of the latter, involving a reconfiguration of existing materials (walking sticks normally not thought of as to do with 'fitness'), forms of competence (walking skills that need to be taught and learnt) and images (of nature, health and well being). In Finland 20 per cent of the population are said to practise such fitness walking that is viewed by its advocates as far more demanding than ordinary walking (Shove, Pantzar 2005: 48, 51). We can also note the significance of the treadmill in gyms as a 'battery farm for the stressed worker' (thanks to Mary Rose for this observation).

Finally, we can distinguish between walking that involves using products of an existing 'leisure industry' operating in conventional fashion; and walking that transforms the economic and material conditions under which it is undertaken. In the latter case, innovations that affect walking practices, such as high-level Alpine walking or Nordic walking, are not solutions to existing 'needs' as developed by producers but rather they stem from communities of practice of enthusiasts or so-called amateurs (see Shove, Patzar 2005, on the latter). Indeed more generally, the activities of 'innovative, committed and networked amateurs' (such as walkers) are on occasions: 'changing our economy and society' and generating new practices, new products and new forms of knowledge (Leadbeater, Miller 2004: 9).

Conclusion

This chapter has thus revealed an array of social practices with which walking is elaborately entwined. It is part and parcel of multiple economies and socialities, in countrysides, suburbs, parks, promenades and cities. According to the UK Government it is a 'year-round, readily repeatable, self-reinforcing, habit-forming activity and

the main option for increasing physical activity in sedentary populations' (quoted Edensor 2001: 81). Also there is nothing 'natural'
about walking even though walking is naturally everywhere. Walking
for pleasure is a distinctive and curious practice within modern societies, enabled by mundane technologies that afford different possibilities for moving in and through the physical and social world.
These technologies intersect with different capacities to 'walk the
walk' reflecting varied biosocial orderings. There are some walks that
involve moments of adventure when the body is put through its
paces and the bare body painfully physicalizes its relationship with
the external world.

Lying behind this chapter have been various presumptions. First,
extensive affordances for walkers are desirable and a good society
would be one in which walking is far more widespread. Much
evidence suggests that people simply now walk less and expect to
walk less. Many benefits would follow if people were to walk more,
or at least stop walking less; and these include improved health,
richer social capital and reduced disorder. In some ways walking
provides what Thrift terms 'an emancipatory politics of bare life',
standing alone against the elements and against the physical world
(2001: 48).

Indeed, the way in which walking has retreated *inside* the gym and
onto the treadmill suggests that the outside affordances for walkers
have been substantially reduced. The upholstered chair we might by
contrast note has, from its widespread diffusion in Europe in the
sixteenth century, a lot to answer for! It results in high status and
authority being attached to 'supine sedentariness' (Ingold 2004: 323;
see ch. 6 below on the car as a moving armchair). The chapter presumes that places are overall better, the more the affordances provided for multiple walkers, from the mundane to the joyful. Modernity
entails replacing walking with sitting, ranging from the sedan chair
to the pampered chair system in the luxury car.

Also walking is the most 'egalitarian' of mobility systems. So
although walkers are marked by class, gender, ethnicity, age, dis/
ability and so on and have their pedestrianism enhanced by unequally
available technologies, social inequalities are strikingly less than with
other mobility systems. If various other considerations are constant,
then the more powerful the walking system, the less social inequality
there will be in that place or society. Pavements and paths we might
say are much better for 'society' than chairs and cars. But we should
not presume that walking is necessarily found in predictable places;
Solnit describes the surprising scale of pedestrianism in contemporary Las Vegas (2000: 285–7)!

In future chapters I will describe some characteristics of increased social networking, stretching across work life, friendships and family life. And this involves a range of mobility and communication systems, forms of access, competences and novel times. This networking we might view as a major component of global consumerism, that at least for the rich third of the world, partners, family and friends are a matter of choice and increasingly a choice spreading itself out around the world. There is a 'supermarket' of friends and acquaintances; and they depend upon an extensive and growing array of interdependent mobility systems. And hence walking to see friends and family is most of the time not an option. Lives are not lived within the relatively 'little boxes' experienced by the family and friends of Wordsworth in early nineteenth-century England (although actually their friendship patterns were national). The choice of friends and partners are not confined to those with whom one can walk to see and this is because walking systems have become subordinated to other mobility systems as I now examine. Wordsworth stated in *The Prelude*: 'I love a public road' (Book XII, quoted Solnit 2000: 111), a place in his time ideal for the *public* to walk steadily along and to have power over one's imagination. And some such public roads remain, places for the public to be moving their body against resistances. Here and there public paths and pavements are still there, providing moments of joy and surprise, effort and endurance, at least for the able-bodied.

5

'Public' Trains

> Railway travelling is travelling for the Million; the humble may travel, the rich may travel . . . To travel by train is to enjoy republican liberty and monarchical security.
>
> (Thomas Cook, quoted Brendon 1991: 16)

Moving in Public

The previous chapter described the significance of feet and the array of social practices with which moving feet are elaborately entwined. Walking was shown to be part and parcel of multiple socialities, in countrysides, suburbs and cities. And walking for pleasure in and through the physical and social world is a particularly distinctive practice within modern societies, one enabled by various mundane technologies.

I turn in this chapter to some bigger technologies, involving huge historic shifts away from travelling by feet (and indeed by horse), to travelling by train, bus and coach. I tell this story in part through the prism of private and public realms, notions that, as shown elsewhere, are immensely complex and difficult to disentangle (Sheller, Urry 2003). The history of walking is the history of principally private, self-directed and endogenous action that helps to constitute the self especially through the kinaesthetic sense. Such walking does, however, depend upon various public facilities, especially paths and pavements that afford new ways of doing that walking. In particular, publicly paid for and provided pavements shift the potential forms and modalities of that 'private' movement of walking.

Broadly speaking, the nineteenth century sees the emergence of new public spaces that involve different forms and capacities for such movement. We noted in chapter 4 the pavements of London and Paris; and we can add 'public' gardens, squares, monuments, bridges, towers, promenades, museums, galleries and *railway stations*. The heyday of capitalist entrepreneurialism is also the heyday of a huge expansion of public space and the structuring of private mobility through 'public' mobilization. Nineteenth-century Europe (and then North America) involves a dramatic 'public mobilization' of private life. An extensive array of new public spaces develops, most of which afford novel or extended kinds of movement, both directly through new places to walk and indirectly through creating objects of the tourist gaze to be 'seen' for oneself (Urry 2002c). The nineteenth century can thus be described as the century of 'public mobilization' through new times, spaces and sociabilities of public movement.

Although this chapter will especially focus upon the railway and its transformative consequences for modern life, it was not the first 'public' form of transport. In Europe the horse-drawn coach was a significant early form. Sombart notes that by the end of the seventeenth century: 'travel by coach had finally established itself as equally acceptable as travel on horseback' (cited Schivelbusch 1986: 73). And this was said to encourage conversation between those passengers sitting opposite each other in the coach. By late eighteenth-century England, many regular coach services were established. By 1830, forty-eight coaches a day travelled between London and Brighton with the journey time reduced to 4.5 hours (Walvin 1978: 34; Thrift 1996: 264). In North America the railway took over some characteristics from public transport that occurred on river steamers that transported people and goods along natural waterways. There was no pre-existing network of roads that in Europe enabled the coach system to develop. In North America railway tracks in fact often followed the line of the natural waterways *and* the railway compartments mirrored the design of river steamers facilitating movement of passengers around the carriages (Schivelbusch 1986: ch. 6).

The railway mobility system connects people located in different places through new mechanized mobile routeways. Part of this public mobilization involves a new *connectedness*, as masses of people are newly and extensively mobilized along routes that enable them to move and imagine moving through extended times and spaces. Public space becomes mobile and connected, a set of circulating process that undercuts the spatial divide of the 'public' and the 'private' (Sheller,

Urry 2003). There is a new connectedness of places based upon the notion that people could and should have the capacity and right to move between multiple places, at least from time to time. The private spaces of everyday life get connected through a public circulating mobilization across a society, through what Peters terms 'passages' (2006).

Such public spaces of connectedness are not always *owned* by public bodies but they are public in certain other senses. First, they are subject to new forms of public *regulation*, often with Acts of Parliament regulating their use, safety, access and so on. Second, these spaces are open to the members of the *public* if they have the means to pay. Access is not restricted by reason of ascriptive criteria. Third, there is a public *organization* of such movement especially through the publicly available timetabling of such mobilization. And finally, new ways of appropriate *behaviour in 'public'* come to develop especially within the public places of the station and railway compartment.

So this chapter explores some different components of this public mobilization, beginning with new modalities involved in the mechanizing of movement. I then examine the re-orderings of times, spaces and sociabilities that the railway system brings about as a precondition of its expansion. I end with examining some implications of contemporary machine *systems* for the concept of public movement. I consider what systemic properties the railway possesses.

Mechanizing Movement

This chapter will show just what a radical innovation the railway system constituted, re-ordering the contours of time, space and everyday life. It initiated a long durée in which human life is dependent upon, and enormously entwined with, machines. These machines do various things but especially they facilitate movement, not just in the factory but much more broadly across social life. Increasingly, through inhabiting machines, humans come to 'life' and especially to a life intermittently lived on the move in the company of various machines of movement.

In this section I set out a simplified periodization of the last two to three centuries in terms of the dominant 'mode of machine'. It is the nineteenth century (beginning in western Europe) that marks a point of massive and irreversible bifurcation. A series of mechanized systems came into play each depending upon steam power. These can be described as 'industrial machines', machines that make other machines or other material objects, or which transport such machines or objects across distance. These industrial machines are interdependent with each other. It is the steam engine that begins a long process of human life becoming a life that is irreversibly interconnected with and dependent upon machines. This is what I mean by 'modernity', that moment when enormously powerful machines are imbricated within human experience. From then on, machines are not something on the side but they serve to constitute a 'human' life that cannot be *lived* without them. The relationships with these machines constitute a Faustian bargain – machines extend in unimaginable fashion what humans can do but only at the expense of robbing humans of powers to do many things, such as some kinds of walking, thinking, reading, knowing, directly experiencing.

Such industrial machines are mainly inhabited by *experts* who are knowledgeable about that specific machine, such as the engine driver, the power loom operator, the iron smelter, the crane operator and so on. These machines are typically confined to specific and highly regulated sites residing outside everyday life, such as the factory, workshop, railway track, dock and so on. When the machine is not in motion they are stored within specialized, guarded sites with the public kept out. The organizing principle is that there should be appropriate machines 'just-in-case' they are required (as with the Revd Awdry's steam engines all lined up in the engine shed ready to be selected: 2002).

It is the railway machine that is distinct in all this, locking together the route and the vehicle and forming an indivisible entity (Schivelbusch 1986: 16–7). Such a machine pulls carriages full of people (at first alongside wagons of coal) and it pulls these people at speed through the very towns and villages in which people live and work. The passenger railway system escapes from places of industry, toil and security, not being confined to those sites outside of everyday life. Indeed the railway machine *enters* and reshapes everyday social life in striking ways, especially moving at consistent speed through the countryside. For the first time machinery is brought *into* the foreground of most people's everyday experience. An incredibly powerful, speeding mechanical apparatus is foregrounded as a relatively familiar feature of everyday life even within places otherwise made up of green and pleasant land. This is a nineteenth-century phenomenon in Europe, a late nineteenth-century phenomenon in North America and an early twentieth-century phenomenon in much of India, Africa and Latin America (Vaughan 1997; Richards, Mackenzie 1986: ch. 9).

And unlike horses, these machines can go on for long periods, only needing intermittent stops for fuel and water (every 150–200 miles: Richards, Mackenzie 1986: 121). They move swiftly, sometimes described as being like projectiles slicing through the landscape on level, straight tracks, deploying new building technologies of multiple cuttings, embankments, bridges and tunnels. The railway restructures the existing relations between nature, time and space, with its building flattening and subduing the countryside, although this is more marked in Europe and Japan than North America.

The railway system moreover involves propelling passengers through space as though they are parcels. The human body becomes like an anonymized parcel of flesh, 'shunted' from place to place, just like the other goods that get moved around the system (Thrift 1996: 266). The tracks and trains come to constitute a great machine covering the land. This is especially so in England from 1842 when the railway companies created a co-ordinating authority to deal with through traffic moving across tracks owned by different companies (Schivelbusch 1986: 29). From then on, a complex tightly coupled system develops. But from time to time machines crash, and when they crash humans die and the system as a whole shudders to a grinding halt. Complex machine systems create big accidents when systems malfunction, unlike the small accidents when a walker falls, a horse dies or a coach overturns. The powerful system can crash when one small part of it malfunctions. The railway system initiated the development of tightly coupled systems where accidents become 'normal' and systems may no longer function if one small part goes awry (Perrow 1999; Jack 2001, on 'the crash that stopped Britain').

The pedestrian and horse mobility systems are what I term a *series* system, in which each component is roughly like every other component. They mirror each other or are mimetic, a series. The railway by contrast initiates a *nexus* system. Laing defines a nexus as: 'a group, whose unification is achieved through the reciprocal interiorization by each of each other . . . t[T]he nexus is everywhere' (1962: 12). With the railway there is a pronounced division of labour in which the different parts (tracks, trains, stations, signals and so on) *have* to work together as a tight nexus, without the nexus the separate elements do not exist. The whole is only able to function if every component works. There is no simple mirroring as with the series but the complex specialization *and* integration of the different components. The railway initiates the first major nexus system with regard to mobility.

In the twentieth-century, two new categories of machines come to compete with these industrial machines. First, there are familial machines, including the four-person family car, telephone, white-space goods, radio, household TV/VCR, PC, heating appliances and the camera/camcorder. Almost all these familial machines depend upon electricity that gets produced and circulated in western Europe and North America following the development of networks of grid lines that transport electricity far away from points of production. Electricity most successfully overcomes the friction of space and time (Thrift 1996: 270–2). The spread of these familial machines is particularly pronounced within the United States and is much slower within Europe (Thrift 1996: 275–6). Such machines are stored within the home/garage and have formed twentieth-century family life especially within North America (see Shove 2003, on some of these familial machines). Most family members can operate most of these machines since they do not require special expertise. These machines are stored in the home so that they are accessible; they come to life when the family requires them and not when experts determine that they should. These family machines are just-in-time, more like a series system than a nexus. The most significant of such machines is the car that more or less uniquely is not powered by electricity (see ch. 6 below).

A second set of non-domesticated machines that develop are 'war machines' mainly owned and developed by states or by corporations closely linked to states. Such machines include machines of mass destruction, jet transport, nuclear power, space travel for science, and virtual reality for simulations of work, pleasure and science. These machines are stored in highly specialized camps or bases where the public is forbidden and systems of surveillance are particularly enhanced. Such machines involve highly significant contestation between different mobilities, with air power providing exceptional power to those employing planes and weaponry able to fly the fastest, the highest, or for the longest time (see Kaplan 2006).

I turn now to the railway system, the first of the systems that mechanized movement. H.G Wells predicted that future historians would take: 'a steam engine running on a railway' to be the nineteenth century's central symbol (quoted Carter 2001: 8). I consider how a steam engine running on a railway dramatically reorganized times, spaces and sociabilities, paving the way for other subsequent ways in which humans and machines have entered passionate and enduring liaisons.

Timetables

In chapter 1, I noted the exceptional significance of the period around 1840 when modernity gets moving through the interdependencies between various new mobility and communication systems. The railway system is central to modernity's appearance. As Carter writes: 'the qualitative break came with the modern railway when, for the first time in history, people travelled faster than any galloping horse could manage' (Carter 2001: 11). The railway initiated a stunning array of time–space effects as part of the increasing interpenetration of 'speed, light and power' (see Thrift's 'inhuman geographies' in 1996: ch. 7).

One English commentator suggested in 1839 that the new railways were having the effect of 'compressing' time and space; if railways were established all over England, then the whole population would: 'sit nearer to one another by two-thirds of the time which now respectively alienates them . . . As distances were thus annihilated, the surface of the country would, as it were, shrivel in size until it became not much larger than one immense city' (quoted Schivelbusch 1986: 34). Likewise, the poet Heine talked of the tremendous foreboding that he felt with the opening of the rail link between Paris and Rouen. He said that 'the elementary concepts of time and space have begun to vacillate. Space is killed by the railways' (quoted Schivelbusch 1986: 37). He goes on to say that the railway is a providential event (a tipping point?) that 'swings mankind in a new direction, and changes the colour and shape of life' (quoted Schivelbusch 1986: 37). J. W. M. Turner's iconic painting *Rain, Steam and Speed* that was first exhibited at the Royal Academy in 1844 (note the date) perhaps best captures this providential event, this changing of the colour and shape of life as a black speed machine slices through a myriad of pre-industrial orderings of time–space (see Carter 2001: ch. 2). Karl Marx too thought that the circulation of commodities through new forms of transport and communications (train, mail, telegraph) represented an upward shift within capitalist industrialization, involving 'the annihilation of space by time'. This becomes a 'necessity' as production more and more rests upon exchange value and hence upon speeding up the conditions of exchange through mechanized movement (Marx 1973: 524; Carter 2001: 8–9).

One particular pre-industrial characteristic was how most towns kept their particular local time, Reading time, Exeter time and so on. The coach guard and later the railway guard had to adjust the time-piece in order to cope with the different times in the towns that the vehicle would pass through. But clocks and watches were becoming widespread, and these devices were bringing timetables into people's everyday lives (Thompson 1967; Glennie, Thrift 1996). The clock provided a common and homogenous time reference by comparison with localized variance of church and monastery bells (Nowotny 1994). Moreover, the clock provided not only a general way of synchronizing activity, but it also measured a precise duration. Increasing attention was paid to smaller distinctions of time and the need to use those moments productively (Thrift 1996: 265). The equal 'empty' units of clock-time became highly valued especially through the increasingly common adage that 'time is money' (Adam 1995). And yet, as noted different times were kept in the various towns through which trains passed. The Great Western Railway timetable of 1841 contained the following useful information: 'London time is kept at all the stations on the railway, which is about 4 minutes earlier than Reading time; 5 minutes before Cirencester time; 8 minutes before Chippenham time; and 14 minutes before Bridgewater time' (quoted in Thrift 1990: 122).

Large numbers of the 'labouring classes', as well as the more affluent, began to travel very significant distances both on business and increasingly for leisure (Thrift 1996: 264; Urry 2002c: ch. 2). This lack of national time-keeping could not survive and by around 1847 the railway companies, the Post Office and many towns and cities adopted Greenwich Mean Time (colloquially known as railway time: Mackenzie, Richards 1986: 94–5). A standardized clock-time was established at a national level, something that helped to enhance mass mobility during the Victorian period. Thus the existing patchwork of local times came to be replaced with a standardized clock-time based upon Greenwich, although various towns held out against this imposed national time (Mackenzie, Richards 1986: 94–5). The second half of the nineteenth century saw further co-ordination of time between European countries and then between Europe and North America (see Zerubavel 1982, on the standardizing of time).

Making appointments for those travelling between towns and cities developed the need for punctuality, precision and calculability in social life stretching across an extended spatial scale (see ch. 2 above on Simmel). Especially significant here was the development of the railway timetable, one of those apparently small innovations that makes possible a public system of transport. The development of modernist clock-time, and indeed of the station clock, is based upon the timetable that all travellers must follow as it structures the scheduling of events and journeys. The objective clock-time of the modernist railway timetable constitutes a public mobilization, squeezing trains and people we might say into a given and circulated time-table. According to Sachs, the station clock meant that 'the cult of punctuality overtook the whole of society' (1992: 162).

The first of these timetables was the iconic *Bradshaws Railway Guide* in England, first published in 1838/9 (Mackenzie, Richards

1986: 96–9). Subsequently the timetable that is public and which constrains both operators and passengers develops into a technology that sits alongside the railway machine. It becomes ubiquitous, ready-to-hand enabling the journey to be attempted, to know when to get to the station, to know when to be met, to know how long it would take. The timetable is in a way *the* nineteenth-century innovation, bringing together the railway machine, accurate clock-time, mass publication and scheduling across a *national* system.

Work practices on the railway were also structured through this omnipresent timetable. Gamst shows how a whole array of time notions orchestrate working on the American railways: the notion of the train 'on time', the concept of 'schedule time', 'time-critical' trains and the general disciplining based on strict hierarchy in which actions almost always take place at specific timed moments and locations (1993). The timetable is a powerful system of governmentality that normatively locates trains, people and activities at specific places and moments.

Railways and their precise timetabling initiated a new regime of time based around the power of clock-time. This involves the gradual displacement of kairological time, which is the sense of time when it is said that *now* is the time to do something irrespective of what any clock indicates. Kairological time is based upon using the experience of the past in order to develop the sense of when a particular event should take place in the future, of just when it is the right time for something to occur (Gault 1995: 155).

Lefebvre more generally claims that lived time experienced in and through nature gradually disappears. Lived time he says 'has been murdered by society' (Lefebvre 1991: 96). Time is no longer something visible and inscribed within space. It has been replaced by measuring instruments, clocks, which are separate from natural and social space. Time becomes a resource, differentiated off from social space, consumed, deployed and exhausted. There is the expulsion of lived (and kairological) time as 'clock-time' comes to dominate. The main characteristics of clock-time are not only simply produced by the widespread use of clocks and watches; indeed clocks of some sort had been in existence for some millennia. Rather clock-time: 'is a time that is abstracted from its natural source; an independent, decontextualized, rationalized time. It is a time that is almost infinitely divisible into equal spatial units . . . and related to as time *per se*' (Adam 1995: 27; and see Adam 1998; Glennie, Thrift 1996; Urry 2000).

Clock-time is time as timetabled and with the spreading of the railways this began to transform modern societies. Such societies came increasingly subject to a regime of clock-time – this possesses the following characteristics: the breaking down of time into a very large number of small precisely measured and invariant units; the disembedding of time from meaningful social practices and from the divisions of night and day and the seasons; the widespread use of various means of measuring and indicating the passage of time: clocks, watches, timetables, calendars, hooters, schedules, clocking-on devices, bells, deadlines, diaries, alarm clocks, and so on; the precise timetabling of most work and leisure activities; the widespread use of time as an independent resource which can be saved and consumed, deployed and exhausted; the orientation to time as a resource to be managed rather than to time as activity or meaning; the scientific transformation of time into mathematically precise and quantifiable measures in which time is reversible and possesses no direction; the synchronized time-disciplining of travellers, school-children, employees, inmates, holidaymakers and so on; and the permeation of a discourse around the need for time to be saved, organized, monitored, regulated and especially to be *timetabled* (see Urry 2000: ch. 5).

And clock-time initiates the dream of speed both in travel and in a much more general way throughout society. Before the railway and its mechanization of movement, speed was mostly not a great issue. Travel by feet and by horse did not vary that much. There were physical limits and relatively little variation between the fastest and the slowest. There were less marked social inequalities generated by differential rates of movement between those on horse and those on feet.

The mechanization of movement through the railway initiates the valuation of speed and especially the value that faster trains are better than slower trains (see Virilio 1986, 1997, more generally on dromology). It follows that new railway and other transport building is justified if journey times are speeded up, that technologies that improve speed are those that should be valued, that speeding traffic aids economic competitiveness, and that high speed and the latest technology equals high status (except perhaps with the British nostalgic love of the steam engine; see Adam 1998; Augé 1995: 98–99; Harris, Lewis, Adam 2004).

Also lying behind these assumptions is the notion that journey time is dead time and that any new technology or infrastructure that reduces journey times should be developed since it minimizes such wasted time. The emphasis upon 'speed at all cost' means that no consideration is paid to the pleasures and uses of 'travel time', to what people might productively do while 'on the move' (for research, see Lyons, Urry 2005; Lyons, Jain, Holley 2007). Harris, Lewis, Adam summarize this prioritization of speed: 'Faster is seen to be better, as it achieves more in a given time frame. High-speed is viewed as less time consuming and therefore less costly and thus more efficient and profit creating or enhancing' (2004: 6; for details, see Whitelegg, Hultén, Flink 1993).

Thus the nineteenth-century mechanization of movement through the railway initiated a concern both for timetabling and for speed. These have had immense consequences for the nature of future transport developments, for the character of an increasingly timetabled social life, for a transformed governmentality, for economic progress and for the overall ways in which humans cohabit with machines. Such concerns created an irreversible set of processes that are further reproduced and spread as each new mobility system comes to the fore. We will see later how the car system appears to be both faster and also more convenient since cars are less constrained by public timetables. The railway is thus in part overtaken by new speed machines as the twentieth century unfolds. The nineteenth-century railway initiates a drive to speed and to the timetabling of social life that cast long shadows over the forms of movement that emerge in subsequent centuries.

Spaces

The railway initiates two powerful spatial effects that have been further magnified by subsequent mobility systems. First, railways seem to shrink space through bringing some places closer together and to eliminate many places in between; and second, the railways expand space by connecting places that otherwise would have never been connected (Schivelbusch 1986: 37). In this section I examine these two contradictory spatial processes that the railway system initiated.

Up to the eighteenth century visitors to other places, especially the rich young men on Grand Tours, got to know a place in its particular form, as spatially individual and unique (Schivelbusch 1986: ch. 13; Spring 2006). This knowing a place involved physical and intellectual effort. Treatises on travel at the time emphasized touring as an opportunity for discourse via the ear, by talking and getting to know a place in what Schivelbusch terms their 'spatial individuality' (1986: 197). Places we might say following Benjamin possessed a distinct 'aura' (1992).

But during the later eighteenth century, travel increasingly developed as involving observation, justified not through science but through connoisseurship via the 'the well-trained eye' (Adler 1989: 22). A connoisseurship of buildings, works of art and of landscapes developed into the nineteenth century based upon various visual technologies of reproduction: camera obscura, claude glass, guidebooks, routes, sketchbooks, guidebooks, photographs, postcards, gas- and electricity-lit arcades, cafés, dioramas, and especially the train and its windows (Ousby 1990). Places began to lose their uniqueness or aura according to Schivelbusch (1986: 41–3).

Thus those areas of wild, barren nature, once sources of terror and fear, became transformed, waiting at a distance for *visual* consumption by those visiting by train from towns and cities of 'dark satanic mills'. In mid nineteenth-century France: 'Nature has largely to do with leisure and pleasure – tourism, spectacular entertainment, visual refreshment' by those getting out of Paris by train (Green 1990: 6).

The railway then is part of a changing relationship of people to environments that get visited by outsiders. The railway makes places relational, on the way from or to other places, and better or worse in terms of values of connoisseurship or consumption. They begin to lose their aura, as Wordsworth famously lamented with the planned building of the railway to Keswick in the English Lake District in 1844 (Schivelbusch 1986: 42). Particular places became less known for their auratic 'beauty and character of seclusion and retirement' (Wordsworth 1876: 326), and more known as being like or unlike other places or being on the way to, or on the way from, somewhere else. Thus it is said that: 'localities were no longer spatially individual or autonomous: they were points in the circulation of traffic that made them accessible' (Schivelbusch 1986: 197). They are elements of an expanding system or what I termed above a nexus. Indeed we might say that the exceptional mechanical power of the railway appeared to create its own space linking many different places (while of course excluding others) into ever more complex and extended systems of speeded-up circulation. Railway travel thus became a 'value in and for itself as speeds increased, another country with its own distinctive practices and culture' (Thrift 1996: 267).

Such travel is a reflection of, and contributes to, the general circulation of goods and services that nineteenth-century industrialization ushers in. Schivelbusch argues that: 'traffic was the physical manifestation of the circulation of goods. From that time on, places visited by travellers became increasingly similar to the commodities that were part of the same circulation system' (1986: 197). Traffic and the conquest of space determined what belonged where. The railways turn places into a system of circulation, transforming what had been distinct places into commodities. By the twentieth century the world has become one large department store of countrysides and cities, places to consume and laid out for the delectation of potential visitors (Schivelbusch 1986: 197; Urry 1995). The railways bring about this modern world through the notion of circulation, of people, goods, places and increasingly photographic images (Larsen 2004).

The railway is key in the transformation from people 'dwelling' in the natural environment, to viewing the environment as a separate entity and thereby creating 'a fictional relationship between gaze and landscape' (Augé 1995: 98). It reflects what I term the shift from land to landscape. *Land* is a physical, tangible resource to be ploughed, sown, grazed and built upon, a place of functional work. Land is bought and sold, inherited and left to children. To dwell is to participate in a life where productive and unproductive activities resonate with each other and with tracts of land, whose history and geography are known in detail. There is a lack of distance between people and things (Ingold 2000). With *landscape* there is what Williams terms 'humanity's decision to unbind itself from the soil' (1990: 2). Landscape is an intangible resource whose key feature is its appearance or look. This unbinding of humanity from the soil developed in western Europe from the eighteenth century onwards, part of the more general emergence of a specialized *visual* sense. The notion of landscape prescribes a visual structure of desire to the experiences of different places: as Miss Bartlett paradigmatically declares in *A Room with a View*: 'A view? Oh a view! How delightful a view is!' (Forster 1955: 8; see ch. 12 below).

And in particular the speedy trajectory of travel *through* the landscape generated many new views, a panorama of new, fast moving landscapes. Schivelbusch suggests that Victorian rail passengers lost control of their sensory perception, as the speed of travel and the confined vision disembodied the traveller from the 'land'. It was 'landscape' that came to be viewed as swiftly passing framed panorama, involving a 'panoramic perception' rather than something lingered over, sketched or painted (Schivelbusch 1986: 58; Kern 1983). The railway choreographed a new kind of landscape, taken in at a glance and in which impressions were captured at speed. There is less 'a room with a view' and more a framed window providing a swiftly changing series of panoramic impressions. Victor Hugo wrote in 1837 as to how 'the towns, the steeples, and the trees perform a crazy mingling dance on the horizon' (quoted Schivelbusch 1986: 55; see Larsen 2001, on the 'tourist glance').

More generally people's identities came to be constituted through their longer-term *connections* with other places. Henry Thoreau in his mid nineteenth-century return to living with 'nature' on the banks of Walden Pond did not complain about the sound of the railway – he considered himself: 'refreshed and expanded when the freight train rattles past me, and I smell the stores which go dispensing their odours all the way from Long Wharf to Lake Champlain, reminding me of foreign parts . . . and the extent of the globe. I feel more like a citizen of the world' (1927: 103; Raymond Williams' novels contain similar sentiments).

Indeed this connectedness seems especially significant in the 'railroading' of America. Verstraete notes how de Tocqueville pronounced mobility as an American national characteristic (2002). To be an American is go somewhere, especially to go west. So in 1862 in the midst of the American Civil War, Congress decided to connect the Atlantic and Pacific oceans by means of a transcontinental railroad (Verstraete 2002). This enormous project involved the affirmation of national identity in the middle of the civil war, as well as enabling the transport of munitions to be used against the native Indians and the transport of goods to the west and on to Asia. Using thousands of Chinese workers the line from Sacramento, California to Omaha, Nebraska was completed in an astonishing seven years. Its completion was recorded on camera. The pictures of the west, of this unknown national land, were brought back to the east and this generated trust and excitement in this shared land of the American nation. The railroad building photographs were essential to the evolving imagined community of the United States; creating and reproducing an 'imaginary heroic national space' although the nation that was affirmed was one that excluded many including especially the Chinese who actually built the railway (Verstraete 2002). These pictures enable the shared imagining of a national community, analogous to the processes Anderson describes with regard to the role of print capitalism within European societies (1991).

The development of the railroad had particular consequences for early tourism within the American frontier. Travellers made specific references to how the railroad annihilated space through its exceptional speed that was not fully sensed because of the railway carriage's unusual comfort. The railway journey produced an enormous sense of panoramic vastness, of scale, size and domination of the landscape that the train swept through (Retzinger 1998: 221–4).

But the railway also initiates some novel micro-spaces and it is to two of these that I turn in the next section, which is concerned with the sociabilities afforded by new spaces of the nineteenth century.

Sociabilities

The nineteenth-century railway initiated two immensely significant new sites of sociability, the railway compartment and the station. Their significance stemmed from how the new rail passengers were seen as being thrown together with large numbers of 'strangers' within such novel, enclosed spaces. These compartments and stations led early commentators to believe that there was something democratic about rail travel since it took place with masses of other people, mainly strangers. Thomas Cook, for example, thought that travelling with others by rail was a democratic and progressive force: 'Railway travelling is travelling for the Million; the humble may travel, the rich may travel' (quoted Brendon 1991: 16; Schivelbusch 1986: ch. 5). Cook, the 'Emperor of Tourists', maintained that travel 'promotes universal brotherhood' (quoted Brendon 1991: 31–2). This mass travel was particularly reflected in the 1851 Great Exhibition when an extraordinary six million visits were made to London, many by train from especially the north of England (total population was only 18m at the time).

Interestingly, at first the railway companies did not realize the economic potential of the mass, low-income passenger market since railways were initially designed for goods and elite passengers (Richards, Mackenzie 1986: 167). It required a specialist in the *social* organization of rail travel, namely Thomas Cook who simplified, popularized and cheapened travel, turning the technological innovation of the railway into a social innovation. He initiated the provision of tickets in advance for different lines, the negotiation of block bookings so as to obtain favourable rates, the development of the railway coupon, the sending of luggage in advance, and hotel coupons and circular notes (Lash, Urry 1994: 263–4). He pronounced that: 'To remain stationary in these times of change, when all the world is on the move, would be a crime' (quoted Brendon 1991: 65).

However, although the new railways did permit remarkable increases in mass travel many social distinctions came to be made between travellers (as well as between those who could and could not travel; see on Britain Richards, Mackenzie 1986: chs. 6, 7). In Europe the rich and the humble were increasingly confined to different railway compartments (and indeed types of carriage). These railways not only simply reflected but more significantly played their part in institutionalizing the stratified class system that was emerging with industrial capitalism. As modernity went on the move, so it did so within different compartments and trains. Class was imbricated within access to these different categories of rail compartment. The sociabilities were increasingly experienced intra-class rather than across class.

Britain set the pattern with three classes of traveller and the concomitant gradation of train and station facilities (see Richards, Mackenzie 1986: ch. 6, for extensive detail). Distinctions developed between classes of compartment and of trains, between the 'social tone' of where one travelled to; and between those able and not able to designate servants to take luggage to the station and to collect tickets (on servants and travel, see Richards, Mackenzie 1986: 141). There was also a major issue to do with men and women travelling together and the harassment experienced by the latter. In the 1840s some British train companies provided Ladies Only waiting rooms and carriages especially for 'Ladies' travelling without escort. By the 1880s however this seems to have become less common and during the First World War many jobs on the railways came to be undertaken by women (there are still women-only carriages in Japan).

In the United States although trains were specified as classless there were significant differences in accommodation styles that could be purchased; and there were also different classes of trains and indeed of waiting rooms (Richards, Mackenzie 1986: 146–7; Carter 2001: ch. 1). So class distinctions resulted less from formal status and more from differences in purchasing power.

Overall, as railways initiated a massive increase in long distance mobility, so social class came to be reproduced through various forms of 'network capital' (see ch. 9 below). One increasingly important international form of such capital for the European rich was the development of a complex circuit of spa towns with entry available only to those able to afford the limited number of expensive apartments and hotel rooms. Spa towns were places where a sociable cosmopolitan elite gathered from all over Europe, now able to travel between them by train. New sociabilities emerged through the growing circuit of travel between such fashionable places drawn 'closer' together via the railway. These spas provided cultural capital and enabled taste setters to indulge in new consumer practices within such places (Blackbourn 2002: 15).

Rail travel involved new sociabilities as men and women found themselves in the company of strangers, even if they were roughly of the same class. Up to the 1860s most European rail compartments were built as though they were like stagecoaches and could only be entered from outside; thus people were literally trapped with others and this gave rise to some notorious crimes (Schivelbusch 1986:

79–84). American carriages were from the beginning built with corridors down their centre, making them more like river steamers, enabling passengers (and train robbers) to move around the train with ease (Schivelbusch 1986: ch. 6).

There has been much debate about how strangers within such novel environments maintained appropriate social distance. Raymond Williams wrote in the twentieth century of how on a station platform there was: 'this moving away [from other passengers], a habit no less his own because it was the habit of this crowded society' (1988: 315). Compared with the stagecoach where strangers regularly conversed with fellow passengers, it is thought that train passengers found new ways of keeping social distance (see Schivelbusch 1986: 74–5). Simmel helpfully makes the following contrast: 'Before the development of buses, trains and streetcars in the nineteenth century, people were quite unable to look at each other for minutes or hours at a time . . . without talking to each other. Modern traffic increasingly reduces the majority of sensory relations between human beings to mere sight' (quoted Schivelbusch 1986: 75). And forms of social distance become widespread, even involving ways of minimizing the viewing of the close-to body of one's fellow passengers. Goffman describes the importance of developing 'civil inattention', being in public but minimizing attention to others. This is a necessity in a train compartment he says but can be difficult to achieve. 'To not stare requires looking very pointedly in other directions' or finding 'some activity for himself [*sic*] in which he can become visibly immersed' (Goffman 1963: 137). Goffman highlights how newspapers and magazines allow us 'to carry around a screen that can be raised at any time to give ourselves or others an excuse for not initiating contact' (1963: 139). However, from their early beginnings rail travel has been associated with reading books as well; indeed it is suggested that Victorian reading habits were significantly developed because of the huge growth of 'railway' reading materials following the establishment of bookstalls on most stations (Richards and Mackenzie 1986: 298–303). The computer or mobile phone screens are contemporary examples of screening oneself from the attention of others and explaining silence (likely to be deployed by women to avoid male harassment). Goffman also notes that conversations between strangers will tend to be 'impersonal' and by declining to reveal names (or email addresses or mobile phone numbers): 'guaranteeing that some kind of nonrecognition will be possible in future' (1963: 139). He particularly emphasizes the 'thinned-out' nature of conversations that typically take place between strangers in compartments and stations.

In research recently conducted with a sample size of 25,000 UK rail passengers we found that just over half spend *some* of their travel time reading for leisure, and over one-third spend *most* of their time doing so, this being the most popular use of time overall (Lyons, Jain, Holley 2007). Working or studying is the activity most prevalent among those travelling on business; they are more than twice as likely as commuters to spend most of their time doing this, this being the single most likely occupation of business travellers' time. By contrast, leisure travellers are twice as likely to spend most of their time window gazing/people watching. The passing scenery may indeed be part of their leisure experience, reflecting the 'tourist gaze' (Urry 2002c). In terms of communication, while one per cent of all passengers spend most of their time making phone calls or sending text messages, 19 per cent spend *some* time on personal calls/messages and 8 per cent on work calls/messages. Overall passengers felt that the travel time was not dead time; however, the younger the person the more likely they were to consider such time as wasted. It is interesting that Virgin trains now advertise their trains on the London Underground in terms of how they provide of 'valuable thinking time'.

We also considered whether passengers planned for their journey. Thirteen per cent planned 'a lot', 41 per cent 'a little' and 47 per cent 'not at all' (Lyons, Jain, Holley 2007). More first-class passengers plan a lot in advance (24 per cent) than other passengers (12 per cent). Those passengers who consider their travel time to have been wasted are more than twice as likely to have done no advance planning (70 per cent), compared with those who consider their travel time very worthwhile (31 per cent). Over one-third of passengers are equipped with a book; over-three quarters carry a newspaper; a third have paperwork and over two-thirds have a mobile phone (see Gasparini on 'equipped waiting', 1995). Business travellers are much more likely to have a laptop, PDA/hand-held computer or to have paperwork with them. Commuters are more likely to have a book or personal stereo radio. Leisure travellers are more likely to have a magazine and less likely a newspaper.

Other studies have found the mobile phone to be the most useful device for working on the move, providing an important link to co-workers and clients. Over one-fifth of rail passengers thought that having such devices with them made the time on the train a lot better (though nearly half of all passengers, 46 per cent, considered electronic devices had not made the travel time any better). Business travellers generally saw slightly more benefit and leisure travellers slightly less. Those travelling first class were more likely to consider that such electronic devices had made their time use more effective (Lyons, Jain, Holley 2007).

Related research on the experience and passing of train time shows some interesting characteristics, especially the stretching of and the compressing of time over the course of a journey (see Watts 2006). For periods nothing much can happen as time can be said to drag, to stand still, while at other moments there are intense periods of multi-tasking.

I turn finally to the railway station that was a new kind of public space within nineteenth-century Europe and North America (along with the station hotel). In his review of railway architecture, Edwards states that the: 'great passenger station was one of the most important new building types of the nineteenth century. There were no parallels in terms of feat of engineering, scale of human movement, or complexity of function' (1997: ix; Sachs, 1992: 162, describes them as 'cathedrals'). It is difficult to imagine just how astonishing these new edifices of steel, brick and glass were in the mid to late nineteenth century, comparable only in scale and imposing grandeur to the churches and cathedrals of the mediaeval period.

But more than just their architecture in signifying the modern world (often of course using older classical or gothic styles), stations played crucial roles in the reorganizing of space. Thus stations were often constituted as hubs where travellers from many different places passed through and which generated a large town or city as a consequence. Chicago owed its massive late nineteenth-century growth to being the meeting place of twenty-seven different railway lines (that all terminated at Chicago: Richards, Mackenzie 1986: 219). In Britain Crewe and Swindon owed their existence to being at the meeting point of multiple rail lines. Similar examples include Nairobi in Kenya and Vladivostok in Siberia. This social mixing also occurred because of the nineteenth-century growth of railway hotels, which could now be entered and accessed by the public, including especially women travellers (Mennell 1985: 158). In the nineteenth century these luxurious hotels became places to see and to be seen in, no longer the private clubs that hotels had previously been.

Urban stations were mostly situated on the periphery of built-up city centre areas which then provoked further commercial growth (as in Gröningen), as well as generating a reputation for crime and prostitution among the local population (as in King's Cross, London). Often nineteenth-century competition between railway companies generated multiple termini within major cities (London with 15, Moscow with 9, Paris with 8). This then led to further travel developments so that rail, underground or road connections were developed to take passengers from terminal to terminal. The boulevards linking various new stations were a key feature of Haussmann's rebuilding of the arteries of Paris during the Second Empire (see ch. 4 above).

Furthermore, many different kinds of station have developed, reflected the various sociabilities taking place within them: private stations, racecourse stations, port stations, services stations, factory stations, hospital stations, school stations, milk stations, airport stations, royal stations, iron ore stations, coal stations, commuter stations, pilgrim stations, spa and seaside stations, country stations and so on (Richards, Mackenzie 1986: ch. 8).

And stations probably more than other travel interchanges have been sites of fantasy, fiction and film. Among others, Emile Zola, Thomas Mann, Marcel Proust, Lawrence Durrell, Arthur Conan Doyle, Arnold Bennett, Noel Coward, Charles Dickens and most poignantly Leo Tolstoy in Anna Karenina situate their classic novels in and around stations and trains. These are places of unexpected social interchange as people's lives from distant parts are contingently brought together, often only for 'brief encounters' before the characters move away (or home) again (see Richards, Mackenzie 1986: 360–4, on the film *Brief Encounter*; Carter 2001).

Conclusion

In the next chapter I examine the growth of the car system that has proved so catastrophic for railways. In the nineteenth century the latter had initiated emphases upon speed, timetables and new social spaces (as discussed). But the car system transformed the concept of speed into that of convenience. It provided a way of transcending a public timetable by enabling car-drivers to develop their own time-tabling of social life. And it initiated and reproduced a wide array of other spaces beyond the railway carriage and the station (including the interior of the car as a place to dwell). During the twentieth century, the century of the car, railways in North America and western Europe have lived within the shadow of its brother, once minute but now turned into a very big (and bad) brother.

What happened to the rail system as the car system grew in this way? Why did it not adapt to its growing competitor and put up a sustained resistance? One important point is that railways have typically been organized through hierarchy, often modelled on a military hierarchy with uniforms, titles, a marked division of labour, and high deference levels (see Richards, Mackenzie 1986: ch. 10). This pattern of hierarchy characterized both private companies that typically built the railways and the state railways that became common during 'organised capitalism' in the twentieth century (Lash, Urry 1987). Railway systems have been essentially military machines focused upon the very specific delivery of rail services and as such have shown little capacity to adapt and to co-evolve in relationship to the growing system of automobility (see Featherstone, Thrift, Urry 2004).

We will see how automobility is to be characterized as a complex and adaptive system (see Urry 2004). The car system is more a way of life, a way of organizing economic, social and cultural life that only in part involves the movement of people from place to place. It is, as we will see, an autopoietic system, extraordinarily adaptive, expanding and able to dominate other systems by continuously transforming the environment within which the others operate. The railway by contrast has been a public (even if privately owned) hierarchy only delivering trains intermittently moving from A to B. It is a hierarchy and not a complex, adaptive system.

There have been, however, three limited responses of the rail system – the speed response, the neo-liberal response, and the integrated transport response. The first response of the rail system to the car system has involved the building of new rail lines that permit the running of very high-speed trains, trains that stop only infrequently and therefore by-pass many places en route (Whitelegg, Hultén, Flink 1993). The first of these speed-systems was that of the Shinkansen expresses in Japan initially built for the 1964 Olympic Games in Tokyo, but now constituting the most extensive effort to beat the car at the speed game. The TGV in France and the ICE in Germany are leading European examples following the attempts to create a high speed European space based on the trans-European transport network (see Richardson, Jensen 2003).

A second response to the perceived failure of the public railway has been to advocate a neo-liberal or market solution. The emphasis was on a much more pronounced consumer-orientation; passengers on UK trains being relabelled as 'customers' and being provided with new ticketing and consumer packages adapted to different consumer segments, including especially what Graham terms the growth of 'premium networked spaces' dedicated to high-paying users separated off from the general 'public' (2004). The station too is restructured as a place with retail, social and cultural facilities enclosed within its shell. Where once the station was a transitional space through which travellers passed en route to the train, so now it is another urban venue, a post-industrial site of consumption, fluid functions and pastiched meanings (Edwards 1997: 173).

A third response is an integrated travel system in which trains and stations are part of a reintegrated system of travel. Buses, trains, light rail, cycles are all reintegrated into a revived public system under the auspices of what Vigar terms the 'new realism' in transport planning (2002). The station changes into a public structure where all are free to pass, stations being 'bridges' between different parts of a city. The bus system in Curitiba, Brazil is a model for such a new public mobilization.

In the next chapter I turn to the expanding and self-organizing character of the car system that has had such consequences in transforming the environment within which these public systems have struggled to survive, and in which so far the three responses mentioned here have not been sufficient to displace on a global scale the orchestrating power of the private car predominantly running along publicly maintained and financed roads.

6

Inhabiting Cars and Roads

We talk of nothing but cars
(Virginia Woolf, *Diary*, vol. 3, p. 146)

A Brief History

In this chapter I examine the growth of the car system that has proved so catastrophic for paths, pavements and rail passengers. We saw in the previous chapter how in the nineteenth century the railway initiated new emphases upon machine-speed, timetables, punctuality, clock-time and public spaces. But the emergence of the car system transformed that concept of speed into one of convenience. The car system provided a way of transcending a public timetable by enabling car-drivers to develop their own timetabling of social life. And it initiated and reproduced a wide array of other spaces beyond the railway carriage and the station (including the interior of the car as a place to dwell). During the twentieth century – the century of the car according to Gilroy – the railway system in North America and western Europe has lived in the shadow of its brother, once minute but now turned into a very big (and bad) brother (2000: 81). This chapter documents some of the shifts as automobility came to constitute itself as an autopoietic system. Indeed I might have termed this chapter 'autopoietic automobility'.

I begin by noting how the humble bicycle paved the way for the car and for its subsequent domination of paths and pavements, roads and freeways. The bicycle initiated the 'pleasure in unfettered mobility', freeing cyclists from the train, locality and timetables and generating a sense of autonomous movement and speed. Emile Zola in *Paris* wrote of how the cycle engenders: 'endless hope, the liberation from the all too oppressive fetters, across space' (cited Sachs 1992: 103). The new movement of the bicycle provided a sense of speed, autonomy and liberation especially for women in nineteenth-century Europe (see Sachs 1992: 104, on its implications for female dress). It provided the kind of autonomy from timetables previously provided by horse-based travel. It engendered a desire for speed and for unrestrained movement, something that continued with the growth of motor racing and the setting of new records.

The bicycle also engendered its own problems which the new speed machine of the automobile gradually overcame. The car unlike the bicycle could be heated and boxed in, a 'motorized carriage', so providing some protection from the elements (Sachs 1992: 9; Setright 2003). At first, though, the early developers of the automobile at the end of the nineteenth century did not realize what it was that they were bringing into being. Bertha Benz is often credited with playing a seminal role in the car's development when in 1885 she took her husband's car out of his workshop and went for a drive to visit her parents some 80 kilometres away. This is said to be the first *social* use of the car especially since men at the time mostly conceived of the car as a 'speed machine'. Early cars were less a means of regular movement than as a way of demonstrating social superiority over others and this was reflected in the design features of especially early European cars (Sachs 1992: 10–11).

From an early period the car especially in the United States was something that was deemed to be self-driven, increasingly by women and not requiring a professional driver. The car rapidly became a consumer good owned and driven by private individuals who increasingly demonstrated technological expertise through their capacity actually to get their car from A to B. Especially important in this emerging culture of modern technology were car enthusiasts who in 'tinkering' with these new machines improved the fit between their desires and the mass-produced machine (Franz 2005: 10). Tinkering involved the addition of lights, electric starters, body parts, luggage racks, trunks, beds and heaters. Knowing how to tinker with their car rapidly became an important form of expertise that even many middle-class women were drawn to, challenging notions of the 'passive consumer'. It was only later in the 1920s and 1930s that the corporatization of technology had the effect of reasserting traditional gender roles (see O'Connell 1998, on the early gendering of the car in Britain).

As early as the 1890s there were three main methods of propelling these novel horseless carriages: petrol, steam and electric batteries, with the latter two being more 'efficient' at the time (Motavalli, 2000: ch. 1; Miller 2000b: 7). Petroleum fuelled cars were ultimately successful for small-scale, more or less accidental reasons, partly because a petrol fuelled vehicle was one of only two to complete a 'horseless carriage competition' held in Chicago in 1896. The petrol system came to be established and 'locked' in, with the first model T appearing as early as 1908, more or less as the Futurist Marinetti was proclaiming the new 'beauty of speed' (Platt 2000: 39). US car registrations in the first decade of the twentieth century jumped from 8,000 to 500,000. The Fordist production and consumption system was established at a very early historical moment.

Thus as Arthur describes, small causes occurring in a certain order at the end of the nineteenth century turned out to have irreversible consequences for the twentieth century (1994a). Such a car system, essentially initiated in the fin-de-siècle, came to dominate those other alternatives that were at the time probably preferable (Motavalli, 2000; see Scharff 1991, on the gendering of these different power sources). The 'path-dependence' of the petroleum-based car was 'locked' in although this lock-in was massively facilitated by corporation policies, as in 1932 when General Motors bought up US tramways in order to close them down.

The path-dependence of the steel-and-petroleum car was also aided by extensive government policies initially in North America and northern Europe to build paved roads. Although cars had developed by the early 1900s, they did not have suitable places to go to in the United States until extensive paved roads appeared from 1932 onwards (interstate highways were not started until 1956). Road building in inter-war Germany was especially significant with National Socialism developing the model of car-only roads (Sachs 1992: 12–5; 48–54). Thus we can say that through road building and other infrastructural expenditures each nation-state: 'shapes the possibilities and potential parameters of social and personal relationships' (Cerny 1990: 194).

Predicting traffic expansion and then providing for this through new road building became especially marked during the middle years of the last century (Cerny 1990: 190–4). There was the locking together of the car with utopian notions of progress. The car's unrelenting expansion of, and domination over, other mobility systems came to be viewed as natural and inevitable; nothing it was thought should stand in the way of its modernizing path and its capacity to eliminate the constraints of time and space (Sachs 1992: 26–8). And over the century this naturalization of the car and its increasingly extensive lock-in with multiple organizations necessary for its expansion was facilitated through new discourses, that drivers had to be qualified and appropriately trained and that pedestrians should behave correctly so as to be able to cross roads safely in spite of them being increasingly monopolized by cars.

In the next section I examine some features of the system of automobility that came to cast its long shadow over the world over the twentieth and early twenty-first centuries. With world car travel predicted to triple between 1990 and 2050 and the number of cars to reach one billion by 2030 this remains of profound significance (Hawken, Lovins, Lovins 2000; Motavalli 2000: 20–1). Horvath writing back in 1974 claimed that the 'automobile may prove to be the single most significant innovation in American culture during the twentieth century' (and we can add 'in world culture': 1974: 168; see for comparative research, Kenworthy, Laube 2002).

Automobility and its Self-Expansion

The automobility system comprises a number of components that in their *combination* generate and reproduce the 'specific character of domination' that it has come to exercise over the twentieth century (see original argument in Sheller, Urry 2000; Cerny 1990: 189–95). The car we might say is a way of life and not just a transport system for getting from one place to another. Its distinct characteristics make it unlike any previous mobility-system. First, cars are the quintessential manufactured object produced by the leading industrial sectors and iconic firms within twentieth-century capitalism (Ford, General Motors, Volvo, Rolls-Royce, Mercedes, Toyota, Peugeot-Citroen, Volkswagen and so on). One billion cars were manufactured during this last century and there are currently between 500–600 m cars roaming the world. Country after country is developing an automobile industry with China currently being the most significant. This industry is that from which the definitive social science concepts of Fordism and Post-Fordism have emerged and have structured much theorizing and research about the nature of organized capitalist societies (see Lash, Urry 1987, 1994). The car industry *is* capitalism for much social science, although strangely the focus has almost entirely been upon its production and not the consumption and use aspects of automobility (but see Featherstone, Thrift, Urry 2004).

Second, in most households the car is the major item of individual consumption after expenditure on housing and one that has so far proved ever more popular with each new generation of young adults. It is sign of adulthood, a marker of citizenship and the basis of sociability and networking (see Carrabine, Longhurst 2002). Overall it is a very expensive means of movement, given the cost of the car itself, repairs, servicing, fuel, taxation, accessories, insurance and so on. However, this does not preclude quite poor households in many societies gaining access to a car, owned or borrowed or lent out (Miller 2000; Raje 2004; Froud, Johal, Leaver, Williams 2005). The car disproportionately preoccupies all criminal justice systems, both because of thefts from, and of, cars and because of the multitude of new 'crimes' that the car system engenders. Cars provide status to their owners through their various sign-values that include speed, home, safety, sexual success, career achievement, freedom, family, masculinity and even genetic breeding. The individual car can also be anthropomorphized by being given names, seen to have rebellious features and thought of as 'ageing' gracefully or badly (see Miller 2001, for much cross-cultural variation). Overall there are a range of 'automotive emotions' implicated in the ownership and possession of a car, a libidinal economy 'in which particular models become objects of desire to be collected and cosseted, washed and worshipped', desired and driven (Sheller 2004a: 225).

Third, automobility is a powerful complex constituted through very many technical and social interlinkages with other institutions, industries and related occupations (Freund 1993). The 'car' is not so significant as such but its system of interconnections. Slater argues that: 'a car is not a car because of its physicality but because systems of provision and categories of things are "materialized" in a stable form', and this generates the distinct affordances that the car provides for the hybrid of the car-driver (2001; Dant 2004). The car is interlinked with licensing authorities; traffic police; petrol refining and distribution; road-building and maintenance; hotels, roadside service areas and motels; car sales and repair workshops (Dant, Bowles 2003); suburban and green-field house-building sites; retailing and leisure complexes; advertising and marketing; and urban design and planning so as to ensure uninterrupted movement (see Merriman 2004, on the interlinkages necessitated by the development of motorways in the UK). These interlinkages are 'locked in' and have helped to ensure that this system has increasingly spread around the world. Huge increasing returns resulted for those producing and selling the car and its associated infrastructure, products and services (see Arthur 1994a, 1994b, on increasing returns). The lock-in means that specific institutions structure how this system developed. Such institutions produced a long-term irreversibility that is 'more predictable and more difficult to reverse according to North (1990). Billions of agents and thousands of organizations have co-evolved and adapted to that remaking of the system of automobility as it spread like a virus around the globe.

Fourth, the car-system is the predominant form of mobility for leisure, commuting and holidaymaking and it subordinates the other mobility-systems of walking, cycling, rail travel and so on (albeit with much variation within different continents: see Kenworthy, Laube 2002). The long-term trend is for automobile territory to become 'ever more exclusive' (Horvath 1974: 175). In particular the loose interactions and mobilities of pedestrians give way to the tightly controlled mobility of machines that (hopefully!) keep on one side of the road, within lanes, within certain speeds, following highly complex sign-systems and so on. Overall the car-system reorganizes time and space and thus how people negotiate the opportunities for, and constraints upon, work, family life, childhood, leisure and pleasure (Horvath 1974; Whitelegg 1997). This capacity of automobility to reshape public and private life and time *and* space through a dialectic of freedom/coercion is examined in the next section.

Fifth, car culture has developed into a dominant culture generating major discourses of what constitutes the good life and what is necessary to be a mobile modern citizen in the twentieth century. Barthes suggested that cars are equivalent to gothic cathedrals in the Middle Ages: 'the supreme creation of an era, conceived with passion by unknown artist, and consumed in image if not in usage by a whole population, which appropriate them as a purely magical object' (1972: 88). These magical objects (Rolls Royces, Minis, Jaguars, Ferraris, Mustangs, Mercedes, BMWs) have been especially explored through modernist literary and artistic images and symbols. These include novels by E. M. Forster, Virginia Woolf, Scott Fitzgerald, Daphne du Maurier, Jack Kerouac, John Steinbeck, J. G. Ballard (see Bachmair, 1991; Graves-Brown, 1997; Pearce 2000; Enevold 2000), and films such as *Easy Rider, Rolling Stone, Alice Doesn't Live Here Anymore, Bonnie and Clyde, Vanishing Point, Badlands, Thelma and Louise, Paris, Texas*, as well as those featuring iconic car chases or crashes such as *The Italian Job, Bullitt* or *Crash* (Eyerman and Löfgren 1995). Cars can also be linked to contemporary scientific signs, with a BMW being described as 'automotive DNA for a new generation' (Sheller 2004a: 232). While the whole notion of American society, its suburbs, urban strips, and mobile motel culture, is indissolubly intertwined with a car-based masculinist modernity.

And this is even so in Cuba with its amazing legacy of 1950s American cars that are now central to its post-1989 tourism strategy (see Edensor 2004, on automobility and national identity; and Enevold 2000, on road travel as a male identity project).

Sixth, the car system generates massive environmental resource-use and an extraordinary scale of death and injuries. Transport accounts for one-third of CO_2 emissions; and more generally there is an exceptional range of materials, space and power used in the manufacture and the movement of cars. Extensive air quality, medical, social, ozone, visual, aural, spatial and temporal pollutions stem from the car-system, a system that is playing a major role in generating many wars (Whitelegg 1997; Adams 1999). The car-system also produces its own 'negativity', it produces death and injury on a scale many times greater than any previous mobility system. The book and the film *Crash* examines the dramatically fast deaths and woundings that the car system necessarily produces. World-wide the system generates 1.2 m deaths and 20–50 m injuries a year. The estimated global cost of such a scale of crashes is $518 billion. Crashes are a normal and predictable outcome of the car system although they are typically referred to as 'accidents', aberrations rather than 'normal' features of what Beckmann terms the 'auto-risk society' (2001; Featherstone 2004: 3–4; Perrow 1999).

And seventh, 'automobility' involves the fusion of the humanist inner-directed self as in the notion of autobiography, and of objects or machines that possess the capacity for movement as in something being automatic or an automaton. This double resonance of 'auto' demonstrates that the 'car-driver' is as a hybrid assemblage of human competences and will, and machines, roads, buildings, and signs (Thrift 1996: 282–84; Dant 2004). 'Auto' mobility thus involves the powerful combination of autonomous humans together with machines possessing the capacity for autonomous movement along the paths, lanes, streets and routeways of each society. Automobility is a self-organizing autopoietic, non-linear system that spreads world-wide, cars, car-drivers, roads, petroleum supplies and many novel objects, technologies and signs (Capra, 1996, 2002; Prigogine, 1997; Urry, 2003). The system generates the preconditions for its own self-expansion (Luhmann 1995).

In the next section it is shown just how the car system produces what it uses as a unit through its capacity for self-production. In particular automobility remakes time–space through its peculiar combination of flexibility and coercion. Automobility's restructurings of time and space generate the need for ever-more cars and its further expansion as a system. It is this remaking of time–space that ensures the car system's self-expansion. Social life has been irreversibly locked in to the mode of mobility that automobility both generates and which can so far only be dealt with through its further expansion and restructurings of time and space.

Automobility and time–space

Automobility we might say is neither socially necessary nor was its development inevitable, but having got established it seems impossible to break from. This is because the car is simultaneously immensely flexible *and* wholly coercive.

Automobility is a source of freedom, the 'freedom of the road'. Its flexibility derives in part from how the car waits as a 'standing-reserve', to be immediately on hand, as Heidegger characterizes the airliner on the runway (1993: 322). But the car is so much more flexible than the airliner since it enables most car-drivers to enter that car and to start it without permission or tickets or the expertise of others. It is ready waiting to spring easily into life, so enabling people to travel at any time in any direction along the complex road systems of western societies that now link most houses, workplaces and leisure sites (and which are publicly paid for). In one UK survey, 95 per cent agreed with the statement that 'driving gives me freedom to go where I want when I want' (Stradling, Meadows, Beatty 2002: 5). Cars extend where people can go to and hence what they are literally able to do. Much 'social life' could not be undertaken without the flexibilities of the car and its 24-hour availability. It is possible to leave late by car, to miss connections, to travel in a relatively time-less fashion. Automobility thus irreversibly set in train new flexible socialities, of commuting, family life, community, leisure, the pleasures of movement and so on. The growth in automobility has principally involved new modes of movement and is not the historical replacement of public transport by the car (Vigar 2002: 12; Adams 1999). Begg, Director of the UK Centre for Integrated Transport concludes that: 'Most car journeys were never made by public transport. The car's flexibility has encouraged additional journeys to be made' (quoted Stradling, Meadows, Beatty 2002: 2).

The seamlessness of the car journey makes other modes of travel inflexible and fragmented. So-called public transport rarely provides that kind of seamlessness (except for first class air travellers with a limousine service to and from the airport). There are many gaps between the various mechanized means of public transport. These 'holes' in semi-public space are sources of inconvenience, danger and uncertainty, especially for women, children, older people, those who may be subject to racist attacks, the less able and so on (Raje 2004).

But the car's flexibility is in fact *necessitated* by automobility. The 'structure of auto space' (Freund 1993; Kunstler 1994) or what Horvath terms the 'machine space' of 'automobile territory' (1974) forces people to orchestrate in complex and heterogeneous ways their mobilities and socialities across very significant distances. The car system has reorganized time and space, 'unbundling' territorialities of home, work, business, and leisure that were historically closely integrated. Automobility divides workplaces from homes, producing lengthy commutes into and across the city. It splits homes and business districts, undermining local retail outlets to which one might have walked or cycled, eroding town-centres, non-car pathways, and public spaces. It separates homes and leisure sites often only available by motorized transport. Members of families are split up since they live in distant places involving complex travel to meet up intermittently. Cars are a major 'convenience device' of contemporary society, devices that make complex, harried patterns of social life just about possible, at least of course for those with cars; a complexity that the car itself generates.

Automobility thus coerces people into an intense flexibility. It forces people to juggle tiny fragments of time so as to deal with the temporal and spatial constraints that it itself generates. Automobility is a Frankenstein-created monster, extending the individual into realms of freedom and flexibility whereby inhabiting the car can be positively viewed, but also constraining car 'users' to live their lives in spatially stretched and time-compressed ways. The car, one might suggest, is really Weber's 'iron cage' of modernity, motorized, moving and privatized. People inhabit congestion, jams, temporal uncertainties and health-threatening city environments through being encapsulated in a domestic, cocooned, moving capsule, an iron bubble.

The key process here is the shift from 'clock' time to 'instantaneous' time. I set out the nature of clock-time in the previous chapter. And this pattern has not so much disappeared but is being gradually replaced by a notion of time as instantaneous (or what Castells terms 'timeless time': 1996). Partly this time-regime stems from the following processes: informational and communication changes based upon nanosecond time; technological and organizational changes which break down distinctions of night and day, working week and weekend, home and work, leisure and work; the increasing disposability of products, places and images in a 'throwaway society'; the growing volatility and ephemerality in fashions, products, labour processes, ideas and images; a heightened 'temporariness' of products, jobs, careers, natures, values and personal relationships; the growth of 24 hour trading; extraordinary increases in the availability of products from different societies so that many styles and fashions can be instantaneously consumed; and an accelerating 'pace of life' (Urry 2000: ch. 5).

But also instantaneous time involves the desynchronization of time–space paths. There is greatly increased variation in different people's times that spread, if not over 24 hours, over longer periods. People's activities are less collectively organized and structured as mass consumption patterns are replaced by more varied and segmented patterns. Time–space desynchronization can be seen in the increased significance of grazing, not eating at fixed meal times in the same place in the company of one's family or workmates and hence of fast-food consumption (Ritzer 1992); in the growth of 'free and independent travellers' who specifically resist mass travel in a group where everyone has to engage in common activities at fixed times; in the development of flexitime, so that groups of employees no longer start and stop work at the same time; in the growth of the VCR/digital TV which means that TV programmes can be stored, repeated, and broken up so little remains of the shared watching by the whole family; and in the shift from rail and bus to the car as the predominant means of mass movement. Automobility is central to this shift to an individualistic timetabling of many instants or fragments of time. The car-driver is in instantaneous time rather than the official timetabling of clock-time based upon the public timetable and indeed the station clock and modernist clock-time.

As early as 1902 a car-driver noted how the car brings into being new temporalities: 'Traveling means utmost free activity, the train however condemns you to passivity . . . the railway squeezes you into a timetable' (cited Morse 1998: 117) since the clock-time of the modernist railway timetable 'locks one into a cage' (Sachs 1992: 93). The car system by contrast allows liberation from such constraints; as the President of the German Automotive Industry Association pronounced in 1974: 'The automobile is another bit of freedom' (cited Sachs 1992: 97). People around the world come to live their lives through the car and through its flexible freedom, such as the empty landscapes of American deserts experienced through driving huge distances across them, a 'line of flight' (Baudrillard 1988). Deserts constitute a metaphor of endless futurity, a primitive society of the future, obliterating the past and the triumph of time as instantaneous (Baudrillard 1988: 6).

The car can thus be linked with the increased significance of per-sonalized, subjective temporalities and the reflexive monitoring of the less structured self elaborated by Giddens and others. People, Giddens argues, try to sustain 'coherent, yet continuously revised, biographical narratives . . . in the context of multiple choices filtered through abstract systems' (1991: 6). And maybe the most significant of those abstract systems is that of automobility. People thus assem-ble complex, fragile and contingent patterns of social life, patterns that constitute self-created narratives of the reflexive self. Automo-bility thus forces or coerces people to juggle fragments of time and activities. Indeed automobility produces desires for flexibility and for multiple activities with often distant friends, family and workmates – and paradoxically so far only the car is able to satisfy such desires in most societies across the world (as Miller 2000, also reveals about many developing societies). Such flexibility means that personal times are desynchronized from each other – no longer following a public timetable. Spatial movement is synchronized rather to the rhythms of the road.

More generally, '[M] modernist urban landscapes were built to facilitate automobility and to discourage other forms of human movement . . . [Movement between] private worlds is through dead public spaces by car' (Freund 1993: 119). Indeed large areas of the globe consist of such dead car-only environments – the non-places of super-modernity according to Augé (1995; but see Merriman 2004). About one-quarter of the land in London and nearly one-half of that in LA is devoted to such car-only environments, as well as very large areas of many cities in developing societies. As Joni Mitchell sings 'They paved paradise and put up a parking lot' (Big Yellow Taxi, Joni Mitchell *Ladies of the Canyon*, May 1970); that is, because cars are mostly static, with many cars greedily needing two or more parking spaces – one at home and one at work (plus maybe one at a leisure centre). This appropriation of land is enormously wasteful especially since the only occupants of car parks can be cars (as well as car thieves of course).

These specialized time–spaces exert spatial and temporal domi-nance over surrounding environments, transforming what is seen, heard, smelt and tasted (see Platt's evocative account of this in *Lead-ville*, 2000). They are sites of mobility from which as I discuss in the next section car-drivers are progressively insulated. Horvath refers to these as places as 'ecologically dying or dead' (1974: 184). They represent the victory of a modernist liquidity over older notions of what 'urban' life should be like, perhaps best captured and repre-sented in the American motel. Clifford notes that the 'motel has no real lobby, and it's tied into a highway network – a relay or node rather than a site of encounter between coherent cultural subjects' (as would, he implies, be found in a hotel; 1997: 32). Motels as noted above memorialize only movement, speed, and perpetual circulation (Morris 1988: 3, 5). This 'sense of sameness and placelessness' is accompanied by a 'social organization of space that helps to further auto-dependence and to mask any realistic alternatives to automobility' (Freund 1993: 11). Morse describes the freeway not as a place but as a vector, as direction, as 'in-betweens' where magnitude is measured in minutes rather than miles (1998). *Leadville* describes the car environment of the A40 in west London and its devastating effects upon those unfortunate people trying to live with the streams of traffic rapidly passing next to their houses (see Platt 2000). These houses are increasingly unsaleable as they are given over to the ruthless car system. This is bringing about what Corbusier predicted as an inevitable effect of the movement of traffic, that roads will increasingly be monopolized by cars (Platt 2000: 183).

Such cars display striking levels of linear social order. Traffic according to ethnomethodologist Lynch is a remarkably: 'standardised, predictable, and repetitive order of things, and its order is independent of the particular cohorts of drivers whose actions compose it' (1993: 155; and see Laurier 2004). Such an ordering requires 'publics' based upon trust in which mutual strangers are able to follow shared rules, communicate through common sets of visual and aural signals, and interact even without eye-contact in a kind of default space available to all motorized 'citizens of the road' (Lynch 1993). This is an example of Goffman's concept of unfocused interaction dependent upon the glance (1963).

In this linear system, car-drivers are excused normal etiquette and face-to-face interactions with others inhabiting the road. Lefebvre argues that the driver: 'is only concerned with steering himself to his destination, and in looking about sees only what he needs to see for that purpose' (1991: 313). And in this single-minded pursuit car-travel interrupts the taskscapes of others (pedestrians, children going to school, postmen, garbage collectors, farmers, animals and so on), whose daily routines are obstacles to the high-speed traffic cutting mercilessly through slower-moving pathways and dwellings. Indeed Adorno wrote as early as 1942: 'And which driver is not tempted, merely by the power of the engine, to wipe out the vermin of the street, pedestrians, children and cyclists?' (1974: 40). Junctions, roundabouts, and ramps present moments of carefully scripted inter-car-action during which non-car users of the road constitute obstacles to the hybrid car-drivers intent on returning to their normal cruising speed deemed necessary in order to complete the day's many tasks in time. To inhabit most roads of the world is to enter of world of anonymized machines, ghostly presences moving too fast to know directly or especially to see through the eye (but see Edensor 2004, on the roads of India).

Thus the individualized desire for privatized flexibility, as opposed to the public timetable of the railway, has resulted in a car system that generates extensive time space de-synchronization. That de-synchronization can only be dealt with by the further extension of the car and especially of the spaces to which the car gets increasingly monopolistic access, what Illich referred to as early as 1974 as a 'radical monopoly' (1974: 45; Sachs 1992: 192). Such a system is so far the only solution to the very problems that cars in their masses have created. Moreover, as roads are no longer the privilege of the rich but are driven along by millions even with modest incomes in at least rich societies, so those roads become increasingly crowded and are some of the most dangerous of places on earth (with over one million deaths a year). These are the 'killing fields' of late modern societies. And in order for car-drivers and passengers to protect themselves in these places of danger and death so the car itself becomes transformed, into a place of securitized dwelling. It is a place of comfort and pleasure so offsetting long journey times and inter-minable delays and congestion. The car as a place of security, emotion and dwelling is thus explored in the next section.

Dwellingness

In using the term dwellingness I am loosely relating my argument to that of Heidegger (1993: 347–163). He distinguishes between a truck driver inhabiting the highway and a person who dwells within their home. In developing a brief historical typology I suggest that the road and especially the car increasingly become places of contemporary dwellingness sharing some at least of the characteristic of Heidegge-rian dwelling within the home (see Urry 2000, for related arguments). I suggest that there have been four characteristic modes of dwelling with regard to the car, what I term 'inhabiting-unmade-roads', 'inhab-iting-the-paved-road', 'inhabiting-the-car', and 'inhabiting the intel-ligent car'. I briefly examine the first three of these and then consider the fourth in chapter 13 within the context of a discussion of alter-native mobility futures. All these modes involve the extension and elaboration of the move towards the sitting society and a kind of seated dwellingness discussed in chapter 4.

First, then there is the inhabiting of unmade roads at the beginning of the twentieth century. I have already noted the significance of the ways that cars were tinkered with in order that they could be made more suitable for dealing with the uneven, muddy and unmade spaces that they had to travel along (Franz 2005). Most cars were open so there was no separation from the sights, smells and sounds of the road. Drivers and passengers inhabited these unmade roads and the places through which they went through. Cars were in part built and especially tinkered with so that we might, following Heidegger, view these as forms of *bauen*, to build (1993: 348). In their building and dwelling many men viewed cars as speed machines and much less as the regular basis of commuting or even social life. There was a preoccupation with engineering the car to break speed records, especially since records could now be recorded by increasingly precise pocket watches. Sombart referred to this period as the 'age of the record' (Sachs 1992: 119). The car constituted as a speed machine, enabled rather rich men to travel fast and many motorists at the time described their experience in mystical terms, as though this were an experience that expressed the inner forces of nature. The author Filson Young wrote of the sensuous experience of riding in a racing car: 'It is, I think, a combination of intense speed with the sensation of smallness, the lightness, the responsiveness of the thing that carries you, with the rushing of the atmosphere upon your body and the earth upon your vision' (quoted Liniado 1996: 7). The rushing of the atmosphere stemmed from how there was no separation between the car and its environment and such dwellingness is still found in those in open top sports cars and riding motorbikes. As Pirsig writes on the latter: 'You're completely in contact with it all. You are *in* the scene, not watching it anymore, and the sense of presence is overwhelming' (1974: 4).

The second stage is 'inhabiting-the-paved-road'. The car-driver is part of the environment through which the car travels and the technologies of insulation do not fully exist. The car-driver dwells-on-the-paved-road and is not separated from its multiple sensuousness. Especially significant in inter-war England was the notion of the 'open road' and the slow motor tour. Motor touring was thought of as a voyage through the life and history of the land. As ownership of cars became more widespread there was an increasing emphasis upon slow means of finding pleasure. To tour, to stop, to drive slowly, to take the longer route, to emphasize process rather than destination, all became part of the performed art of motor touring. Filson Young wrote of how 'the road sets us free . . . it allows us to follow our own choice as to how fast and how far we shall go, to tarry where and when we will' (quoted Liniado 1996: 10). Such a novel spatial practice was facilitated by organizational innovations partially taken over from cycling clubs. These 'paved' the way for the inter-war transformation of the motor car, from alien threat to a 'natural' part of the rural scene. Light notes how 'the futurist symbol of speed and erotic dynamism – the motor car – [was turned] into the Morris Minor' in the inter-war years (1991: 214; O'Connell 1998). In that period motoring for leisure became an apparently 'natural' yet hugely fateful way of moving through and experiencing the countryside (see Koshar 2002: 216–7, on the German leisure culture).

In the United States, car ownership became 'democratized' so that even the dispossessed of the Great Depression travelled by car or truck (Graves-Brown 1997: 68; Wilson 1992: ch. 1). Movement itself became a measure of hope; the road itself seemed to offer new possibilities, of work, adventure, romance. *The Grapes of Wrath* tells the story of hope and opportunity travelling along perhaps the most iconic of roads, Route 66, a mighty symbol of movement and (male) freedom (Enevold 2000: 410; Eyerman and Löfgren 1995: 57). Up to the Second World War automobility mostly involved men and sometimes their families 'inhabiting the road'.

The third stage begins with the inter- and especially post-war period of massive suburban housing in North America and then western Europe. This suburban pattern was predicated upon low-density family housing with a sizeable garden, many domestic production goods for the 'wife' to use, and a car to enable the 'husband' to travel long distances to get to work. This resulted in 'auto sprawl syndrome' and in so doing forced those living in such areas to depend upon car use. The massive programme of road building beginning in 1952 in the United States was thought to be importantly democratic. In this stage the car-driver in the west comes to dwell-*within*-the-car rather than on the road. Those inhabiting the car can prevent most of the smells and sounds of the road from entering; thus 'through the car window everything you see is more TV. You're a passive observer' (Pirsig 1974: 4). The car-driver is surrounded by control systems that allow a simulation of the domestic environment, a home-from-home moving flexibly and riskily through strange and dangerous environments. As one respondent to Bull expressed it: 'The car is a little bit of a refuge. . . . although people can see into the car . . . it's almost as if this is my own little world, (2004: 247). The car is a sanctuary, a zone of protection, however slender, between oneself and that dangerous world of other cars, and between the places of departure and arrival. The car becomes rather less fun according to longitudinal Danish research (Beckmann 2001: 204).

The driver is strapped into a comfortable if constraining armchair and surrounded by micro-electronic informational sources, controls and sources of pleasure, what Raymond Williams calls 'mobile privatization' (see Pinkney, 1991: 55). The Ford brochure of 1949 declared that 'The 49 Ford is a living room on wheels' (Marsh, Collett, 1986: 11), the VW camper is described as a 'Room with a View', while advertising for the Lexus IS200 states that 'It's the feeling inside' (Sheller 2004a: 224). The car is a room stimulating particular senses and emotions. Once in the car there is almost no kinaesthetic movement from the driver. So although automobility is a system of mobility it necessitates minimal movement once strapped *into* the driving seat (the ultimate in the 'sitting society'). Eyes have to be constantly on the look-out for danger, hands and feet are ready for the next manoeuvre, the body is gripped into a fixed position, lights and noises may indicate that the car-driver needs to make instantaneous adjustments, and so on. The other traffic constrains how each car is to be driven, its speed, direction, its lane and so on. The driver's body is itself fragmented and disciplined to the machine, with eyes, ears, hands, and feet, all trained to respond instantaneously and consistently, while desires even to stretch, to change position, to doze or to look around having to be suppressed (see Merriman 2004, on how the motorway driving body had to be taught and internalized during 1960s Britain).

The car we might thus see as an extension of the driver's body, creating new subjectivities organized around this disciplined 'driving body' (see Freund 1993: 99; Hawkins 1986; Morse 1998). As early as 1930 a Californian city planner declared that 'it might be said that Southern Californians have added wheels to their anatomy' (cited Flink 1988: 143). The car can be thought of as an extension of the senses so that the car-driver can feel its very contours, shape and relationship to that beyond its metallic skin. As Ihde describes: 'The expert driver when parallel parking needs very little by way of visual clues to back himself into the small place – he "feels" the very extension of himself through the car as the car becomes a symbiotic extension of his own embodiedness' (1974: 272). An advert for the BMW 733i promised the 'integration of man and machine . . . an almost total oneness with the car' (quoted Hawkins 1986: 67).

The machinic hybridization of the car-driver extends into the deepest reaches of the affective psyche. A libidinal economy has developed in which subjectivities get invested in the car as an enormously powerful and mobile object, what Sheller refers to as the co-constitution of motion and emotion (2004a: 226). There is a sexualization of the car as an extension of the driver's affects, carried to one extreme with the superfast sports car and to the other extreme with the ultra-dominant Hummer. The car is implicit within especially male driver's ego-formation as competent, powerful and masterful (as advertisers shamelessly exploit). Various 'coming-of-age' rituals revolve around the car, with car-sex becoming an element of fantasy in everything from music videos to 'crash culture' (see Ballard 1995). The car is both all-powerful *and* simultaneously feeds people's deepest anxieties, ranging from the fear of accident and death to the intense frustration of being stuck behind a slow vehicle and hence wasting tiny fragments of time.

The body of the car extends the human body, surrounding the fragile, soft and vulnerable human skin with a new steel skin, but one that can scratch, crumple and rupture once it encounters other cars in a crash (see Brottman 2001, on 'car crash culture'). Within the private cocoon of glass and metal intense emotions are sometimes released in otherwise unacceptable forms. With 'road rage' emotions of aggression, competition and speed come to the fore although automobility is always polysemic, encouraging one to be careful, considerate and civilized *and* to enjoy speed, danger and excitement (Michael 1998: 133). There is multiple scription and hence different elements of the hybrid car-driver lurking behind that steel skin, apparently so hard but one which easily crumples. According to motoring organizations the road rage driver should not be purified by changing the human–machine hybrid but rather the pathological 'road-raging' human (analogous to the presumed pathology of the 'drunk driver': Hawkins 1986: 70–1). What is not proposed by motoring organizations is that the hybrid should be transformed, such as by the fitting of long sharp spikes sticking out from the centre of every steering wheel pointing to the heart of each driver. Such a transformed hybrid would not 'rage' or be alcohol-impaired (see Adams 1995: 155)!

Moreover, that steel skin provides an environment affording the possibilities for sociability. Car-drivers control the social mix in their car just as homeowners are mostly able to regulate those visiting their house. The car is a 'home from home', a place of affect to perform business, holidays, romance, family, friendship, crime, fantasy and so on (although most car journeys are in fact solitary). Some writers argue that the car partly enhances certain kinds of sociability especially around leisure (see Löfgren 1999). Unlike 'public' transport, the car facilitates a domestic mode of dwelling and one in which there are many examples of giving and receiving lifts to others. Walter emphasizes that central to understanding car use is that of gift-giving between family members and between friends (1981). Also though because of the linking together of the car and mobile communications, the car is increasingly an office and a site of multi-tasking. Laurier describes the doing of office work on the motorway, including desk work, dictating letters, making appointments, keeping in touch, sorting papers and rearranging meetings (Laurier 2004: 264).

Central also to dwelling within the car is its soundscape, as technologies of the radio, the cassette player and the CD player increasingly ensure that this mobile home is filled with sound. The twentieth century was not only the century of the car but also of mechanically produced sounds (Bull 2004: 247). The car radio connects the 'home' of the car to that world beyond, a kind of mobile connected presence. Almost better than 'home' itself, the car enables a purer immersion in those sounds, as the voices of the radio (and the hands-free phone) and the sound of music are right there, in the car, travelling with one as some of the most dangerous places on earth are negotiated. Various respondents to Bull described how: 'It's lonely in the car. I like to have music on'; 'I suppose I feel at ease, I put the radio on, put the keys in the ignition and I'm away'; 'I'm in a nice sealed, compact space . . . I like my sounds up load, it's all around you' (2004: 246–7). Music and voices in the car fill the space and substitute for other forms of sociality and life, especially as 75 per cent of car journeys in the United States are now solitary (US Census 2000, cited www.grist. org/news/daily/2003/06/17/). Being in the car is to inhabit a place of sound and of being hybridized with those technologies connecting people to the world beyond, as well as to their memories and dreams (see Pearce, on the emotions of home, family and nation that can be encountered on long car journeys: 2000).

Thus this is a strong kind of contemporary dwelling. Car-drivers, while moving at speed, lose the ability to perceive local detail beyond the car, let alone to talk to strangers, to learn local ways of life, to sense each place. Sights, sounds, tastes, temperatures and smells get reduced to the two-dimensional view through the car windscreen and through the rear mirror, the sensing of the world through the screen being the dominant mode of dwelling in the contemporary world. What lies beyond that windscreen is an affective other, kept at bay through privatizing technologies incorporated within cars. These technologies in theory ensure a consistent supply of information, a relatively protected environment, high quality sounds and increasingly sophisticated systems of monitoring. They enable the hybrid of the car-driver to negotiate conditions of intense riskiness on high-speed roads (roads are increasingly risky because of the reduced road-space now available to each car). And as cars have increasingly overwhelmed almost all environments, so everyone experiences such environments through the protective screen and increasingly abandons streets and squares to omnipotent metallic iron cages.

The Politics of the Car

Indeed so all-embracing is automobility as a system that we can suggest that civil society in most countries should now be re-conceptualized as a civil society of 'car-drivers' and 'car-passengers'. Cerny writes that the 'car, as nexus of public and private, is not exceptional, but characteristic of the paradox of civil society in today's world' (1990). There is thus not a civil society of separate human subjects autonomous from these all-conquering machines. Such a hybrid of the car-driver is in normal circumstances unremarkable as civil society comes to be organized around such hybrid entities. Notions of public and private life are reorganized on the basis of automobilized humans, humans mostly unable to function within civil society without their wheels. And an automobilized civil society is almost certainly one of the most unequal of such societies that we have so far seen at least (Sheller, Urry 2003).

But such a civil society has also become over the past four decades sites of intense contestation (see Böhm, Jones, Land, Paterson 2006). Civil society's mobilization around automobility began in relation-ship to consumer protection. In the United States, consumer advocates such as Ralph Nader, represented 'the public interest' in demanding car safety, road safety, 'lemon laws' to protect consumers against unscrupulous car-salesmen, and industry-wide standards for re-calls of defective models and fair pricing (Nader 1965). The oil-crisis of the 1970s sparked public concern over energy-use and the growing demand for 'greener' cars with higher fuel economy and in some instances interest in recycling the metals, plastics, and rubber that make up the car. In the 1970s, urban quality of life became a crucial political issue as cities were choked with fumes and smog, as well as beset by traffic flow and parking problems. In this period the car began to be viewed as more polluting than the train (Liniado 1996: 28). Many cities such as Amsterdam, Stockholm, and Portland, Oregon developed explicit policies to upgrade and prioritize cycle lanes and public transport, in order to challenge the car system (see Peters 2006: ch. 6). Later, cities such as Athens attempted to control access of private cars in and out of the city centre, while others imposed commuter restrictions, or incentives such as park-and-ride schemes, or enforced car-pool lanes with four occupants required per car, or congestion charging. More symbolically, some European cities have instituted an annual 'leave your car at home' day. The debate over better provision of public transport (and overall urban design) has moved front-stage in a number of societies, as states wrestle with controlling traffic and some drivers seek alternative means of travel. Integrating better mass transportation into urban design has been crucial to some new metropolitan cities such as Singapore and Hong Kong (Owen 1987).

And as the environmental movement developed, the oil industry became the target of protest. There were campaigns against the expansion of oil extraction into wilderness areas such as Alaska or various off-shore sites; there were protests against pollution caused by oil extraction, processing, and shipping (Exxon Valdez oil spill); and there were protests against the transnational oil corporations especially the Greenpeace campaign against Shell Oil in the early 1990s. With the Gulf and Iraq wars, many critics of the car system were able to identify very direct ways in which American and European foreign policies are driven by global oil interests. In the United States, the desire to increase access to oil sources from outside the United States, since with its decline in oil production since 1971, meant that the politics of the car as a system became increasingly centre-stage in public debate, debate now global with the perceived significance of 'peak oil'.

Further, questions of congestion pricing systems, taxation of car-use and of petrol have become key aspects of government transport policy from California to Britain. It is only in thinking about what it would take to get people out of their cars that we can see the enormous transformations that automobility has wrought in the social organization of time, space, and social life. Overall, although many people may 'love' their car, the system that it presupposes is often unloved, resisted and raged against. Civil society is remade through contestations over the power, range and impact of the system of automobility. The same people can be both enthusiastic car-drivers, as well as being very active protestors against schemes for new roads (see Macnaghten, Urry 1998: ch. 6, on how cars generate intense ambivalence).

By the mid 1990s in the UK the scale of grass-roots protest against the construction of new roads had so developed that it was described as 'the most vigorous new force in British environmentalism' (Lean 1994). There were by then at least 250 anti-road groups, a movement significantly impacting upon civil society. The array of direct actions has also diversified as protesters have become more expert, through the use of mass trespass, squatting in buildings, living in trees threatened by road programmes, and digging tunnels. Stopping traffic has itself become a significant form of symbolic direct action, as practised in 'Reclaim the Streets' events. Protesters also became more sophisticated in the use of diverse technologies, including mobile phones, video cameras and the internet. These enabled almost instantaneous dissemination to the media (Macnaghten, Urry 1998: ch. 2). As the control of mobility into and out of regions of the city becomes a central concern of the state, the 'tactics of mobility' emerge as a potential form of resistance (Thrift 1996).

Indeed living without a car has become a significant lifestyle choice for both environmentalists and a small cosmopolitan elite able to live in expensively gentrified city-centres. Experiments in restricting car use in cities have been proliferating recently. Car-free days have been promoted throughout Europe, with leadership from Italy in particular. Many town centres have been pedestrianized or have attempted to ban cars from their roads (e.g., Oxford). The choice of an alternative lifestyle with voluntary limitations on car-use is most feasible in medium-sized regional towns where a mix of cycling, walking, and public transport can develop (as in Cambridge, UK but especially in The Netherlands: Peters 2006: ch. 6). Nevertheless, such towns remain clogged with both moving and stationary cars apart from those small 'pedestrian zones' of civility left to the walker. Attempts to introduce pedal-rickshaws and more bike lanes are still constrained by the imperatives of the car-driver system against which they must compete (but see Peters 2006, on the Netherlands). Thus the politics of automobility generates new forms of public protest and changing civil society's repertoires of contestation.

We can further note gender differences within this automobilized civil society. The automobilization of family life not only brought the newest and most expensive car models to the male 'heads of families', while women had to settle for second-hand models or smaller cars, but also led to the uneven gendering of time–space. While working, men became enmeshed in daily commuter traffic while suburban 'housewives' juggled family time around multiple child-related schedules. Once family life comes to be centred within the moving car, social responsibilities push women, now driving in very significant numbers, towards inhabiting 'safer' 'family' models including most recently SUVs (Sheller 2004a: 231). By contrast men often dwell within sports cars or impractical 'classic cars' and indulge in individualistic fantasies recycled from American road movies with their sexualized objectification and infantilization of women (Enevold 2000: 407). Male drivers show a much greater tendency to speed in their cars and hence are likely to externalize risks onto others and hence to maim and kill others (Meadows, Stradling 2000; but see Laurier 2004, on fast driving by women who view the road as their workplace). Cars were originally designed to be inhabited by the average male body and only recently are adjustable to drivers of various heights and reaches. The distribution of company cars has also benefited men more than women, due to continuing segregation in the job market which means most women are unable to inhabit such cars.

Thus for many women exclusion from automobility has become a crucial issue, both because it limits their capability to work outside the home and because it makes movement through public spaces difficult. In most countries women became eligible to be licensed drivers later than did men, and in some countries they still face severe restrictions on their ability to drive (impossible in Saudi Arabia). Women working in domestic service jobs face gruelling journeys on unreliable public transport between the city and suburbs. Single mothers without cars are among the groups most dependent on public transport and most likely to find their particular 'taskscapes' full of gaps, dangers and inconveniences (Cass, Shove, Urry 2005). The male drivers' domination of public space appears in 'kerb crawling' in the city, a form of prostitution that compounds the difficulties of women as *flâneuse* (Wilson 1995). But simultaneously women's 'emancipation' has been partly predicated upon 'accessing' the car which afford a sense of personal freedom and a relatively secure form of travel in which families and objects can be safely transported, and fragmented time schedules successfully intermeshed. Women's access to cars has helped to integrate women into the labour market by better enabling the juggling of the conflicting time disciplines of paid and unpaid work (Wajcman 1991). Women have therefore struggled to claim the rights to automobility and in doing so have in part re-shaped but paradoxically enhanced the car system.

Conclusion

The power of automobility is the consequence of its system charac-teristics. Unlike the bus or train system it is a way of life, an entire culture, as Miller establishes (2000). It has redefined movement, affect and emotion in the contemporary world. Sheller emphasizes 'the full power of automotive emotions that shape our bodies, homes and nations (2004a: 237; Gilroy 2000).

Such a car system possesses distinct characteristics: it changes and adapts as it spreads along the paths and roads of each society, moving from luxury, to household, to an individual item; it draws in many aspects of its environment which are then reconstituted as components of its system; the car system became central to and locked in with the leading economic sectors and social patterns of twentieth-century capitalism; it changes the environment or fitness landscape for all the other systems; it promotes the notion of convenience rather than speed; the car system is a key component in the shift from clock to instantaneous time; it seems to provide the solution to the problems of congestion that it itself generates; it is able to externalize dangers onto those outside the system as it provides enhanced security for those 'within the system'; it is central to the individualist, consumerist embodied affective culture of contemporary capitalism; and the car system mobilizes the shift from the pedestrian labyrinth to smooth motorized passages (see Sachs 1992: 192, on *The Love of the Automobile*).

In chapter 13, I return to this car system and consider the implications of a fourth stage of inhabiting the car, inhabiting the intelligent car. For most of the twentieth century the revolutions in communication technology took place separate from the physical means of transportation. However, the current trend is toward the re-embedding of information and communication technologies (ICT) into moving objects. At the same time that information has been digitized and so released from location; so cars, roads, and buildings are rewired to send and receive digital information (ITS). I consider what effects the convergence of ICT and ITS will have on cities, in particular with whether this could represent an epochal shift as cars are reconstituted as a networked system rather than as separate 'iron cages', as a potentially integrated *nexus* rather than as a parallel *series*. This could produce a shift from the modern divided traffic flow to what Peters terms the organic flow in which all traffic participants are able to survive and co-exist, aided by new kinds of communications regulating the overall system as a whole (2006). It may be that as a networked system it will be possible to tame or at least reorganize automobility that has so far 'driven' out all challenges to its omnipotent taking over the world.

7

Flying Around

I suppose we shall all travel by air-vessels; make air instead of sea-voyages; and at length find our way to the moon, in spite of the want of atmosphere

(Lord Byron 1822, cited Caves 2002)

In this chapter I turn to the emergence of air travel and air systems. Flying commenced at the very beginning of the twentieth century with the Wright brothers' first flight in 1903, and symbolically culminated at the end of that century on September 11th 2001 in which planes were central 'actants' in a deadly network of spectacular globally watched destruction (see http://en.wikipedia.org/wiki/Wright_brothers, accessed 18.03.06, especially on the many controversies as to who actually 'flew' first). Air travel went from small beginnings on a sand dune in North Carolina, to become the industry that stands for and represents the new global order. The history of flying is a remarkable history of various ingenious ways of transcending two-dimensional spatial constraints, and it now produces an exceptional sorting and resorting of populations within countries and around the world. As Castells notes, geographical proximity in most countries no longer shapes social relationships (2001: 126), and this is in part because some people can sometimes fly rapidly from, over and past such spatial proximities, forming new time-distanciated proximities.

In this chapter I examine various aspects of the growth and significance of 'aeromobility', beginning with a brief periodization of some of the striking changes that have occurred in the nature of airspaces over the past century.

Second, I examine the changing risks of air travel and the development of intersecting expert systems that make such movement through the air contingently possible. I demonstrate that more significant than the planes themselves were the systems that enabled that space *above* the ground to be regularly, safely and predictably moved through by very large numbers of travellers. Contemporary developments involving systems of 'code-space' within airports and air travel are outlined.

Third, the character of air spaces is explored; it is argued that they are neither 'non-places' as some argue but nor are they places of conventional rooted dwellingness. Rather airspaces are typical of the 'places' that the global order is ushering in, showing many overlaps and similarities with diverse other places from around the world. The systems of air travel thus move out and increasingly populate many other kinds of place.

So finally, I turn to the ways in which flights, aeroplanes, airports and airport cities are central to the contemporary global order and show that without the complex systems of mass air travel, what is now termed 'globalization' would be utterly different. Indeed not only do passengers increasingly fly across borders forming new social time-distanciated social networks, but the systems that make possible their travel also fly around and land in many towns and cities that become subject to a 'airspace makeover'. Air travel, although still the practice of a small minority of the world's population in any one year, is thus shown to be implicated in the global remaking of places in their current re-ordering and the contingent securing of mobile populations in a world of global riskiness.

A Brief Periodization

Aircraft are nothing without airspaces and airspaces are nothing without 'the impeccable machine making use of its splendid expanses' (Pascoe 2001: 21). They are indissolubly linked, in a complex relationality with each other (see Adey 2006b: 87–8). And the history of flight has been the history of massive transformations in the 'splendid expanses' of such airspaces, of fields, runways and terminals over the twentieth century. Airspaces shift from airfield, to transport hub, and then to global hub.

First, early airfields in the beginning of the twentieth century were places of spectacle, record making and voyeurship, with frequent crashes and risks for those both flying and watching on the ground (Pascoe 2001: ch. 1; Perrow 1999: ch. 5). Initially various inventors developed individual flying machines, machines often setting new records, akin to how cars developed as individual speed machines (see ch. 6 above). These new flying machines were astonishingly clever in leaving the airfield for short periods, so transcending the physical two-dimensional limits of land-based movement. According to Le Corbusier aircraft were the greatest sign of progress that had so far been seen during the twentieth century although at first the airfields did nothing to reflect this modernity (Pascoe 2001: 127). Simultaneously flying machines transformed the nature of warfare as the new realm of airpower developed, including especially the innovation of machines able to bomb from the air (Pascoe 2001: 127; Kaplan 2006). But for all this there was nothing inevitable about this development of air travel; even as late as the end of the First World War the *Manchester Guardian* stated that aviation was a 'passing fad that would never catch on' (quoted Thomas 2002: 3). Crucial to the development of air travel was the generation of what Adey terms 'airmindedness' (2006a).

The airfield stage had already been initiated by 1914 with the first ever commercial flight. Passengers paid $5 to fly for eight miles with the St Petersburg – Tampa Airboat Line in the United States (Morrison, Winston 1995: 3). While the first international scheduled services took place in 1919 from Hounslow in west London, close to where Heathrow is now located (Pascoe 2001: 81). Early airports were oriented around the flying machines. They were mono-modal and concerned with transporting people and goods from one place to another by air. Aviation-related activities defined the meaning of these airspaces, with other activities playing a minor role. There was more or less nothing of the contemporary 'terminal' and its multiple buildings and complex intersecting activities.

In the second period airports developed into transport hubs with the increasing interconnection between different modes of travel (planes, trains, metro and cars). Le Corbusier especially promoted the airport as a machine for travellers rather than as a field oriented to the plane (Pascoe 2001: 120–1). This quantum leap, stemming from the growth of interwar airmindedness, involved airspaces being turned into complex and integrated infrastructures, often with a futuristic design (Jarach 2001: 121; Adey 2006a). The airport was no longer isolated and specialized but developed into a multimodal hub so that passengers: 'are given within airport boundaries the chance to connect in a seamless way from air to ground, railway and sea ferry' (Jarach 2001: 121). However, the core business of such air-spaces still involved managing the complex logistic services involved in the boarding and the de-boarding of people and objects; increasingly these processes were governed by the concept of 'turnaround' time and the need for systems to minimize such time (Pascoe 2001: 125). Such multimodal hubs were typically owned by public bodies and there was a close relationship between that body and so-called national carriers also often owned by the state. Such airports and airlines often arose out of military facilities within the era of organized capitalism in which national transport interests and their inter-modalities were planned and implemented by the national state (see Lash, Urry 1987, on organized capitalism).

The third stage is described by Jarach as the further quantum leap from the traditional to the 'commercial airport' or what I would term the global hub (2001: 123; see Kesselring 2006b). Airports move away from being mainly transport hubs and have become sites for mass travel, with most airports being built on the edge of cities, as places or camps of banishment (Serres 1995: 19). According to IATA there are 1195 international airports, with 225 currently undergoing expansion (quoted Fuller, Harley 2005: 35). There are 1.9 billion air journeys each year (*Economist* 2005; Fuller, Harley 2005: 9). One half of British adults report taking an flight during 2001, with about one-half of that 50 per cent travelling once, one-quarter travelling twice and one-quarter travelling three or more times (Lethbridge 2002; British adults make *on average* 1.3 air trips per year: DfT 2002: 12). The annual number of air passenger kilometres flown in the UK rose sevenfold from one billion in 1962, to seven billion in 1996 (DfT 2002; the UK is the fourth largest airflying nation after the US, Japan and Germany). Airports are developing into small-scale global cities in their own right, places to meet and do business, to sustain family life and friendship, and to act as a site for liminal consumption less constrained by prescribed household income and expenditure patterns. Airports are locations for meetings, as they develop into 'destinations' in their own right, ambivalent places, of multiple forms of transport, commerce, entertainment, experience, meetings and events. Such airports are variably organized: through vertical public management (such as Munich), horizontal public management (such as Manchester), private–public management (such as Düsseldorf), and private corporation (such as Heathrow). But in all such cases airports develop as strategically important within the global competition of places, cities and regions (see Kesselring 2006b). Certain airport operators such as the Schiphol Group in the Netherlands, Fraport in Germany or BAA in the UK operate on a global scale, establishing and managing new airports and sets of airport services around the world.

Thus airspaces have thus moved through two 'leaps', from a mono-modal 'field' to a multimodal transport hub, and more recently to a multifunctional commercialized global hub. There are of course many airspaces that remain at the two earlier stages. Further dimensions of these shifts will now be explored, beginning with the notions of risk and system.

Risks and Systems

Large technical systems such as airports and the global aviation industry are sites of riskiness and this has been so since early planes ventured into the sky a century ago. Flight is risky for those flying, for those organizing and managing those flights, and for those on the ground as viewers or innocent bystanders. The riskiness of air travel is of course the stuff of novels and movies, such as Arthur Hailey's *Airport*, Michael Crichton's *Airframe*, or Jodie Foster in *Flightplan*, which have explored many of the possible risks in prescient detail. A wide array of software-based 'expert systems' have been developed to deal with this riskiness and contingency of air travel. These have remarkably transformed the hazards and physicality of taking off, cruising and landing. Mass air travel is mostly a kind of 'motionless motion', where the body becomes so light and insignificant that it can fly away like an 'angel' (Serres 1995: 262).

Various non-human actants and especially much computer code are combined with rule-following humans to enable this wonder of relatively safe mass air travel. Air traffic control systems effect high levels of safe take-offs and landings, while the Boeing 777 contains some 79 different computer systems requiring four million lines of code (Dodge, Kitchin 2004: 201). Indeed if as Thrift and French argue software conditions existence in the city, this is so in a much deeper and extensive form within airspaces (2002; Adey, Bevan 2006). There is no airspace and there are no smoothly flying citizens without vast amounts of computer code. There has been the development of pervasive, consistent and routinized 'code/space' producing the 'real virtuality of air travel' (Dodge, Kitchin 2004). In these various code/

spaces the code is so significant that without code the space fails. There is no alternative to the code even though it typically remains in the background and unnoticed until of course the computer crashes (see Adey 2006b: 80). Thus an airline passenger ticket is the material embodiment of such code/space on which are printed several data codes that both describe what the passenger is doing but also simulate and predict other actions the passenger may undertake (Dodge, Kitchin 2004).

The extremely complex management of multiple movements at airports involves various expert systems. These computer software systems, which have developed in a piecemeal way, are intended to orchestrate take-offs, landings, ticketing and reservations, baggage handling, schedules, cleaning, weather forecasting, in-flight catering, security, multiple employment patterns, baggage X-ray, waste management, environmental impact and so on (there are twelve such systems at Schiphol: Peters 2006: 115).

Such systems have built into them risk assessments of events such as delayed flights, sick crew, damaged planes, adverse weather, computer crashes, terrorist bombings and so on. The central resources involved in managing airflights are time, money and capacity. Peters shows how continuous modifications and adjustments are made between these different resources in order to keep the system moving and especially to get the planes airborne on time (Peters 2006: 122–4).

What is central to all these systems is the notion of time and especially of Universal Time that synchronizes the actions of people and countless organizations around the world (see Peters 2006, on the following). Dispersed and heterogeneous flows of different categories of peoples and objects are all synchronized and this synchronization is based upon a universal measure of time; this is necessary so that each plane in each airport in each air sector can get 'airborne on time' (or more or less on time: Peters 2006). Synchronization has to be global and based on a system of time reckoning that is also global.

In *Normal Accidents*, Perrow examines air safety arguing that air travel involves non-linear, 'quite complex', 'tightly coupled' systems, although they are less coupled than those operating in for example nuclear power (1999: 128). Over time there have been large reductions in air travel fatalities, partly because of technological improvements and partly by introducing forms of redundancy into the systems (four engines rather than two). However, although such developments have improved air safety technically, the historic reduction in the number of fatalities and injuries has slowed down because, according to Perrow, various commercial and military demands have substantially increased. Airline operators have sought greater speed, reduced 'manning' levels, higher altitude flying, reduced fuel use, greater traffic density, reduced separation between planes, and more operations to take place in all-weathers. These heightened requirements have engendered a tighter coupling of the systems and an enhanced workload on the crew and on air traffic control at very specific moments, moments that push the system to its limits (Perrow 1999: 128–31, 146). Hochschild analysed some dimensions of this in the work of flight attendants who responded to the intensification of their work with a slowdown and especially with a tendency to smile less often and less deeply and thereby to reduce their 'emotional labour' (1983). She describes how the: 'workers respond to the speed-up with a slowdown: they smile less broadly, with a quick release and no sparkle in the eyes, thus dimming the company's message to the people. It is a war of smiles' (Hochschild 1983: 127).

Indeed in the third period air travel has developed into a globally competitive industry (or set of industries) since the previously organized capitalism with protected national flag carriers has mostly dissolved. There is global competition within what elsewhere I term 'disorganized capitalism' (Lash, Urry 1987, 1994) and this engenders a massive push to minimize especially the turnaround time of planes and of crews. Many interrelated events must be synchronized so as to minimize the periods in which planes and the crew are unproductively on the ground. Significant changes in this have been especially initiated in the last decade or two by the budget airlines of North America, western Europe and now India and China; they have reduced profit margins per passenger by reducing turnaround times, developed exclusive internet bookings, deployed demand responsive pricing, used cheaper airports, simplified check-in procedures and reduced labour costs. These airlines mostly fly point-to-point and this has led to some reduction in the number of systems that have to be synchronized (such as planes needing to wait for connecting flights).

In general the tight coupling of such interactively complex systems makes airlines and airports especially vulnerable to small disruptions that produce cascading and positive feedback effects when things go slightly wrong. Perrow dissects various aircraft crashes resulting from small events often through 'management' error, as well as many involving positive feedback loops where 'humans' or 'systems' respond either to the wrong aircraft or to its insertion into the wrong sequence or to a false interpretation of information upon a display and so on (1999: 141, 160). Gleick summarizes more generally about such tightly coupled systems: 'everything depends on everything else. Vibrations can be felt everywhere' (1999: 223–4).

There are also huge risks involved in building megaprojects of which airports are some of the largest and most contentious contemporary examples. Airports are one of the key ways in which cities and societies seek to enter or develop their positioning within the global order, and increasingly cities seek to compete with other cities through building the largest, newest, most expensive, or most stylish airports. For example, Beijing is currently being turned into the world's largest airport in time for the 2008 Olympics. However, Flyvbjerg, Bruzelius, Rothengatter show that on such megaprojects, there is: 'a calamitous history of cost overrun', greater financial expenses than predicted and lower than expected revenues (2003: 11). Partly this is because risk assessments are carried out in terms of a simple cause-and–effect and not in terms of the complex systems involved in such developments in which almost all other aspects are simultaneously changing over the course of the very long timescales involved in such megaprojects (see Flyvbjerg, Bruzelius, Rothengatter 2003: ch. 7). In particular airports are almost always sites of intense contestation especially around the environmental, economic and social impacts of new runways and airports, cheap flights, and the security issues involved in managing the complex flows of millions of bags and passengers.

The aviation industry is thus a fragile but tightly connected system of places, private corporations and state actors, interrelated with almost all other sectors of the economy. There is a multiplicity of structural, economic, political and social risks associated with global aviation, indicating how the making of 'aero-mobilities' is also political. As Foucault argued, the sorting and resorting of populations is fundamentally political and bound up with central issues of power and knowledge within and increasingly across 'societies' (1991). Compared with other mobilities air travel involves much sorting and resorting of disparate populations across national borders.

Mobility always involves some ambivalence but it is heightened with international air travel; it is the prime example of how the modern world involves systemic forms of ordering but where that ordering is impossible partly since there are potentially over six billion air passengers and no one system can spot which three to four individuals out of those 6+ billion could have murderous intentions (Bauman 2002). Indeed, one set of risks not been widely envisaged until September 11th 2001 was the use of passenger airlines as massive bombs, an event that cast its long shadow upon airports, airlines and air passengers, as well as upon those regimes and societies now subject to the 'war on terror'. The whole world watched the surreal moment as planes with live passengers flew into and demolished two of the largest buildings in the world. The World Trade Center, a city in the air, was with two strokes bombed out of existence, an 'uncanny' moment when the distinction between fantasy and reality was effaced in astonishing images, eclipsing anything Hollywood has generated (Urry 2002a). The fiery collapse of the twin towers destroyed multiple mobility systems and disrupted the global discourse of unfettered mobility (Little 2006). A huge node in the global financial trading system was shut down; a major station in the metropolitan transportation system was obliterated; a significant hub in the telephonic and electronic communications systems fell silent; the mobile phone network was overwhelmed; bridges and tunnels were closed to traffic; crowds fled Manhattan on foot unable to contact loved ones; and most astonishingly air traffic within US airspace simply ceased for a period (see Hannam, Sheller, Urry 2006; Aaltola 2005: 273; and the changing map of US airspace during September 11th: Fuller, Harley 2005: 47). The attacks were thought of as targeting the United States at 'empire', New York as a 'global city' and mass mobility as a predictable and safe practice (and see ch. 12 below).

The awesome power of the terrorist act stemmed from the linking together of people, objects, and technologies in a deadly non-failing network. Using modest communication devices, twenty men supported it seems by an extensive network, unleashed a unique 'war' involving a few knives, twenty odd suicide bombers and a number of planes in the appropriate place and time. This event involving fairly old technologies, especially small knives as weapons caused far-reaching global side effects, upon the global economy and the flows of money, objects and people, but especially upon the former certainties of modern life of 'walking through an airport' (Aaltola 2005: 273; Urry 2003a). When civilian aeroplanes are turned into weapons, time–space gets 'curved' into new complex configurations with the 'whole world' being brought dramatically closer. Terrorist attacks and the fear of such attacks show how air systems are especially vulnerable to such risks (Urry 2002a; Hannam, Sheller, Urry 2006; Ahmed 2004: 73, on the affective politics of fear). Systems of interconnected material worlds produce new moments of unintended and dangerous co-presence. The 'gates' designed to prevent networks from colliding, and the narratives of security that underwrote the building of those gate-keeping processes, may not be sustained as flows of terrorists slip under, over and through various borders, eliminating the invisibilities and screens that kept networks apart.

September 11th thus exacerbated: 'the imbalance between demand and capacity when the fear of flying was heightened and increased security measures imposed significant time delays on travelers' (Golaszewski 2003: 58; Kesselring 2006b). Airlines and airports struggle with how: 'small changes in traffic have large impacts on revenue' (Golaszewski 2003: 57). These unpredictable risks of the global risk society, such as terrorist attacks, SARS and other global pandemics, wars, produce positive feedback that enhance the 'fear of flying', the sense of escalating danger and the increased securitization of mobile populations. In particular there developed the 'war on terror', of which Aaltola states: 'i[In] several ways the war against terror is obsessed with aeroplanes and airports' although actually there has been no repetition of the spectacular use of planes as bombs (2005: 262).

The events of September 11th so mark contemporary discourses and practices of security especially 'in the air', that new measures are turning the 'state of emergency', or the exception, into the 'rule' (Benjamin 1992: 248; Agamben 1998; Diken 2005). These measures include in the United States the surprising 'nationalization' of airport security within the Department of Homeland Security so as to standardize systems of person and baggage securitization. The US Government has also been developing its programme of Total Information Awareness (later revised to Terrorism Information Awareness) so as to integrate and co-ordinate many forms of public and private data including biometric technologies able to recognize humans at a distance and the mapping of people's multiple connections across their social networks (Dillon 2003: 552–3). While the UK Government has been developing its ID card scheme that will contain and integrate 49 separate pieces of personal information (http://news.bbc.co.uk/1/hi/uk_politics/4630045.stm, accessed 20.03.06). The EU has been forcing airports to be massively restructured so as to separate out their outgoing from their incoming passengers.

The banality of terrorist lives, what Noble terms *Bin Laden in the Suburbs* (2004), means that suspicion is cast on any and every individual (Diken 2005: 139). Thus, novel securitization techniques that are trialled within airport environments move into general securitization within the wider society, moving from an exception to becoming the rule as literally anyone might be the next Bin Laden (Adey 2004). The adage to 'know thy enemy' means that after September 11th almost anyone on any train, street, bus and especially in that seat next to one on the plane could be thy 'enemy' that indeed cannot be known (see Watson's critique as to whether any of these measures will actually improve 'airport security': 2001).

What is also significant is that as people and artefacts become more mobile, other people and objects become relatively less mobile. Overall the greater the extent, range and significance of mobility around the world, the more elaborate and complex the consequential patterns of immobilization (see discussion of the relativity of this in Adey 2006b). An enormous fixed and immobile infrastructure affords the mobilities of people and objects, through directing, checking, monitoring, ensuring security, providing hospitality, entertaining, ground transportation, engineering, air traffic control and so on. As mobilities have become larger in scale and significance, more global, so the immobilities of people and artefacts have also increased in scale, organization and complexity. Sassen writes that the increase in 'capabilities for enormous geographical dispersal and mobility' go hand-in-hand with 'pronounced territorial concentrations of resources necessary for the management and servicing of that dispersal and mobility' (2002: 2). These territorial concentrations involve a tremendous reworking of social and physical relations, obliterating or erasing all kinds of life previously existing in such a place (see Pascoe 2001, on Narita; Adey 2006b: 81). Airports are 'terraformers', reconfiguring geography according to the 'spatio-temporal rhythms and cross-modal standards of global capital' (Fuller, Harley 2005: 102–3). Especially striking are the massive Asian airports designed on a vast scale by celebrity architects and sometimes located upon newly formed islands built in the sea and designed to operate on global time 24/7 (see Fuller, Harley 2005, on Kansai, Chep Lap Kok, Pudong). But as Adey emphasizes, airports are always on the move, with endless accretions, extensions, new runways, re-themings, makeovers; places almost literally we can say on the move (2006b: 81–2). All fifteen airports studied by Fuller and Harley in their photographic essay *Aviopolis* were being upgraded just before or during their research (2005: 114).

And within such airspaces, immobilities are themselves organized around various kinds of limited movement; of planes, fuel, luggage, passengers, staff, objects, services, trolleys, consumer goods and so on, intermittently proceeding along *mostly* pre-determined routes through the airport-city. These objects proceed around the place of the airport; on occasions having to be combined (passengers to get access to trolleys) and on other occasions kept apart (luggage not yet security checked must not get near planes), but with a lot of waiting. In order to deal with these complex intersecting systems, immobile people and artefacts are both highly inflexible – not allowing certain people or objects onto the plane – and highly flexible to deal with the concentrated flows of people and objects in the remarkable compressions of time and space in order to combine in a fragment of time the exceptional flows necessary in order to get those planes 'airborne' (see Peters 2006: ch. 5).

These dialectical processes help to realize globality as a social phenomenon. In other words, there must be people and objects that stay in certain relationalities of flexibility and inflexibility in order that other peoples and objects can be contingently on the move. To create mobility, transition and modernity there are flexible systems of people and materials that provide the specific mobility potential (motility) in the form of services, infrastructures, technologies and person power. There is thus a *binding* character to mobility (Sheller 2003).

In the next section I turn to the nature of the airspaces themselves, spaces designed to organize the different modes of time that are juxtaposed within the complexities of air travel.

Airport Spaces

The most common conception here is that airports are a leading example of 'non-places'; and non-places particularly mark social relations of 'supermodernity' (Augé 1995: 75–9; Kirn 2001). Supermodernity involves: 'entirely new experiences and ordeals of solitude, directly linked with the appearance and proliferation of non-places' (Augé 1995: 93). In particular airports are a new generic space similar to shopping malls, business hotels, service stations, supermarkets and so on. They are all characterized as placeless. Such non-places are spaces: where people coexist or cohabit without living together; they 'create solitary contractuality' (Augé 1995: 94). Airports are indistinct since nothing distinguishes one from the other. And people within such non-places barely need to interact in order to negotiate their passages through the airspace; people pass but do not meet or as John Berger states: 'a[A]irports are too polite; reality is always at one remove in an airport' (cited Pascoe 2001: 229). This approach to airspaces also emphasizes the design aesthetic that is becoming global – such an aesthetic enables visitors to airports to 'find their way' with relative ease (see Pascoe 2001, on the history of such designs). Much of the sign language used is international (especially 'English') and many experiences are similar across airports within different countries. Certain corporations have developed expertise in airport design and management and this also helps to homogenize international airports around the world, turning

them all, it is said, into non-places (Lloyd 2003; see the phot
Fuller, Harley 2005).

This claim that airspaces are to be understood as non-places
recently been critiqued from two directions. First, even if airspaces
are less distinct as places and share many characteristics in common,
there are various ways in which airspaces are nevertheless different
from each other and where they are not characterized solely by a
'solitary contractuality'. Second, this claim that airports are non-
places rests upon a far too sedentarist notion of place as though
'places' are given and unchanging and share no characteristics with
airspaces. Rather what is striking is how places are increasingly *like*
airports.

First then, airspaces are places of material organization and considerable social complexity. They are not simply 'non-places'. They
are characterized by: 'the boring, everyday, routine, but essential
operations, processes, systems, and technologies, that enable global
mobility to occur' (Parker 2002: 16; see the entertaining Baskas 2001).
Airspaces are characterized by various distinct system features that
constitute it as a place, features that are engineered through design
and material layout, through the sign system, through the various
code-spaces, and through various social patterning. These system
features include how there can only be one-way traffic of passengers
and that they can almost never reverse; that each passenger is transformed through a series of planned and timed steps although these
vary depending upon 'class'; that passengers have to find their un-
escorted routing from entry to plane often involving lengthy walks
and changes of terminals and where airports are never quite the same
as each other; that there are strict rules relating to the parallel movements of baggage that are sometimes co-present with the passenger
and sometimes separated from them; that there is a central control
room which means that the staff dealing with passengers are autho-
rized to change only a subset of information appearing upon their
screens; and that workers are always dealing with 'situated actions'
involving monitoring and adjustment of actions and timings in relationship to rapidly changing and often unpredictable external events
(see Peters 2006: ch. 5; Cresswell 2006: ch. 9).

Moreover, in and around such complex material and semiotic
organization, various sets of social relations are afforded possibilities for development. Gottdiener argues that: 'the implosive articulation of a many-purposed pedestrian crowd creates a critical mass
of social density, much like the busy downtown district of a large
central city. With enough interacting people, the scene itself emerges

as a distinct feature of place' (2001: 21–2). And of course many airports are being redesigned to make them more like destinations. Airspaces are also places of work for often thousands of workers, and air terminals are becoming more like small cities (Gottdiener 2001; Pascoe 2001). People spend considerable amounts of 'dwell-time' in these places and thus it is argued that: 'i[I]nstead of experiencing waiting time as wasted time . . . the urban traveller is invited to use transit time to accumulate useful experiences of leisure and work' (Lloyd 2003: 94; Lyons, Urry 2005; and see the next chapter). And such airspaces in the third period are full of commercial and tourist services for passengers, for visitors and for the hundreds or thousands of employees. These services include bars, cafés, restaurants, and hotels, business centres, chapels and churches, shopping centres, discotheques (Munich, Frankfurt), massage centres (Changi), conference centres (Munich), art galleries (Schiphol), gyms (Los Angeles) and casinos (Schiphol). Also and most significantly, there are many instant offices and airport hotels, allowing travellers to arrive, stay over, do their 'business' face-to-face and depart, especially as many airports are now organized on the hub-and-spoke model (Doyle and Nathan 2001). Airspaces are thus full of meeting places, they are places of 'meetingness' that transform them into strategic moments in constructing a global order. Airspaces provide multiple sites for developing and sustaining 'global microstructures' (Knorr Cetina 2005).

Some writers thus view airspaces as new kinds of public spaces, albeit with very particular characteristics. Thus Sudjic writes:

> The airport, alongside the museum, and the shopping mall, is one of the key public spaces that serve to define the contemporary city . . . It is a surrogate for the public realm, one that offers at least the illusion of a meeting place in which the rich and poor are in closer proximity than almost anywhere else in an increasingly economically segregated world. (1999)

Thus there is a general trend from hubs to ambivalent places of movement and mobility, commerce, experience and events. Airspaces are places of 'dwelling in mobility', sites of rest, activity, meeting and consumption rather like many other places across the world, no longer the exception but the rule.

Second, therefore, cities are becoming more like airports, less places of specific dwellingness and more organized in and through diverse mobilities and the regulation of those multiple mobilities. Indeed the more apparently 'cosmopolitan' the place, the more that place is produced and consumed through multiple mobilities very much akin to the multiple ways that airports function and are organized. Also, airports are themselves increasingly vast cities which may well harbinger a particular conception of future urban form (Fuller, Harley 2005). And all cities are increasingly like airports in how forms of surveillance, monitoring and regulation are being surreptitiously implemented as part of the global 'war on terror'. In the 'frisk society', the use of detention centres, CCTV, GPS systems, iris-recognition security and intermodal traffic interchanges, once trialled within airports, move out to become mundane characteristics of towns and cities, places of fear and contingent ordering within the new world order. Hence, Martinotti writes that airports and the like: 'are the places of the city we live in today. Non-places are nothing less than the typical places of the city of our times' (1999: 170). Thus airspaces are the future not just for those who are literally *Up in the Air* (Kirn 2001). Diken and Laustsen describe the nature of current societies: 'in which exception is the rule, a society in which the logic of the camp is generalized' (2005: 147); and my argument here is that it is global air travel and its specific 'mobilities and materialities' that are turning spaces of exception (airspaces) into the generalized rule around the world (Sheller, Urry 2006b).

Global Lines of Flights

Monumental terminals of glass and steel designed by celebrity architects, gigantic planes, contested runway developments, flights massively cheaper than surface travel, new systems of 'security', endless queues – these are the new global order, points of entry into a world of apparent hypermobility, time–space compression *and* distanciation, and the contested placing of people, cities and whole societies upon the global map (see Edwards 1998, on such airport design). There are many ways in which flights, aeroplanes, airports and airport cities are central to an emergent global order. Without the rapid development of the complex extended systems of mass air travel, what is now termed 'globalization' would be utterly different, possibly non-existent (Urry 2003a).

Regular and safe air travel is centrally implicated in producing global ordering, which is to be understood as enacted as process and through multiple performances, more as effects and less as 'causes' (Franklin, Lury, Stacey 2000: 1–17). Global space is something that is made (Law, Hetherington 1999). This global space constitutes its own domains through multiple processes including those technologies and systems that afford relatively risk-free long distance air travel. Air flights are central to performing the global order; airports can be viewed as 'global transit points' that promote and guarantee the flows of significant numbers of people, goods and information around the world, making possible connections with those who are otherwise distant and absent (see Kesselring 2006b).

Such an umbilical cord between air travel and the global can be seen in a distinct set of way that I now detail. First, there is the sheer scale of the air travel industry, of international travel flows and of the monumental scale of airports, all being major components of the emergent global economy. The 1.9 billion air journeys that take place each year occur within increasingly massive and iconic airports. Thus Beijing's Terminal-3, designed by celebrity-architect Norman Foster, possesses a: 'soaring aerodynamic roof [that] will reflect the poetry of flight. Passengers will enjoy a fully glazed single, lofty space, day lit through roof lights and bathed in colour changing from red to yellow as you progress through it' (cited in *The Hindu* www.hindu.com/2006/03/03/stories/2006030301412000.htm, accessed 18.3.06). The completion of the terminal will make Beijing Capital International airport the largest in the world, outdoing both the current largest international airports, Chek Lap Kok in Hong Kong and Heathrow in the UK, although the building there of Terminal 5 may alter that again in this incessant global competition for airspaces, cities and societies.

Second, air travel presupposes the notion of a global or Universal Time. Such a time synchronizes the actions of all organizations and people involved in air travel around the world. It is thus an 'industry' presupposing a global ordering and employing a notion of time that synchronizes air flights through the heterogeneous ordering of aircraft, passengers, crew, baggage, fuel, freight and catering that are assembled so that planes can be 'airborne on time' (Peters 2006: ch. 5). This synchronization of flights is also effected by the more or less universal interconnectedness of the multiple computerized booking systems and by the general use of English as the language of airspace (Peters 2006: 105).

Third, air travel is a quintessential mode of dwelling within the contemporary globalizing world, a world of arrivals and departures, lounges, duty free, English signs, pre-packaged food, frequent flyer programmes, and what Andy Warhol terms 'the airport atmosphere' (1976: 145). Many iconic signs and practices associated with the global order derive from international air travel and a widespread familiarity that is especially spread through film and TV (see Iyer 2000, on the 'global soul'; Makimoto, Manners 1997, on the 'nomadic urge'). J. G. Ballard describes the symbolic aspect of the global display seen in airport concourses which: 'are the ramblas and agoras of the future city, time-free zones where all the clocks of the world are displayed, an atlas of arrivals and destinations forever updating itself, where briefly we become true world citizens' (cited Pascoe 2001: 34). Moreover, airspaces teach people through contemporary 'morality plays' the appropriate categories by which to navigate the conflicts and dilemmas of the contemporary world. These categories include business class passenger, terrorist, Third-Worlder, suspect Arabs, Westerner, budget traveller, illegal migrants and so on. Aaltola maintains that the 'airport provides a particularly well-suited place in which to learn the hierarchical world-order imagination . . . Placed in the airport, a person recognizes the types and remembers their own respective position among them' (2005: 275). We can describe this particular well-trained eye as that of the 'airport gaze' in which since 2001 it is legitimate to be ever vigilant since air travellers differ greatly in their perceived threats to the new world order and increased securitization is deemed essential for life in a global era.

Fourth, air travel transmits people into global relationships through what Gottdiener terms a 'space of transition' (2001: 10–11). Air travel is the key 'space of flows' that moves people around the world, especially connecting hub airports located in major 'global' cities (Castells 1996; Urry 2000; Aaltola 2005: 267). This system of airports is key to the constitution of global processes, permitting travel so that people encounter other people and places from around the world 'face-to-face'. Air flights are centrally significant micro-structures within the performances involved in the global order. This *system* links together places, forming networks and bringing those connected places closer together. Two hub airports are 'near' in the network of air travel, even if they are thousands of miles apart. The 2003 Global Airport Monitor identified fifty-one hubs, twenty-five European, fourteen American, nine Asian-pacific and three African (Aaltola 2005: 267). Simultaneously these networks distance those other places, the spokes that are not so well connected, not part of 'hub civilizations' as Huntington puts it (1993). As one commentator notes: 'Jumbos have enabled Korean computer consultants to fly to Silicon Valley as if popping next door, and Singapore entrepreneurs to reach Seattle in a day . . . But what about those they fly over, on their islands five miles below? . . . Air travel might enable businessmen to buzz across the ocean, but the concurrent decline in shipping has only increased the isolation of many island communities' (cited in Massey 1994b: 148). Thus the development of complex networks of air travel (with at least 300 airlines world-wide who are members of IATA) produces areas of very dense air traffic (between the hubs) and other areas (the spokes) characterized by sparse networks that have the effect of peripheralizing people and places away from the hubs of the global order (Graham, Marvin 2001). Airports are thus we might say machines that very significantly *move* places throughout the world.

Fifth and relatedly, air travel and its visible inequalities are a synecdoche of the increasingly global pattern of inequalities deriving from huge variations in network capital. Globalizing systems are highly differentiated by the kinds of travellers moving through these semi-public airspaces. In particular the global or kinetic elite experiences: 'the construction of a (relatively) secluded space across the world along the connecting lines of the space of flows' (Castells 1996: 417). For first-class passengers, air travel is integrally interconnected with limousines, taxis, air-conditioned offices, fast check-in and fast routing through immigration, business-class hotels and restaurants, forming a seamless scape along which nomadic executives making the global order can with less effort travel. For countless others, their journeys are longer, more uncertain, more risky, and indicative of their global inferiority in a world where access to network capital is of major significance within the emerging global stratification system. Moreover, automated software for sorting travellers as they pass through automatic surveillance systems, such as iris-recognition for Privium passengers at Schiphol, reinforces the 'kinetic elite' whose ease of mobility differentiates them from a low-speed, low mobility mass (Wood, Graham 2006). Privium is described as 'a select way to travel', 'an exclusive membership for frequent travellers who appreciate priority, speed and comfort and who like to start their journey in style' (www.schiphol.nl/schiphol/privium/privium_home.jsp#anchor3, accessed 20.03.06; all UK passengers can now apply for membership of the Iris Immigration System). And the enhanced mobility of this elite is at the expense of the slowing down and greater time that is made possible in order to interrogate those not within the privium elite (Adey 2006b: 89).

Sixth, airports are complex places since peoples and cultures from around the world overlap within them through the intersection of enormously elaborate relays. These relays come together especially within the departure lounge of airports, places of intense sameness produced by the systems of the aviation industry *and* of intense hybridity as mobile peoples and cultures unpredictably intersect through various modes of 'dwelling-in-transit'. As Serres writes: 'On the departure board, the list of destinations reads like a gazetteer of the world . . . Via the operations of this particular message-bearing system, men and women part company and come together, re-arrange themselves and create new human mixes. Here we see them at rest; in a short while people who are now standing next to each other will be a thousand miles apart, and strangers will converge into neighbourliness' (1995: 258). And daily flows through airports contribute to the production of contemporary urbanism, including diasporic cultural communities, 'ethnic' restaurants and neighbourhoods, distant families and cosmopolitan identities, and exclusive zones and corridors of connectivity for the fast-tracked kinetic elite.

Seventh, international air traffic makes possible very many different mobilities, of holidaymaking, money laundering, business travel, the drug trade, infections, international crime, asylum seeking, leisure travel, arms trading, people smuggling and slave trading (Hannam, Sheller, Urry 2006: 5–9). These render visible the already existing chaotic juxtapositions of different spaces and networks that air travel affords. For example, global diseases rapidly move so that the: 'world has rapidly become much more vulnerable to the eruption and, more critically, to the widespread and even global spread of both new and old infectious diseases . . . The jet plane itself, and its cargo, can carry insects and infectious agents into new ecologic settings' (Mann, cited Buchanan 2002: 172). Only a few long-range random transport connections are necessary to generate pandemics, such as occurred among those threatened by SARs, as during 2003 it spread across the very mobile Chinese diaspora especially between south China, Hong Kong and Toronto (Sum 2004; Little 2006; Urry 2004; Hannam, Sheller, Urry 2006: 7).

Eighth, air flight affords a god's eye view, a view of the earth from above, with places, towns and cities laid out as though they are a form of nature. In Ingold's terms, air travel generates 'map-readers' rather than 'wayfinders' (2000). While way-finders move around *within* a world, map-readers move across a surface as imagined from above. And air travel colludes in producing and reinforcing the language of abstract mobilities and comparison, an expression of a mobile, abstracted mode of being-in-the-world. And through this mode places get transformed into a collection of abstract characteristics in a mobile world, ever easier to be visited, appreciated and compared even from above, but not really known from within (see Szerszynski, Urry 2006, on how a vision from above is engineered through the iconic pictures of the earth taken from space).

Thus we can say that air travel is indissolubly bound up the new relations of empire that according to various authors increasingly replace nation-state sovereignty or 'society' (Hardt and Negri 2000; on empire and air travel, see Aaltola 2005). By 'empire' is meant the emergence of a dynamic and flexible systemic structure articulated horizontally across the globe, a 'governance without government' that sweeps together all actors within the order as a whole (Hardt and Negri 2000: 13–4). Empire involves a system of nodes and connecting lines that is in effect replacing the world atlas. However, elsewhere I argue through the prism of complexity theory that such an 'empire' functions more like a strange attractor more than a complete system (Urry 2003a). Thus societies are drawn over time into the 'basin' of empire where empire is to be understood as a 'network-based imperial hierarchy' without necessarily strong co-present territorialities (Aaltola 2005: 268). Contemporary societies increasingly possess a visible imperial *centre*, with iconic buildings, world heritage landscapes, celebrity-designed airports, global brands and so on. Societies are drawn into the attractor of empire upon the world-as-stage, competing for the best skyline, airport, palaces, galleries, stadia, infrastructures, games, sports heroes, skilled workforce, universities and security. While beyond the centre effects spread across nominally distinct national borders as imperial representatives fly to the spokes from the imperial hub. Aaltola summarizes how the 'network-based imperial hierarchy is knit together by the air travel system . . . [it] manages to create an economical, vibrant and political power hub geography . . . [that] signifies a healthy, stable and predictable world order' (2005: 268).

The United States is by far the most powerful empire in this sense upon the current world-as-stage, with various exceptional centres (NY, LA, Washington), many icons of power (Pentagon, Wall Street, Hollywood, Ivy League Universities, Texan oil wells, Silicon Valley, MOMA), a massively dense transportation infrastructure, a porosity of certain borders, huge 'imperial' economic and social inequalities and networks linking it through travel and communications with almost every other society. Yet each society as empire produces its opposite, a co-evolving other, its rebellious multitude with the US empire generating powerful multitudinous 'others'. Huge transformations are taking place in the production of 'empire-and-multitude' through global fluids of money laundering, drug trade, urban crime, asylum seeking, people smuggling, slave trading, and urban terrorism. These and many other fluids all depend upon the passages of passengers passing through airports and as a result the spaces of multitude and empire are contingently juxtaposed as they were on September 11th 2001 (see Urry 2003a, on global fluids).

Air flights and systems are thus central to the emergent global order generating mass movement, new forms of dwelling, interconnectedness, new inequalities, novel global meeting places, distinct ambivalent juxtapositions, new modes of vision and enhanced relations of 'empire' as attractors. Some other aspects are examined in subsequent chapters, including the interconnections between physical and virtual mobilities in the next chapter and the significance of air travel to climate change in chapter 13.

Conclusion

In this chapter I have examined various aspects of the growth of 'aeromobility', beginning with a brief periodization of some of the striking changes in airspaces over the past century. In chapter 13 I consider some other possible developments, including the development of personalized air transport – what has been described as 'a plane in every garage', as well as the innovation of systems of mass space travel. I also explored further aspects of the risks of air travel and of the intersecting expert software systems that currently make such travel contingently possible, especially in the context of how the new risks of terrorist attack have especially focused upon these fragile flying machines.

I further analysed how flights, aeroplanes, airports and airport cities are central to contemporary global ordering and suggested that without the complex systems of mass air travel, there would not be 'globalization' as currently conceived. Airspaces involve some interdependent systems of immobile fixed moorings that make rapid and far-flung global mobilities contingently possible (Adey 2006b: 87).

In examining the character of air spaces I argued that they are neither non-places but nor are they places of what is understood as conventional dwellingness. Rather and most significantly airspaces are typical of those 'places' that the global order is ushering in, showing many overlaps and similarities with towns and cities from around the world. It is increasingly difficult to distinguish between airspaces and some other places in a global order; there is de-differentiation as systems of air travel move out and increasingly populate many kinds of place, the camp of the airspace has become the rule (Diken 2005: 147). So not only do passengers increasingly fly around the world, but the systems of both movement and securitization that make possible such travel also fly around, landing in many towns and cities subject to an airspace makeover (also of course personal information often escapes and can then be hoovered up by identity thieves and the like). As Fuller and Harley state in *Aviopolis*: 'we know Sudjic and Virilio are right: the airport is the city of the future' (2005: 48), and the forms of automated if contingently malfunctioning surveillance in such cities are also the future.

8

Connecting and Imagining

> Take 73-year old Grace Angel, who was born in Wandsworth
> and has lived in her house in Tooting [London] for over fifty
> years ... She rarely leaves Wandsworth; she enjoys the sense
> of community ... At the same time her life is not confined by
> the locality. She tells how she writes letters to France and the
> United States
>
> (Fennell 1997: 45)

In previous chapters I examined various mobility systems and in part
considered how certain systems have defined the fitness landscape
for those historically developing later. I also noted how mobility
systems are not to be viewed as bounded and autonomous but in part
depend upon how forms of travel presuppose and, on occasions,
bring into being modes of communication and new forms of organization at-a-distance. In chapter 11 noted the exceptional transformations in both transport *and* communications that took place in Europe
around 1840 when modernity got mobilized. Transport systems dating
from that exceptional moment include the first railway age and the
first ocean steamship service; while communications developments
include a national post system, the development of commercial telegram services, the invention of photography and the growth of printed
guidebooks. However, as noted in early chapters the study of travel
and transport within the academy has been largely conducted separately from the analysis of communications, as though these were
different and unrelated systems.

In this chapter I therefore insert communications *into* the study
of travel and transport, and examine some ways in which they are

always intertwined. This can be seen in two respects. First, many communications are actually about travel, arrangements and schedules, about the contingent processes of getting places and meeting up. Some such communications are 'personal' such as a call to a friend to arrange a meeting. Other communications are impersonal and 'socialized', such as Thomas Cook's development of systems for packaged tours beginning in 1841. Second, communications and travel are partially substitutes for each other in that sometimes communications can replace travel while some travel may mean that communications need not take place. Overall I consider many ways in which communications can effect substitution or complementarity in relationship to physical travel.

But I also show that the contemporary world is ushering in some new intimate intertwinings as communications are increasingly freed from location. Communications are themselves travelling and as they travel so they change what it is to be travelling *and* communicating, and indeed what it is to stay at home or to be stationary. I examine aspects of the internet and mobile telephony that are moving communications away from fixed sites and for them to be 'on the move' and indeed to operate within and help to generate in-between spaces and times.

It should initially be noted that communications are of many sorts (see Thrift 1996: 264–7). These range from personal messengers, pigeons, letters, telegrams, books, radio, postcards, special event cards, newspapers, telephones, television, email, text messages, internet, video conferences and so on. A simple categorization of these many forms is between one-to-one communications (the personal letter), one-to-many communications (TV), and many-to-many communications (email bulletin board). Some communications are two-way such as a telephone call while others are one-way such as non-interactive television. Each of these forms of communications presupposes various systems that make it possible to track and to trace objects and people, forming as I have noted a 'technological unconscious' that bends bodies-with-environments to a specific set of addresses without much cognitive input (Thrift 2004c: 177). These forms of address, of persons and objects, enable repetitive actions to occur, mostly without thinking. These systems include address books, timetables, house numbers, diaries, telephone numbers and directories, reservation systems, postcodes, email addresses, barcodes and so on.

In the next section I consider some elements of virtual communications or travel that involve new kinds of entities that form the background to much human life and connections. I point to the exceptional significance of various transitions that occurred around 1990 th.. initiated new kinds of address and connection. In the following section I briefly examine 'imaginative travel' especially via the TV, before turning to the development of 'mobiles' which have dramatically released communications from fixed points and amplified the body through prosthetic incorporation. This analysis of the mobile provides useful ways of analysing 'inhabiting machines' of which the mobile will prove to be an early primitive example. There is a brief conclusion.

My account here is mainly designed to examine these communications channels in so far as they interconnect with modes of physical travel. In particular I attend to how systems are assembled that combine together elements of physical movement *and* modes of communications. I also try to avoid an epochal hubris that presumes that one's own epoch is such a moment of transition where changes in the present are more important and fateful than those that happened at other times and places (see ch. 13 below on futures).

Virtual Travel

Nevertheless I begin by noting the contemporary emergence of powerful, interdependent knowledge-based systems that through new software are increasingly organizing production, consumption, travel and communications around the world.

I develop here Thrift's distinction between various modes of the apparently 'natural order' that constitute the background to human life, the background that is there because it is there (2004b). There are I argue three such backgrounds. First, there is the 'natural world' of rivers, hills, lakes, storms, soil, snow, earth and so on, that provided the taken-for-granted background for most of human history. Second, there is the background made up of the 'artificial' objects of the industrial revolution such as trains, pipes, steam, screws, watches, paper, radio, cars and so on. And third, there is the background constituted through the emerging world of 'virtual' objects resulting from the revolutions in computer hardware and software, such as screens, cables, mice, signals, satellites, ringtones and so on.

This chapter explores the last of these natures, a virtual nature that has many implications for a world of 'movement'. These inescapable and mundane virtual objects possess a 'fugitive materiality' that is often observable only when they break down, as they periodically do. Such objects are hard to examine since they tend to be realized through their very performances. They each require systems of address so that each person or object is known to the others within the system. Small bits of hardware and software work away in countless unexpected locations and are often themselves on the move. GIS and GPS are potentially able to 'track and trace' in a covert and simulated fashion very many objects and persons around the world as they leave virtual traces (see Thrift 2004b).

So in the background of twenty-first century lives are virtual objects, hovering and mostly taken-for-granted, and which express and capture flows, or what Knorr Cetina calls 'flow architectures' (2003). Such backgrounds are not simple or fixed environments for actions; they are increasingly sentient environments that adapt to and transform lives without being noticed or necessarily remarked upon. Such sentient environments will in the future include affective computing to sense the emotional state and potential stress levels of drivers. And central to those lives are numbers and calculations, what Thrift terms 'qualculation' based upon systems that enable speedy counting, measuring, ranking and archiving without humans necessarily knowing about such calculations or being cognitively able themselves to do many (any?) such calculations (2004b).

These systems, predominantly developed and embedded within the private sector, are software-based and mostly have the effect of making certain actions seem unexceptional and unproblematic. The software makes it more or less certain that the product can be purchased, the meeting will happen, the components will arrive at the factory, the plane will be waiting, the message will get through, the money will arrive and so on (Thrift, French 2002). These software-based systems make repetitive or iterative actions possible and mostly effected without much cognitive thought and intervention.

Such systems distribute economies, peoples, activities across the world. Castells describes this resulting pattern as that of the 'network society'. Its social structure is made up of networks that are powered by microelectronics-based information and communication technologies (2004). Historically there have always been networks but until the microelectronics revolution they were, according to Castells, organizationally inferior to vertical-hierarchical organizations. Networks have their strength in flexibility, adaptability and a self-organizing character but beyond a certain size they had been a much less efficient mode of organization, partly because of the time lags involved in communicating across the network in question. According to Castells it is the growth of micro-electronics based communications technologies that transforms the potential for networks, offering new advantages of flexibility, scalability, survivability and increasingly portability. Castells see the strength of networks as resulting from their self-organizing and often short-term character and not from centralized hierarchical direction as with older style rational-legal bureaucracies. He shows the 'chaotically' subversive effects of the *personal* computer upon the *state* bureaucracy of the Soviet Union that historically controlled all information flows including access to the photocopier (Castells 1996: 36–7; 2001). Although the notion of network here is too all-inclusive a term there seems little doubt that there is a shift from more hierarchical to more networked modes of economic and social organization, and that this shift is linked with the development of micro-electronics based communications technologies that permit new, fast communications especially one-to-many and many-to-many (Castells 1996; 2001).

What accounts for this rapid development of the networked mode driven by micro-electronics and new software? 1989–1990 is the key moment in this development (as significant as 1840–1; see ch. 1). What happened in this moment? First, Soviet Communism collapses almost overnight partly according to Castells because of its failure to develop new informational technologies and hence its emerging dependence upon US computing technology (1996). This collapse of the Soviet empire consolidates the American 'empire' and makes almost the whole world open to new systems of virtual communications (also apartheid disappears in South Africa so 'opening up' Africa).

Second and more specifically, Tim Berners-Lee 'invents' the world wide web which through the concepts of URL, HTTP and HTML enable (mostly) seamless jumps from link to link without regard to conventional borders of country, language, subject or discipline. This novel language and architecture initiates an astonishing array of new projects, services and sociabilities.

Third, there is the early development of mobile telephony especially at Nokia, as it turns from a toilet paper producer to the world's leading mobile phone manufacturer, and at Vodafone, now the world's largest mobile telecommunications network company by turnover.

Fourth, all major financial markets move to on-line real time trading accessible somewhere or other 24 hours a day. This early use of virtual communications dissolves many national markets and national suppliers for most forms of finance and for many financial services.

And fifth, during the Gulf War in 1991 systems of 24-hour real time reporting using new virtual communication technologies are developed and become especially notable; and quickly turn into 24/7 real time news reporting across multiple and intersecting TV and internet channels.

These various interdependent systems dating from around 1990, firstly, have the effect of both massively spreading virtual connections *and* of bringing virtual objects into the background of much social life. This can be described as the shift from the stationary, wooden, fixed 'desk' occupied by the individual scholar, to the ephemeral, mobile and interchangeable 'desktop' that can be occupied by anyone (paralleling the shift from the religious 'icon' to the computer 'icon'). With digitization, information adopts modes of mobility that are substantially separate from material form or presence (Hayles 1999: 18–20; Urry 2003). Information is everywhere travelling (more or less) instantaneously along fluid networks. Its repositories cannot be burnt down as with the Mediaeval library. Central to this human experience are those flickering 'screens' and the pervasiveness of living on those screens (Turkle 1996). And on those screens that inhabit workplaces, homes, airports, shopping centres, post offices, stores, garages, trains, aircraft and even cars there are almost always 'strangers', lurking and indexing other worlds and alternative possibilities (see McCarthy 2001, on 'ambient television').

Secondly, these systems seem to usher in worlds that are less based upon predictable and given co-presence, upon what I term below communities of propinquity. Specific others are not so simply 'there'; or rather they are or may be there but mainly through the mediation of what I term virtual nature, the panoply of virtual objects distributed in relatively far flung networks. The apparently different domains of work, family and social life becoming more networked, more similar to each other and more interdependent. I examine in chapter 9 and 10 how through such communications technologies weak ties spread from domain to domain especially with the growth of network capital that enhances the power of some nodes and relatively weakens other positions. Castells summarizes how:

> What is specific to our world is the extension and augmentation of the body and mind of human subjects in networks of interaction powered by micro-electronics-based, software-operated, communication technologies. These technologies are increasingly diffused throughout the entire realm of human activity by growing miniaturization [and we may add portability]. (2004: 7)

This book argues that these information and communication technologies and especially new kinds of software do indeed transform networks and social life through transforming the background within

which human movement takes place, through new '
objects that remodel the 'technological unconsciou

These bodily augmentations also enable and effect ι
out of social networks that increasingly depend, even for h
and family life, upon these virtual objects lurking in the backgrь
and often unnoticed. But what is important here is intermittent physical travel and especially the meetings of incredibly diverse sorts that
these new 'movement-spaces' make possible and indeed are partial
constituents thereof. Castells' account is overly cognitivist in which
the new 'network society' is seen through the lens of 'informationalism' and its liberation from places, borders and location (the shift
from the 'desk' to the 'desktop').

But at the same time that Castells' argument is too cognitivist (and
hence is a kind of nomadism), other analyses of virtual objects are
too nostalgic for pre-virtual 'communities' with characteristics seen
as being irredeemably and negatively transformed by new communication processes (hence are a form of sedentarist argument; see
Putnam 2000; Urry 2004a; and ch. 1 above). In order to get beyond
both nomadic *and* sedentarist positions and to establish the nature
of the 'pre-virtual' world supposedly being transformed, three senses
of 'community' should be distinguished (Bell, Newby 1976). First,
there is community in a topographical sense. This refers to settlement
based upon close geographical *propinquity*, but where there is no
implication of the quality of the social relationships found in such
settlements of intense co-presence. Such propinquitous, co-present
'communities' are statistically now less common.

Second, there is the sense of community as any *local* social system
in which there a localized, relatively bounded set of systemic inter-
relationships of social groups and local institutions.

Third, there is *communion*, human association characterized by
close personal ties, belongingness and emotional warmth between its
members. The last of these is what is conventionally meant by the
idea of 'community' relationships that are in decline or are threatened by decline in part because of new communication technologies
(see Putnam 2000). This is community as 'affect'.

Moreover, in relationship to virtual objects and communications
it has been claimed that virtual communities are not real (or affective) communities (Jones 1995: 24; Sardar 1996). In the early days
of internet development it was common to argue that although
virtual communities involve more connections (more weak ties)
these connections: 'grow more fragile, airy, and ephemeral' as electronic space supplants the rich complex diversity of pre-existing
social space (Heim 1991: 74). Virtual communities were thought

to lack the substance of 'real communities' providing only 'a life on the screen' rather than emotional, affective 'communion' (Turkle 1996).

However, there are some important points to make here against such a claim. First, Bell and Newby argued (thirty years ago!) that communion, an emotion of community, is not necessarily produced by any particular settlement type and it can be emergent even where its 'members' do not dwell in close physical proximity. There are many ways of affirming affective communion and some of these involve physical movement and not stasis. This movement can take place both within boundaries, such as travelling along well-worn paths or roads, or beyond boundaries, to many other places through travel, communications and imagined travel. Raymond Williams in the *Border Country* captures: 'the networks men and women set up, the trails and territorial structures they make as they move across a region, and the ways these interact or interfere with each other' (Pinkney 1991: 49; Williams 1988). Massey argues that the identity of a place is derived in large part from its interchanges with other places that may on occasions be what she calls 'progressive' (1994b: 180). Travel and communications, we might say, can be central to affect.

Second, it seems that intermittent co-presence is important even within virtual spaces (Baym 1995: 157). Meeting up can reinforce the: 'magical, intensely personal, deeply emotional bonds that the medium had enabled them to forge among themselves' (Rheingold 1994: 237). Virtual spaces seem to depend upon moments of face-to-face co-presence for developing trustful relationships. People meet up from time to time, dwelling together in a shared place. There is not a fixed amount of travel that has to be met in one way or another, and that there is not be the straightforward 'substitution' of virtual travel for corporeal travel. It seems that virtual and physical travel transforms the very nature and need for co-presence. Koku, Nazer, Wellman argue on the basis of research on research scholars that: 'f[F]requent contact on the internet is a complement to frequent face-to-face contact, not a substitute for it' (cited Putnam 2000: 179). Other research suggests that those who are on-line are those most active in voluntary and political work within their immediate neighbourhood (Wellman 2001: 10). Their range of contacts may be predominantly local but significantly broader than those who are not online. Virtual connections can thus promote more extensive local connections and hence more and not less corporeal travel.

In research on the geographies of social networks of young adults in NW England, email enables everyone within a network to share and to have equal access to the same information (see Larsen, Urry, Axhausen 2006: ch. 8). Thus the responsibility for organizing events gets more equally distributed. Moreover, everyone has access to the documentation about dates and venues stored in their mailbox that they are able to consult later. Thus email seems to produce more meetings and not fewer:

> It makes it easier to meet up with people because, there is less effort involved in writing a small message and sending it out to a number of people in terms of coordination and getting people together . . . For instance, when it was my stag do a couple of years ago my best man did it all by email and it worked wonderfully well because you get this kind of coordination of dates when people are available, when they are not . . . So rather than that kind of confusion that occurs when you are going from one person to another and then going back . . . you have got this situation where everything is . . . transmitted to everybody from one source. (male architect, early thirties; Larsen, Urry, Axhausen 2006: 115)

Moreover, with certain forms of information being able to travel the world in seconds, it is argued that face-to-face meetings are changing. Weber and Chon suggest that:

> [S]ince more information can now be exchanged via technology, there is a greater need to build relationships when getting together for face-to-face meetings. Consequently, meetings in the future will focus more on social aspects rather than on business, which may be conducted mainly via technology. (2003: 206)

Face-to-face meetings will thus be less concerned with traditional (one-way) presentations of information and passive listening and more with building and sustaining networks and exchanging social goods. Future business meetings may well be more participatory and affective, involving networking, two-way communication, hands-on experiences and workgroups (Davidson, Cope 2003: 139).

And this is because in 'real' meetings Collis maintains that:

> The social drink, the impromptu meeting, can be pure gold. It is nothing you can quantify; it's intuitive; gut-feel; keeping faith with serendipity. Who, for example, goes to a conference to listen to the presentations? It's networking that counts. Or the chance to bond with your boss or other colleagues for an extended time (2000: 64)

More generally, Mintzberg describes this as the *ritualistic* aspects of co-presence:

> Gossip about peers in the industry is exchanged; comments are made
> on encounters the participants have recently had or on published
> material they have recently read; important political events are
> discussed and background information is traded. It seems reasonable
> to conclude that the manager collects much information in these
> discussions, and that this fact makes the formal, face-to-face meeting
> a powerful medium. (cited in Schwartzman 1989: 75; and see Lodge
> 1983)

An ethnographic study of virtual teams operating on a global scale
highlights some similar affective characteristics. As a manager of a
virtual team remarks:

> We are having a global team meeting in two weeks time ... the big
> joke is – 'can't you do this virtually?' ... I say no we can't do it virtu-
> ally, we can get so far virtually but before we have a real good drink
> and a good meal and a good social chat at length we are not going to
> be a 'real team' ... We can then use technology to maintain it. (cited
> Nandhakumar 1999: 53)

Echoing Boden, Nandhakumar suggests that personalized trust relationships are essential for virtual team-working, and while trust
relationships can be to some degree sustained virtually, face-to-face
sociability is required to establish trust in the first place (1999: 55;
Boden 1994; see ch. 10 below).

Indeed networking and showing one's face directly seem important in business meetings especially those working in information and
communication industries! The ideal spaces of such multifaceted networking are said to be places with a cultural buzz. Workplaces move
away from the formal office occupied for work nine–five, to a 'club'
full of informal conversation, brainstorming and gossip. Indeed new
office buildings are increasingly designed around 'club space' that is
more for meeting up with colleagues on those days of co-presence
(Thrift 2000; Laurier, Buckner 2004). Co-present affective conversations are moving into the café scene some two centuries after Lloyds
Insurance of London first began in a coffee house and only later
acquired its own office buildings. Laurier and Buckner analyse how
stylized cafés are 'busy meeting grounds' where business and professional people meet up and hang out with workmates and conduct
informal meetings with clients and business partners, although lurking
in the background and 'ready-to-hand' will normally be various
virtual objects (2004; Wittel 2001). In networking places some distinctions between social life and professional life, friends, workmates and
clients get blurred. There is a proliferation of urban places of cool,

creative sociality and community where social networks travel to meet up, to do business and to have shared fun. Crucially, such face-to-face sociality and meeting places make small worlds of affective communion in otherwise impersonal 'big worlds'. One interviewee in Wittel's study stated:

> So these meetings and these conferences for me are about being seen and seeing other people again, saying hello being sort of on the back of their mind and it's usually like a two-minute conversation like how are you doing, how is your business and that is all it needs. (Wittel 2001: 67; Amin, Thrift 2002; Florida 2002)

So far moreover videoconferencing is a thinner version of physical meetings in terms of bodily idiom, sociality and affect. They are not *yet* like face-to-face meetings. As one virtual project team reflected: 'Because of the lack of eye contact we did not know when they watched us . . . it felt more like watching television' (Sarker, Sahay 2004: 11). Thus while virtual conferences may substitute for some face-to-face travel it seems that virtual meetings will mainly *supplement* traditional meetings, lectures, plenary sessions and conferences (Cairns et al. 2004: 290). Some argue that: 'videoconferencing is a perfect second tool after the first handshake' (Standage 2004). Video conferencing is sometimes more about global team working in that it enables people to be brought into meetings who would not normally attend if they had to travel (Collis 2000: 68).

A related development is that of teleworking. In the UK 7.4 per cent of all those in employment describe themselves as 'teleworkers' for all or part of each week. In recent years there has been a 13 per cent per annum increase (Hotopp 2002: 315). Other research shows that there has been a striking increase in businesses in the UK who provide remote access capability to their workers, almost doubling to around 60 per cent by 2000, higher than any other major economy (PIU 2002: 16). Teleworking seems to be increasing most rapidly among those who possess or at least have access to an 'office' at their 'real' workplace (Reeves 2002; PIU 2002: 16). This means that employees may live further from their notional workplace but such workplaces are intermittently visited by teleworkers. Indeed, as noted above: 'the opportunity to socialize with work peers is a key factor in job satisfaction. Work is about companionship as well as compensation' (Reeves 2002; Gillespie, Richardson 2004). Intermittent teleworking may alter workplaces, shifting from that of the formal 'office' occupied for 'work' from 9–5, to more of a 'club' where informal conversation, brainstorming and gossip are the main activities when staff are present. Thus some offices: 'have become a bit like clubs, in which employees can talk, brainstorm, meet people and catch up on gossip' (Cairncross 1997: 41).

Paralleling this has been the proliferation of diasporic 'communities' which extend the range, extent and significance of all forms of travel for far-flung families and households. Currently each year 200 m people in the world migrate, double the number in 1980 (http:// news.bbc.co.uk/1/hi/programmes/newsnight/4995388.stm/accessed 25.6.06).

For example, the internet is central to being a real 'Trini' in Trinidad. The use of the internet in Trinidad 'has permeated all sectors of society' being seen as hot, stylish and fashionable (Miller, Slater 2000: 27; and see Hiller, Franz 2004). As virtual travel becomes part of everyday life so it transforms the sense of who is near and far, present and absent. It changes the character of co-presence and thus we should regard: 'i[I]nternet media as continuous with and embedded in other social spaces, that they happen within mundane social structures and relations that they may transform but that they cannot escape into a self-enclosed cyberian apartness' (Miller, Slater 2000: 5). Here the very distinction between on-line and off-line is gradually dissolving since: 'many community ties are complex dances of face-to-face encounters, scheduled get-togethers, dyadic telephone class, emails to one person or several, and broader online discussions among those sharing interests' (Wellman 2001: 11).

This 'de-differentiation' between the virtual and other channels and communication technologies is particularly demonstrated in the 'social networking' internet sites such as Bebo, MySpace, Friendster, Faceparty and so on. These are huge 'communities', MyFriend having 40 m members in 2005. It is said that these sites blur the distinctions between online and offline. This MySpace generation of mainly teenagers and college students: 'live comfortably in both worlds at once' and indeed simultaneously use, move and multitask between many different types of media (www.businessweek.com/magazine/content/ 05_50/b3963001.htm: accessed 29.06.06). In the United States it is said that social networking sites shows the largest increases in computer use among young people. These seem to be relatively novel affective places.

Many of the backgrounded virtual objects I have so far referred to, and are further examined in chapters 9–11, are stationary and located within immobile boxes that lurk in the corner of offices, houses and other public spaces. There is therefore a distinction between mobile people (and mobile objects) and relatively immobile machines, even if the two are contingently assembled from

time-to-time to effect various social practices that
on the move.

Imaginative Travel

Historically the most influential 'stationary' machine has been the
television lurking in the corner of a billion or so rooms around the
world and providing extraordinarily heightened access to other
places, cultures and peoples. As early as the 1950s Heidegger foresaw
much of speeding up of social life through the 'shrinking' of the distances of time and space, the importance of 'instant information' on
the radio and the way that television is abolishing remoteness and
thus 'un-distancing' humans and things (Zimmerman 1990: 151, 209).
TV alters the very possibilities of interaction and dialogue, remaking
the public sphere through mediated forms of quasi-interaction, producing new ways of conceiving of self and identity (Gitlin 1980;
Meyrowitz 1985; Thompson 1995).

However, there have been many other forms of imaginative travel,
as people 'travel' elsewhere through memories, texts, guidebooks
and brochures, travel writing, photos, postcards, radio and film. Such
travel can sometimes substitute for physical travel (see de Botton
2002), but more often seems to generate the desire for travel and
for being bodily in other places. In the nineteenth century principally, written texts including guidebooks were crucial for imaginative travel; in the first half of the twentieth century, photographs and
the radio were central; while in the second half of the twentieth
century, film and TV became the main media for such travel (on the
cinema and travel, see Tzanelli 2004; Beeton 2005). I now consider
TV in more detail.

TV functions as object, media and culture (see Urry 2000: ch. 3).
First, it is an *object* to be purchased and that dwells in a particular
place within the layout of a given room. In its chosen location
it constitutes what is the home and where and how household
members should dwell within it (the TV also increasingly constitutes many other spaces: see McCarthy 2001). The TV set and
the rest of the furniture are mutually constituting, being part of the
background of everyday existence; 'ready-to-hand', unremarkable
and everyone knows what it does and how to use it (Scannell 1996:
ch. 7).

Second, the TV provides an exceptional array of *media*, of many
services, sources of information and modes of entertainment. These
media flow constantly and indiscriminately, constituting a televisual

low (Meyrowitz 1985: 81–2). Such media are consumed individually and co-operatively. Such outputs are time-of-the-day-coded (and in which there is a different attending to time at different moments). Part of this temporal-coding involves disclosing certain events as 'live'. The consuming of a live event enables one to be in two places. We can imaginatively travel and be at the World Cup, or New York as the 'twin towers' are destroyed, or the Asian Tsunami (Scannell 1996: 172).

Third, radio and TV generate the dominant communicational interchanges between households and the world beyond. TV is *culture*. The notion of TV as such a powerful yet differentiated culture parallels Heidegger's comment about the radio:

> I live in a dull, drab colliery village . . . a bus ride from third rate enter-
> tainments and a considerable journey from any educational, musical
> or social advantages of a first class sort. In such an atmosphere life
> becomes rusty and apathetic. Into this monotony comes a good radio
> set and my little world is transformed. (quoted Scannell 1996: 161)

Heidegger describes how the radio 'has so expanded its everyday environment that it has accomplished a de-severance of the "world" ' (quoted Scannell 1996: 167). By this he means bringing close, within range, abolishing distance or farness with events, places and people. 'Heidegger interprets the possibility of radio as transforming spatiality; as bringing things close and hence within the reach of concern; as making the . . . the great world beyond my reach . . . as accessible and available for me or anyone' (Scannell 1996: 167). TV thus *discloses* the public world of events, persons and places. People are thrown into the public world disclosed upon radio, television and now the internet. That public world travels into one's own 'little world' and brings them together (see Morley 2000). TV thus produces a something of a global village, blurring the private and the public, frontstage and backstage, and what is near and far. Little remains hidden from view as TV in particular makes almost everything public, on display, enabling one to travel imaginatively almost everywhere (see Meyrowitz 1985, Thompson 1995, on 'para-social interaction'). In particular, there are global events in which the world views itself from afar. Such extraordinary events get placed upon the world's stage. With such events, especially dating from after 1990 onwards, striking images of death, heroism, fame, tragedy or excess, come to be globally circulated, recognized and consumed, images central to the iconography of citizens of the globe able to travel to and consume 'the globe' itself (Szerszynski, Urry 2006).

Mobile Communicative Travel

However, in recent research in Britain young people reported that their mobile phone is in fact more important to them than their TV (Carphone Warehouse 2006: 8). In this section I examine how communications are now on the move, often travelling and corporeally interwoven with the person (and indeed with TV programmes also accessible on those mobile machines).

An early 'mobile machine' was the Sony Walkman that travelled with the user/wearer. It is:

> virtually an extension of the skin. It is fitted, moulded, like so much else in modern consumer culture, to the body itself . . . It is designed for movement – for mobility, for people who are always out and about, for travelling light. It is part of the required equipment of the modern 'nomad' . . . it is testimony to the high value which the culture of late-modernity places on mobility. (du Gay et al. 1997: 23–4)

The original Sony Walkman was provided with two headphone sockets so that, used indoors and in a stationary mode, two people could listen together. However, it soon became clear that the Walkman would be used more individualistically especially outdoors as people were on the move, walking, travelling by train, plane and car. Thus as with many developments examined here, the Walkman:

> was not simply presented as a device for individual listening – it became this through a process in which production and consumption were articulated . . . Consumer activities were crucial to the introduction, modification and subsequent redevelopment and marketing of this product. (du Gay et al. 1997: 59)

The iPod, the laptop computer, the DVD player and the use of the mobile phone for TV have all drawn upon and developed further this 'privatised' augmentation of the moving body. It should though be noted that the book, magazine and newspaper, which developed as earlier means of communications, were also portable.

Mobile telephony has taken this personalized portability to new limits. There are now more new mobile phones than landline phones around the world. It is thought that two billion of the world's population are mobile phone users (compared with one billion in 2004). Nokia predicts that about two-thirds of the world's population will be mobile phone users by 2015 (www.guardian.co.uk/g2/story/0,,1806639,00.html#article_continue: accessed 29.06.06). These mobile communications are generating new affordances: to produce a new set of fashionable objects that are 'ready-to-hand' even while people are on the move; to make corporeal movement almost always needing to be augmented by mobile communication devices; to shift relationships further to a person-to-person connectivity; to produce major new components of 'network capital'; to engender new sociabilities on the move; to develop 'interspaces' between home, work and leisure sites; and to shift time systems from that of 'punctuality' to a more informal 'fluid' system of coordination. I begin with the last of these before examining these various other novel social patterns.

In chapter 2 I noted the significance Simmel attached to the watch. He maintains that:

> if all clocks and watches in Berlin would suddenly go wrong in different ways, even if only by one hour, all economic life and communication of the city would be disrupted for a long time. Thus, the technique of metropolitan life is unimaginable without the most punctual integration of all activities and mutual relations into a stable and impersonal time schedule. (1997: 177)

Thus complex systems of relationships depend upon meetings and activities being punctual, timetabled, rational, a system or 'structure of the highest impersonality' often involving distance-keeping politeness (Simmel 1997: 178; Toiskallio 2002: 171). This 'system-ness' of mobility is crucial and results in the individual becoming 'a mere cog in an enormous organization of things and powers'; as a result 'life is made infinitely easy for the personality in that stimulations, interests, uses of time and consciousness are offered to it from all sides' (Simmel 1997: 184).

Mobile telephony may be changing this. In research reported elsewhere it is shown that a shift is taking place, from time as 'punctuality' to time as 'fluid and negotiated' (Larsen, Urry, Axhausen 2006). Communication technologies more generally play a major role in facilitating co-present meetings. Most telephone calls are brief concerned with coordinating face-to-face meetings and desynchronized social life more generally (Ling, Ytrri 2002; Ling 2004). And recent research shows that coordination can take place during meetings, when people have already met up (Larsen, Urry, Axhausen 2006: ch. 8). Some respondents do not 'go out' with one group but with a larger mobile phone connected network of both strong and weak ties. People text each other about 'happening' places, 'private' parties and interesting people, and they are likely to meet with people that they did not go out with in the first place. As a respondent describes:

If I'm in one bar and they're in another, I might text them and say it's not very good here, really quiet or really busy, we'll come ... where are you and you'll go oh I'm in Varsity and it's really really good. So I'll go to Varsity then. It's just like having a constant network between all of you. (male doorman, early twenties; Larsen, Urry, Axhausen 2006: 121)

Thus 'going out' can involve continuous coordination, negotiation and movement with people who are present as well as those who are absent. This provides opportunities to meet new people and come across 'happening' places. Texting is often impromptu and informal, and one text will often be sent to several people. This also affords fluid meeting cultures with recurrent circulating invitations to 'join in' (see Hulme, Truch 2005):

It might be like you're sitting in the office or 5 or 6 offices around Liverpool and say we're all going out for a drink, do you want to come. And it happens instantaneously sort of thing. It is more manageable because you've got that instant communication. (male architect, early thirties; Larsen, Urry, Axhausen 2006: 122)

With mobile connectivity, there is less need to wait for people to 'return home' before arrangements can be made. Respondents explain how they often call friends to say that they are in the neighbourhood and ask whether they fancy meeting up for a quick beer or coffee. The clock-time of pocket/wrist watches is thus supplemented by a negotiated 'network' or fluid time of mobile communications. Now people can not only be on time or running early or late, but also 'refuse to accept' clock-time by texting to say they are late or by suggesting a new place or a later time. While some respondents were annoyed that many people are less bothered about being on time, most agree that people are more relaxed about running late as long as they call or text to say they are behind schedule. 'I think because everybody carries their mobile with them, it doesn't matter if you are late for something' (fitness trainer, early thirties; Larsen, Urry, Axhausen 2006: 119). There is less of an obligation to be on time but rather to inform others if one is going to be late. Whereas coordination was once finalized before departure, it is now often negotiated and performed on the move. Thus clock-time is increasingly supplemented by a negotiated 'network' or fluid time of mobile communications. Now people can not only be on time or running early or late, but also 'refuse to accept' clock-time by emailing or texting that they are late or suggesting a new place or a later time.

A recent survey has suggested two-thirds of people are regularly late when meeting people, with the mobile phone particularly blamed (http://news.bbc.co.uk/1/hi/magazine/5128394.stm: accessed 29.06.06). Thus mobile phones can moreover eliminate the need for rigid pre-coordination as people can be in 'perpetual contact' regardless of physical location (Katz and Aakhus 2002). Mobile 'phonespaces' afford fluid and instantaneous meeting cultures where venue, time, group and agenda can be negotiated with the next call or text.

Research further shows that people may be bolder in whom they invite to events if they can hide behind the informal and/or collective nature of emails and text messages. Mobile phones, with their multi-destination messages, multiple contacts and informality, are effective at distributing casual invitations to 'join in', and information about 'happening' places, to many weak ties. One young architect explains how he sends cinema invitations by text every week to a large network of people at the college where he works, and people just text if they wish to 'join in' (this also preclude the potential awkward experience of having one-to-one phone conversation with 'weak ties'; Larsen, Urry, Axhausen 2006: 123). The significance of 'weak ties', informal co-presence and 'new faces' seem to increase dramatically in the era of text messages and email (Wittel 2001).

This is further facilitated by 'flexible car systems'. Whereas trains and pocket watches were early modern twins, mobile phones and cars are the late modern twins in an era where social networks are dispersed and coordination and travel are necessary for social life (Larsen, Urry, Axhausen 2006: ch. 7).

Mobile phones in providing the affordances for a fluid, mobile meetings culture reinforce 'person-to-person' communities and 'networked individualism', the person is the portal (Wellman 2001: 238; see on Japan, Ito, Okabe, Matsuda 2005). Whereas the emblematic technology of 'place-to-place' connectivity was the fixed landline telephone, the mobile is emblematic of 'person-to-person' networks. 'Mobile phones afford a fundamental liberation from place' (Wellman 2001: 238). While landlines eliminate the necessity for physical proximity, they reinforce the need to be present at specific places. Personalized, wireless worlds afford 'networked individualism', each person is, so to say, the engineer of his/her own ties and networks, and always connected (batteries and masts permitting), no matter where she/he is going and staying. As Licoppe reports: 'the mobile phone is portable, to the extent of seeming to be an extension of its owner, a personal object constantly there, at hand . . . Wherever they go, individuals seem to carry their network of connections which could be activated telephonically at any moment' (2004: 139). The mobile phone frees people from spatial fixity, is the node for each person's social network and is one of the most common items used on train journeys (Lyons, Jain, Holley 2007; Geser 2004: 4). This pattern of networked individualism: 'suits and reinforces mobile life-styles and physically dispersed relationships' (Wellman 2001: 239). Or as mobile phone researcher Townsend puts it:

> The old schedule of minutes, hours, days, and weeks becomes shattered into a constant stream of negotiations, reconfigurations, and rescheduling. One can be interrupted or interrupt friends and colleagues at any time. Individuals live in this phonespace they can never let it go, because it is their primary link to the temporally, spatially fragmented network of friends and colleagues they have constructed for themselves. (2004)

Such a widespread mobile phone culture affords small worlds of communicative co-presence in the midst of widespread patterns of absence, distance and disconnection. Absent others are only a call or text away so people can be in communication with significant others while moving through a sea of strangers (Roos 2001). A Cellnet-funded study suggests that mobile phoning and texting are about networked gossiping, 'anytime, anyplace, anywhere', of living in 'connected presence' with one's more or less dispersed social network (Fox 2001). Perpetual gossip at-a-distance helps people live in fragmented worlds where they will not bump into their weak ties on a regular basis. Fox enthusiastically argues that:

> We no longer live in the kind of small, close-knit tribes or communities . . . where we would naturally be in daily contact with the members of our social network . . . Families and friends are scattered . . . We are constantly on the move, spending much of our time commuting to and from work either among strangers on trains and buses, or alone and isolated in our cars . . . [before the mobile phone] there was no telephonic equivalent of the regular brief and breezy encounters in a village or small community, where frequent passing exchanges . . . ensured that everyone felt connected to their social and support network . . . Mobile phones are re-creating the more natural, humane communication patterns of pre-industrial times: we are using space-age technology to return to stone-age gossip. (2001)

So, widespread mobile phone ownership enables individualized yet connected small worlds of communication in the midst of absence, distance and disconnection. However, as noted previously there appears to be simultaneously both more individualization *and* more

dependence upon others and upon communicative systems. It is difficult to escape these systems given the significance of communications for the coordination of a flexible social life including visits with
significant others. Human agency and social networks are thus com-
plexly interwoven with mobile phones, email and the means of corporeal movement.

People are especially busy calling and texting when in motion
and transit, and modern cities are less characterized by 'isolation'
but by connectivity, of private worlds of distant talk. Trains, buses,
cars, streets and waiting lounges are places of much communication
and where travel time can be made 'productive' (Lyons, Urry 2005).
The mobile phone seems to be most useful for those working on
the move, providing important communications with co-workers
and clients (Laurier 2004). Over one-fifth of rail passengers thought
that having such devices with them made their train journey a lot
better. Those travelling first class were especially likely to consider
that such communication devices improved their time use (Lyons,
Jain, Holley 2007). Mobile phones have become 'travel partners' to
such extent that people feel incomplete if leaving for a journey
without it:

> I'll know about it if it's not there because you know you can't leave
> the house and you think something's missing. It's got to be with me
> definitely. It's got to be with me. (male sales advisor, late twenties;
> Larsen, Urry, Axhausen 2006: 113)

These young adults describe their mobile phones as prosthetic, as
physically coterminous with their bodies. Mobile phones allow them
to be 'proper' social beings. Without them, they are 'lost' being
dependent upon such systems:

> I've lost it once. This sounds so bad, but it was the worst week of my
> life. I didn't have a clue what I was doing or anything . . . the worst
> thing was all my numbers were on it. (doorman, early twenties; Larsen,
> Urry, Axhausen 2006: 113)

I have noted related research that suggests that new social routines
are engendering novel spaces that lie 'in-between' home, work and
social life, forming 'interspaces'. These are places where different
'fields' or 'domains' of activity overlap. Interspace is important for
the reorganizing of 'life' or what we might describe as the 'overheads'
of maintaining social networks. This merging and overlapping of
fields engenders simultaneity rather than linearity and also means

that identities may well be less place-based and more engendered through relations made and sustained on the move, in liminal 'inter-spaces' (Hulme, Truch 2005: 141). The use of phones, mobiles, laptops, SMS messaging, wireless communications and so on, involve both making arrangements and doing the business of social life while 'on the move' (see data in Hulme, Truch 2005: 142–3). Thus particu-larly important is how 'impression management' is now multi-channel and something that can be worked out in physical absence from the 'other'. So 'face-work' is accompanied by text-work, email-work, phone-work (Hulme, Truch 2005: 144–5; not forgetting previous letter writing-work as in Marx's voluminous letter writing).

Thus mobile technologies affect social interactions even when people are 'face-to-face'. Co-presence and distant communications increasingly intermingle. Unmediated body-to-body talk is dwindling in modern societies that are saturated with machines, images and communication devices being ready-to-hand (Fortunati 2005; Thrift 2004b). People are increasingly 'face-to-face-to-mobile-phone' as the mobile phone is brought along even when people meet socially (Katz, Aakhus 2002a: 2). Face-to-face meetings transform into face-to-interface interactions when computer documents are worked upon, PowerPoint presentations begin, mobile phones ring and so on. Face-to-face meetings are mediated and connected to other meet-ings; they are typified by 'absent presence' (Gergen 2002; Callon, Law, Urry 2004). As Wittel says:

> it is impossible to separate face-to-face interactions from interactions over distance. In urban spaces the idea of an uninterrupted face-to-face sociality, disentangled from technological devices, is becoming a myth. More and more, we are experiencing an integration of long-distance communication in our realms of face-to-face interaction . . . It is hard to imagine a dinner of, let's say, four businessmen without a mobile ringing. (2001: 70)

Thus people increasingly can be described as 'face-to-face-to-mobile-phone', with the mobile phones brought along even to 'purely' social events (Katz and Aakhus 2002a: 2). Plant notes how:

> Several Birmingham entrepreneurs say they use their mobiles as means of deliberately absenting themselves from their present environments and so keeping other people at bay: 'If I arrive at a meeting where I don't know anyone, I play for time and composure by doing things with my mobile'. This sends out other messages to the room as well: it says that one is busy and not to be disturbed, and temporarily extends one's personal space. (2000: 62)

Thus face-to-face meetings are no longer just face-to-face; they are becoming virtual meetings. Face-to-face meetings are mediated and connected to other meetings; they are typified by the 'absent presence' of others. As Callon and Law maintain more generally, 'presence is not reducible to copresence . . . copresence is both a location and a relation' (2004: 6, 9). Meetings are now rarely a sequence of purely face-to-face-encounters within specific physical spaces (Katz, Aakhus 2002b; Licoppe 2004; Ling 2004).

One particular set of emergent relations engendered through the affordances of mobile devices are 'underground' social gatherings or what Rheingold terms 'smart mobs' (2002). There are emergent phenomena which possess some similarities with flocks of birds: 'Like a well-choreographed dance troupe, the birds veer to the left in unison . . . The flock is organized without an organizer, coordinated without a coordinator' (Resnick 1997: 3). Mobiles engender new kinds of crowd that have significant roles in contemporary politics, as in the Battle of Seattle in 1999, the change of government in the Philippines in 2001, the UK fuel protest in 2000, the many critical mass cycle rallies, and the anti-globalization movement (Rheingold 2002: ch. 7; Chesters, Welsh 2005). Thus what Rheingold terms the 'power of the mobile many' engenders 'mobile ad hoc social networks' (2002: 169). And the instantaneous responsiveness of the communications on the move means that such mobile social networks can very quickly form as tipping points are encountered and very large numbers of people can tip into a smart mob, a moving swarm of people walking, running, cycling, driving, flying and so on.

One consequence of these various developments is that mobile phones (and increasingly blackberries and communicators) are not 'extravagant' and 'frivolous' but 'necessary evils', naturally interwoven with the human body and always at-hand so making a mobile, communicating life (just) possible. So when people misplace their mobiles they are 'lost', physically disabled because they have had removed their 'natural' ability to talk with absent others, and socially, because they are disconnected from their networks. Among young adults mobiles are 'lifelines' between network members because few remember more than a few phone numbers. A landline connection cannot satisfactorily substitute a 'lost' mobile phone. People are lost in a no-man's land of nonconnectivity; without tools for coordination they would experience less corporeal travel and reduced face-to-face encounters.

Some mobile affordances can be seen in 'mobile offices'. Work activities once mainly carried out in offices are sometimes now conducted in cars. The car combined with the mobile phone produces significant affordances as it is re-assembled as an office (Laurier 2005). Work materials can be synchronized and connected up to other company members while 'on the road'. The mobile and car-based telematics function as actants, taking messages as voice-mail, screening calls and providing information about traffic delays and alternative routings (especially with the increasing merging of various car-based mobile communications). This 'mobile office' appears to be a system of multiple and overlapping mobilities constituting a fluid and flexible workforce. The mobile is regularly used to rearrange the day as traffic often impedes the smooth planned for series of meetings and encounters, involving what has been called a 'playful opportunism'. And even traffic jams can be used to make numerous phone-calls, preparing for subsequent meetings. Team working is achieved by the skilful use of mobile telephony so as to maintain connections both with those back at the office (including making meeting arrangements, dictating letters and so on), as well as with others elsewhere on the road.

Transport *and* communication technologies are thus 'travel partners', components of 'network capital'. We might see this as a process of co-evolution, between new forms of social networking on the one hand, and extensive forms of physical travel, now normally enhanced by new communications, on the other. These sets of processes reinforce and extend each other in ways that are difficult to reverse. This also means that crucial to the character of modern societies is that of 'network capital', comprising access to communication technologies, affordable and well-connected transport and safe meeting places. Without sufficient network capital people will suffer social exclusion since many social networks are more far-flung (see ch. 9).

The mobile phone is an early forerunner of many other miniaturized machines discussed further in chapter 13. For the present I sketch one aspect of the argument to be developed in detail in that chapter. The twenty-first century will be the century of 'inhabited machines', machines inhabited by individuals or very small groups of individuals. They include walkmans, mobile phones, PDAs, the individual TV, the networked computer/internet, the individualized smart car/bike, virtual reality 'travel', tele-immersion sites, helicopters and smart small aircraft and other micro-mobiles yet to emerge. Such machines are desired for their style, smallness, lightness and demonstrate a physical form often closely interwoven with the corporeal. It is through inhabiting machines that humans will come to 'life'. Further, machines only function because they are so inhabited; such machines come to 'life' when they are humanly inhabited. These machines are miniaturized, privatized, digitized and mobilized.

These machines depend upon *digital* power that is substantially separate from material form or presence and involves exceptional levels of miniaturization and portability. These machines re-order Euclidean time–space relations, bending, stretching and compressing time–space. Such machines means that inhabiting them is to be connected to, or to be at home with, 'sites' across the world – while simultaneously such sites can monitor, observe and trace each inhabited machine. These machines are producing a 'liquid modernity' of interdependent flows of text, messages, people, information and images (Bauman 2000).

Many nineteenth and twentieth-century machines will survive into this new century – such as film, the family car, the railway, air travel – but they will be transformed in part as inhabiting machines (film as medium for internet, or email located within the car, for example). The global reach of such machines means that inhabiting them is to be connected to, or to be at home with, 'sites' across the globe. And there is heightened convergence between all such machines, as innovations from one chaotically flow into the other.

Such mobile machines thus reconfigure humans as physically moving bodies and as bits of mobile information and image, as individuals exist both through, and beyond, their mobile bodies. These inhabiting machines enable people to be more readily mobile through space, or to stay in one place, because of the capacity for 'self-retrieval' of personal information at other times or spaces. People inhabit networks of information, image and movement through such machines. 'Persons' thus occur as various nodes in these multiple machines of inhabitation and mobility. Such machines are inhabited, not just used and not just enabling or constraining. The machines only work when they are inhabited and when they are on the move. To employ such machines is to become in effect physically incorporated within them.

Conclusion

Thus the dichotomies of real/unreal, face-to-face/life on the screen, immobile/mobile, community/virtual and presence/absence are not helpful here and need to be dispensed with. While as Nokia says 'It's good to connect' there are many interdependent ways of so doing and consequences thereof. I examined the contemporary emergence of powerful, interdependent knowledge-based systems that increasingly through new software are organizing production, consumption, travel and communications around the world. I developed the distinction between various modes of the apparently 'natural order' that constitute the background to human life. And this was linked to the apparently 'networked' character of the global order. And I showed that almost because of that networked nature of work, friendship and family, meetings are especially significant and have so far not been much replaced by virtual communications. Imaginative travel especially via TV was also examined and plays a significant role in the 'de-severance' of the world.

Mobile communications were then examined and it was noted that these fashionable objects are 'ready-to-hand' especially in augmenting corporeal movement. They shift relationships further to a person-to-person connectivity and engendering new kinds of sociabilities on the move. They develop 'interspaces' and shift time systems from 'punctuality' to a more informal 'fluid' system of coordination. These mobile means of communications are increasingly combined with humans, forming new material worlds and inhabiting machines. These machinic hybrids involve 'a contradiction between nearness and remoteness, or mobility and fixation . . . at the push of a button, territories dissolve, oppositions of distant and close, motion and stasis, inside and out, collapse; identities are marginalized and simulated, and collectivities lose their borders' (Bogard 2000: 28). Bogard characterizes such a collapse of distance as an impure or indeterminate relationship, neither one nor two, as a fractal space: '[t]his blurring of boundaries between the monad and the dyad is an excellent image of the rapidly evolving symbiosis of bodies and computers, groups and communications networks, societies and cybernetic systems' (Bogard 2000: 40). Connections and communities are simultaneously private and public, intimate and distant. These could be described as new fractal social spaces, as each realm folds over, under, through and beyond each other in striking new social topologies. These are oscillatory, flickering, both here-and-there, both inside and outside, rather like a Mobius strip.

This chapter thus concludes the second part of this book. Various forms of movement have been explored and I especially examined the interconnections between them. In the next part I turn to some of the more general issues that the mobility paradigm also addresses, where these interdependent, dynamic mobility systems are shown to have profound consequences for different social practices, for emerging patterns of socio-spatial exclusion and for the contours of social networks, meetings and places, now and into the future. I examine various mobility scenarios.

Part 3

Societies and Systems on the Move

9

Gates to Heaven and Hell

> Mobility is one of the aspects of freedom, and as such it is some-
> thing new and exciting for women: being free to move around,
> to go where one wants to is a right that women have only just
> started to gain
>
> (Rosi Braidotti 1994: 256)

In the second part of this book I elaborated various mobility systems
and briefly examined some interconnections between them. A wide
array of materials were deployed to bring out the centrality of these
systems to the nature, character and emergent features of contemporary social life. In the remaining chapters I use this material to 'recon-
struct' the social sciences along the lines of argumentation I first
presented in *Sociology Beyond Societies* (Urry 2000). In this chapter
I consider some of the relationships between social inequality and
mobilities.

Historically much literature on social inequality ignored the
complex ways in which the notion of 'space' makes significant differences to understanding economic, political and cultural processes
that produce and reinforce social inequalities (see the classic critique
by Massey 1994b). However, over the past two decades various
analyses of social inequality have begun to address such deficiencies,
critiquing national 'social mobility' studies and drawing upon various
sources to reveal the specificities of various non-national class and
other structures and cultures (see Devine, Savage, Scott, Crompton
2005).

More generally it is increasingly understood how various mobilities fragment national societies through the emergence of local,

regional, sub-national, networked, diasporic and global economies, identities and citizenships (see Urry 2000). Scott concludes that there are: 'no longer any territorial coincidence between the political forms of states, the flow of economic transactions, and the cultural and communal boundaries of "societies"' (1997: 253). Especially significant are the flows of people, monies, environmental risks, taxation-revenues and information which partially evade control by national states who increasingly function as 'gamekeepers' or regulators rather than 'gardeners' (Majone 1996; Bauman 2000; Urry 2000).

These changes transform the analysis of social class that has been historically rooted in both data and arguments derived from the 'golden age' of organized, national capitalism (see Lash, Urry 1987; 1984). Up to the early 1970s in a dozen or so north Atlantic rim societies it was reasonable to investigate 'nationally' organized and structured social classes and also that such classes were nationally inflected through the social divisions of gender, age and ethnicity (see Walby 2008). However, in what Lash and I term 'disorganized capitalism' conditions are very different. National states fragment or are drawn into supranational entities so this: 'adds a further potential challenge to the [historic] association between class structures and national states' (Breen and Rottman 1998: 16). With regard to the capitalist class, Scott argues that: 'national capitalist classes themselves are being increasingly fragmented along the lines of the globalized circuits of capital and investment that they are involved in' (1997: 312). Some claim that there are emergent 'transnational capitalist classes' that are highly mobile, detached from national class contexts and that will through their 'mobile habitus' develop global solidarity and cohesion (Sklair 1995; Scott 1997: 312–13). Likewise there has been the growth of powerful professions whose taskscapes are partially global and who can be said to dwell in many places located along diverse routeways. Reich argues that as: 'b[B]arriers to cross-border flows of knowledge, money, and tangible products are crumbling; groups of people in every nation are joining global webs' (1991: 172). As a further consequence, determinants of status within a given 'society' are as much derived from these global informational and cultural flows as they are from status processes endogenous to each society. There is what Lash and I term 'disorganized capitalism' with a powerful, structuring 'economy of signs and spaces' (1987; 1994).

Specifically multiple mobilities become central to the structuring of inequality within contemporary 'disorganized' societies. Bauman summarizes what he sees as the significance of this:

Mobility climbs to the rank of the uppermost among the coveted values – and the freedom to move, perpetually a scarce and unequally distributed commodity, fast becomes the main stratifying factor of our late-modern or postmodern times. (1998: 2)

However, what is absent in this analysis – especially within sociology – is exactly how these multiple mobilities do in fact make a difference to the contemporary nature of social stratification, to entering the gates of heaven or hell. How can such mobilities be theorized? What are the consequences for social inequality beyond that of social class? What kind of evidence is available to support these claims? This chapter seeks to examine in more detail the mobile processes that engender and reinforce social inequality in contemporary societies, beginning in the next section with some connections between various notions of citizenship and inequality. In the following section I consider the main way in which mobilities have entered this debate and this is through the notion of 'access' to activities, values and goods. I argue however that there are many dimensions of such access and that in order to develop this notion it is necessary to deploy the concept of network capital. This I set out in the fourth section where I seek to establish network capital alongside other forms of capital elaborated by Bourdieu. I also note some recent changes in the ways in which states and private corporations are securing populations in ways both structured by social inequalities and which reinforce such inequalities. In the conclusion I examine some issues concerned with the rights to movement and whether and in so far these rights can or ought to be realized. I argue that the rights to certain kinds of movement are exclusionary and that such rights should be recouched in terms of various capabilities of economic and social life. The empirical importance of mobilities paradoxically means that our understanding of rights should be de-mobilized. I argue against the fetishism of movement, paralleling Marx's nineteenth-century critique of the fetishism of commodities.

Citizenship and inequality

In this section I document the 'classic' notion of citizenship that lies behind the conventional national framing of social stratification. T. H. Marshall characterizes citizenship as: 'the claim of all to enjoy these conditions [of civilized life] is a claim to be admitted to a share in the social heritage, which in turn means a claim to be accepted as full members of the society, that is, as citizens' (Marshall, Bottomore 1992: 6; Urry 2000: ch. 7). According to Marshall such a citizenship was established in England over a number of centuries: civil rights acquired in the eighteenth century, political rights during the nine-teenth century, and social rights in the first half of the twentieth century (Marshall, Bottomore 1992: 17; Bulmer and Rees 1996). Marshall describes citizenship as a 'developing institution' that creates an image against which achievement can be measured and towards which people can aspire for further gains. It is thus partly normative – that citizenship ought: 'to embrace the majority of the population [in a society] in a supportive system of social security' (Turner 1993b).

This kind of citizenship is based upon national risks that face anyone living within a specific territory, national rights that those possessing full membership should receive, and national duties that are appropriate for all that society's citizens. Central to this notion of citizenship is both the nation-state providing a single, stable and exhaustive national identity and a civil society organized around a single nation. These features ensure a nation-state that is able to striate the space surrounding it, clearly distinguishing its people and institutions inside its borders from those outside. Especially impor-tant in this is what Billig terms 'banal nationalism', a set of practices and discourses that articulates in various forms the identities of each society through its mundane differences from each other. These dif-ferences are articulated thorough waving celebratory flags, singing national anthems, flying flags on public buildings, identifying with national sports-teams and heroes, being addressed in the media as a member of a given society, celebrating its independence day and so on (Billig 1995; Smith 1986: 228).

This national, organized capitalist society presumes a citizenship of stasis, of the rights and duties attributed to, and available to, those living and working within a given territory by virtue of their long-membership. 'Citizenship went hand in hand with settlement' (Bauman 2000: 13). Underlying this is social governmentality or what Rose terms: 'Government from "the social point of view"' (1996: 328). In Britain:

> codifiers such as Beveridge and Marshall constructed a vision in which security against hardship, like hardship itself, was social and to be provided by measures of benefit and insurance that, in name at least, were to be termed 'universal', including all within a unified 'social citi-zenship'. (Rose 1996: 345)

Marshall presumes that social citizenship is the ultimate stage of societal achievement.

However, with the development of 'global complexity' there is a hollowing out of this national social domain (Rose 1996; Urry 2000, 2003a; Walby 2008). In chapter 1, I noted twelve different modes of international movement in the global order, modes that depend upon and presuppose new modes of travelling and espe-cially of communicating. These modes of corporeal travel that I elaborated are asylum and refugee travel, business and profes-sional travel; discovery travel of students, au pairs and other young people; medical travel; military mobility; post-employment travel; 'trailing travel'; travel across the key nodes within a given diaspora; travel of service workers; tourist travel; visiting friends and relatives; and work-related travel. These modes of international movement do not so much weaken the state (see Hirst, Thompson 1999) but to hollow out civil *society* and its organizing power over both the life-chances *and* the life-styles of its 'members'. Through the transformations of corporeal, communicative, virtual and imaginative travel that especially develop from around 1990 (see ch. 8), sets of social relations no longer primarily flow within and through a national economy, state and especially its civil society. The everyday practices of civil society are less *societally* structured through the interlinking impact of these modes of international movement in the global era. It should be noted that civil societies were never societally organized in much of the world outside the north Atlantic rim.

This hollowing out of the social has many consequences but I note two here (see Urry 2000, for an earlier formulation of a 'sociology beyond societies'). First, many citizenships and identities proliferate, competing with and in cases undermining a national identity and citi-zenship. These include minority citizenship involving the rights to enter another society and then to remain there and receive rights and duties; consumer citizenship concerned with rights to be provided with appropriate goods, services and information by private and public organizations; mobility citizenship concerned with the rights and responsibilities of visitors to other places and other cultures; and various identities of gender, sexual orientation, ethnicity, generation and so on (Urry 2000: ch. 7). These are all in part at least citizenships of flow, concerned with the mobilities across various borders, of risks, travellers, consumer goods and services, cultures, migrants and visitors, and of the rights and duties that such mobile citizenry should enjoy.

Second, the idea of national citizenship loses some ground to more universal models of membership located within a de-territorialized notion of a person's universal rights (Soysal 1994: 3; Bauböck 1994; Walby 2005). The hesitant emergence of something of a post-national citizenship stems from greater global interdependence, increasingly overlapping memberships of different kinds of citizenship, and the emergence of universalistic rules and conceptions regarding human rights formalized by various international organizations, codes and laws, including both the rights to movement and the rights to an ecological citizenship concerned with a citizenship of the earth (UN, UNESCO, ILO, EU, Council of Europe, Geneva Conventions, European Human Rights Convention and so on). But to be clear here. I am not suggesting that empirically there are rights to receive unconditional hospitality in each country around the world. Rather my claim is that there are various rights, institutions and rules that enable claims to be made about such movement and these post-national rights, institutions and rules implicate entities that are not simply 'nation-centric' (Derrida 2001: 20–2).

I now consider how to analyse the effects of such new mobilities and citizenships upon some aspects of social inequality and to the realization that citizenship should not be formulated in a static, societal fashion. I begin with various UK debates engendered out of the concept of 'access'.

'Access'

This formulation in UK debates has opened up the examination of citizenship and inequality through something of a mobilities lens (see Cass, Shove, Urry 2003, on the following). A lack of citizenship or new kinds of social exclusion are said to be resulting not only from social inequality *per se*, but also from a combination of distance, inadequate transport and limited ways of communicating. It is also maintained that these socio-spatial exclusions are unfair or discriminatory and that local and national governments should reduce such socio-spatial inequality (SEU 2002; Ferguson 2004; Kenyon 2006). In *Making the Connections: Transport and Social Exclusion* the UK's Social Exclusion Unit argues that: 'We are analysing the nature of transport barriers to accessing work, learning, healthcare, and other key services and activities; and developing policies to remove them' (SEU 2002; Cass, Shove, Urry 2005). *Inter alia* the Report notes that young people with driving licenses are twice as likely to get jobs as those without; that nearly one-half of 16–18 year olds experience difficulty in paying for transport to get to their place of study; that almost one-third of car-less households have difficulty in accessing their local hospital; that children from the lowest social class are five times more likely to die in road accidents than those from the highest social class; and that twice as many people without a car find it hard to 'access' their friends. This Report concludes both that: 'social costs have not been given due weight in transport policy', and that 'local authorities do not routinely assess whether people can get to work, learning, health care or other activities in a reasonable time or cost' (SEU 2002: 4). Various other reports and studies similarly document a 'poverty of access' resulting from various mobility-relevant aspects of social exclusion (Church, Frost, Sullivan 2000; Kenyon, Lyons, Rafferty 2002; Kenyon 2006: 104–5).

I argue elsewhere that there are in fact four components to the notion of 'access'; these are economic, physical, organizational, and temporal (see Cass, Shove, Urry 2003, for more detail; Church, Frost, Sullivan 2000; Kenyon, Lyons, Rafferty 2001; Kenyon 2006). Thus first, all mobilities require *economic* resources and this is the largest constraint upon social equality (even walking needs decent shoes or boots: see Michael 2000). Economic resources are necessary in order to own or use a car/taxi, although there are in many western societies the 'motoring poor' (Froud, Johal, Leaver, Williams 2005); to access a 'point of contact' through ownership or availability of telephone/ mobile/ 'secretary'/ email (see Brown, Green, Harper 2002); to purchase intermittent long-distance travel by car/ coach/ train/ plane/ ship; and to stopover and meet up with friends, family or workmates while 'away' (Larsen, Urry, Axhausen 2006). Roughly speaking those with most access to travel are also those with best access to communications 'at-a-distance', although the low entry cost of the mobile phone, the minute costs of SMS messaging and the cheapness of internet cafes is altering some of this.

Also, there are various *physical* aspects of access: an inability to get into or to drive a car; the difficulties involved in walking certain distances or within particular kinds of unsafe, unlit, uneven environments; the physical difficulties involved in entering particular sites; limitations on the capacity to read timetabled information; physical constraints upon carrying or moving large or weighty objects and so on.

Moreover, people's ability to access services and facilities depends upon how they are *organized*, such as the ability to negotiate lifts with others (Raje 2004, on UK Asian households). With regard to public transport, not only is it important to be near a bus stop or railway station but also to reach various destinations, to be provided with safe, secure and productive travel experiences, good conditions of waiting and interchange locations, and high frequency, reliability and punctuality (Cass, Shove, Urry 2003). Moreover, the increased 'privatization' of public transport and simultaneous capitalist commercialization a 'splintering urbanism' develops between 'hot' zones, where most consumers are located and whose custom is desired, and cold zones (Graham, Marvin 2001; Cass, Shove, Urry 2003; see Pennycook, Barrington-Craggs, Smith, Bullock 2001, on the complexities of mapping such zones in Bradford). The travel poor and time-dependent in the cold zones have few choices waiting in unsafe bus stops or unstaffed stations or lacking the smart cards necessary for premium places (see Hamilton, Jenkins, Hodgson, Turner 2005, on the gendering of these zones).

Access also depends upon temporal *availability*. Thus many people find no 'public' transport before or after working hours, or that services to cheap shopping centres are unavailable when they are free to shop, or that leisure activities have to be curtailed because of the time and frequency of services. Also there is the question of 'time sovereignty' and the degree to which people do or do not have control over, or flexibility built into, their temporal regime. The 'socially excluded' may include those who have extensive resources of time (and therefore a high degree of flexibility), but also the low-paid, for whom the pressures of punctuality reduce their 'time sovereignty' and for whom temporal co-ordination is highly important (Breedveld 1998). Access is therefore also a matter of timing, time resources and time management especially in relationship to the patterning of domestic schedules and the routines of co-ordination around which household life revolves.

Thinking about the mobility processes that engender social exclusion is a major step forward. But the idea that social exclusion might be reduced through improving *access* encounters various problems. First, 'accessing' other people, places and services at geographical distance is not something that is fixed but is continuously changing since what is necessary for 'social' inclusion depends upon the mobility systems themselves and how they develop. Changes in mobility systems transform what is 'necessary' for full social inclusion. 'Keeping up' with such technologies will be hard to achieve.

Indeed establishing exactly what people's preferences are for travel and communications is difficult to determine since there may be 'blocked desire' if people cannot meet obligations. Research conducted on a partially 'demand-responsive' bus service reveals otherwise invisible patterns of demand (see Cass, Shove, Urry 2003, on the following). While elderly users describe their journeys as 'just' for shopping, or just to 'pop into' the 'hub', our research identified many other 'needs' that people had, to visit a spouse in a care home, to visit friends, to go to a café, to attend a community centre, art classes, to get to work, to go on a pleasure trip, to go a pub and so on. Thus the range of what it is that the otherwise 'excluded' are trying to access may only be revealed through new infrastructures that 'realize' such latent demand.

Furthermore, there are important temporal as well as spatial dimensions of exclusion. One consequence of the breakdown of predictably scheduled events (fixed meal times, specific times for social interaction and times for work) is that people are more obliged to negotiate meetings and social encounters, even by event. For some, scheduling social life appears increasingly 'do-it-yourself', arranging encounters around flexi-times, and searching for common slots between people with equally idiosyncratic schedules (Shove 2002; and see ch. 8 above on mobile telephony). There is for many the need to organize ever more complex diaries, more complex *because* other people's times are more fragmented and less formally controlled.

Finally, governments normally conceive of access in terms of whether certain social groups can get to work, hospitals, schools, courts and so on (Cass, Shove, Urry 2003: ch. 2). Emphasizing these *public or formal* aspects of contemporary life, the SEU Report refers to the need to access: 'work, learning, healthcare, and other key services' (2002: Summary NC). However, this view of 'access' neglects the maintenance of friendship, family ties and informal connections, the socialities that constitute everyday life.

Overall as Kenyon shows there are many elements of mobility-related social exclusion (2006: 105). They are disparate. It is necessary instead to consider what are the underlying bases of such restrictions upon access. In the next two chapters I examine in more depth how networks seem central to many aspects of social life; people have to 'access' networks if they are to participate in a complex, multiply networked society. Where nodes in such networks are located at geographical distance from where people live or work, access involves communications and intermittent travel. Hence social inclusion is a matter of overcoming constraints of space at particular moments of time so as to gain access to the informal networks of work, leisure, friendship and family. There is an unavoidable 'burden of mobility' in order to sustain social networks (Shove 2002). Thus to determine whether there is social inequality as engendered through mobility constraints it is necessary to know what people want or might want to do, where they want to go, and what are the constraints upon making and forming networks and the holding of diverse 'meetings' (Kenyon, Lyons, Rafferty 2002; Cass, Shove, Urry 2005). In relating notions of a networked society to an analysis of how leisure, family and work life have (on average) become more far-flung, more extended and less overlapping, I noted some implications for the concept and discourse of 'access'. How then to capture the concerns that the notion of 'access' raises but to do so in a way that overcomes the issues I have raised?

Network Capital

In this section I turn specifically to develop the notion of network capital. What I propose here is that the various aspects of access set out earlier should be (loosely) reconceived through analysis of the forms of capital that Bourdieu sets out, but that there is a major extra form of capital that he neglects and this is what I term network capital. I suggested above that there are four aspects of access, the economic, the physical, the organizational and the temporal. I propose that the economic aspects refer to what it typically understood as the divisions of social class, and of gender, age and ethnicity to the extent to which these are economically structured, while the other elements, the physical, organizational and temporal, are all components of what I term network capital.

There are three key features of Bourdieu's approach which I set out briefly before turning to network capital per se. First, the structured 'spaces of positions' (in class and other structures) are conceived of as 'fields' and that classes and other social forces are not to be understood as simply realizing pregiven 'interests'. All such forces are engaged in multiple and fluid struggles (Devine, Savage, Scott, Crompton 2005: 13). Second, these struggles involve many different sites and terrains including especially those around aspects of 'culture' where taste is never 'pure' and people seek to distinguish themselves symbolically from others. There are multiple forms of capital with no necessary homology between them, and especially between economic and cultural capital, although there are normally correlations between holdings of different capital forms (Bourdieu 1984: 186). Third, central to such struggles is the habitus of each social force. Habitus is: 'the capacity to produce classifiable practices and works, and the capacity to differentiate and appreciate these practices and products (taste), that the represented social world, i.e. the space of life styles, is constituted' (Bourdieu 1984: 170). Such habituses stem from and generate bodily expressions of taste. The body, says Bourdieu: 'is the most indisputable materialization of class taste' (1984: 190) and, as he shows with regard to eating, of what we may term 'gender taste' as well as many other taste wars as well.

So how do these notions of field, culture and habitus connect to my thesis of another form of capital? Bourdieu's *Distinction* (surely the best book in post-war sociology) is very national-centric and overly static in its understanding of social struggle, although in passing it deals with an astonishing array of distinctions of taste including business tourism (1984: 306–8). *Distinction* also presents a non-ethical and a-moral conception of struggle and interest (thanks to Andrew Sayer for bringing this home to me). So my question is how to 'mobilize' Bourdieu's argument and specifically capture the importance of network capital?

I have consistently argued against the notion that mobilities are simply new. However, what are new are the following: the scale of movement around the world, the diversity of mobility systems now in play, the especial significance of the self-expanding automobility system and is awesome risks, the elaborate interconnections of physical movement and communications, the development of mobility domains that by-pass national societies, the significance of movement to contemporary governmentality and an increased importance of multiple mobilities for people's social and emotional lives. One consequence of this emergent 'mobility complex' is that many people are we might say 'forced' to exercise choice and are less determined by overarching *social* structures, of class, family, age, career and especially propinquitous communities (Giddens 1994; Beck 1999). And as people move around and have to develop these personalized life projects through 'Freisetzung', setting the individual free from *these* structures, so they extend and elaborate their social networks which are more personalized, more specific to them and less shared (see chs. 10 and 11, and Beckmann 2001).

Simultaneously contemporary capitalism presupposes and generates some increasingly expressive bodies, bodies characterized by habituses that are emotional, pleasure-seeking and novelty acquiring. Some such bodies are on the move, buying and indulging new experiences in new places and with new people. Capitalist societies involve new forms of pleasure and intermittent excess, with many elements or aspects of the body being commodified (for those that can afford to pamper their body!). Expressive capitalism develops into a mobile and mobilizing capitalism with transformed, and on occasions, over-indulged bodily habituses (May, Thrift 2001).

Capitalism involves power as a mobile entity and able to constantly produce the new and then to take advantage of it. Even when at work some new modes of management are in part about engendering pleasures to work more intensely but simultaneously to find it 'fun' (Thrift 2000). And many ways in which the body is commodified is in and through it moving about and being moved about. As some bodies are subject to the 'new' so being subject to the new is elsewhere, on the move, somewhere else, in between home and away. Newness in the twenty-first century often thus involves moving and commodified bodies. Thus life for some within the contemporary capitalist order presupposes intermittent movement, and this involves bodies newly flowing and intermittently encountering others in rich, face-to-face (and embodied) co-presence.

As a consequence, multiple mobilities set up new kinds of distinctions of taste, between the modes of movement, the classes of traveller, the places moved to, the embodied experiences of movement, the character of those who also moving and so on. More generally, mobilities develop into a distinct field with characteristic struggles, tastes and habituses. It is site of multiple intersecting contestations. This field has spun off from economic, political and cultural processes and is now self-expanding and gives rise to an emergent form of capital, network capital, that is a prerequisite to living in the rich 'north' of contemporary capitalism (Kaufmann 2002; Kaufmann, Manfred and Joye 2004).

I call this network capital to bring out that the underlying mobilities in themselves do nothing. What are key are the social consequences of such mobilities, namely, to be able to engender and sustain social relations with those people (and to visit specific places) who are mostly not physically proximate, that is, to form and sustain networks. So network capital points to the real and potential social relations that mobilities afford. This formulation is somewhat akin to that of Marx in *Capital* where he focuses upon the *social* relations of capitalist production and not upon the *forces* of production *per se* (1976). My analogous argument is that it is necessary to examine the social relations that the means of mobility afford and not only the changing form taken by the forces of mobility.

Also Marx examined how the appearances of capitalist societies were different from their 'real relations'. So while the wealth of societies: 'appears as an immense collection of commodities' (Marx 1976: 125), actually what is crucial are the social relations of capital and labour-power that lie behind and structure the form of such commodities and also generate what he terms the fetishism of commodities (Marx 1976: 163–7). Analogously I argue here that the proliferation of mobilities that new mobility systems generate is not in itself so significant as the novel social relations or sociabilities that such new means or forces of circulation can produce. It is the social relations that stem from mobilities that are crucial. Concentrating upon the means of mobility is analogous to focusing upon the proliferation of commodities, upon their fetishism and not upon the 'real relations' (Marx 1976: 165). We can thus critique the 'fetishism of movement' that parallels Marx's critique of the fetishism of commodities.

What then are the key social relations here? Is there a distinct new form of capital? Wellman suggests the contemporary importance of: 'knowing how to maintain a networked computer, search for information on the internet and use the knowledge gained, create and sustain online relationships and use these relationships to obtain needed resources, including indirect links to friends of friends' (2001: 248). However, this formulation overly emphasizes access to the computer for networking and ignores an array of other 'mobility' requirements (see Axhausen 2002; Church, Frost, Sullivan 2000; Kenyon, Lyons, Rafferty 2001).

I argue that it is the 'social relations of circulation' or network capital that is key. Network capital is the capacity to engender and sustain social relations with those people who are not necessarily proximate and which generates emotional, financial and practical benefit (although this will often entail various objects and technologies or the means of networking). Those social groups high in network capital enjoy significant advantages in making and remaking their social connections, the emotional, financial and practical benefits being over and above and non-reducible to the benefits derived from what Bourdieu terms economic and cultural capital (1984). Or network capital comprises eight elements that *in their combination* produce a distinct stratification order that now sits alongside social class, social status and party (Weber 1948: chapter 7). These eight elements are:

1. *array of appropriate documents, visas, money, qualifications* that enable safe movement of one's body from one place, city, country to another
2. *others (workmates, friends and family members) at-a-distance*: that offer invitations, hospitality and meetings so that places and networks are maintained through intermittent visits and communications
3. *movement capacities*: to walk distances within different environments, to be able to see and to board different means of mobility, to be able to carry or move baggage, to read timetabled

information, to be able to access computerized information, to arrange and re-arrange connections and meetings, the ability, competence and interest to use mobile phones, text messaging, email, the internet, skype, etc.

4. *location free information and contact points*: fixed or moving sites where information and communications can arrive, be stored and retrieved, including real/electronic diaries, address books, answerphone, secretary, office, answering service, email, web sites, mobile phones)

5. *communication devices*: to make and remake arrangements especially on the move and in conjunction with others who may also be on the move

6. *appropriate, safe and secure meeting places*: both en route and at the destination (s) including office, club space, hotel, home, public spaces, street corner, café, interspaces, that ensure that the body is not exposed to physical or emotional violence

7. *access* to car, roadspace, fuel, lifts, aircraft, trains, ships, taxis, buses, trams, minibuses, email account, internet, telephone and so on

8. *time and other resources to manage and coordinate 1–7*, especially when there is system failure as will intermittently happen

I have thus set out this emergent form of capital, network capital, resulting from the proliferation of new mobilities. Such network capital is not to be viewed as an attribute of individual subjects. Such capital is a product of the relationality of individuals with others and with the affordances of the 'environment'. Together these constitute a relational 'assemblage', an emergent network moving through time–space and concretized in moments of co-present meetingness within specific places for particular moments (see Delanda 2002: 63–4).

I now relate my formulation to that of Putnam who develops the related concept of *social* capital which: 'refers to connections among individuals – social networks and norms of reciprocity and trustworthiness that arise from them' (Putnam 2000: 19; Urry 2002; Larsen, Urry, Axhausen 2006: ch. 2). He sees such capital as being fostered within propinquitous communities. Such communities with high social capital are characterized by dense networks of reciprocal social relations, well-developed sets of mutual obligations, generalized reciprocity, high levels of trust in one's neighbours, overlapping conversational groupings, and bonds that bridge across conventional social divides. Social bonds and especially involvement in civic work *within* neighbourhoods generate social capital (see Putnam 1993, on how high social capital correlates with stronger economic growth across different Italian regions; see Klinenberg 2002; Layard 2005: 179–80).

Regretfully for Putnam local face-to-face socializing, church-going, political rallying, volunteer work, and philanthropy have declined over the last few decades in the United States, particularly because of the widespread growth of TV, urban sprawl and more extensive travel. Thus:

> Just as frequent movers have weaker community ties, so too communities with higher rates of residential turnover are less well integrated. Mobile communities seem less friendly to their inhabitants than do their more stable communities ... So mobility undermines civic engagement and community-based social capital. (Putnam 2000: 204–5)

Two-thirds of car trips involve driving alone and this figure is growing; each additional minute in daily commuting time reduces involvement in community affairs by both commuters and non-commuters; and spatial fragmentation between home and workplace is especially bad for community groups that historically straddled class, ethnic and gender divides (Putnam 2000: 212–4). One way he says to counter this is to: 'spend less time traveling and more time connecting with our neighbors than we do today ... and that the design of our communities and the availability of public space will encourage more casual socializing with friends and neighbors' (Putnam 2000: 407–8).

Thus for Putnam social capital is principally generated within propinquitous 'communities'. Three criticisms of Putnam's thesis need to be made here. First, recent research has deconstructed the notion that local cultures and places are fixed and sedentarist (Albrow 1997; Durrschmidt 1997; Urry 2000; chs. 1 and 2 above). Places are constructed through, as Clifford says, routes as well as roots (1997: Massey 1994a, 1994b). Travel is central to communities, even those characterized by relatively high levels of apparent propinquity and communion.

Second, Florida shows how social networks of casual friends among mobile city-dwellers can generate social capital. In what Florida calls 'the creative class', youngish well-educated people prefer tolerant and diverse communities of principally weak ties and seek to escape Putnam's preferred tight-knit small-town communities (2002: 269). In UK research it is shown that the supposed decline in voluntary membership is mostly true of men and especially through the reduced appeal of predominantly *male* working men's clubs and trade unions. Women's membership and participation in voluntary association seems to have increased, as does the propensity of the service class to join and participate in voluntary associations (Li, Savage, Tampubolon, Warde, Tomlinson 2002). Indeed paralleling Florida, Li et al. conclude that the more mobile service class is more likely to participate within voluntary associations, and as a side-effect to proliferate weak ties and have greater social capital (2002: 17).

Third, and most relevant here, it seems implausible to argue that trust and reciprocity is only generated within propinquitous communities. Putnam ignores what his own practice as an academic shows, namely the widespread *growth* of longer range mobility especially by car and air, as conferences, holidays, family connections, diasporic relations, and work, are increasingly internationalized. Certain kinds of social capital seem to depend upon extensive long-range travel or network capital, especially exploiting the opportunities provided by 'structural holes' that arise in-between different social networks (Burt 1992). Social capital can depend upon the range, extent and modes of mobility. Physical travel is especially important in facilitating those face-to-face co-present conversations, to the making of links and social connections, albeit unequal, that endure over time (see the following chapters). Indeed the means of movement are themselves places of conversation and social capital, as research on 'community transport' and lift-giving both reveal. Local social networks can confer mobility on certain groups through the regular provision of lifts; and indeed even where there is a good bus service receiving lifts from others is still a key element of social networks and capital. Gray, Shaw, Farrington maintain that the vehicle providing access to local shops and services is as important an arena for social interaction as the destination itself (2006). In chapter 11, I describe some of the uses made of travel time and in particular its functioning as an in-between time and space central to making and remaking networks and connections (see Lyons, Urry 2005).

Putnam's concept of social capital is thus unsatisfactory since it presumes that only small scale communities can generate face-to-face proximities and relations of trust. By contrast the more general concept of network capital brings out how co-presence and trust can be generated at-a-distance, and this presupposes extensive and predictable travel and communications and the emergence of a distinct new field of 'mobilities'. It is this field that engenders network capital as a major new form of capital. However, I return to Putnam's argument in the conclusion of this chapter when considering some normative issues concerning the role that travel plays in ensuring that people can keep talking. Inequality is in part an inequality with regard to the possibilities of good conversation.

I conclude here with some further points about the dimensions and workings of network capital. I already noted in previous chapters the importance of mobility systems and the relations between them. These are matters of contestation within civil society, especially notable in recent decades being the struggles to resist the automobility system and to reclaim the streets for the pedestrian system. This engenders new forms and styles of struggles within civil society (see Figueroa 2005). While in chapter 7, I described how the growth of the aeromobility system sets up a new realm of network capital, especially with the differentiation between the kinds of travellers moving through such semi-public airspaces. For first class passengers air travel is like a seamless scape along which nomadic executives making the global order can with travel. For countless others their journeys are indicative of their global inferiority in a world where network capital is of major significance within the emerging stratification system.

Bauman also notes how one key element of such a stratification order is that of 'exit'. The prime technique of power he says is 'escape, slippage, elision and avoidance, the effective rejection of any territorial confinement' and the possibility of escape into 'sheer inaccessibility' (Bauman 2000: 11). There are many examples of such 'exitability' for a kinetic elite but especially significant is the capacity to minimize tax payments by temporarily living in a low tax country and yet being able to travel frequently to, and communicate with, the country of one's upbringing. High levels of network capital enable smooth and painless exiting from where obligations and in this case higher tax payments would be extracted. The mobile elite can be increasingly seen as 'absentee landlords' with high mobility and high potential for exit mobility if the 'going gets tough' (Bauman 2000: 13; many donors to political parties in the UK have encountered political difficulties because they live 'abroad'). By contrast Bauman's concept of the vagabond points to the opposite kind of 'traveller' who are unable to escape and avoid obligations as they are pushed and forced to move about, be surveilled and sometimes pinned down (1993; and see Beckmann 2001: 251).

Indeed the kinds of automated software for sorting travellers discussed in chapter 7 expands the notion of network capital; the iris recognition systems being a select way to travel that provides an exclusive membership for frequent travellers (Wood, Graham 2006).

More generally as I note with regard to aeromobility, information about human beings is increasingly left behind in traces. Indeed movement now is almost never without traces left on computers, including mobile phone records, ATM use, creditworthiness ratings, CCTV images, differentiated insurance rates through GIS software, hotel bookings, GPS data, fingerprints, travel itineraries, biometric data and so on. Much of what was 'private' already exists outside of the physical body and outside the 'self'.

As those bodies are on the move so the world is increasingly organized to control and regulate personal schedules. Human life comes to depend upon sorting systems, systems of increasingly detailed detection, to determine who or what should enter and exit, including cyber-imagery of 'strangers' and 'familiars'. Systems are morphing into a Big Brother that would have George Orwell turning in his grave. Rather than there being a single 'observing tower' of the panopticon as described by Foucault, there now is a ubiquitous panopticon in which no single sovereign or state official is in control. Everyone is inside what we might describe as a 'global panopticon' with multiple systems necessary for 'security'. As populations are on the move so what Foucault terms societies of security develop fluid systems of 'mobile security' (1991).

More generally, while network capital appears to engender increased freedom (as Microsoft says: 'where do you want to go to today?'), there is simultaneously dependence upon systems that strip people of certain human powers, sense of the self and abilities to move around unnoticed. There is shifting from 'face-to-face security' to 'e-security' and, as social networks are increasingly used for identifying 'threats', a further stage is emerging that we could call 'network-security'. In this stage models of social networks are used to identify those who are regarded as security threats, in a way deploying the kind of analysis of networks developed in chapters 10 and 11 below.

Overall there is a pervasive and increasing switching *between* different systems that lie behind and sustain high levels of network capital. These systems include massive search engines; databases of information storage and retrieval; electronic money flows; financial and other audits especially through a 'spreadsheet culture'; intelligent transport systems; GIS/GPS systems; CCTV and other vision machines; and systems of tracking movement with five billion barcodes being carried each day (Rheingold 2002: 100). As people increasingly lament it is almost impossible to get 'lost' these days if one possesses some network capital because of the interconnectedness of these multiple, intersecting systems.

But there are two limits on this. First, those without network capital can indeed get lost as with many economic and political refugees who are not 'connected' (and occasionally with young backpacker travellers whose network capital is often fragile and parent-dependent!). Second, network capital depends upon code-space and thus upon the non-failing nature of such systems. But I have noted how systems that are closely coupled do crash as a relatively routine happening (Perrow 1999; Law 2006). When systems begin to crash then the consequences can be catastrophic as with the 2001 attacks on the World Trade Center and in effect upon mobility as a way of life. And Hurricane Katrina in New Orleans in 2005 showed the extraordinary distributional consequences of uneven levels of network capital within disasters, with predominantly middle class whites able to flee in advance because of their ownership of cars, contacts and communications, while the network capital poor were left both to the Hurricane but especially to the network capital-weak resources of the federal, state and city authorities (see Hannam, Sheller, Urry 2006: 7–9). It was only the TV pictures taken from low-flying helicopters that demonstrated to the world that was watching just what happens to those living in large areas of a major city when network capital 'sinks' to zero.

Conclusion: Mobility and Freedom

In conclusion I examine some issues concerned with whether there are rights to movement and whether and to what degree such rights can or ought to be realized. I will argue that the rights to movement are intrinsically exclusionary and that such rights should be recouched in terms of the capabilities to engage with and to enjoy various qualities and dimensions of co-presence.

I return first to Putnam's *Bowling Alone* that deals with what I take to be the major benefit of travel and of social life more generally. Putnam is concerned with the social causes and consequences of 'conversations' within everyday life, an unusual topic for a macro social scientist (2000; Miller 2006). He specifically laments how declining social capital within the US is reflected in there being far less frequent face-to-face conversations. For Putnam the quantity of co-presence is not a given but has declined since the 1960s. He maintains that TV and large-scale mobility: 'privatizes leisure time . . . TV watching comes at the expense of nearly every social activity outside the home, especially social gatherings and *informal conversations*' (2000: 236–7; my emphasis). Americans talk less frequently face-to-face. This is also born out by research reported by Layard into the causes of happiness and how the growth of TV seems to reduce overall happiness levels (2005: 78). And Miller describes the contemporary development of a plurality of 'conversation avoidance devices' which have a negative effect upon people's conversational skills.

And yet according to Putnam it is 'good to talk' face-to-face; this minimizes privatization, expands social capital, makes people live longer and promotes economic activity, in mutually self-sustaining ways. Living a life 'on a screen' is not a satisfactory substitute for good conversation (Turkle 1996). If more relationships are conducted on-screen then this produces less conversation, poorer social interaction and a weakening of social capital. For Putnam it is undesirable for people to live mainly 'on the screen'. Miller's recent history of *Conversation: A History of a Declining Art* provides much supporting documentation of the negative effects of this long-term decline in talk (2006).

This argument is also born out by Klinenberg's research on the 1995 Chicago heat wave reported in chapter 4 above (2002). In areas of Chicago that afforded opportunities for people to get out and about, to visit shops and local services, deaths from the heat wave were much lower. The connectedness of houses with habitable streets, accessible parks, shops, cafes, neighbours and so on provided affordances for everyday walking and especially for talking. Where affordances were rich and diverse then people would go out and about even in very high temperatures and survive. In such areas where people were walking and talking they were much less likely to die from heat.

But in countless ways 'walking and talking' is simply impossible for many. In the following two chapters it is shown just how the contemporary social world is networked and increasingly lived at-a-distance (at least in the prosperous 'global north'). So the walking will often have to be combined with other mobilities. The rights and duties of multiple mobilities are then key to debates about what makes a good society, both now and especially in an increasingly uncertain yet mobile future. I suggest that a good society is one that maximizes the possibilities for good conversation! In order then for people to meet and talk is there or should there be a 'right to mobility'? And should such a right be unrestricted? Is 'right' the correct term here?

Kant wrote that anyone should be free to travel both for conducting trade and 'to offer themselves for social contact with established inhabitants of any territory' (cited Bauböck 1994: 321–2; Cohen

2004). Adam Smith wrote similarly that a merchant 'is not necessarily the citizen of any particular country' (cited Jordan, Düvell 2002: 242), while Marx and Engels famously advocated that workers of the world should and increasingly would unite (1952). And most attempts at restricting the 'right' to mobility have been associated with forms of state intervention that stigmatize certain groups on the basis of colour, religion, ethnicity or cultural practice. States routinely hold that there are good movers and bad movers and that the latter should be limited, penalized, extradited or thrown into prison. Often such distinctions between friend and foe stem from and enhance the fear of the mobile, which harks back to the fear of the 'mob' (see ch. 1). And in a world of global risks there are increasingly few restraints upon states and private corporations seeking to, and succeeding in, monitoring, regulating and limiting people's rights to movement, even where as in the case of the 'borderless' European Union it had been presumed that all citizens are entitled to travel within and across all EU territories (Verstraete 2004; Cohen 2004; Stephenson 2006; except for new accession states).

So responding to these various illiberal restrictions on movement, it seems that we should favour the notion that there should be freedom of movement or a generalized right to mobility (but see Sager 2006, on freedom and mobility). Famously Article 13 of the UN Universal Declaration of Human Rights recognized this freedom of movement through three separate rights: to leave any country, including one's own; to return, to one's own country; and to have freedom of movement and residence within the borders of each state (UDHR 1948). Similar EU objectives are expressed in Article 8a(1) of the Maastricht Treaty and reinforced in the Amsterdam Treaty of 1997 (Stephenson 2006).

However, expressing this in terms of rights to movement, the negative freedom from restraint, is a limited way to formulate this as Sheller shows (2006). Recent debates about positive freedom, the nature of progress and the good society can illuminate the deficiency of this formulation (see Walby 2005, on the following). More broadly it is claimed that GDP per capita provides one of the best measures of progress across different societies. This is the measure adopted by the World Bank and the IMF. And part of the justification of the 'freedom of movement' is to enhance the scale of economic development since there is a reasonable relationship between expenditure on 'mobility' and GDP per capita. And indeed the EU with its four freedoms of movement demonstrates at the level of a new 'polity' the close connections between personal mobility and economic growth.

However, recent formulations of the so-called human capabilities approach provide another way of thinking through some connections between mobility and freedom. The capabilities approach first developed by Sen focuses upon what people are able to do, what capacities they have, rather than what people's average income is (1999). This is similar to the notion of 'positive freedom', of the freedom to, of the alternative opportunities of various functions that people can develop (see Sager 2006: 466). The capabilities approach draws upon research that shows that social inequalities in nevertheless rich societies can produce a lower level of capabilities and more general wellbeing than in more equal societies. Thus the society with the highest GDP per capital (the US) does not produce the greatest longevity of life or the greatest happiness. This may be because people's capabilities are less developed there compared with some more 'equal' societies. Indeed happiness levels have been falling in the United States while income per head has risen, bearing out in some ways Putnam's pessimistic analysis of the United States discussed earlier (Walby 2008; Layard 2005: 30).

Nussbaum elaborates what these specific capabilities might be (2006). She suggests the following heterogeneous list: life, bodily health, bodily integrity (including being able to move freely from place to place), senses, imagination and thought, emotions, practical reason, affiliation, other species, play (including enjoying recreational activities) and control over one's environment.

In order to explore this capabilities approach, I now consider one context where the right or freedom to mobility has been most developed, namely in relationship to automobility (see ch. 6 above; Sager 2006: 467–9). Many people and orgnizations assert that there should be a freedom to drive, the freedom of the open road, and that governments should not restrict but rather enhance this freedom to drive. Such a discourse has lain behind much of the expansion and development of road building and automobility over the past century; and the car industry has been a massive 'driver' of change and development especially in generating the car-based USA as the society with the highest income per capital (see ch. 6 above).

However, for various reasons formulating this in terms of a right or a 'freedom from' seems an unhelpful formulation. It is an extraordinary 'freedom' that all road users have to inhabit roads (as drivers, cyclist or pedestrians) that are full of cars being driven by *any* 'adult' (over 16/17/18) who passed a modest test at a previous moment in time (and which could be fifty years or so earlier in time). Also in many societies some or all 'drivers' are unqualified. The so-called freedom to drive involves the freedom to control objects that are big and powerful; one ton objects that move at fast speeds and are not even channelled along particular routes (such as rail tracks). These objects can and do kill with predictable regularity.

This 'freedom to drive' involves astonishing inequalities. 3,000 people die *each day* from car accidents and 30,000 are injured (WHO 2004; Featherstone 2004). By 2020 road crashes will be third in the world ranking of disease and injury and yet most of these victims do not actually own a car. Crashes we should note are not accidental but are features of the automobility system (see Beckmann 2001). The death and injury rates around the world are what Durkheim termed a 'social fact', stemming from consistent and predictable social processes (1964). There are what Elias describes as very different social standards of self-regulation on the roads effected through variations in the 'civilizing process' (1995; death rates per 100,000 population vary from forty to six per year, with China normally reckoned to have one of the very highest: Featherstone 2004: 4–5). We might say then that the freedom to drive is the freedom to die.

Further huge inequalities are effected between car owners/users (high in network capital) and those who are cyclists and pedestrians and especially children (who are much lower in network capital). This freedom produces exceptional levels of socio-spatial inequality; an inequality that stems from a car-based hypermobility that results in a massive scale of death and injury effected upon the hugely vulnerable bodies of pedestrians and cyclists. Their freedom is that of the 'bare life' opened up through a kind of mass slaughter that results in deaths greater than the number of bodies slain in warfare since the end of the Second World War (Featherstone 2004). Very many capabilities are thus damaged by the freedom to drive.

How then to reconcile not restricting the rights to move while preventing the astonishing system effects of death and injury that stem from the untrammelled growth of the car system (ignoring here automobility's role in global heating: see Lovelock 2006, and ch. 13 below)? Focusing upon the rights to movement (the freedom from) is to fetishize *movement*, in a similar way to that Marx in which critiques how capitalism produces the fetishism of *commodities*.

So we can make a distinction between income per person and the rights to mobility *and* the distribution of capabilities. My suggestion here is that one set of capabilities should be seen as the opportunity to engage in co-present conversations with those in one's various networks. Mobilities enable such conversations, to making links and social connections that endure over time. All social groups around the world should be able to 'meet and talk', to be able to exercise this positive freedom. This is a crucially important capability that is only rather implicit within Nussbaum's list of capabilities and especially within that of 'affiliation' (2006).

Moreover, because of the networked nature of social life communication and travel at a distance will be 'necessary'. People need to experience sufficient travel so that the pleasures of meeting and talking to people are sustained and developed, and this will have further beneficial effects that Sheller characterizes as 'civic freedom and mobility' (2006). Thus if all else were equal, a 'good society' would not limit travel, co-presence and resulting good conversations. Such a society would extend the capabilities of co-presence to every social group and regard infringements of this as undesirable. As the airline BA puts it: 'there's no substitute for face-to-face contact'. But if so then this 'contact' should be available for all social groups at least from time to time and not just to those who are currently easily able to meet 'face-to-face'. A socially inclusive society would elaborate and extend the capabilities of co-presence to all its members. It would minimize 'coerced immobility'. Initiatives in transport, planning and communications should promote networking and meetingness (and limit missingness). This is a dynamic notion of citizenship that values 'freedom to' rather than 'freedom from'. Such a notion means that zero friction, the death of distance and the untrammelled pursuit of movement are undesirable goals (see Sager 2006: 471).

However, this capabilities agenda for mobilities is of course massively difficult to implement. First, obviously it would not follow that this specific capability should mean that people should be able to move long distances *every* day. There would have to be a temporal rationing. So I am proposing here *intermittent* travel and co-presence as a capability. And it may be that significant reductions will occur in the frequency of such 'desirable' co-presence if oil supplies were to decline rapidly before alternative fuels develop or global climate change begins to impact sooner rather than later (Stern 2006; ch. 13 below). Overall the capabilities approach needs us to determine whether there should be priority between the rates of 'intermittent co-presence' for some social groups, for those living in some geographical areas or for some kinds of organizations. However, the prima facie starting point would be that *all* social groups should have *similar* rights of co-presence. For many groups this would entail very significant reductions in their capabilities to effect work, friendship and family co-presence. We might even, analogously with the development of the concept of food miles, think there should be something called 'friendship miles' and the need to constrain friendship choices within national or local boundaries. The growth of young people's travel (students, au pairs, and being on their 'overseas experience') greatly increases the range of friends to choose from, their geographical spread and as we will see in the next chapters the likely future travel in order to keep those friendship networks warm. More generally here there is a paradox of choice according to Schwarz: 'Freedom is essential to self-respect, public participation, mobility, and nourishment, but not all choice enhances freedom', even I would suggest the choice of friends (2004: 4).

More generally there needs to be a methodology, apart from the willingness to pay, to value different forms of travel for co-presence, for family life or work or education or religion or friendship or pleasure or shopping or business or gambling? The urgent need to develop a post carbon economy and society makes developing this methodology a priority.

Las Vegas, with a population of one million, attracts thirty million visitors a year, two-thirds visiting by plane (Gottdiener 2001: 2). It would be difficult to imagine in any formulation of the 'need' for 'co-presence' that such a rate of travel to engage in what we might call 'parallel gambling' was justifiable. But this is a relatively easy example. A methodology should here enable not only the current opportunities for co-presence to be distributed more 'fairly' but also to enable decisions to be made about new investments to enhance the physical co-presence of some groups which will be at the expense of others. Overall travel would need to be rationed on the basis of need, reducing the frequency for many travellers while enhancing the co-presence of many others. It would also be necessary to ensure that opportunities are distributed, not only more fairly within current societies, but especially between current and future generations whose lives are likely to be even more networked and lived 'at-a-distance'. The capabilities approach does not refer to the responsibilities entailed within citizenship and so a major consideration here would be the responsibility to ensure that future generations possess at least equal rights to co-presence. Finally, I have so far presumed that there is a simple relationship between movement and co-presence but because of positional competition this is not the case. Movement is partly a good whose significance and appeal depends upon how much access to co-presence other people have (see Mishan 1969). So the notion of the capabilities for co-presence is here relative, contested and not simply absolute.

In the next chapters I discuss the significance of this capability of co-presence in more depth, particularly drawing out the importance for distributed social networks of meetings of many diverse sorts. I hope though to have shown that the capabilities for conversation through travel and meetings provide at least a way of overcoming the narrow conceptualization of 'movement from'. I have also shown in this chapter the theoretical and empirical significance of network capital in enabling the deciphering of some lineaments of stratification, inequality and power in the emergent global order. The gates to heaven depend upon access to sufficient network capital while hell waits those who are network deprived in this strange new world dis/order.

10

Networks

Everybody on this planet is separated by only six other people.
Six degrees of separation. Between us and everybody else on
this planet
  John Guare *Six Degrees of Separation* (cited Watts 1999: 11)

In the previous chapter I developed the concept of network capital. In
this chapter I discuss networks more explicitly before considering
in the following chapter the significance of meetings of many different
sorts. I have at various places in this book developed some notions
from complexity thinking to develop and enhance my argument. I
begin in the next section with some discussion of the complexity-
inspired small worlds literature. I show that although this is an interesting contribution to deciphering networked relations around the
world such a literature does not deal sufficiently with what is meant
by 'knowing' others. This is discussed in the following section in relationship to work, friend and family relations that are I show increasingly 'networked'. I consider briefly how those networks are distributed
across space and the ways in which such networks can be sustained
often across very significant distances.

Small Worlds

I have noted how various theorists at the beginning of the twenty-
first century are developing and applying the physics of complexity
to contemporary social science. Sociological work analysing global
processes increasingly deploys the physics and mathematics of

complex, non-linear adaptive systems (Urry 2003a, 2005). And physicists and mathematicians seeking to analyse networks partly turn to the sociology of social networks in their examination of so-called small worlds phenomenon (see Watts 1999). Thus it has been argued that 'Where small-world ideas will lead us in five or ten years is anyone's guess, but they may reveal something about the way our ideas link up with one another, how discoveries in biology, computer science, sociology and physics can be so intimately connected' (Buchanan 2002: 208).

In general networks can be massive in scale, those of social relationships across the globe involve 6–7 billion people or 44,000 transnational corporations, those involving the weather presuppose 1 million interdependent variables, those of the human brain entail ten billion nerve cells and 1,000 billion synapses (Casti 1994: ch. 3). Capra argues that *networks* are the key to late twentieth-century advances in science concerned with investigating the 'web of life . . . Whenever we look at life, we look at networks' (Capra 1996: 82). And as noted in chapter 8 Castells argues that 'structures' that imply a centre, a concentration of power, vertical hierarchy and a constitution are empirically now less significant. Rather *networks*: 'constitute the new social morphology of our societies, and the diffusion of networking logic substantially modifies the operation and outcomes in processes of production, experience, power, and culture . . . the network society, characterized by the pre-eminence of social morphology over social action' (Castells 1996: 469). Castells argues that the 'network society' is made up of networks that are powered by microelectronics-based information and communication technologies (2004). These various interdependent systems dating from around 1990 spread virtual connections around the world and bring very many virtual objects into the background of much everyday social life, especially through those flickering 'screens' and how life increasingly occurs upon those screens (Turkle 1996; and ch. 8 above).

However, most importantly these systems seem to usher in worlds that are less based upon predictable and given co-presence, upon communities of propinquity. Specific others are not so simply 'there'; or rather they are or may be there but mainly through the mediation of very many virtual objects distributed in relatively far-flung networks. There are various consequences. First, there is increasingly 'connected presence' where small gestures or signs of attention are significant in indicating that others are there but at a distance. Second, family and friendship becomes networked rather like much economic life; network membership becomes crucial. Indeed the apparently different domains of work, family and social life becoming more networked, more similar to each other, more self-organized and more interdependent (see Larsen, Urry, Axhausen 2006). Likewise, organizations, enterprises, states (the European Union) and civil society organizations are increasingly networked. Third, there are increasingly significant global microstructures: 'structures of connectivity and integration that are global in scope but microsociological in character' (Knorr Cetina 2005: 215). Such microstructures are constituted as light, effective, thick, rich relations, as with Al Qaeda or global trading networks. And fourth, these networks generate small-world effects (Watts 1999). Weak ties connect people to the outside world, providing a bridge other than that provided by the densely knit 'clump' of people's close friends and family. Bridges between such clumps are formed from weak rather than strong ties, as I now examine in detail.

It's a Small World

So far detailed analyses of the patterns and implications of such networks *within* social life are less developed (see Scott 2000, on the technical social network modelling literature). I turn to a new version of network analysis much influenced by complexity theory. This emerged during the late 1990s and is concerned with the mathematics of social networks that stretch across the world and can result in a 'small world' (Watts 1999, 2003; Barabási 2002; Gladwell 2002; Buchanan 2002; Capra 2002). Watts examines the dynamic complexity of social networks that are neither perfectly ordered nor fully random, they are poised between order and randomness (1999). Networks are dynamic, evolving, changing and self-constituting over time (Watts 2003). He explains the empirical finding demonstrated by various researchers that everyone on the planet, whatever their socio-spatial location, is separated by only six degrees of separation. It is questionable if this is literally correct but there seems little doubt that people across the world are linked through relatively few connections of knowing others (see Watts 2003: ch. 5, on the difficulties of empirically testing this). Thus it is common for people who believe that they are strangers to discover if they discuss the matter that they are connected along a relatively short chain of acquaintanceship. Surprisingly then: 'even when two people do *not* have a friend in common they are separated by only a short chain of intermediaries' (Watts 1999: 4; Barabási 2002: 27–30). Thus it is theoretically possible to get messages rather quickly to anyone else across the world through one-to-one contacts even though the sender and the ultimate receiver appear to have no connections. How are such networked connections so organized that they make it seem that we live in a small world?

The key idea here is the 'strength of weak ties'. Granovetter's famous research showed that a striking 84 per cent of job searchers were able to acquire a new job, not through someone they knew well, but through someone that they did not know particularly well and saw only occasionally (1983). The extensive *weak* ties of acquaintanceship and informational flow were central to successful job searches and to other social processes such as rumour spreading (and see Burt 1992: 24–7; Barabási 2002: 43; Gladwell 2002). These important weak ties have the effect of connecting people to a world outside, so providing a bridge not provided by the densely knit 'clump' of people's close friends and family. Bridges between such clumps are formed through long range weak ties.

If people were only connected to their small group of close friends and family, then there would be a very large socio-spatial separation of the world's 6+ billion people. In an ordered network where each person is only connected to his or her nearest fifty neighbours, actually probably an over-estimate, then there would be sixty million degrees of separation in order to be connected to even half the world's population (Buchanan 2002: 54–5; see Wellman et al. 2005, for estimates of how many people we actually know).

However, Erdös shows that only a few long-range random links or weak ties connecting these different 'clumps' neighbours dramatically reduce the degree of separation. Erdös' mathematics of random graphs shows that a small percentage of randomly placed links ties together a network of points on a graph in a more or less completely connected whole (see Buchanan 2002: 36–8, Watts 2003: ch. 2). And the proportion of links that is required to connect such a network together reduces, as the network gets larger. Thus the more extensive the network of points, the smaller the proportion of those points that have to be linked through random ties. The percentage of the network necessary to link it together reduces to a tiny fraction. There is a critical switching point. If there are just three random links out of each 10,000, then the degree of separation of the world's population falls from 60 million to 5. This is the small world phenomenon – a few long-range random links, combined with densely knit lumps, produce a low degree of separation of each person from everyone else around the world. There is a 'phase transition' from small *clumps* to small *worlds*.

Watts goes on to argue, contrary to Erdös, that there is a normal distribution of individuals across the world with the overwhelming majority of people relatively weakly connected and a few only moderately connected. And recent research using email shows that messages had to be forwarded between five and seven times to get from a starting point to the target-person, a pattern showing that connections depend upon many people and not only upon exceptionally well-connected hubs which all messages have to flow through (www. sciencenews.org/articls/20030816/fob8.asp; accessed 4.8.03). Other networked phenomena, from film stars to electric power interconnections, also demonstrate a similar patterning of tight clumps with a few random long-term connections that turn the world from 'large' to 'small' (for further detail, see Urry 2004b).

The world wide web would also *appear* to be so organized. There is a 'small world of the web' where one appears to be present with an entirely different person through making just a few clicks (Buchanan 2002: 118–19). Research on its architecture suggests that there is between 4 and 10 degrees of separation from one 'side' of it to the 'other' side (Buchanan 2002: 81). Information travels from one point to any other point with apparently only a handful of steps in between. However, research shows that web sites are not at all normally distributed. A tiny number of nodes, Microsoft, CNN, Google, Yahoo, BBC, AOL, possess an enormous number of links and hence dominate the web (Buchanan 2002: 54–5, 82, 84–5). This distribution has come to be known as a 'power law' distribution that is somewhat similar to the typical Pareto income distribution in any society (Barabási 2002; Watts 2003: ch. 4). This is referred to as a scale free distribution. Each time the number of links is doubled, the nodes possessing those links falls by about a factor of five (Buchanan 2002: 83; Watts 2003: ch. 4). The web is thus described as an aristocratic network, in which the connected get ever more connected and the less connected get even less connected. The connectors or hubs dominate such web networks because of what Barabási terms: 'the flocking sociology of the world wide web' as opposed to the presumption of randomness (quoted Buchanan 2002: 85). Moreover, the dominance of these main connectors would appear to be increasing over time (http://news.bbc.co.uk/1/hi/sci/tech/428999.stm; accessed 11.8.03).

There thus seems to be a hidden self-organizing character to the web. Even though its development was unplanned, uncontrolled and amorphous, it seems to take on the autopoeitic character of a dynamic system (see Fox Keller 2005). Indeed Barabási argues that this aristocratic network where the rich get richer and the poor poorer characterizes a vast array of networks. This scale-free state is thought to be a generic property of complex systems in genetics, neuroscience, power grids, transportation systems, epidemiology and the global financial flows that proceed through the three main hubs of London, New York and Tokyo (Fox Keller 2005: 1060–1). Thus the use of complexity arguments paradoxically here results in a reductionism in which all systems seem to migrate to the power law model, with some authors even claiming that there is a new 'law of nature'.

Fox Keller though argues that although there are systems that do seem to grow according to the principle of preferential attachment and self-organize in a power-law distribution, this is not entirely new. Moreover, it results in a spurious search for the universal and it ignores the specific architecture of particular systems (Fox Keller 2005: 1066). In the case here it is necessary to ask how social networks are organized. Is either the small world model or the power law model correct or even useful in modelling social networks? What are the specific features of social networks as they spread across space?

So far the main commentator on small worlds who deals with these issues is Batty. He notes that: 'the small worlds research has tended to discuss the spatial dimension as being too hard to handle but it is now clear that it must be treated in terms of growth of networks ... small worlds always exist but, as the network grows, technologies have to be in place that enable long-distance ties across its span to be realized' (2001: 638; and see the rest of the *Environment and Planning B* 2001 collection edited by Batty). Thus technologies of transportation and communications are crucial to the nature of small worlds type connections. However, Batty presumes that space is only a matter of extended scale. But what I show in the next chapter is that crucial to networks is the *intensive* scale and especially intermittent meetings, the performing of temporary 'localness', involving people from near and far. Meetings are enabled by such spatially extending technologies but should not be reduced to them. People's travel and communications practices extend the short and weak ties within and especially across networks. Meetings are costly in terms of time, money and effort but they may result in network enlargement, reinforcement and the pleasures of co-presence. Travel and communications provides resources, particularly enhanced network capital, and this will magnify inequalities away from small-world egalitarianism. Networks also depend upon material infra-structures especially to do with changing technologies of travel and communications that afford potential movement or motility and connections across distance (Kaufmann 2002). Such mobility notions animate the somewhat formalistic notion of network present within the small worlds and power law literatures (and most other network analysis; Scott 2000; McCarthy, Miller, Skidmore 2004).

This importance of meetings clarifies Watts's critique of Barabási when he says that the: 'essential limitation with the scale-free view of networks is that everything is assumed to come for free. Network ties . . . are treated as costless, so you can have as many of them as you are able to accumulate, without regard to the difficulty of making them or maintaining them' (Watts 2003: 113). Watts uses this point to question the empirical significance of the aristocratic model, a model that that may be apposite in the case of the web because of how search machines costlessly 'travel' across billions of pages. But establishing and maintaining ties for social groups is according to Watts not at all cost free. However, they are costly because of the 'work' of communications, travel and meetings that are involved in 'performing' social networks. This costly work constitutes the very stuff of social life involving time, space, money, resources, risks, pleasures and so on, as shown in Larsen, Urry, Axhausen (2006).

Moreover, much of the social network literature presumes that information is the key resource in the making and extending of connections. But there are in fact many different components of social networking practices of which information is only a minor element in the 'knowing' of others, as will now be discussed.

Knowing

I begin here with setting out a simple classification of network clusters, each having different implications for how, when and where people are 'known'. First, there is the line or chain network where many nodes are spread out in more or less linear fashion. Messages or relationships proceed from one to the other node along such spaced out and distributed nodes. Some work-related or friendship networks are linear with relatively few connections that go out of line (Laurier, Philo 2001). One may know those close to one in the 'line' but not necessarily those located 'further' away.

Second, there are star or hub networks where important relationships move through a central hub or a very small number of hubs. In this case being in or near the hub is highly valued. An example would be the financial services industry where trading floors in London,

New York and Tokyo comprise three such hubs through which messages and relationships disproportionately flow. Some family networks are also of this clustered star pattern where the patriarch or matriarch occupies a central 'starring' or winner-takes-all role (see Barabási 2002: 103). If one knows the central figure then one probably knows of many others in that network.

Third, there are all-channel or distributed networks in which communications proceed simultaneously in more or less all directions (Arquilla, Ronfeldt 2001: 7–8). An example here would be the network relationships among those working within the cultural industries in the centre of London (Wittel 2002). There are also variations in whether network relationships are tight, with most nodes connected to most others, or loose as is more typical these days (Ohnmacht 2005).

Network clusters also vary as to whether obligations and reciprocities across the network members are one-way or all-ways. These patterns will be particularly reflected in decisions as to how the network may meet up and who decides the location, timing and length of 'meetings' and especially who gets to be invited.

Overall the small worlds and power law literatures presumes a binary division, that x either does or does not know y. And this is what counts. But we have already seen that many contemporary developments undermine this binary division; increasingly it would seem that people are 'dimly' aware of very many 'others' since fewer worlds are literally 'enclosed'. I have noted various ways in which invited and especially uninvited guests come into one's world as visitors and as celebrity figures upon various screens (McCarthy 2001). The billion TVs, the billion telephones and the internet with a billion users world-wide discloses people, events and happenings from elsewhere on an astonishing scale (much 'news from nowhere'). Thus communications are re-ordering the nature of 'knowing' and 'knowing of' people through a huge expansion of (very) weak ties. Thus people might be said to 'know' everyone in their email or mobile phone address book or the members of an internet chat room or the current members of a 'family history' set out on the family web site. There seems to be major increases in *very* weak ties in which others are dimly known in one limited respect. Wellman et al. suggest that the median number in people's personal community network is 23, with between 200 and 1,500 very weak ties (2005: 20).

Also we should note that it is difficult to establish the sociological significance of 'knowing' or 'knowing of' someone else in the small worlds sense. Such 'knowledge' of someone who is three steps away may have no significance whatsoever for the patterning of social life or the forming of 'imagined communities' at-a-distance. The concept of social network can be too formalistic being based on 'who knows (of) whom' as opposed to the social practices of who does what with whom, when and why.

In the following I consider whether network connections seem to demonstrate something of an aristocratic network pattern more like the web (rather than a networked 'small world').

It seems that networks disproportionately flow through well-connected nodes. It might be noted that the richest and most mobile 300 people in the world receive the same income as the poorest least mobile three billion and this *prima facie* suggests an aristocratic model of networked relationships. Thus connections across the globe are not at all random but highly structured. What seem significant are hugely dense connections between those awesomely well-connected nodes, combined with an exceptional thinness of connections between those that are relatively less and less connected (overall data in UNDP 2004, suggests such a pattern). Complex systems thus produce an aristocratic pattern through system interdependencies.

Such a pattern can also be seen in how very powerful connectors (individuals or organizations) play a pivotal role in how systems dramatically tip from one condition to another (Gladwell 2002). The notion of social contagion and sharp tipping points presuppose a small number of extremely powerful connectors located at key points within certain networked relationships. Such connectors possess a disproportionate number of social ties. As a result of such connector concentration, systems suddenly tip. Social contagion spreads through the exceptional influence of a few very powerful connectors. This aristocratic pattern is one where the rich get richer and exert disproportionate influence (Buchanan 2002: ch. 7; Watts 2003: ch. 4).

It is thus necessary to research the changing nature of social networks and in particular the spatial and social characteristics of such networks in work, family and friendship. The small worlds literature ignores research on such issues.

Social Networks

I have in previous chapters noted the shift away from 'little boxes' to a more spatially distributed series of social networks. Family life in at least parts of Europe and North America in the first half of the twentieth century was predominantly lived within a 'little box'; family members regularly encountered each other within their immediate neighbourhood. There was an informal co-presence of family members who often also worked within the same neighbourhood (Wellman 2001).

Classic studies that documented this at least up to the 1950s were conducted in many rural areas (see Frankenberg 1966), in the East End of London (Young, Willmott 1962) and in various Italian-American 'urban villages' (Gans 1962). Significant others were encountered through walking about such neighbourhoods, through 'door-to-door' connectivity as Wellman expresses this (2001: 231; 2002). People walked to visit one another and there was much overlap of family life, work and friendship. People encountered each other within their neighbourhoods that were yet to be transformed through car-based commuting, TV, the telephone and other home-based technologies described in Putnam's lament for the loss of such casual co-presence (2000; see ch. 9 above).

A wide array of research suggests many transformations have occurred in such patterns, transformations related to the internet but which significantly commenced before then (see Wellman et al. 2005). People's residences, workplaces and leisure places are now at greater distance from each other, although people do not necessarily move very far from where they are born. Those who have experienced higher education tend to live further from their place of origin and then to have friends located at very significant distances (PIU 2002; Larsen, Urry, Axhausen 2006). They may also 'live' in more than one place with a kind of 'distributed' family life.

As a result, networks seem to overlap less, so there is a reduced chance of bumping into those one knows without planning. There are fewer quick, casual meetings of the sort that occurred when there was much overlap between social networks and walking was the main mode of travel (Axhausen 2002). The relatively far-flung nature of contemporary social networks is shown by the very extensive travel patterns of dollar bills across the United States (see /www. wheresgeorge.com/ accessed 14.09.06).

People thus have to spend much time planning and sustaining meetings with a fairly small proportion of those who are 'known', communicating and then travelling from a distance so as to 'keep in touch' (see Larsen, Urry, Axhausen 2006). Planned meetings are central to many people's lives and this seems true of many kinds of networks. I also suggested above that people actually know an increasing number of other people in a very weak sense, but that relatively little effort is spent in 'keeping up' with many of these very weak ties, who may mainly remain as names in various electronic directories (Axhausen 2002; 2003).

Research on new media workers in central London shows a vision of such networking patterns. They have high levels of geographical mobility, many social contacts, and non-linear DIY work biographies rather than planned and nurtured careers (Wittel 2001: 65–6; Beck 1999; Sennett 1998). This pattern is 'individualized' so that people are 'forced' to construct social bonds. As Wellman et al. argue:

> This individualisation of connectivity means that acquiring resources depends substantially on personal skill, individual motivation and maintaining the right connections . . . With networked individualism, people must actively network to thrive. (2005: 4)

Moreover, ties tend to be ephemeral but intense, focused, fast and overloaded. As these spread, the networks of weak ties are extended. As one respondent noted: 'So these meetings and these conferences for me are about being seen and seeing other people again' (Wittel 2001: 67). There are said to be no real 'strangers', only potential members of people's ever-expanding networks. And because of mobility and speed, network sociality is less based upon a shared common history and narrative, as Sennett laments about the resulting 'corrosion of character' in the contemporary world (1998). Rather what is key in the network is information, the immediacy of the particular, of what each person can offer in the quick exchange and the active production of trust (Wittel 2001: 67–8). This produces further 'network capital' especially stretching across societal borders.

In this networking pattern, work and play are to some degree assimilated. Indeed workplaces are increasingly designed to look like play places and leisure places, though a kind of designed 'Starbuck-ization' are sites for much work. This overlap is especially marked where 'nomadic workstyles' have developed and this is having extensive effects upon the design and use of 'offices' which are increasingly distributed and diversified (see Harrison, Wheeler, Whitehead 2004).

Wittel describes how the times of play and the times of work are less tightly drawn, as especially the 'party' and other 'networking events' are transformed into and become part of 'work' (2001: 68–9). The categories of friend and colleague merge and cross over from one to the other. Moreover, this network sociality depends upon network capital: 'the use of cars, trains, buses and the underground, of airplanes, taxis and hotels, and it is based on phones, faxes, answering machines, voicemail, video-conferencing, mobiles, email, chat rooms, discussion forums, mailing lists and web sites' (plus old-fashioned business cards as key tokens of exchange: Wittel 2001: 69).

With network sociality clumps of persistent ties almost disappear and connections are long range but with intense obligations for intermittent meetings. As these connections spread, so the networks of weak ties and the power of 'network capital' come to be further extended.

Such a network sociality is particularly noticeable within highly globalized industries. Employees in the building design industry are increasingly transnational, with few employees having a single nationality (and many are in mixed nationality relationships). Most do not think of themselves as 'company people' since their primary loyalty is to their profession. Companies are partly chosen because they demonstrate a 'cosmopolitan culture' (Kennedy 2004). Specifically with regard to networking, social networks are predominantly multinational with few being wholly expatriate or local. They possess a 'post-national' character (Kennedy 2004: 176). These employees are enmeshed in a pool of post-national friends transcending strong feelings of nationhood.

Also, there are powerful overlaps between work and friendship networks with work-based leisure-time socializing very significant for these mobile professional workers. The 'project' and the work team are key organizing features of work *and* leisure networks. Links once established tend to stick and people keep in touch with overseas friends from different nationalities. Networks endure through visits and other communications (Kennedy 2004: 175). And as friends move and form other networks with similar people, more friends are added to the revolving circuits of a 'post-national' social life characterized by density, connectivity and multiplicity (Kennedy 2004: 172, 176). 'Eventually, as friends move and form, or join, other networks with more like-minded individuals in the next host country, and because previous contacts are maintained, yet more friends are added to the revolving circuits of transnational social life' (Kennedy 2004: 176). Although this kind of 'nomadic networker' is not yet typical it is likely to become empirically much more significant and has the effect of further distributing friendship internationally (see studies in Burawoy 2000).

And this reflects the more general process by which accumulation within networks – that is *who* you know – becomes apparently more significant than *what* you know (Durbin 2006). And this is because of the importance of new kinds of knowledge management within and between organizations. To the extent that some knowledge is tacit, that is informal and individually embodied through specific experiences, then organizational success will result from how people can access such information. The more that people construct formal and especially informal networks, then the more opportunity there is to create, circulate and share such tacit knowledge and to build new capital. Durbin describes the importance of the 'social networks that exchange tacit knowledge and allocate developmental and financial resources' (2006: 1); she especially notes how such networking socially discriminates against especially women (and others) who are unable to enter or sustain membership of such networks. More generally, Reich describes each firm not as a single 'rational actor' but as a social entity: 'a façade, behind which teems an array of decentralized groups and subgroups continuously contracting with similar diffuse working units all over the world' 1991: 81). And it is argued that integrating networks into the production of knowledge is beneficial for generating new kinds of knowledge, through what Seufert, Krogh and Bach term 'knowledge networking' (1999).

One consequence is that many travellers find it more difficult to escape the 'office'. No longer is the person in transit also *incommunicado* (Ling, Yttri 1999). Now that laptops, PDAs, blackberries, communicators and mobile phones are standard equipment among business people, and as airports, hotels, cafés, planes and trains are to an uneven degree designed as workspaces with internet and laptop connections, many travellers have fewer opportunities for 'escape'. Places-in-transit become 'a high-tech command centre' from which business people communicate with clients and colleagues. It is expected of many travellers that their office can reach them in real time and that they will respond to phone calls, text messages, emails, faxes and so on. 'Taking off on a business trip used to mean getting away from it all. But corporate downsizing and new information technology (which both allow and require you to be totally wired at all times) have forced travellers to be more accountable and productive when they're away' (Collis 2000, 112; Lyons, Urry 2005). 'As many HP [Hewlett-Packard] virtual team members work at home, or on the road, mobile technologies such as cell phones and wireless networks make it possible to conduct virtual meetings from (almost) anywhere, anytime' (Jones, Oyung, Pace 2002).

Mobile communication systems and 'personalized networking' are doubled-edged swords that simultaneously allow contact with absent others as well as monitoring by absent others. They allow 'for a sense of presence at a-distance that allows the traveller to be always available, and therefore always under surveillances' (Molz 2006). To inhabit such machines is to be connected to, or to be at home with, 'sites' across the world, others being uncannily present *and* absent, here and there, near and distant, home and away, proximate and distant (Urry 2004b, 35).

Specifically, many people use travel (and waiting) time to keep in touch with one's 'personalized network', restoring trust, maintaining 'absent presence' and rearranging events (see Katz, Aakhus 2002b, on 'perpetual contact'; Licoppe 2004, on 'connected presence'). Much mobile phone use thus occurs in between events and sometimes this in-between time–space is more important than the actual events. As I have argued these 'interspaces' and the activities conducted there can be highly significant (especially with SMS texting: Truch, Hulme 2004: 2). Various social groups spend a large amount of time in transit and while in transit people text and call, both for work and especially for friendship. Much mobile phone involves arranging and rearranging 'events' on the move, in transit. Network capital thus can get extended while in interspace, in the interstices in between the fields or domains of work, friendship, family. And this is partly according to Vilhelmson and Thulin because regular work at fixed places is beginning to fade away (2001).

Such networking practices also seem to be present within much family life. This is partly because families are being plugged into an ever-expanding array of communication technologies that connect family members to one another and to the outside world. The typical modern family with two teenagers living in the rich 'north' is said to have access to several land-line phones, three or four mobile phones, a couple of computers, cameras (including a digital one) and video cameras, email accounts, at least one car, travel cards, TV sets, DVDs and videos, magazines, a newspaper and various credit cards. The family is a communications hub, a centre of network capital: 'No longer a sanctuary where the family was relatively shielded from intrusions from the outside world, the home is now a communication hub, infused with messages of diverse and increasingly global origins' (Bachen 2001: 1). Yet these 'machines' also enable local ordering as the co-ordination of seemingly endless journeys to work, school, recreational and domestic activities that would be practically impossible without email, text messages, telephone calls and diaries. 'Families and technologies in households are inter-connected as elements of the same system' (Bachen 2001: 2). So high network capital families are able to mobilize social networks through the making and sustaining of many connections at-a-distance (see Larsen, Urry, Axhausen 2006).

But such 'families' are also being transformed through growing divorce rates, single parenthood, the rising age of first marriage, joint custody, co-habitation, singles, stepfamilies and gay couples (Allen, Crow 2001: ch. 2; see Weston 1991, on 'families we choose'). Families are becoming networked and are not so much nuclear as 'unclear'

(Bauman 2003). In particular among couples without children, long-distance relationships are common, especially because women pursue careers more-or-less like men (Holmes 2004, 190; Walby 1997). Many dual-career couples will at one moment live apart. 'Unclear' families are fragmented, not only socially but also spatially, with most families moving house after a divorce. Moving back and forth between one's mother's and father's new place of residence involves considerable travel for children and parents, especially if one relocates to another city (Allan, Crow 2001: 132). Thus family life can be increasingly conducted at-a-distance involving 'choice' as to which family members are seen, how often they are seen and the nature of these 'family' connections (Finch, Mason 1993; Allen, Crow 2001). The need for negotiation and deliberation about how, when and by whom family responsibilities are fulfilled is particularly noticeable with 'families' being increasingly diverse and individuated (Beck, Beck-Gernsheim 1995; Beck-Gernsheim 2002).

There are also variations in the nature of networks as people proceed through different stages in the life cycle. As people age, accessing a day-to-day 'support network' from other family members becomes more relevant than the sustaining of more distanciated 'social networks' (Wenger 1997). Such support networks take different forms, providing emotional support, companionship, instrumental help and information on a more or less day-to-day basis. With a more networked family life this support network will often now entail state or marketized provision in order that it is available from face-to-face if close family and friends are at-a-distance. And with families spread out increasingly across the world much family life can only be maintained through extensive travel and communications, combined with formal services increasingly bought through the market but on occasions provided through local or national states.

This networking of family life stems from large increases in the number of households around the world. Between 1985–2000 the annual growth rate in the number of households world-wide was 2.3 per cent, while the world's population grew by 1.3 per cent (see Liu, Daily, Ehrlich, Luck 2003). And many of those smaller households are on the move. The number of international migrants more than doubled between 1960 and 2000 (UNDP 2004: 87). Various cities and societies now have large number of people living within them who were not born there (Miami 59 per cent, Singapore 33 per cent, London 28 per cent, Israel 37 per cent, Switzerland 25 per cent, New Zealand 22 per cent: UNDP 2004: 99, 87). Such migration is rarely an isolated decision pursued by individual agents but rather a collective action involving families, kinships and other communal contacts. Migrants travel to join established groups of settlers who provide transnational arrangements for them in receiving countries, while simultaneously retaining links with their country of origin and with chains of other immigrants (Goulborne 1999; Ryan 2004: 355).

Migration disperses family members and friends across vast areas and thus the intimate networks of care, support and affection stretch over large geographical distances (Chamberlain 1995). There are over 2,000 'transnational communities', most of which are organized on the basis of long-distance communications and travel (see Cohen 1997). This is most striking in the case of the 'society' of 'overseas Chinese' with a global membership calculated between 22 m and 45 m, bigger than most countries. This community has produced an array of Chinatowns that are nodes in extensive travel patterns, involving both the overseas Chinese community and their close patterns of family life and as core elements of 'global tourism' (Ma, Cartier 2003). Such transnational communities could not prosper without large amounts of travel both to the homeland and between the various Chinatowns where family members are distributed (Ong, Nonini 1997). Recent research in Trinidad shows that about 60 per cent of nuclear families having at least one family member living abroad (Miller, Slater 2000: 12, 36). To-and-fro travel, as well as extensive email communications, are necessary to sustain family life between Trinidad, the US and the UK, producing a 'brain circulation' across the globe. While the British Pakistani community is transnational and cosmopolitan, engaging in a complex traffic in 'objects-persons-places-sentiments' between the UK and many locations across Pakistan. Pakistanis returning home are obliged to take objects from the UK to their relatives and friends still in Pakistan (Werbner 1999: 26).

There are thus complex connection between forms of transport, particular 'family events' and the general sustaining of family life at-a-distance. There have been huge increases in the scale of world-wide communications through telephone calls and the internet. The overall volume of international telephone calls increased at least tenfold between the early 1982 and 2001 (Vertovec 2004: 219). This is so in most countries, partly through various innovations such as prepaid cards and mobile technology. Thus for migrants and their kin within the world today: 'transnational connectivity through cheap telephone calls is at the heart of their lives' (Vertovec 2004: 223). Empirical studies of phone calls show that the greater the distance between callers the longer the calls that are made but the more infrequent they are (Licoppe 2004: 142–3). Such calls often presume a certain ritualistic character. To have an open conversation is a sign of the bond between family members often living very far away from each other (Licoppe 2004: 143). Thus geographical proximity or distance do not correlate straightforwardly with how emotionally close relatives feel to one another, nor indeed how far relatives will provide support or care for each other' (Mason 2004: 421). Intimacy and caring can take place at-a-distance, through letters, packets, photographs, emails, money transactions, telephone calls, as well as intermittent visits.

Such issues were examined in recent research already reported upon (Larsen, Urry, Axhausen 2006: chaps 6–8). Respondents were asked to name up to 10 'non-local friends'. These were found to be widely scattered with on average only one in the north-west region, with the *average* distance between them and their 'non-local friends' being 1,402 km. All respondents have 'non-local friends', the mean being 6.5 (Larsen, Urry, Axhausen 2006: Table 7, Appendix B). Three could have listed more than ten such places. They have on average friends in two foreign countries and over half of the sample of youngish people have friends in non-European countries. Several of the university graduates made friendships while studying abroad or with exchange students; some met English and foreign friends when working or travelling abroad; and some made English friends while touring the world or working abroad (Larsen, Urry, Axhausen 2006: Table 8, Appendix B).

Also respondents live far away from their 'close family members'. Indeed there are almost as many family ties abroad as within the respondents' immediate neighbourhood. Many of them have 'close family members' abroad (Larsen, Urry, Axhausen 2006: ch. 6). Very few possess family networks nearby. Respondents thus have to journey to another city or town when meeting up with three out of four of their close family members. Extensive travel to meet up with their nearest family is unavoidable and almost always necessary.

We also asked respondents to identify the locations of those people (up to ten) that they consider 'most important' to their present life and where they now live. Some of these people that the respondents are closest to and most dependent upon in fact live abroad (Larsen, Urry, Axhausen 2006). The 'strong ties' of care, support and affection are thus significantly dispersed geographically.

Even though many friendships are stretched out and much communicative travel in-between meetings sustains them, few of these respondents talked about friendships that occurred without intermittent co-presence. Most interviewees agreed with this statement:

It is easier to keep in contact with people with text messages and emails. You can have a broader range of friends and it doesn't matter where they are in theory. [Yet] I don't think that good friendship is as good only via a message. That's not a proper friendship really . . . I couldn't really stay friends with somebody if I am just messaging them and never seeing them. I would have to see them now and again in the flesh and do things. (Larsen, Urry, Axhausen 2006: 79)

'Strong ties do depend upon communications. All respondents have regular communications with each of their identified 'most important people', through email, phone or text message (but not necessarily all three). The respondents talk on average every other day on the phone or text or email with their 'most important people', so they have more frequent interaction with them at-a-distance than face-to-face. Distance though affects the differential frequency of use. As distance increases, face-to-face contact declines (see ch. 11 below) as does the rate of texting and phoning. But the use of email increases with distance (Larsen, Urry, Axhausen 2006: figure 1, 2)

These various studies show that people's spread-out lives are nevertheless relational, connected and embedded. They are individualized in that each person's networks and relations are specific to that individual. But they are social in that these networked lives are enmeshed in social dramas where their actions depend upon negotiation, approval and the feelings of others often at-a-distance and they have social and emotional consequences over distance. People are enmeshed in networks that both enable and constrain possible actions. And interestingly this is true not only for people in relationships and families but also for 'singles' that increasingly form tight-knit groups of friends where somewhat analogous forms of care and support can flourish, according to Watters (2004).

Conclusion

I began by examining the small-worlds literature. Although this is an interesting contribution to deciphering networked relations around the world such a literature does not deal sufficiently with what is meant by 'knowing' someone else. This I discussed in relationship to work, friendship and family relations that are increasingly 'networked'. The apparently different domains of work, family and friendship have each become more networked and hence issues of distance, communications and intermittent meetingness are present within each. Furthermore, networks within these domains increasingly overlap so movement between and across them is significant. Network capital and weak ties seem to spread from domain to domain especially with the growth of more 'personalized network' patterns. And most significantly here these domains generate high levels of travel between often far-flung network members because meeting up is still so significant. In the next chapter, I directly consider the significance of physical co-present meetings.

11

Meetings

And it is rather peculiar to think of the happy person as a solitary person: for the human being is a social creature and naturally disposed to live with others
(Aristotle Nicomachean Ethics IX.9)

In the last chapter I discussed the small worlds literature and noted its failure to examine what is really meant by 'knowing' someone and especially the significance of meetings to these knowing processes. This importance of meetings clarifies Watts' critique of Barabási when he says that the main limitation with the scale-free view of networks is that everything is assumed to come for free. Network ties are treated as costless (Watts 2003: 113). But establishing and maintaining ties for social groups is according to Watts not at all cost free. However, he does not realize that they are costly because of the 'work' of communications, travel and meetings that is involved in 'performing' social networks. This costly work constitutes the very stuff of social life involving time, space, money, resources, risks, pleasures and so on.

These many processes are illuminated in David Lodge's novel *Small World* (1983). It describes how networks of professionals have to spend time travelling to meetings, with in effect the network only reproducing itself through periodic meetings to cement its weak ties. The novel especially focuses upon 'conferences' where the most common refrain is of course 'it's a small world'. Lodge describes the complex, multi-layered and richly gossipy nature of conferences and other 'occasioned meetings'. *Small World* brings out that what gets exchanged through intense and dynamic conversational interactions are rich social goods. These include friendship, power, projects, markets, information, rumours, job deals, sexual favours, gossip and so on. Central to networks then are very 'costly' meetings, communications and travel through time–space, these being necessary to 'form' and to 'cement' weak ties at least for another stretch of time.

Thus the connections between people as examined by the network literature presuppose intermittent meetings. They are not cost free. Although people may 'know' others in a short chain of acquaintance-ship, this produces less affect than if they intermittently meet up. Indeed in some senses people might be said only to 'know' each other if they do intermittently meet. However, intense meetings at one time, say as students, can then carry that particular network without so frequent further meetings. Affect we might then say can be mobile through time/space.

Also it would seem that those with the largest number of weak ties will be advantaged in such meetings so producing many more weak ties in a virtuous circle, what is known as the 'Matthew effect' ('For unto everyone that hath shall be given . . . but from him that hath not shall be taken away even that which he hath'; Watts 2003: 108). There are then positive feedback mechanisms whereby the network rich get richer and the network poor poorer, so producing greater inequalities between people. Meetings are essential to network capital (being one of the components I elaborated in ch. 9) and thus to enhancing through positive feedback, aristocratic rather than egalitarian patterns of network capital. The world-wide inequalities in structured access to the infrastructural resources necessary for travel, communications and meetings would *prima facie* suggest more of an aristocratic rather than an egalitarian model (see ch. 10).

And this is necessarily part of networking practices. A network only functions if it is intermittently 'activated' through occasioned co-presence from time to time. *Ceteris paribus* 'network activation' occurs if there are periodic events each week, or month or year, when meetingness is more or less obligatory. Examples of this obligatory meetingness include hourly meetings of a teenage friendship group, daily meetings of a couple, weekly meetings in a project team, monthly strategy meetings in a company, annual Thanksgiving celebrations within families, bi-annual conferences in an international professional organization, and so on. These are often unmissable, obligatory and make or *perform* the network in question. And these meetings necessitate physical travel by some or all of the participants; there is a 'mobility burden'. In order to continue to be within a given network there are obligations to travel, to meet up and to converse. These obligations cannot be evaded at least within a particular period of time. Meetings are thus important components within diverse complex systems especially because those systems have been 'networked' as seen in the previous chapter. It is precisely because of that networking of work relations, family life, friendship, leisure and so on, that face-to-face meetings then are so significant. Meetings can be both effective and affective (see the review in Mina 2002).

Moreover, Van Vree's analysis of the development of 'modern meeting behaviour' and various 'meeting regimes' show how: 'power, status and property are largely being distributed in and through meetings to an unprecedented degree' (Van Vree 1999: 278). Particularly important in the twentieth century has been the 'professionalization' of meetings among various networks – and these seem characterized by more informal modes of behaviour. And we can add that these modes will entail overlaps and interchanges with meeting behaviour within family and friendship networks. Overall it seems that 'national meeting regimes' are giving way to 'continental and global meeting regimes' (1999: 332). Van Vree suggests that Marx's 'c[C]lass struggle has largely been translated into meeting activities', while 'the invisible hand' of Adam Smith is the entirety of unpredictable and unexpected results of meetings and negotiations' (1999: 314).

I use the single term here of 'meeting' to refer to both the highly formalized with 'agendas', structure and timetables *and* the informal, to where the specific place and time are planned in advance to where they are negotiated en route, and to the enormous number of different contexts in which two or more people gather together and orient themselves to those others for some period of time. Apart from Van Vree, Goffman and Schwartzmann this has been an overlooked topic in contemporary sociology/social science. Part of the argument of this chapter is to re-instate 'meetings' within sociology and especially to see how and in what ways meetings make social networks that in a sense can only be said to exist if they are intermittently performed.

In this chapter I examine various aspects of such proliferating and network-productive meetings. First, I develop an analysis of five bases of co-presence that engender travelling and meeting. I then specifically consider how and why face-to-faceness is so significant in engendering such meetingness, drawing especially upon Simmel and Goffman. I then examine studies of meetings at work and within families and between friends, drawing in part on recent research. There is a brief section on those meetings that take place on the move and how these meetings are coming to generate new kinds of times and spaces. There is a short conclusion.

Why Meet?

I elaborate five processes within social networks that engender travelling, meeting and normally much talk (this is drawn from Urry 2002b, 2003b). I am not suggesting though that especially the 'home' is not also a place of co-presence and rich complex conversation. As Ellegård and Vilhelmson maintain, the home can be a 'pocket of local order' (2004). But to move outside that pocket it is important to distinguish five analytically separate processes that engender intermittent movement and co-present meeting.

First, there are legal, economic and familial obligations which mean that it is intermittently necessary for people to travel and be within some other place. These formal obligations include travel to work or a job interview; to attend a family event (wedding, christening, Thanksgiving, marriage, funeral, Christmas, birthday); to visit a lawyer or court; or to attend a school or hospital or university or public office. Often such a 'mobility burden' involves complex inequalities of power with the less powerful 'having to' travel at specific times along certain routeways. Changes in the location of various kinds of office and organization often increase the scale and complexity of journeys undertaken especially by those whose mobility is particularly dependent upon the mobilities of others.

Second, there are less formally prescribed social obligations often involving strong normative expectations of being present *and* attentive. Such mobility burdens involve seeing 'the other' 'face-to-face' and sometimes 'body-to-body' (which in turn ranges from the formal handshake to sexual intimacy). This mutual presencing among those with weak ties intermittently enables network members to 'read' what the other is thinking, to observe their body language, to hear 'first hand' what they have to say, to sense their overall response or to undertake emotional work. 'Co-presence renders persons uniquely accessible, available, and subject to one another' (Goffman 1963: 22). Such social obligations to networks of friends or family or colleagues are necessary for sustaining trust and commitment that will have to persist during periods of distance and solitude. Such social obligations can be associated with obligations to spend 'quality' affective time often within specific locations away from normal patterns of work and family life. There can be a distinct temporal feel to the moment, separate from and at odds with 'normal' life ('take time out' as the advertising goes so as to re-establish a close relationship). On occasions the experience of this affective togetherness can involve a kind of collective 'effervescence' (Durkheim 1915; Chayko 2002: 69).

Third, various material objects are often central to specific social networks and entail a temporary occasioned encounter. It is may be necessary to be co-present with others to sign specific *contracts*, to work on written or visual *texts*, to give *gifts* to distant others, to devise solutions to *ill-functioning objects* or to devise new *instruments* for scientific purposes. These objects may have a specific location or they can move and those involved will 'meet up' at some specific place to work upon them (as in the laboratory, the family home, the office, the workshop and so on). Increasingly this involves 'elbow to elbow' working, facing with others the same or parallel computer screens either in a fixed location (study, internet café, office, airport lounge) or anywhere that the software and documents can be accessed (but see Knorr Cetina, Bruegger 2002, on how financial traders increasingly share materials on physically distant screens). Actor network analyses in technology studies have brought out the central role of 'objects' in the social networks of science, and how those objects are typically located in place but may also move between places while contingently keeping their shape (Law, Mol 2001).

Fourth, places are often central to a networked social life. There are obligations to be in a place 'directly', to walk a city, to be 'by the seaside', to climb a mountain, to view that sunset and so on. Such 'leisure places' may be experienced 'directly' through a 'face-to-place' co-presence with people's bodies immersed in that 'other' place. Such facing of place normally involves travel over, and beyond, some non-places, to get to these distinct places, normally in the company of 'significant' others. Such places help to constitute social networks. They are that place where the family goes on holiday, where the leisure group fishes, where the professional organization holds its conference, where rock climbers are especially drawn to and so on (Macnaghten, Urry 2001; see the next chapter).

Finally, many networks are organized around the experience of a 'live' event that happens at a specific moment and place. These include political rallies, concerts, plays, meetings, matches, celebrations, film premières, conferences, festivals and so on. Such events in real time generate intense moments of simultaneous travel and co-presence. For specialized social networks known as 'fans' these are moments that cannot be 'missed' and which produce mass movements at specific moments to 'catch' the event 'live'. This can be an awesome 'burden'. Certain places are distinct sites for such events. They may well be: 'unique places due to the fact that such places stage these globally unique events' such as particular sporting, artistic or festival events (Roche 2000: 199, 204, on mega-events).

So there are these diverse obligations within social life that entail co-presence and hence intermittent travel. Networks thus come together though a mixture of formal and informal obligations, as well as through the significance of objects, place and events. What this normally generates are co-present meetings and conversations between some set of network members. These conversations are at least intermittently necessary to solidify weak ties 'at-a-distance'. Gladwell notes the importance of such 'word of mouth' communications in systems tipping from one state to another. But contrary to notions of a virtual world rather the opposite seems to be the case: 'we are about to enter the age of the word of mouth . . . to rely more and more on very primitive kinds of social contacts' (Gladwell 2002: 264–5). As BT argues it is 'good to talk' but why is this so and especially why is it *contra* BT still good to talk *face-to-face* and not through a telephone or mobile phone?

Talking Face-to-Face

In chapter 2, I noted Simmel's analysis of how the eye is a unique 'sociological achievement' (1997: 111; see Jensen 2006). The look between people produces moments of intimacy since: '[o]ne cannot take through the eye without at the same time giving'; this produces the 'most complete reciprocity' of person to person, face-to-face (Simmel 1997: 112). The look is returned and trust can get established. Goffman terms these eye-to-eye looks that enable people to develop encounters, displaying attentiveness and commitment and detecting where there is lack of trustful commitment in others (1967: 169; Schutz 1963: 92). Goffman more generally noted the importance of the: 'realm of activity that is generated by face-to-face interaction and organized by norms of co-mingling – a domain containing weddings, family meals, chaired meetings, forced marches, service encounters, queues, crowds, and couples' (1971: 13; Urry 2002b). Such 'face-to-face interactions', such focussed encounters presuppose the *movement* of one, some or all of the participants, to such weddings, family meals, chaired meetings, forced marches, service encounters, queues, crowds, couples and so on.

So what happens within conversations? They are a performance or achievement of the participants, especially if there are inequalities of power between the participants. Such conversations are often necessary to talk *through* problems, especially the telling of 'troubles'. 'When the eyes are joined', conversations normally flow, typically beginning with small talk (Goffman 1963: 92). Face-to-face conversations are produced, topics can come and go, misunderstandings can be quickly corrected, commitment and sincerity can be directly assessed. Participants often protect the other in order not to embarrass them, and much loose talk involves helping to construct and mould the conversational flow, to get the conversation 'going' (Boden, Molotch 1994). Mische and White describe the increasing importance of conversation as a specific form of social discourse characterized by free-floating discursive exchanges as indexed by the term 'making conversation' (1998: 696). The outcomes of the conversations are stochastic and uncertain (Mische, White 1998: 700; Miller 2006).

Especially significant in conversation is the developing of trust (Boden 1994). This has to be worked at through a joint performance by those conversing. 'Thick' intermittent co-presence involves rich, multi-layered and dense conversations. Some exchanges of information or decisions or affect are only possible face-to-face. There are also some networks, such as crime networks, where information must be spoken and not written down (so no written record remains). Again this entails a significant obligation for everyone to be there, to display attentiveness and to stay talking face-to-face. And producing such trust becomes especially significant as relationships get to be conducted at a distance and with less day-to-day information and reinforcement (although e-Bay is interesting here as a counter-example with various mechanisms to effect trust).

Conversations consist of not only words but also indexical expressions, facial gestures, body language, status, voice intonation, pregnant silences, past histories, anticipated conversations and actions, turn-taking practices and so on. As Montaigne wrote about the special effects of face-to-face talk: 'g[G]estures and movements animate words . . . Our bearing, our facial expressions, our voice, our dress and the way we stand can lend value to things' (quoted Miller 2006: 287).

Such a face-to-face 'interaction order' presupposes turn-taking. A tilt of the head indicates a willingness to receive an utterance. Such turn taking is highly structured. The ebb and flow of talk is a simple but highly effective system. Turn-taking thus: 'worked like a revolving gate, demanding and facilitating deft entry and exist, and effectively managing the flow of talk by spacing speakers and pacing topics' (Boden 1994: 66). Such turns are valued, they are distributed between participants and they normally involve only one speaker talking at a time. Turns are not allocated in advance, turn transition is quick and there are few gaps and overlaps in turn transition.

Conversations also often involve touch. There is a rich, complex and culturally variable vocabulary of touch. The embodied character of conversation is thus: 'a managed physical action as well as "brain work"' (Boden, Molotch 1994: 262). Goffman describes how information within talk is 'embodied'. Thus when:

> one speaks of experiencing someone else with one's naked senses, one usually implies the reception of embodied messages. This linkage of naked senses on one side and embodied transmission on the other provides one of the crucial communication conditions of face-to-face interaction. (Goffman 1963: 15)

There are two key features of such co-present encounters: the richness of information flow between the participants and the ongoing feedback from each that results from being able to see the face of the other. According to Thrift the face is the chief site of affect and hence to see the face produces an unmediated access to the affective register of the other person (2004d: 61). Such affects organize how bodies are disposed for actions; and they depend upon relationships. This view of affect is anti-individualistic and opposes itself to the idea of deep-rooted emotional drives. Affects arise from relationships and so it is not a question of simply seeing the other. It is the relationship that effects affect we might say (Thrift 2004d: 63). Affects is an emergent effect of bodies in relationship to each other and especially through their distribution in time and space.

In particular there are co-present encounters located within time–space when bodies are brought into affective proximity. We can term these a meeting or a 'gathering' in which people sense that they are bodily close enough to be seen and to see others, and especially to see the face of the other (Goffman 1963: 17). Participants meet together, they each commit themselves to remain there for the duration of the interaction, and each uses and handles the timing of utterances and of silences to perform talk. Almost always meetings will entail travel by some or all of the participants, since conferences, family get-togethers, parties, symposia, bonding events, camps, a 'night-out' and so on are often located on 'neutral territory'. As Boden writes: 'The drums beat and from far and near the chosen foregather, face-to-face across the shiny table' (1994: 82). And partly those present at each meeting offer their time to be there. There are various kinds of travel time gift to those others who are present. Meetings often involve very significant exchanges, contestations and expressions of guilt over 'travel time' as the key resource (see Jain, Lyons 2006, on various 'gifts' of travel time).

In particular sites come alive through the 'constant cacophony of talk' (Amin, Thrift 2002: 86), or 'Talk, talk, talk and more talk' (Boden 1994: 82). And talk here is not only a means of representation or the functional exchange of information. Talk comprises sets of utterances that often carry out tasks or do things. Such performative utterances include agreeing contracts, forming trust, doing deals, repairing relationships, celebrating family life, getting married, making new contacts and so on.

With talk there is an expectation of mutual attentiveness and this is by contrast with the 'civil inattention' normally found between 'strangers' who happen to be in the same space (Goffman 1963: 84–5). Meetings are complex encounters, 'ritual affairs, tribal gatherings in which the faithful reaffirm solidarity and warring factions engage in verbal battles . . . When in doubt call a meeting. When one meeting isn't enough, schedule another' (Boden 1994: 81). Beyond making decisions, meetings have various other functions: seeing how one is heard, executing procedures, distributing rewards, status and blame, reinforcing friendship, judging commitment, and having an enjoyable time (Schwartzman 1989; Boden 1994). Meetings are especially important in what Goffman terms 'face-work' between people in interaction. Thus: 'the person tends to conduct himself [sic] during an encounter so as to maintain both his own face and the face of other participants' (Goffman 1972: 9). But meetings are often also where one's 'face' is put on the line, one's face will be threatened intellectually, organizationally or emotionally and that serious repair work may be necessary to restore one's face. Also Mische and White note how conversations contain the potential for switching, with changes in speech register indicating abrupt transitions of networks (1998). So different networks can be drawn upon within the same conversation; a chance comment or reference moves the conversation from in effect one network to another.

This face-to-face talk sustains the normal patterns of social life that involve long periods of distance and of solitude. So far face-to-face communication is the richest, multi-channel medium because it engages all the senses: 'all the technology in the world does not – as least yet and maybe never – replace face-to-face contact when it comes to brainstorming, inspiring passion, or enabling many kinds of serendipitous discovery' (Leonard, Swap 1999: 160: Amin, Thrift

2002: 38; generally see Hutchby 2001). Nor can those technologies necessarily sustain periods of absence that can get too long and the weak ties can gradually decay (although those distant others may still be 'known of'). What are deemed to be appropriate periods without co-presence will vary partly in terms of the 'material worlds' that potentially connect network members. And if there are such material connections (motility rather than actually mobility) then the mobility burden will probably be higher with more obligations to make that visit.

The networks of weak ties discussed in chapter 10 depend upon two main forms of intermittent meetings: those where *specific* others are encountered (parents, best friends, particular colleague and so on); and those where *generalized* others are met. The latter depend upon being within specific places that are good for encountering sets of weak ties without knowing exactly who will be present. Many different networks come together at such places: at festivals, sports clubs, hobby events, special interest holidays, new age camps, seminars, beaches in Rio, protest camps and so on (Szerszynski 1997). Such places are good for 'networking' within particular groups, although it will not be known who will actually be there. This co-presence often involves 'showing one's face' within such places and that face then is reported to others. Travel and weak ties within far-flung networks generate what we might call 'presentism' that in turn further extend weak ties.

Meetings at Work

First, we can further note how important face-to-face work is within organizations. US research shows managers spending up to half of their time in face-to-face meetings, with much of this work involving collaboration with and evaluation of colleagues through lengthy and intense periods of co-presence and talk (Boden, Molotch 1994: 272; Van Vree 1999: 279). Face-to-face talk and phone talk can occupy three-quarters of an executive's working time (Boden 1994: 51). The higher the organizational position, the more significant is establishing and nurturing 'complex interpersonal networks' through rounds of face-to-face meetings (Boden, Molotch 1994: 273). There is a high frequency of face-to-face meetings where the emotional, personal or financial aspects of work are involved.

So why meet? Strassmann summarizes: 'there are meetings, and meetings about meetings, and meetings to plan reports, and meetings to review the status of reports. And what these meetings are about is people just trying to figure out what they are doing' (cited in Romano, Nunamaker 2001, 4). Moreover, the ubiquitous meeting tool, 'the personal diary', makes sure that a new meeting is arranged, as the current meeting is ending:

> One of the unstated protocols of modern work is that those attending meetings should bring their diaries and schedule into their future the circle of forthcoming meetings. Indeed, this forms part of the ritualistic end of meeting: the entry into the diary of the next meeting. Indeed, the notion 'diarize' has been coined to describe this ritual. (Symes 1999: 373)

Schwartzman distinguishes between two types of meetings according to 'time, formality and representation': scheduled and unscheduled meetings. Scheduled meetings are pre-arranged, scheduled for a specific time and place, having an explicit agenda, perhaps materialized as a paper document, with more or less formal turn-taking and minutes. By contrast, unplanned meeting talk is loosely regulated and informal in conversational style and there is seldom a need to report back. Unplanned meetings often involve bumping-into-each encounters and especially 'knock-on-the-door' meetings when problems and enquiries have to be solved immediately face-to-face. Both types of meetings are communicative events with specific norms of speaking and interacting, oratorical genres and styles, interest and participation (Schwartzman 1989). The commonsense notion of what meetings are and do in organizations is mistaken since:

> Instead of accepting task-focused assumptions that suggest that decisions, crises, conflicts, and the like are what meetings are about, the opposite is proposed here, that is, that meetings are what decisions, problems, and crisis are about. Meetings reproduce themselves by the volume of decisions, crises and the like that an organisation produces. (Schwartzman 1989: 9–10)

Decisions, problems, and crises occur because they produce meetings and meetings produce organizations. So organizations are about meetings, organizations are made and remade through the performances of meetings (Schwartzman 1989: 40–1, 86). Schwartzman defines a meeting as:

> A meeting is a gathering of three or more people who agree to assemble for a purpose ostensibly related to the functioning of an

organisation or group. The event is characterised by multiparty talk that is episodic in nature, and participants either develop or use specific conventions for regulating this talk (1989: 63).

Important aspects here are the physical coordination and assembling of these three or more people at the same place, their roles and their speech performances.

More generally meetings are especially significant because of changes in how organizations now work. Organizations have shifted from an emphasis upon the 'individual work ethic' to the 'collective team ethic' especially with the development of 'project working' (see Grabher 2004). Face-to-face social and leadership skills are especially valued in such organizations (Sennett 1998: ch. 6). This is especially so in those organizations whose structure is 'blown to bits' by new informational technologies. Such organizations are more distributed, with the extensive out-sourcing of function and activity away from a 'head' or 'main' office where core staff would have been located (Evans, Wurstler 2000; Harrison, Wheeler, Whitehead 2004). Project working is significant as organizations are 'deconstructed' through new networking technologies; according to Grabher 'projects are cool' (2004: 1491).

Such 'de-constructed' organizations rely more upon networking at a distance and extensive travel in order to achieve intermittent face-to-face co-presence especially where much of the knowledge involved is tacit (Evans, Wurstler 2000: 217; Boden 1994: 211). In particular: 'only via personal travel can members of top management teams position themselves for important face-to-face interactions' that are necessary in dispersed organizational structures (Doyle, Nathan 2001: 13). This is especially important within 'project-based networks'. Thus software developers project-working in Ireland rely upon intense 'team' working in order to seek to offset two features of their experience (Ó Riain 2000). First, the workforce involved in software development in Ireland is multi-cultural so forms of face-to-face bonding are necessary in order to deal with otherwise potentially disruptive 'differences' between people from varied national and ethnic backgrounds. And second, these developers have very mobile careers and relatively fleeting associations with each other. So what is required for a project is: 'an intense experience of a shared space and culture in order to create a cohesive work team' (Ó Riain 2000: 189). Such places of intensity: 'are increasingly "between" other places' and in the Irish case is part of the 'innovative regional milieu' found in the Dublin area, a place of meetingness (Ó Riain 2000: 189).

In parallel research on the organizational and knowledge management processes by which photocopiers get repaired a key role was played by the breakfasts that the engineers all took together before starting their work each day (Brown, Duguid 2000). These informal co-present discussions enabled a vast store of practical or tacit knowledge to be circulated and exchanged and this would not have happened without regular informal talking though issues over breakfast.

Indeed many work related meetings take place in interesting locations away from the office. Davidson and Cope's examination of conferences, conventions, incentive travel and corporate hospitality bring out how business trips often have what we might term touristic qualities and therefore business travel and tourism are being de-differentiated (2003; Weber, Chon 2003; Larsen, Axhausen, Urry 2006). Davidson and Cope maintain that: 'for some forms of business travel, the leisure and pleasure element is absolutely crucial' (2003: 256). Partly as a consequence the amount of such travel remains fairly consistent and resilient over time (Davidson, Cope 2003: 13).

Normal business trips become touristic when they expand into weekend breaks (Davidson, Cope 2003: 257). Academic conferences are being organized in more exotic places with conferencing functioning as a form of conspicuous consumption through which power is displayed, networks are sustained and interesting places are seen face-to-face (Høyer, Næss 2001). Many (long-distance) meetings have a 'leisure' component to them. Davidson and Cope argue that seeing the other place is what keeps them alive (2003). While Collis argues that:

> perhaps the strongest argument against conferences being in danger of being replaced by Internet or videoconferencing technology is the very simple one ...: 'Delegates enjoy them!' ... due to the fact that they are often located in cities of tourist interest, and offer other peripheral pleasures such as the social programme, the partners programme ... (2003: 139)

These processes have generated an explosive growth in conference centres, meeting rooms, instant offices and airport hotels around the world. Such hotels allow travellers to stay put, stay over do their 'business' and then return far and wide (Doyle, Nathan 2001). And similar patterns seem to characterize many business lounges at airports, since business trips are shorter and involve a greater precision of timing, coordination and meeting.

More generally, I have noted the proliferation of 'inter-spaces', new public and semi-public spaces of bars, cafes, leisure clubs, restaurants, pubs, campuses and clubs with often extensive 'cultural exchange' (Hajer, Reijndorp 2002). Both information and people circulate rapidly but come regularly together in meetings. This 'tyranny of proximity' seems to be functional for developing and sustaining knowledge work in the so-called new economy (see Amin, Thrift 2002: 59, 73). Indeed it seems that the weaker the ties, the more important is meetingness and the more significant are places of exchange within city centres, campuses, conferences and camps for conversational co-presence, for intense networkers working and 'living on thin air' and whose main resource is not what is known but who is known (Leadbetter 1999; Grabher 2004, on not 'know-how' but 'know-whom').

Surveys of businesses demonstrate that 'urban sociability' (sites for good meetingness) determines the location of business services and knowledge industries. Singapore's financial sector shows the intensive use of bars, restaurants, clubs, sporting clubs, parties, sponsored events and business associations. It seems that sociability: 'is the bases on which contacts and opportunities are made, trust and reliability is tested, knowledge and jobs are exchanged, business deals are tested and sealed, reputations are tracked and business is made sociable . . . There, the sites of pleasure in the city come alive as business institutions' (Amin, Thrift 2002: 75; Amin, Cohendet 2004).

Where there are virtual teams that operate world-wide longitudinal research shows that face-to-face meetings brought about through corporeal travel are exceptionally important. Thus the temporal rhythm of such teams: 'is structured by a defining beat of regular, intense face-to-face meetings, followed by a less intensive, shorter interaction incidents using various media' (Maznevski, Chudoba 2000: 489). Indeed virtual business communities seem to require very frequent trips and meetings (Doyle, Nathan 2002: 8–10). Overall so far it seems that email and other virtual travel increases the 'need' for face-to-face interaction rather than substituting for it (Hampton, Wellman 2001; Castells 2001: 122).

Global financial traders show similar patterns. As the world financial system is progressively disembedded from specific places, so the traders seem to need richer face-to-face relationships in order to exchange appropriate information, knowledge and trust (Boden 2000; Knorr Cetina, Bruegger 2002). The fragility of the symbolic communities in electronic money-space, mean that re-embedded intense meeting-places are necessary for trustful relationships where much knowledge is tacit. 'Surrounded by complex technology and variable degrees of uncertainty, social actors seek each other out, to make the deals that, writ large across the global electronic boards of the exchanges, make the market. They come together in tight social worlds to use each other and their shared understanding of "what's happening" to reach out and move those levers that move the world' (Boden 2000: 194). The City of London shows the importance of meetings even with the disappearance of the 'pit' based system of trading. The intense communicative role of the 'square mile' and other financial centres has grown with increased travel. Thus the City: 'has become a global node of circulating stories, sizing up people and doing deals . . . much of the City's population will consist of visitors, but they are not incidental . . . They are part of the communicative commotion that places the City in the electronic space of global finance' (Thrift 1996: 252).

One increasingly common place of 'intensitivity' or 'effervescence' in the contemporary world is that of the university campus, a specific place that students, staff, visitors and employees 'go to' or even in the UK 'go up to'. Recent attempts to develop *virtual* universities have encountered difficulties because of the physical and symbolic role of a physical campus and the need to demonstrate to prospective students what experiences they will receive for their fees (Cornford, Pollock 2001; universities being part of the 'experience economy'). If university is only seen in terms of the production, assembling, storage, transmitting and assessing information flows, then it is possible to eliminate the physical campus. But if the campus is understood as a place of intense 'meetingness' then no amount of virtual connectivity can really replace it. This would explain why many attempts at developing virtual learning environments have failed or been far less successful than predicted. The physical campus is a place of lateral relationships and meetings between students, and between lecturers, and between students and lecturers (and indeed other staff). Thus Amin and Cohendet state that: 'occasions such as conferences and their murmurings, chatter, and social display, are as deeply implicated in knowledge exploration as work in the laboratory' (2004: 81). The campus (and its conferences) is thus to be understood as a 'community (or communities) of practice' characterized by multiple, overlapping lateral relationships effected through the intense promiscuity of meetings (Wenger 1998; see Chayko 2002: 72, on 'collective resonance').

In concluding therefore that people work in a networked 'connecting economy', the UK Henley Centre argues that: 'few of us actually make anything: we have meetings, we make presentations, we encourage people'; hence 'our work is based on the influence we have over our networks' (Justin Worsley, Associate Director, quoted *Leisure Week*, 15 June 2000; reported Henley Centre press centre). Accessing meetings when the network meets up is crucial for contemporary working, for sustaining and enlarging network capital. In the next section I turn to meetings within families and between friends.

Family and Friendships Meetings

I noted above how Wellman argues that there is a further shift taking place in the networking of social life, towards person-to-person connectivity (2001). The shift to a 'personalized, wireless world affords truly personal communities that support sociability, information and a sense of belonging separately to the individual' (Wellman 2001: 238). Each individual and their specific network is key, while place, home and context are less significant in structuring networks. This shift to personalized networks is accompanied by the claim that leisure time is increasingly 'harried' and therefore that meetingness is increasingly difficult to bring about (Linder 1970; Southerton 2001). This is because of increases in hours worked (Layard 2005); the heightened fragmentation of working hours so people's leisure times coincide less; increases in the variety and complexity of leisure activities; and the greater need for multi-tasking of leisure time to maintain friendships across distance. These processes result in an increasing 'society of the schedule' as people's daily time–space patterns are somewhat desynchronized from work, community and place and hence from each other (Shove, Southerton, Warde 2001). Organizing meetings becomes demanding, as there is a loss of collective coordination; some suggest this is especially marked in the United States and explains 'why Americans have no pals' since few are free at the same time (Jenkins, Osberg 2003; Putnam 2000). Organizing leisure becomes especially problematic if few are free. One needs 'somebody to play with' and simultaneous free time (Jenkins, Osberg 2003).

Thus people have actively to maintain their sparsely knit ties and dispersed family networks. 'Active networking is more important than going along with the group' (Wellman 2001: 234). A sense of normal co-presence of family members requires increased if intermittent travel in order to keep in touch. In Sweden it is thought that about one-half of all travel stems from meeting up with friends and family (O'Dell 2004: 15). While a UK Report states: 'There are social customs, obligations and activities that substantial majorities of the population . . . identify as among the top necessities of life'; among these necessary events are: 'celebrations on special occasions such as Christmas' (83%) and 'attending weddings, funerals' (80%), 'visits to friends or family' (84%), especially those in hospital (92%) (Gordon et al. 2000). This Report captures the socialities involved in people's everyday lives, showing that travel and communication will be required to maintain and reproduce familial relationships (see Sutton 2004, on the family reunions of African Caribbean transnational families).

Increasingly these sociabilities entail the pleasures of 'eating out'. In a world of 'geographic mobility, small households, smaller and unstable families, discontent with traditional divisions of labour, eating out is a rich source of . . . conviviality and co-operation' that plays a particular role within family life (Warde, Martens 2000: 227). Such events are according to UK research almost universally enjoyable and are especially marked for familial celebrations. Being present is a major indicator of social belonging within that network. Apologies are necessary if one is unable to be present. Thus: 'it is important to be present, if it is possible, because the meal symbolizes a socially significant, temporally specific occasion. To have eaten the same meal the day before or the day after would not be a satisfactory substitute, even if many of the same people were present' (Warde and Martens 2000: 217). Such are the obligations of familial and friendship co-presence.

Similar arguments have been developed with regard to shopping. Miller shows that much shopping is not simply individualistic but is directed towards others, especially family members and friends (1998). Shopping is dependent upon relationships with others in two senses. First, it often is carried out with others; it is therefore a kind of mobile meeting. And second, it is oriented to others through expressing love and friendship. It is guided by moral sentiments and thus expresses significant socially embedded values.

In UK research reported in the previous chapter it was noted that there is increasing geographical distance between network members, and this is due to residential migration especially among those who have been in higher education, the accumulation of friends elsewhere and often abroad, and the complex structuring of families and households often through proliferating 'family fragments' (Smart, Neale 2004; Larsen, Urry, Axhausen 2006: ch. 6). Overall this results in less frequent face-to-face contact with friends and family. The respondents socialize with their locally most significant people every other day or so; those living up to 30 km away every fourth day or so; those living 30–80 km away almost once a week. While distant ties are less likely to meet up, they do so intermittently, no matter what the cost it seems. Moreover, the research graphically showed that 'strong ties' cannot sustain themselves without occasional physical co-presence. Indeed the respondents meet all their 'most important people' at least once a year.

Moreover, often these 'meetings' will be 'somewhere else' and so involves a combination of travelling to another place with a co-present meeting with friends or family. Trips abroad to catch up with busy friends in the UK are common. Long work hours, commitments to partners and dispersed social networks make it difficult for friends to meet up spontaneously at the same time, so meetings are coordinated in advance and travel elsewhere brings networks together:

> My friends from back home in Chester, everyone does their own thing. It's quite difficult to all meet up at the same time. We've all got like our partners and things like that, and our partners aren't really from the same area so they don't really know each other very well. Quite often, if we are going to meet up, we try and go away or something together. (Male sales advisor, late twenties, Larsen, Urry, Axhausen 2006: 100)

This is how another sales advisor explains a recent extended weekend trip to Amsterdam:

> It was more of a touristy holiday, a relaxing holiday. I went with four other friends as well. People I hadn't seen for a while. It was a catching up holiday. They mainly came from London. It was people that I hadn't seen while I was away in Barcelona. I had come back but they were living in opposite sides of London so it was still far enough. And then we decided to get together and go for a holiday. (Male sales advisor, late twenties, Larsen, Urry, Axhausen 2006: 100)

This kind of trip can also be seen within families. A male architect explains how:

> The last [holiday] . . . was my mum's 60th birthday . . . we really couldn't afford it but we were keen to make it a special birthday for her so we got cheap flights . . . So we went to Rome for three or four days . . . my sister, who didn't come, did contribute towards the price of the flights and things like that (Male architect, early thirties, Larsen, Urry, Axhausen 2006: 96).

Another respondent explains how she and her partner invited her parents to Las Vegas to see the singer Celine Dion on their 35th wedding anniversary:

> My mum and dad are big fans of Celine Dion . . . It was actually their 35th wedding anniversary and it was kind of a Christmas present, anniversary present and birthday present all rolled into one – just a very nice treat. (Female personal trainer, early thirties, Larsen, Urry, Axhausen 2006: 96)

These 'gifts' represent a desire for being with their parents and having quality time, and for experiencing the place and event *together* as a family. The concert in Las Vegas does not only offer proximity to a famous star, but also to family members. The following illustrates how an extended family that all live close to each other nonetheless embark on tourist travel so as to bring the family 'a little closer together' after it suffered 'a couple of deaths':

> The second time it was like a big family holiday. There was like 19 of us who went. So it was kind of organised for everybody really . . . We'd had a couple of deaths in the family and it was in quite a short space of time, within a couple of weeks of each other. It kind of brought the family a little bit closer together. (Male sales advisor, mid-twenties, Larsen, Urry, Axhausen 2006: 97)

Also distant connections enable people with more modest incomes to travel further than their income would otherwise allow. A male porter has a 'rich' uncle in San Francisco:

> I have been to San Francisco twice [within the last couple of years] . . . I stayed at my uncle's place . . . Yeah, he's always got things planned, like we'll go and watch a baseball or basketball game. He's always got tickets there waiting for us, so it's quite cheap when we get there. (Male university porter, mid-twenties, Larsen, Urry, Axhausen 2006: 97)

Free accommodation means that people living in what are deemed to be interesting places are especially likely to receive visitors (sometimes against their will!). One respondent taking advantage of this states that:

> I'm organising a trip to Mexico because I know he's [friend] only there for another year, so there's no point on missing out on free accommodation . . . You know, say it was somewhere like Azerbaijan, I don't

think I would be that keen on going, but you know Mexico, I'd quite like to go there. (Male architect, late twenties, Larsen, Urry, Axhausen 2006: 97)

Much of this travel thus involves combining together of significant places *and* people. People travel with their partner to visit parents in their hometown or their migrated parents in Spain or their best friend now living in London or an old university friend now working in Berlin or a stag night in Amsterdam with a group of friends. So when people travel to friends or kin they simultaneously travel to particular places, and these places will be especially experienced through the host's social networks and accumulated knowledge of its cultural scene or its 'nature'.

Such travel is especially significant for migrants and members of diasporic cultures who possess particularly stretched-out networks. As Mason notes with regard to her research on Pakistani migrants in the north west of England, everybody went back to Pakistan for periods that might last between two weeks to several months (2004). Almost all respondents were enthusiastic about their visits to Pakistan, whatever their age. They were something planned with relish, looked forward to and remembered fondly until the next time. Such visits had to be regular occurrences, and involved joint activities.

In our research, an Irish male architect returned to Ireland three times in 2004 (Larsen, Urry, Axhausen 2006). He toured various places to see friends, family members and the national rugby team playing crucial games, thus combining obligations to significant people *and* being at live events (Larsen, Urry, Axhausen 2006: 98). For a doorman and his family who lived 25 years in South Africa before returning to the UK, annual holidays to South Africa are deemed essential (Larsen, Urry, Axhausen 2006: 98). They 'have' to go to South Africa to stay in contact with, and introduce their daughter, to their family as well as to the distinct landscapes of South Africa. These visits also enable them to reunite with friends living in Cape Town, elsewhere in UK and Europe, as their transnational circle of friends and their families coordinate their holidays to Cape Town at the same time. Intimate networks of care, support and affection thus move across geographical distance.

While caring at-a-distance works in some cases, the death of a Russian architect's grandfather means that 'she really has to be there', to be proximate with the rest of her family. She has to care in a more embodied and social way than is possible by phone and email (Larsen, Urry, Axhausen 2006: 99). Timing is everything; this woman has to be on time for the funeral and she is therefore in an acute rush to fulfil her work obligations and arrange the journey. This illustrates how flexible and efficient coordination and travel depend upon access to, and skilful use of, network capital.

Meetings on the Move

I turn now to the increasingly significant pattern of meetings that take place in some sense on the move. In much analysis of travel it is usual to ignore such practices. It is presumed that the time that is spent traveling is unproductive and wasted; that activity time and travel time are mutually exclusive; and that people will always prefer to minimize journey times and hence even tiny increases in speed and reduced time are highly valued (Lyons, Urry 2005).

However, it now seems that time spent travelling is not necessarily unproductive and wasted; there are activities conducted at the destination; activities conducted while travelling including the 'anti-activity' of relaxing, thinking, shifting gears; and the pleasures of travelling itself, including the sensation of speed, of movement through and exposure to the environment, the beauty of a route and so on (Mokhtarian, Salomon 2001: 701; Featherstone, Thrift, Urry 2004, on the car). In one survey more than two-thirds of the respondents disagreed that: 'the only good thing about travelling is arriving at your destination'; while nearly half agree that 'getting there is half the fun' (Mokhtarian, Salomon 2001: 709). Thus travel times and activity times are not simply separate from each other and mutually exclusive. There are many ways now in which such times seem to overlap and become de-differentiated from each other (Lyons, Urry 2005). New technologies (akin to the book in the mid nineteenth century) are developing which are 'mobile' and hence provide new affordances for activities now possible and appealing on the move.

New social routines are engendering spaces 'in-between' home, work and social life, forming 'interspaces' as already noted (Hulme, Truch 2005). These are places of intermittent movement where groups come together, involving the use of phones, mobiles, laptops, SMS messaging, wireless communications and so on, often to make arrangements 'on the move'. Interspace is the space and time between two or more 'events' resulting from how the boundaries between travel time and activity time seem to blur. Travel time comes to be converted into activity time within 'interspace'. In turn, less of the individual's travel time is used, enabling more travel to occur or encouraging greater use of those modes that may enable activities to be undertaken en-route, including developing or maintaining network capital. This pattern is increasingly found among relatively prosperous young professional people working (and playing) in various city-centres. German research shows that for young people: 'mobility and communication play a prominent role in the way young people organize their everyday lives' (Tully 2002: 20).

The importance of meetings on the move can be seen with new mobile workers. Such workers are regularly on the move to meet clients (Laurer 2004). Face-to-face meetings occur in 'interspaces' such as motorway service stations, roadside cafes, pubs, clubs, restaurants and so on. Thus service stations, as well as airport lounges and hotel lobbies, are full of 'meetings' where colleagues or associates come together often to work on documents, to engage in talk. Team working is achieved by the skilful use of mobile telephony so as to maintain connections both with those back at the office (including making meeting arrangements, dictating letters), as well as with others elsewhere on the road and with whom 'meetings' can be arranged and most significantly re-arranged (Truch, Hulme 2004; Brown, Green, Harper 2002). The mobile is regularly used to rearrange the day involving a 'playful opportunism' especially in Europe or South East Asia where it is presumed that ownership is ubiquitous within certain social groups (and Sherry, Salvador 2002). Interspace is thus central to the development and extension of what elsewhere I characterized as 'network capital'.

Conclusion

In chapters 10 and 11 I have shown that work, family and friendship have each become more distanciated and networked. Moreover, networks within these domains increasingly overlap so movements between and across them are significant. In all such cases networks have intermittently to meet up, and various aspects and functions of such meetings have been elaborated. Network capital and weak ties are spreading especially with the growth of 'personal networking' and the resultant complex scheduling (and rescheduling) of social life in part conducted on the move. The growth of multiple mobilities, new technologies and extended networks is bringing into being the 'field' of 'interspatial' social life where network capital is a major resource.

In the next chapter I turn to the question of place directly and consider the mobilities of place and some of the unusual places that contemporary travellers feel the need to move to. But such places will often be part of and help to constitute the patterning of social networks with work, family and friendship.

12

Places

How sad it is! I shall grow old, and horrible, and dreadful. But this picture will remain always young . . . If it were only the other way! . . . For that . . . I would give everything! . . . I would give my soul for that

(Oscar Wilde 1951: 31)

In many locations in this book the issue of place has been encountered. In a simple sense almost all mobilities entail movement between specific places and there is something about places that are complicit within that movement. Processes of placing we can say are central to corporeal, imaginative and virtual travel. Especially places can be loci of affect that draw or repel particular kinds of residents or visitors.

I am particularly concerned in this chapter with places of attraction, for various reasons people find some place the reason for moving, for being 'drawn' there. I referred to this above as 'facing-the-place', by analogy with the importance of 'face-to-face'. What is it that makes one want to see that place for oneself, to be immersed within it, to feel its affective register (Thrift 2004d)? When Freud finally got to Athens in his forties he found the Acropolis he had known about from his childhood took his breath away. He could not believe that it really existed and he was actually there in its overwhelming presence (Rojek 1997: 56–7). Many other visitors to places often find it hard to believe that they are in the affective presence of that particular 'wonder of the world' or special city or iconic landscape of their dreams. Other places are places of affect because there is something about it that makes it appropriate for particular social encounters to occur, they are places of meetingness. I have noted in this book many different examples of the importance of the situatedness of such meetings. Other places have to be travelled to because that is where people are being exiled to, or have to migrate to.

In various chapters I noted the significance of affect in all this. Place and movement are enormously bound up with affect. I begin with an array of observations about the history of travel and note some characteristics of those places that get to be visited. Central to my claims here are that places are not fixed, given or unchanging but depend in part upon the practices within them. Those relations have to be affectively performed. Places entail various kinds of performances (as shown in Sheller, Urry 2004), and therefore without those performances over time that place will change and become something else. Places and performances are bound up with each other in exceptionally complicated and diverse ways. In particular I begin with the strange performances that took place within spa towns and beaches, performances that laid down certain ways of physically behaving in certain contexts that established a way of being 'leisured'.

I then consider the importance of the senses to how places came to be affectively enjoyed and suggest that the shift from land to landscape marks a particular way of being in the world, that places can be compared, contrasted and collected, visited from afar.

In the following section I consider one particular kind of affect and that is how some places are central to the emotion of national identity. They are we might say places of national affect.

Following this I turn to various ways in which multiple globalizing processes are engendering an exceptional global competition between places over various stakes but especially to attract many if not all kinds of 'visitors'. This global competition to be attractive to certain 'strangers' is transforming places. They are remade as spectacle so as to attract various kinds of strangers while repelling other kinds such as asylum seekers or terrorists. There are now certain global icons that the whole world wants to see, to be close to, within their lifetime.

I do not say much about the modes of travel involved because these were encountered in detail in Part 2. But often the mode of travel and particular places are conjoined together, the place presupposes travelling there in specific kinds of way, they are joined at the hip we might say. Examples of this would be train journeys to the resorts of south west England, cheap air flights to Thailand from Australia, travelling by car to the Grand Canyon and so on.

Places of Affect for the Sick

I begin with a brief reprise on the history of European travel. Apart
from pilgrimages and the Grand Tour for rich young men, organized
European travel began with the provision of services for wealthy
sick people (Urry 2004d). During the eighteenth and nineteenth
centuries very many spa towns developed across Europe, including
Wiesbaden, Vichy, Baden-Baden, Harrogate, Budapest, Bath and so
on (Blackbourn 2002). Taking the waters and being immersed within
them promised recovery to the ill and the dying. These were sites to
perform recovery from various crippling illnesses. 'Taking the waters'
became a fashionable performed therapy within various medical
regimes. Water, internal and external, was seen as the antidote to the
multiple 'diseases' of civilization (Anderson, Tabb 2002).

These spa towns were socially select places with visitors limited to
those who could afford housing in the town (as reported in Jane
Austen's novels) or later to those who could stay in the limited
number of expensive hotels. And most spa towns have retained a
place image as socially select, often hiding their many workers from
view. Spa towns were places where a newly formed cosmopolitan
elite gathered across Europe, increasingly able to travel by train and
where there was a growing circuit of travel and meetings between
these fashionable places that were drawn 'closer' together. These
spas provided cultural capital and enable the European wealthy
to meet each other while being provided with multiple services
(Blackbourn 2002: 15). Spas increasingly developed into places of
luxurious pampered pleasure (see Switzer 2002, on Budapest).

And early seaside resorts also originally developed as places of
medical treatment. The beach was initially a medical zone, as Shields
describes in the case of Brighton (1991). In the eighteenth and early
nineteenth centuries beaches were places where the ill and the
infirmed were 'dipped' into the sea because of the sea's presumed
health generating properties. 'Dippers', large apparently sex-less
mature women, provided this distinct performed 'service'. Beaches
have often been populated with the infirmed seeking to perform
recovery and convalescence. In *Death In Venice* the aging and disap-
pointed writer Aschenbach dies in his deck chair on the beach as the
object of his paedophilic desire walks out into the sea (Mann 1955;
Visconti 1971; Urry 2004d). Even the Caribbean was seen as a place
for the wealthy infirmed from Europe. Cuban air was strongly
recommended for treating tuberculosis as early as the 1830s, while
Jamaica in 1903 was described as a 'veritable Mecca for the invalid'

(Sheller 2003: 65). Many seaside resorts have remained as places for the ill to take the waters and the air, to receive treatment and to convalesce. Such reports were typically visited by train with the resort being constructed at the end of the railway line. Only later did beaches turn into zones of pleasure and especially places to perform pleasure, a paradise on earth as I discuss below (and global travel has led to the rapid movement of modern mobile plagues: see Farmer 1999).

The Affect of Vision

The more general desire to be in 'other places', which could be places of affect, stemmed from certain historic shifts in the material practices of everyday life. These practices move from the social practices of *land* to those of *landscape* (Milton 1993; Urry 2002c). *Land* is a physical, tangible resource to be ploughed, sown, grazed and built upon, a place of functional work. Land is bought and sold, inherited and left to children. To dwell is to participate in a life where productive and unproductive activities resonate with each other and with tracts of land, whose history and geography are known in detail. There is a lack of distance between people and things in agriculture, timber growing, quarrying, mining and so on. Affective emotions are intimately tied to place (see *Haweswater*: Hall 2002; Ingold 2000).

With *landscape* an intangible resource develops which is that of appearance or look. This notion developed in western Europe from the eighteenth century onwards, part of the more general emergence of a specialized *visual* sense separate from the other senses and based upon novel technologies. There is nothing inevitable or natural about this organizing power of vision; indeed there was a centuries-long struggle for visuality to break free from the other senses with which it had been entangled. Febvre argues that in sixteenth-century Europe: 'Like their acute hearing and sharp sense of smell, the men of that time doubtless had keen sight. But that was just it. They had not yet set it apart from the other senses' (1982: 437). As a result people were said to live within a fluid world where entities rapidly changed shape and size, boundaries quickly altered and where there was little systematic stabilization of the social or physical worlds. 'Interaction' describes the fluid, changing forms of perception that characterized sixteenth century life (Cooper 1997).

Over the next couple of centuries there were many changes. Visual observation rather than the *a priori* knowledge of mediaeval cosmology came to be viewed as the basis of scientific legitimacy. This subsequently developed into the very foundation of the scientific method of the west, based upon sense-data principally produced and guaranteed by sight. A number of such sciences of 'visible nature' developed organized around visual taxonomies, including especially Linnaeus (Gregory 1994: 20). Such classifications were based upon the modern epistème of the individual subject, the seeing eye, and the observations, distinctions and classifications that the eye is able to make (Foucault 1976).

Treatises on travel consequently shifted from a scholastic emphasis on touring as an opportunity for discourse via the ear, to travel as *eyewitness* observation. And with the development of scientific expeditions (the first recorded in 1735: Pratt 1992: 1), travellers did not expect that their observations would become part of science, Travel came to be justified (since it needed plenty of justification given its enormous relative costs) not through science but through connoisseurship, 'the well trained eye' (Adler 1989: 22). A connoisseurship of buildings, works of art and of landscapes developed especially in the late eighteenth century with the growth of 'scenic tourism' in Britain and then across Europe. Such connoisseurship came to involve new ways of seeing: a 'prolonged, contemplative [look] regarding the field of vision with a certain aloofness and disengagement, across a tranquil interval' (Bryson 1983: 94; Taylor 1994: 13). This visual sense enables people to take possession of objects and environments, often at a distance (as Simmel argued; see ch. 2 above). It is by seeking distance that a proper 'view' is gained, abstracted from the hustle and bustle of everyday experience (see Pratt's account of 'imperial eyes': 1992). Areas of wild, barren nature, such as the English Lake District or the Alps or the Danish island of Bornholm, had been sources of terror and fear, places of repulsion (see Bærenholdt, Haldrup, Larsen, Urry 2004: 72, on Bornholm as 'Denmark's Switzerland'). But they became transformed into places of positive affect, what Williams terms 'scenery, landscape, image, fresh air', places waiting at a distance for the tourist gaze by city-dwellers with new notions of sublime and picturesque landscapes (1972: 160; Barrell 1972; Green 1990; Perkins, Thorns 2001).

Over the next century nature of all sorts came to be widely regarded as scenery, views, and perceptual sensation (Urry 2002c: ch. 8). By 1844 Wordsworth was reporting that the idea of landscape had recently developed, and he promoted both the Alps and the Lake District as landscapes of affect. Previously barns and outbuildings had been placed in front of houses: 'however beautiful the landscape which their windows might otherwise have commanded' (Wordsworth 1984: 188). But by the mid nineteenth century, houses were being built with regard to their 'prospects' as though they were a kind of 'camera' (Abercrombie, Longhurst 1998: 79). The language of views thus prescribed a particular visual structure to the experience of nature. The building of piers, promenades and domesticated beaches enabled the visual consumption of the otherwise wild, untamed and 'natural' sea (Corbin 1992). While I noted above (ch. 4) how Haussmann's rebuilding of Paris enabled people for the first time in a major city to see well into the distance, their eyes being seduced by the sights in question, and they could envisage where they were going to and where they had come from, so making Paris: 'a uniquely enticing spectacle' (Berman 1983: 151).

New technologies of the gaze began to be produced and circulated, including postcards, guidebooks, commodities, arcades, cafés, dioramas, mirrors, plate-glass windows and especially photographs. In particular from 1840 onwards tourism and photography came to be welded together and the development of each could not be separated from the other. Both sets of practices remake each other in an irreversible and momentous double helix (Osborne 2000). From then a 'tourist gaze' enters and helps to *make* the mobile, modern world (Urry 2002c; Löfgren, 1999). Places are 'kodakized', desired and fixed through the objects of camera, film, photograph and initially the 'kodak system' (West 2000; Baerenholdt, Haldrup, Larsen, Urry 2004: chs. 5 and 6; Larsen 2004). New photographed places of affect include the Mediterranean (Pemble 1987), the Alps (Ring 2000), the Caribbean (Sheller 2003), the Grand Canyon (Newmann 2002), the exotic Nile (Gregory 1999), stinking fishing villages (Lübbren 2001) and water generally (Anderson, Tabb 2002). Thus from the nineteenth century onwards the 'world as exhibition' is established and this 'seeing the world as a picture' has then cast its long shadow over countless places and peoples (Larsen 2004). And it gives rise to yet another mobility, of light pieces of photographic paper that can be passed from hand to hand, sent around the world, given as presents.

It is thus said that Wordsworth's poem *The Brother* signifies the beginning of a time when people stop belonging to a culture and increasingly can only tour it, so as to compare, contrast and collect, to see Venice and die (Buzard 1993: 27; Szerszynski, Urry 2006). A specialized visual sense characterizes the modern world. As E. M. Forster wrote: 'Under cosmopolitanism . . . Trees and meadows and mountains will only be a spectacle', landscape not land (1931: 243).

Places are known about, compared, evaluated, possessed. A place is not so much a place with its own associations and meanings for those dwelling or even visiting there, but each is a *combination* of abstract characteristics that mark it out as more scenic or cosmopolitan or cool or exotic or global or environmentally degraded than other places. This language of abstract characteristics is a language of mobility, the expression of the life-world of mobile groups of tourists, conference travellers, business people or environmentalists. This is a consumption of movement, of bodies, images, and information, moving over, under and around the globe and subjecting it to abstract characterizations (see Szerszynski, Urry 2006).

Perhaps the most iconic of such places of consumption has been the beach. As Rachel Carson writes, the 'edge of the sea is a strange and wonderful place' partly because it is never quite the same from one moment to the next (1961: 2). It is an in-between place, neither quite land nor sea. And over the past two centuries the beach went from a place of repulsion and danger to one of attraction and desire. It became a place to be dwelt upon by visitors, a place of landscape rather than land and especially of leisure rather than work. There was a long process of domestication whereby the beach was emptied of disrupting local practices. Locals were 'tamed' and transformed into objects of the tourist gaze (Corbin 1994: 232). This is reflected in shifts in styles of painting, whereby the beach moves from a place of work and toil to a place of leisurely promenading (Bærenholdt, Haldrup, Larsen, Urry 2004: 55–7; Crouch, Lübbren 2003).

And as such especially the golden beaches of the Mediterranean and the Caribbean become thought of as paradises on earth (Caletrio 2003; Sheller 2003). Beaches became the classic place for visitors to place themselves temporarily, with an assortment of unusual props and in a state of considerable undress, certainly compared with the dress codes of the time. For the affluent classes of Europe and North America in the early decades of this century, the beach became a place of immense affect, of paradise and excess. And over the twentieth century this strange liminal place became desired much more widely, the beach signifying a symbolic 'other' to factories, work and domestic life. The beach became widely desired around the world as the place where near naked bodies would be caressed by the sun and where the icon of the tanned body meant that the body more generally becomes a 'mask' or 'sign' (Ahmed 2000). This initiates many other forms of bodily adornment and physical and chemical modification that de-stabilize the self and make bodies themselves 'mobile' and subversive of conventional hierarchies of (clothed) wealth and power.

This thin line between the sea and the land is indeterminate and has to be transformed into a stage for bringing about multiple kinds of leisurely performance (Bærenholdt, Haldrup, Larsen, Urry 2004: ch. 4). On the beach, according to Shields 'all are actors, not spectators' (1991: 85). This thin strip becomes a central stage for multiple, contested and on occasions marginalized performances of contemporary leisure and tourism (Lencek, Bosker 1998). Visitors have to turn themselves into performers on the beach as a tourist stage. As a stage it comes to life when visited and dwelt upon with visitors doing those things appropriate to that particular place. Overall the beach is: 'the emblematic space for a life of leisure' (Bærenholdt, Haldrup, Larsen, Urry 2004: 50). The transformation of this strip into a global icon signifies the shift in societies from land to landscape, from work to play. And for some societies the beach is emblematic of nationhood, such as Bondi beach in Australia or those beaches surrounding various West Indian islands, nations in which play and pleasure are central to identity (and in which many work at providing play for others).

But beaches come and go, some becoming more desired and others less so. Some of the beaches of northern Europe and North America have become 'old fashioned', dating from another era before automobility and air travel enormously heightened the national and global competition between beaches. Spas and resorts often developed images of being places of regret, that one was visiting that place because one could not be elsewhere and especially on a new beach of paradise (see Urry 2002c, generally here).

As fast therefore as places are produced so they are consumed, wasted, used up as they are so 'toured', only in the end a set of abstract characteristics. Travel practices can thus move on and leave behind places that are no longer of positive affect. In such a 'touring' world, places come and places go, some places speed up and others slow down or die. People may try to escape from where there is a 'drudgery of place', of being inexorably tied there and where time is fixed and unchanging. Such places remain heavy with time and are left behind in the 'slow lane', as with many old-style beach resorts in northern Europe and America (Urry 2002c). However, they may be reincarnated as places for the performances of nostalgia (the Isle of Man) or of gambling (Atlantic City).

All such places are places for consuming goods and services (Urry 1995). Such goods or services are often metonymic of the place, with the part standing for the whole. The consuming of place may involve consuming goods or services that are culturally specific to that place. As Molotch says: 'touristic stuff has a more definite placeness' (2003:

677). Products can be folded into place and places come to be as they are through products. People eat, drink, collect, gamble, scuba dive, surf, bungee jump the 'other' (Urry 2002: 3). Some such places are places of excess, where consumption is performed to dangerous extremes, so temporarily differentiating that place from the rest (Sheller, Urry 2004).

But often places are often full of bitter disappointment, frustration and despair, where its performances cannot be realized. This is captured in *The Beach* (Garland 1997; and see Campbell 1987). People's fantasies of a place compared with what performances it actually affords are a constant trope in tourist tales. Thus the objects of performed consumption are not available (Cyprus closed for the winter: Sharpley 2004), the service quality is degraded compared with the destination's place-image (as in 'English' Harrogate: Cuthill 2004), the place to-die-for is overrun with cheap souvenir stalls (the Taj Mahal: Edensor 2004), eco-tourists discover the pristine coral reef has been destroyed by earlier mass tourism (Duffy 2004, or middle aged business people find their city centre is over-run by promiscuous, drunk 'party-goers' (Chatterton, Hollands 2003). The performances of place often cannot be realized or there are contested performances or 'emotional geographies' of place (Bondi, Smith, Davidson 2005).

Places and Nations

In this section I consider one specific set of performances of place, namely, with when a particular place is central to nationality. Overall national histories tell a story, of a people passing through history, a story often beginning in the mists of time (Bhabha 1994). Much of this history of its traditions and icons will have been 'invented' and results as much from forgetting the past as from remembering it (McCrone 1998: ch. 3).

The late nineteenth-century Europe was a period of remarkable invention of such national traditions. In France, Bastille Day was invented in 1880, *La Marseillaise* became the national anthem in 1879, July 14th was designated the national feast in 1880 and Jeanne d'Arc was only elevated from obscurity by the Catholic Church in the 1870s (McCrone 1998: 45–6). More generally, the idea of 'France' was extended: 'by a process akin to colonization through communication (roads, railways and above all by the newspapers) so that by the end of the nineteenth century, popular and elite culture had come together' through these diverse mobilities (McCrone 1998: 46). Key in this process was the mass production of public monuments of the nation especially in the re-built Paris. These monuments needed to be travelled to, to be seen, talked about and increasingly shared through paintings, photographs, films and the emerging European tourism industry. Multiple mobilities came together to reproduce places central to national identity.

This collective participation and the more general nation-inducing role of travel had been significantly initiated with the 1851 Great Exhibition held at London's Crystal Palace. This is arguably the first-ever national tourist *event* and hence demonstrated the importance of what I earlier referred to as 'facing-the-event'. While the British population was only 18 m, 6 m visits were made to the Exhibition in London, many by train visiting the *national* capital for the very first time. In the second half of the nineteenth century similar mega-events of nationhood took place in capital cities across Europe with attendances sometimes reaching 30 m or so (Roche 2000). In Australia a Centennial International Exhibition was held in Melbourne in 1888 and it is thought that two-thirds of the Australian population attended this event (Spillman 1997: 51).

More generally, since the mid nineteenth century, travel to places housing the key sites, texts, exhibitions, buildings, landscapes, restaurants and achievements of a society has reproduced the cultural sense of a national imagined presence (Urry 2000). Particularly important in the genealogy of nationalism has been the founding of national museums, concert halls, theatres and galleries within specific towns and cities and the development of the historiography of specific places seen as nationally significant (McCrone 1998: 53–5; Kirshenblatt-Giblett 1998; Edensor 2002).

More recently a global public stage has emerged. Upon this stage almost all nations have to appear, to compete, to mobilize themselves as spectacle and to attract large numbers of visitors to key places. This placement particularly operates through mega-events such as the Olympics, World Cups and Expos that are held in specific 'global' cities (Harvey 1996; Roche 2000). These international events are based upon mass travel. The staging of such events presupposes corporeal and imaginative travel especially to the 'Olympics and Expos in the Growth of Global Culture' (Roche 2000).

And this connects to the changing nature of nationality (Maier 1994: 149–50; McCrone 1998). Once nationality was based upon a homogenous and mapped national territory, in which law was defined, authority claimed and loyalty sought within that territorial boundary. But now frontiers are permeable and much cultural life is interchangeable across the globe through extensive corporeal and imaginative travel. Thus 'territory is less central to national self-definition' and more important are specific places, landscapes and symbols (Maier 1994: 149; Lowenthal 1985). What are central are icons pivotal to that culture's location within the contours of global travel, such as visiting wine fields in France, the 'highlands' within Scotland, beaches within the 'Caribbean', the skyline in New York, Shakespeare's birthplace within England, Machu Picchu in Peru and so on. Theses are some of the key places of national affect upon the global public stage.

In the next section I turn to the global competition between places more generally.

Global Travel and Places

In the first chapter I listed the twelve major forms of travel practice in the contemporary world. Each of them entails being attracted to *and* repulsed by different places as I will now briefly indicate.

First, there is asylum and refugee travel where people seek to escape from many places of famine, persecution and poverty. Such migration will involve often very risky, complex and expensive travel to get to certain rich places around the world which might offer a contingent 'hospitality' (Marfleet 2006). Overall there is a profoundly 'unequal access to foreign spaces' and this will particularly impact upon mobility escapees (Neumayer 2006). With the shift towards digital societies of control the border is less literally at the border and is more virtual and de-localized (Walters 2006: 193).

By marked contrast business and professional travel generally takes place to places known for their cosmopolitan buzz as well as being housed in safe and efficient hotels and conference facilities (such as occurs to many North American, European or major Asian cities; see ch. 8 above).

The discovery travel of students, au pairs and other young people on their 'overseas experience' generally involves going to civilizational centres but often where many others also go, so forming 'backpacker enclaves' (Williams 2006). And once one has been there one moves on, driven by what has been called an 'experience hunger' as the 'backpack' gets lugged on to the next place by the money poor, time rich young 'traveller' for whom backpacking is a rite of passage for the young middle class (Richards, Wilson 2004: 5).

Medical travel to spas, hospitals, dentists, opticians and so on occurs increasingly within certain cities located in developing countries which have come to specialize in high quality medical care (such as Havana, Delhi).

The military mobility of armies, tanks, helicopters, aircraft, rockets, spyplanes, satellites and so on generally moves from dominant societies to poor and developing place and societies, while the reverse flows of terrorists move towards what I termed imperial centres.

Post-employment travel and the forming of transnational lifestyles within retirement normally involve movement to cheap sun-blessed beaches and 'safe' small towns There is often a high level of movement between the place of origin and the destination place, for example between places within Sweden and Spain (Gustafson 2001; O'Reilly 2003). The 'trailing travel' of children, partners, other relatives and domestic servants normally moves from poor towns and cities to those more prosperous. In the latter there is normally high quality work for the partner/parent of those being trailed (Kofman 2004).

Travel across the key nodes within a given diaspora moves in multiple directions but where large cities figure highly since they tend to be hosts for such diasporic nodes (Cohen 1997; Coles, Timothy 2004; Hannam 2004). There are complex relations between diasporic migrations patterns and return visits (Duval 2004).

Service workers travel from poorer often rural places and go especially to global cities where such work is concentrated because of the concentration of high earning, time pressed professional workers who are most likely to employ service works, often semi-illegally (Sassen 2000).

Tourist travel to visit places and events has historically been to cities and countrysides in western Europe and North America, although this is changing significantly with the growth of leisure travel within Asia (Urry 2002c).

Visiting friends and relatives occurs to very many different places and especially on occasions to places that have no especial 'tourist appeal' (Conradson, Latham 2005; see chs. 10 and 11 above). More generally much travel involves moving with or to be with significant family and friends within particular places; sociabilities are thus core to much travel as I explored in earlier chapters.

Finally, work-related travel including commuting takes place to very many different workplaces, especially for high level workers mainly moving between workplaces within global cities (Grabher 2004; Beaverstock 2005). Some such work related movement increasingly takes place via what I termed 'in-between spaces' (ch. 8).

The interplay between these twelve different 'flows' produces an enormously complex structuring and restructuring of places. Generally because of mobilities the relations between almost all places across the globe are mediated by flows of visitors, as place after place is reconfigured as a recipient of some such flows. There is an omnivorous producing and 'consuming [of] places' around the globe (Urry 1995). Places are situated at different stages and locations within these flows – and there are places that go 'with the flow' and those that are left 'behind' and these rapidly change. Some places 'move' closer to various global centres (which are themselves in play). While others move farther away from the global stage upon which towns, cities, and countries appear, to compete, to mobilize themselves as spectacle, to develop their brand and to attract visitors.

In attracting these flows (apart from those of terrorists and certain kinds of migrant), places are 'on performance' on this relentless global stage. Especially significant is spectacle-ization that is necessary in order for places to *enter* the global order, to somehow be 'recognized'. Such cities can only be taken seriously in the new world dis/order if they are in part places of distinct spectacle. Such places are often hugely complex and there is no single linear experience as networks playfully criss-cross the world, bringing the curtain up and down on place after place.

Some places come to be known as global icons, wonders of the world, places that can take the breath away, worth dying to see, to linger in, to be 'cosmopolitan' because one has been there for oneself. Touring the world is how the world is performed, as a connoisseur of places. Schultz indeed describes the astonishing '1000 Places to See Before You Die' (2003; this book is 972 pages!). This connoisseurship can apply to all sorts of places, good clubs, views, walks, historic remains, food, landmark buildings and so on.

In this global competition buildings are crucial to places of affect, they can make a place worth dying to see, to 'see Venice and die'. Machu Picchu signifies Inca heritage (Arellano 2004), the Taj the 'exotic orient' (Edensor 1998), Palm Island signifies Dubai and so on (Junemo 2004). New landmark hotels, office blocks and galleries built by celebrity architects are global icons with the whole world now increasingly watching (Sheller, Urry 2004).

Also places can be centres of affect if they are centres of sociability. Other peoples' performances give liveliness or carnival or movement to that place. Many moving people with the appropriate habitus, indicate this is *the* place to be, a place to die for, a place that cannot be missed, a place of life. The performances of moving, viewing others are obligatory for the affective experience of place, such as cosmopolitan Hong Kong (Sum 2004), the Barcelona Olympics (Degen 2004), English Harrogate (Cuthill 2004) and so on. Baudelaire's notion of *flânerie* captures this emotional moving performance of place: 'dwelling in the throng, in the ebb and flow, the bustle, the fleeting' (cited Tester 1994a: 2).

This global competition of place presupposes 'place reflexivity', a set of disciplines, procedures and criteria that enable each place to monitor, evaluate and develop its 'potential' within the emerging patterns of global travel. This reflexivity is concerned with identifying a particular place's location within the contours of geography, history and culture that swirl the globe, and in particular identifying that place's actual and potential material and semiotic resources. Many consultancy firms have developed that are interlinked with local, national and international states, companies, voluntary associations and NGOs to enable each 'place' to monitor, modify and maximize their location within the turbulent global order. Such procedures 'invent', produce, market and circulate, especially through global TV and the internet, new or different or repackaged or niche-dependent places and their corresponding visual images (see Urry 2002c: ch. 8). More generally, many types of work are found within these places that get visited: transportation, hospitality, travel, design and consultancy, conferences; mediatizing and circulating images through print, TV, news, internet and so on, the organizing through politics and protest campaigns for or against the construction or development of tourist infrastructures, and sex tourism industries (Clift, Carter 1999). Thus huge numbers of people and places get caught up within the swirling vortex of global travel. There are not two separate entities, the 'global' and 'travel' bearing some external connections with each other. Rather they are part and parcel of the same set of complex and interconnected processes. Moreover, such assembled infrastructures, flows of images and of people, and the emerging practices of 'tourist reflexivity' is a 'global hybrid' made up of an assemblage of technologies, texts, images, social practices and so on, that *together* enable it to expand and to reproduce itself across the globe.

In certain cases becoming a destination is part of a reflexive process by which societies and places come to 'enter' the global order (or 're-enter' as in the case of Cuba or St Petersburg during the 1990s). While most people across the world are not global travellers, the places they live in and the associated images of nature, nation, colonialism, sacrifice, community, heritage and so on, are powerful constituents of the multiple flows of travellers. Such places come to be visited and mostly this entails movement, especially of cars driving around that place or of walkers strolling about. Bærenholdt, Haldrup, Larsen, Urry describe many of the complex micro-mobilities of tourists that take place within different kinds of site, such as a beach, a fishing village, an island or a castle, that are stages for diverse tourism performances (2004).

And there are some strange places which are nodes within certain flows and which are also places for unusual ways of 'strolling' about (see Urry 2004d). Consider the following: the grassy knoll in Dallas where President Kennedy was assassinated, Changi Jail in Singapore, Nazi Occupation sites in the Channel Islands, Gracelands, Dachau, Hiroshima, slave plantations, northern Ireland, west African slave forts, Egyptian pyramids, Pearl Harbour, Robben Island in South Africa, Sarajevo's 'massacre trail', Jim Morrison's grave in Paris, Auschwitz-Birkenau (a UNESCO World Cultural Heritage Site) and so on. These are all places of violent death, of many or of a single icon (such as Diana, JFK, James Dean, Sharon Tate; see Rojek 1993; Lennon, Foley 2000). Indeed part it seems of the allure of certain places is that of death, danger and risk. In the Caribbean 'danger' is just around the corner, just beneath the veneer of the playplaces. Tales of pirates, Rastas, drugs, Yardies all contribute to performing 'dangerous travel' in these paradise islands (Sheller 2003). More recent tourism performances also involve putting the body into other kinds of personal danger (see Bell, Lyall 2002, on adventure tourism in New Zealand). There are many guidebooks now for 'dangerous travel' (Schroeder 2002: 73) as well as a BBC TV series on 'Holidays in the Danger Zone'.

These places of death and suffering often now charge an entrance fee to visitors, provide interpretation and sell various services. Collective witnessing occurs through tourists coming and paying 'their respects' in public. It is as though the visits of strangers, of pilgrims to sacred sites of death, can produce an immortality of those that died in that place or for that cause. So these places entail complex performances for visitors to grieve in public at the memory of the death of a race, a nation, a leader, or a star normally known though mediatized images. These places of death and play are complex, entailing performances of memory, respect, collective grief and emotion. As a prominent notice instructs visitors at the Arlington National Cemetery where Kennedy is buried: 'Silence and Respect' (Lennon, Foley 2000: 88). That is how Arlington is to be performed by visitors to this place where a particular death is to be remembered with respect.

More generally, memories are central to place and can linger with one, days, weeks, years or decades after a place has been encountered. During Wordsworth's 1790 walking tour of the Alps he noted that 'scarce a day of my life will pass in which I shall not derive some happiness from these images' (quoted De Botton 2002: 153–4; see ch. 4 above). These images survived in his memory and as they enter his consciousness they involve imaginative travel to those places from years before. He referred to these flashes of memory as 'spots of time', small critical moments in nature that can be surprisingly reawakened. They 'flash upon the inward eye' transporting us elsewhere and can have a 'renovating virtue' (De Botton 2002: 156; Bærenholdt, Haldrup, Larsen, Urry 2004: 149).

Such memory work, as we would now term it, has been utterly transformed by the fixing of images that occurred with the invention of photography in 1839–40 and the forming of the travel-photography nexus from that moment in the mid nineteenth century (Osborne 2000; Urry 2002c; see above). This fixing of images was described by Fox Talbot as 'natural magic' and immobilizes memories of place and experience. Elsewhere it is shown how such memory work entails tourists using photographs of holidays to eternalize images and to try to stop time in an era of fluid modernity (Bærenholdt, Haldrup, Larsen, Urry 2004: 116–7). Photographs produce the nearness of people and place as: 'the viewer is brought into bodily contact with the trace of the remembered' (Edwards 1999: 118). Such traces can start a memory journey but they do not constitute the destination which can involve recollections, memories and meanings often far from what is literally on the trace. Indeed some respondents in this research describe how photographs evoke memories, not only of sights, but of the smells, tastes, sounds and temperatures of place (Bærenholdt, Haldrup, Larsen, Urry 2004: 119). But they also provoke memories of the death of loved ones, the inexorable ageing of the fragile human body and the complex movement of people and relationships as hearts are broken and dreams are shattered (Bærenholdt, Haldrup, Larsen, Urry 2004: 120). As we argue elsewhere, such transient holiday pictures are not simply transient at all, but they 'have an enduring after-life . . . a vital part of life-stories and spaces of everyday life' (Bærenholdt, Haldrup, Larsen, Urry 2004: 122). Travel is thus more generally about friendship and family life and hence with multiple anticipations and memories of peoples and places.

Conclusion

This chapter has been about affective relations within place and how such places entail various kinds of performances. Without those performances over time that place will change and become some-thing else. Places and performances are bound up with each other. Places are not fixed and unchanging but depend upon what gets bodily performed within them by 'hosts' and especially by 'guests'. Places to play are brought into being through systems of organized and/or informal tourist performance including especially photogra-phy and memory work. Thus places are economically, politically and culturally produced through the multiple mobilities of people, but also of capital, objects, signs and information moving at rapid yet uneven speed across many borders, only contingently forming stable places of spectacle.

In particular I began with the sickly performances that took place within spa towns and beaches that laid the preconditions for a very much wider pattern by which places came to be travelled to for various kinds of emotional pleasure. I analysed the shift from land to landscape and noted how this marks a particular way of being in the world, as places are performed through comparison, contrasts and collections. In the following section I specifically considered how some places and the travelling to such places become central to national identity. I finally analysed the exceptional global competi-tion between places that is transforming the character of places as they struggle for positioning on a global stage.

Thus places are dynamic, moving around and not necessarily staying in one 'location'. Places travel within networks of human and we show non-human agents, of photographs, sand, cameras, cars, souvenirs, paintings, surfboards and so on. These objects extend what humans are able to do, what performances of place are possi-ble. And the resulting networks swirl around, increasingly fluid-like, changing the fixing of place and bringing unexpected new places 'into' play.

But finally here we should note how the swirling vortex of *global travel* is bringing into being its opposite, with terrorism also now going global. Global terrorism challenges the global power of the USA, its allies and a culture of mobility. In this new world dis/order, places that attract western visitors are in the front line of new global warfare, with recent attacks on visitors in Cairo, Luxor, New York, Bali, Mombassa, Jakarta, Kashmir and so on. Potential death and the fear of death especially stalk those places that attract visitors from elsewhere. Some of the time such terrorists are themselves tourists, only intermittently transmuting into terrorists. And the weapon of the weak is fear, to induce panic into those 'innocent tourists' playing away, performing what they are meant to perform in such places. The new fear can be like an epidemic, potentially striking at the airport, on the plane, at the hotel, in the nightclub, on the beach, at the petrol station, on the tourist bus, in the apartment. To be a tourist is to be on the front line in places of positive affect but places that can transmute within a split second into places of carnage (Diken, Laustsen 2002: 14).

However, with the passing of time, such places of death will themselves transmute into new places for visitors. So Ground Zero or the Falls and Shankhill Roads in Belfast are now on the tourist map, waiting for visitors to come (in Belfast there is a Troubles Tour). Places of death are routinely transformed into places for visitors, appearing on ever-new tourist itineraries. And as discussed in chapter 7 with regard to airspace, this new invisible enemy also provokes new forms of surveillance and control in order to keep those visitors moving around the world. In the United States, this requirement provoked the nationalizing of airport security and the general development of control systems over the 550m individual visits made to the United States *every* year (Diken and Laustsen 2003: 3). To enter cities of spectacle for a week means that such visitors have to place themselves within an increasingly global electronic panopticon both within the airport but increasingly moving into the street.

In the final chapter I peer into the future and try to figure out just what are some of the mobile futures likely to emerge, futures that are both unpredictable and for major periods of time irreversible. In particular I draw from chapters 9, 10, 11 and 12 the centrality of the concepts of network capital, networks, co-presence, places and meetings as central to deciphering likely mobility futures. And this future includes new nexus-like forms of control and ordering of moving populations. Not only people, machines and places are on the move as the previous chapters detail but so too are the means of tracking, ordering and governing that are increasingly detached from specific locations and which may well engender a dark future.

13

Systems and Dark Futures

Throughout Crash I have used the car not only as a sexual image, but as a total metaphor for man's life in today's society ... the ultimate role of Crash is cautionary, a warning against that brutal, erotic and overlit realm that beckons more and more persuasively to us from the margins of the technological landscape

(J. G. Ballard 1995: 6)

Most of this chapter is taken up with developing some analyses of future mobilities and in particular with whether the current dominant mobility system, of automobility, might be in some places be superseded by an alternative post-car system. I am concerned especially how to 'think' alternative futures. I deploy the notion of system and tipping points to examine such system futures. I consider various scenarios and conclude that the irreversible consequences of the last 'mobility century' and the extraordinary 'digitization' of life have left an awesome interdependent legacy. I suggest that the world is poised between global heating and 'regional warlordism', and a planet that does mitigate global heating but only through developing a 'digital panopticon'. Before developing analysis of these bleak scenarios I briefly summarize the main themes of this book so far.

Mobilities

My starting point is that human beings are nothing without objects organized into various systems. The systems come first and serve to

augment the otherwise rather thin powers of individual human subjects. Those subjects are brought together and serve to develop significant powers only because of the systems that implicate them, and
especially those systems that move them, or their ideas, or information or various objects. I have examined the character of various
mobility systems and of their adaptive and evolving interrelation-
ships with each other.

In particular I argued that travel and transport should be understood, not as individually determined or principally motivated by
calculations of costs and benefits, but through examining various
system processes analysed via a 'new mobilities paradigm'. This paradigm consists of a number of interdependent features: that all social
relationships involve diverse 'connections' that are more or less 'at a
distance', more or less fast, more or less intense and often involving
physical movement; that there are five interdependent 'mobilities'
that produce social life organized across distance and which form
(and re-form) its contours; that physical travel involves lumpy, fragile,
aged, gendered, racialized bodies encountering other bodies, objects
and the physical world multi-sensuously; that on occasions and for
specific periods, face-to-face connections and meetings occur often
as a consequence of extensive movement; that distance raise massive
problems for states that seek to effect 'governmentality' over their
intermittently moving populations of lumpy bodies; that social life is
constituted through various material objects (including 'nature' and
'technologies') that directly or indirectly move or alternatively block
the movement of objects, people and information; that crucial to
analysing these relationships is how the changing environment
'affords' different possibilities of action, movement and belief; that
it is necessary to analyse the various systems that distribute people,
activities and objects in and through time–space; that mobility-
systems are organized around the processes that circulate people,
objects and information at various spatial ranges and speeds; that
these various mobility-systems and routeways often linger over time
with a powerful spatial fixity; that mobility systems are based on
increasingly expert and alienating forms of knowledge; that interdependent systems of 'immobile' material worlds, and especially exceptionally immobile platforms (transmitters, roads, garages, stations,
aerials, airports, docks), structure mobility experiences through
forming *complex* adaptive systems; and that one important distinction to be made is between series systems and nexus systems. In
earlier chapters I examined the series systems of pedestrianism and
automobility, and the nexus systems of the railway and air. In the
following sections I examine whether automobility might shift from

a series to a nexus system and if so what would be some implications of such a shift.

In developing analysis of hybrid systems and their uncertain futures I mobilize some ideas from the complexity sciences. These have been used to examine especially the non-linear properties of systems as they move unpredictably and irreversibly away from points of equilibrium. Overall I see mobility systems as a subset of powerful, interdependent knowledge-based systems that organize production, consumption, travel and communications round the world. These systems, almost all software-based, ensure and make it seem unexceptional that products can be purchased, meetings will happen, components will arrive at the factory, planes will be waiting, messages will get through, money will arrive and so on. These systems make repetitive or iterative actions possible and mostly happen without much cognitive thought. They produce regular and repetitive 'spaces of anticipation' distributing economies, peoples, activities across the world. I showed how 1989–1990 was a key date in developing many new distinct systems.

These systems have the effect of spreading connections that in all spheres become less based upon predictable co-presence and more upon relatively far flung networks of at least partially weak ties. Thus the apparently different domains of work, family and social life each become more networked – and in a way more similar to each other. Moreover networks within these domains increasingly overlap so movement between and across them becomes significant. Weak ties spread from domain to domain especially with the growth of network capital that dramatically enhances the power of some nodes and overall generate social inequalities that increasingly seem to depend upon relative levels of access to network capital.

And as people are distributed 'far and wide', so meetings are essential for work, family and social life. People have to come together from time to time; this is obligatory and costly. Meetings are crucial and there are huge inequalities in access to the resources, the network capital, through which meetingness is performed and realized. Much travel involves meeting up for business and professional reasons and visiting family and friends within specific places. The geographical distribution of people's business, professional, family and friendship networks structure the forms, rhythms and patterns of such obligatory travelling.

There is a dynamic involved here, the more the proliferation and significance of network capital and hence the greater the networking, the more that such capital is necessary to participate in such networks. More network capital becomes necessary in order 'to stand still' in the capacity to network. There are therefore feedback mechanisms that extend network capital as the range of networking enlarges, and thus further extending the range, extent and heterogeneity of networks.

I also showed how the networking of social life moves from door-to-door to place-to-place to person-to-person connectivity. The person rather than the place or home is increasingly the new 'portal', the new centre of each social network. Each individual and their specific network is key, while place, home and context seem to become less significant in structuring networks. There is also much use of travel (and waiting) time to keep in touch with this 'personalized network'. This involves 'work' often on the move to restore trust, to maintain 'absent presence' and to rearrange events through 'connected presence'. A key transformation of contemporary life is from specific 'movement-spaces', as in daily commuting, or the annual holiday or the weekly family visit, to 'interspaces' or the indeterminate time–space lying in-between home/work/the social and which is more extensive and elaborate. The growth of multiple mobilities, new technologies and extended networks is bringing into being a new 'field' of 'interspatial' social life where network capital is highly significant.

I also showed how this shift to personalized networks is accompanied by the increasingly 'harried' nature of time with people's daily time–space patterns being desynchronized from work, community and home and hence from each other. Organizing co-presence which is utterly central to work, family and friendship becomes especially demanding, as there is some loss of collective co-ordination.

Capitalist societies were shown overall to involve new kinds of pleasure, with many elements or aspects of the body being commodified. Even when at work new modes of management are in part about engendering pleasures, to work more intensely but simultaneously to find it 'sociable and fun'. And many ways in which the body is commodified is in and through it moving about and then being and performing within certain places. As bodies are subject to the 'new', so being subject to the new is elsewhere, on the move, in some other place that 'needs' to be visited and immersed within. Newness in the twenty first century often involves moving and commodified bodies. Life within the contemporary capitalist order presupposes intermittent movement, and this involves bodies newly flowing but intermittently encountering others in rich, face-to-face (and embodied) co-presence within specific places. Places come to be travelled to for various kinds of affect. I analysed the shift from land to landscape and noted how this marks a particular way of being in the world, as places are performed through comparisons, contrasts and collections. I also analysed the exceptional global competition between places that is transforming the character of places as they struggle for positioning on a global stage. Places were thus shown to be dynamic, moving around and not necessarily staying in one 'location'. Places travel within networks of human and non-human agents, of photographs, sand, cameras, cars, souvenirs, paintings and so on. These objects extend what humans are able to do, what performances of place are possible. And the resulting networks swirl around, fluid-like, changing the fixing of place and bringing unexpected new places 'into' play.

And I have discussed how as people are moving about so information about them as human subjects is forcibly left behind in countless traces. Much of what was once 'private' and carried close or on the person as body now exists outside of that body and outside the 'self'. Or the self we can say is hugely distributed across various databases spread through time–space. There has been an irreversible shifting of the social world towards a 'database-ization' that many have examined with regard to the genetic 'coding' of life itself. But in the following I suggest that this 'database-ization' has further implications especially in the context of the potential unfolding planetary catastrophe engendered by irreversible climate change.

In earlier chapters I discussed how humans had unknowingly struck a Faustian bargain with machines that enabled them on a mass scale to do things and go places that were unimaginable within earlier epochs, especially through intersecting system developments dating from around 1840.

But my suggestion now is that a new Faustian bargain was struck around 1990. This has implicated humans in a new embrace, this time with countless digital code and databases. These databases enormously extend what humans are able to do, to travel virtually, to enable instantaneous information retrieval, to communicate with countless others even while on the move and to proliferate may new sources of information and friendship (as in web 2.0). But simultaneously, this 'dance with the digital' locks humans within these interdependent 'databasing' systems. And this process of making public through databasing what had been private to each self has hardly yet begun, but my claim here is that the new technological pathway has been laid down and increasingly many elements of economic and social life are 'locked in' to a path dependent pattern, more of a spider's web than web 2.0.

The very future of human life on the planet as it has been understood depends upon the more extensive *and* intensive 'database-ization' of each self, or what Butakman terms a 'terminal identity' (1993). The only way of taming the utterly dominant car system and hence producing a step change in the significance of mobility machines for global climate change is through the conversion of the car system from a series to a nexus system. But such a nexus system presupposes a massive extension of the database-ization of economic, social and political life, especially the precise bodily location of each 'self' at any moment. One key aspect of this involves the US-based Global Positioning System but this is being taken to a far greater accuracy with the Galileo positioning system being developed by the European Union. For commercial users for a fee the accuracy of what can be identified will be better than 1 metre. This will also be complemented by ground stations to bring the accuracy down to less than an astonishingly few centimetres.

I conclude from the discussion in the next few sections that there is a future stark choice for sustaining a planetary future. On the one hand, there is the dystopic barbarism of unregulated climate change, the elimination of many existing 'civilizing' practices of economic and social life, and the brutal reversal of many mobility and network capital developments of the past few decades. And on the other hand, there is the dystopic digital Orwell-ization of self and society, with more or less no movement without digital tracing and tracking, with almost no-one within at least rich societies outside a digital panopticon and with a carbon database as the public measure of worth and status.

Futures

First though, I make a few observations about futures in general, drawing together points made elsewhere in this book. First, futures are heavily circumscribed and are clearly not at all open. Some of the key determinants of such futures include cognitive and non-cognitive human capacities, the embedded traditions within each society, the power and conserving effect of national and international states, huge global processes operating at multiple levels, the relative fixity of the built environment, various economic, technological and social path dependencies, and large-scale enduring economic-technological, social, environmental and political inequalities around the globe. Thus there are very powerful socio-physical systems, moving in and through different time–spaces, and these produce many constraints upon possible 'futures'. There are countless ways in which different levels and orders are locked in and limit the possibilities of future change.

Moreover, because of the complex interdependencies of these systems it is almost impossible for any small groups of individuals to foresee what would be the appropriate means of effecting change. So although many groups are seeking to realize various projects of social change it is enormously hard to do, especially if the change is or has to be global. Imagining what would engender such global change is almost impossible although countless groups are seeking to do that all of the time, including some exceptionally powerful groups. There are just so many unintended consequences across time and space of economic, social and political innovation; and these consequences themselves engender further adaptive and evolving system consequences. It may be that bombing out of existence the twin towers of the World Trade Center did lead to many of the outcomes around the world that al-Qaeda had hoped for. But there are not many examples of such effective forecasting and implementation of appropriate actions by groups which have anything like the intended outcomes (strikingly unsuccessful were the Pentagon's 'future forecasts' in Iraq).

Nevertheless, there are moments of heightened openness, when the die is less cast and various possible alternatives are structurally placed upon the table. Not that such change is uncaused but it is less reducible to pre-existing systems. Change we might say at some moments is in the air although often this is only known about in retrospect. The period around 1990 seems to have been one of those moments. However, there is a danger here, an epochal hubris that presumes that one's own moment is somehow a special moment of transition and hence that decisions taken in the moment of the now are more fateful than those that have been taken at other times and places (see Laszlo 2006, on the concept of the 'chaos point').

Moreover, not all changes by any means. Certain networks of social relations are stabilized for long periods of time. I have already discussed the importance of path dependence analyses that show how causation can flow from contingent events to general processes, from small causes to large system effects, from historically or geographically remote locations to the general. I showed how path-dependence means that the ordering of processes through time significantly influences the non-linear ways in which they eventually turn out decades or even centuries later. Path dependence is a process model in which systems develop irreversibly through a 'lock-in' but with only certain small causes being necessary to prompt or tip the initiation of the 'path'. Such small causes are mostly unpredictable, difficult to foresee although in hindsight they appear explicable in terms of how they tip the system in path dependent outcomes.

Moreover, I have examined how when change happens it may not be gradual but can occur dramatically, at a moment, all of a sudden, in a kind of rush. If a system passes a particular threshold, switches or tipping points occur with 'punctuated equilibria'. The system turns over, as with a liquid that turns into a gas with small changes in controlling temperatures, or with the internet growing dramatically in the late 1990s as countless people and organizations adapted and co-evolved with it, or where minor increases in global temperature may provoke out-of-control global heating.

Cars, Climates and Catastrophes

We have seen how lock-ins means that institutions matter a great deal as to how systems develop over the long time. Institutions, using this term very broadly, can produce a long term irreversibility that is: 'both more predictable and more difficult to reverse' (North 1990: 104). Abbott argues that while change is the normal order of things and indeed many assessments of contemporary social life emphasize the increasingly accelerating nature of profound changes, there are certain networks of social relations that get stabilized for very long periods of time (2001). One of these is the car-system which I showed in chapter 6 is remarkably stable and unchanging, even though a massive economic, social and technological maelstrom of change surrounds it. The petroleum-and-steel car system seems to sail on regardless, now over a century old and able to 'drive' out competitors, such as feet, bikes, buses and trains. It is a modern day Leviathan: 'automobility stretches its six fingers – production, possession, pipelines, projection, pressure and power – to tighten its global grasp upon humankind' (Latimer, Munro 2006: 35). Such locked-in institutional processes are extremely difficult to reverse as billions of agents around the world co-evolve and adapt to it and built their lives around its strange mixture of coercion and flexibility (see Krugman 1996, more generally on agents and systems).

But it is a key feature of complexity approaches that nothing is fixed forever. Abbott maintains that there is: 'the possibility for a pattern of actions to occur to put the key in the lock and make a major turning point occur' (2001: 257). However, much current government and corporate thinking and practice adopts a linear and not a complexity vision as to the future of the car. In other words, the question becomes a question as to whether one particular aspect of the 'car' can be changed and what will be the consequences of a linear change of improved fuel efficiency or reduced weight to power ratio or increased car sharing. This linear approach is dominant and is found in the UK's Royal Academy of Engineering's Report on *Transport 2050* (2005). In this Report there is no examination of the car as a complex system hugely interconnected with a multitude of economic and social practices or how a set of small changes can provoke system change and the emergence of a new kind of post-car entity. So in order to break with the current car-system, what Adams terms 'business as usual' (1999), I examine what might provoke a 'tipping point'. My claim is that within a few decades the four person, steel bodied and petroleum powered one ton car will be in museums where visitors (if there are still such visitor attractions and physical travel to them) will gawp at this technological dinosaur. The oddity of the car will be housed in displays alongside equally quaint mobile phones, ungainly computers sitting in big metal boxes while outside jumbo jets will be rusting away.

However, this post-car future could come about in two very different ways. Either the catastrophe of global heating (alongside collapsing oil supplies) will have 'washed away' many of the cars, roads and communication systems around the world. There will be a much lower carbon economy brought about by declining population, production, consumption, communications and mobilities. This scenario has been termed that of 'tribal trading' (Foresight 2006). Or alternatively a nexus vehicle system will have emerged, beginning in various rich societies but gradually spreading around the world. This post-car system will involve adaptive and co-evolving interplays between very many systems operating at different temporal and spatial scales. These systems will include the resource/environmental, technological, economic, policy and societal.

Predicting whether the post-car will result from the second set of transformations is exceedingly difficult. In this book I have emphasized that large-scale system change normally results from 'small' changes that occur in what turn out to be the early stages of a socio-technical system. Those small changes that take place in a particular order then lay down a subsequent path dependent pattern.

So I will now briefly detail eight 'small' developments that might in their dynamic interdependence tip mobility into a new system, the nexus vehicle system (see Graham, Marvin 2001, for a contrary view; I am very grateful for Kingsley Dennis' research here). These changes range across many different systems and are not at all a matter of 'technology' per se. My argument here draws upon Hughes' classic study of the growth of the electricity grid system (1983). What he shows is that the successful development of large-scale technologies depends upon the design not just of the devices but of the 'society' into which such designs would fit. In other words a new large scale system (which the post car nexus system would be) requires a vision of the future reconfigured sociology in which that set of devices will be placed. What then are some of the small changes that might provoke system change?

First, there is the small change concerned with the rapidly changing understanding of *global climate change*. Over the past few years that, there has been a remarkable reduction in the uncertainties involved in the multiple sciences of climate change. So although the scale and impact of future temperature changes is still much debated and, especially in the United States and certain developing societies, contested there is growing consensus about the following. World temperatures have risen by at least 0.5°C over the past century and this is almost certainly the product of very many different forms of human practice that raised the levels of greenhouse gases in the atmosphere (Stern 2006: ii). Moreover, these levels of greenhouse gases and world temperatures will increase significantly over the next few decades; and this rise will further increase temperatures through multiple forms of positive feedback including especially the melting of Greenland's ice (Lovelock 2006: 33). These processes are locked in and according to Lovelock: 'there is no large negative feedback that would countervail temperature rise' (2006: 35). The overall economic, social and political consequences of such changes are global and, if they are not significantly mitigated, they will very substantially reduce the standard of living, the capabilities of life around the world and probably the overall population world-wide as the impacts are most felt in poorer countries (Stern 2006: vi–vii). With business as usual the stock of greenhouse gases could treble by the end of the century and there is a 50 per cent risk of more than a 5°C increase in temperatures and the transformation of the world's physical and human geography through for example a 5–20 per cent reduction in world consumption levels (Stern 2006: iii, x). There is thus a growing consensus among scientists and social scientists and among many national and international governments that reducing global carbon consumption is essential and there are very substantial economic reasons for so doing. Within this, bearing down on carbon use within transport is crucial because it uniquely has been rising because of growing car use, rapidly expanding cheap air travel and the increased 'miles' flown by both manufactured goods and foodstuffs. There are potential alternatives to carbon-based systems in powering 'cars' and so reducing carbon use in this area is high up many economic and policy agendas (Motavalli 2000). And such a move away from a carbon-based transport system is increasingly expressed as a relatively short term imperative that will generate long term savings if this can be achieved in time; there is a 'high price to delay' (Stern 2006: xv). This is thus a small but potentially very significant change in the economic and policy landscape around the world.

Second, it is now increasingly realized that *oil supplies* around the world are about to start running down. Peak oil production occurred in the United States as far back as 1971 and it seems that oil production world-wide will peak around 2010 especially because of the failure to discover new fields at the same rate as occurred in the past (Heinberg 2005; Rifkin 2002: ch. 2). Energy will become increasingly expensive and there will be frequent shortages especially with the world's population continuing to rise. There is not enough oil and this will generate significant economic downturn, more resource wars and some claim much lower population levels. The delivery of fresh water also depends on fossil fuels and yet severe water shortages now face one third of the world's population (Laszlo 2006: 28–9). Rifkin claims that the oil age is 'winding down as fast as it revved up' (2002: 174). Indeed the United States seems to have based much of its foreign policy on the concept of peak oil for over thirty years. One interesting consequence is that 'patriotic' American celebrities are currently buying non-oil based 'green' cars so that less 'foreign' oil has to be imported.

Third, *transport policy* is shifting away from predict and provide models (except with regard to air travel) which were based upon increased mobility as a desirable good and in which predictions of future car use were planned for through new road schemes developed by engineers. These schemes provided what had been predicted in the model (Whitelegg 1997; Vigar 2002). 'New realist' policies critique how expanding the road network simply increases car-based travel. The new realism involves many organizations developing alternative mobilities through integrated public transport, better facilities for cyclists and pedestrians, advanced traffic management, better use of land-use planning, real time information systems, and a wider analysis of how transport impacts upon the environment (Vigar 2002). In particular, transport policies increasingly take note of alternative models of transport such that of Curitiba (in Brazil). This model involves separating traffic types and establishing exclusive bus lanes on the city's predominant arteries. As a result there is a safe, reliable, and efficient bus service operating without the hazards and delays inherent to mixed-traffic bus services. And there is the densification of development along these bus routes. Over a thousand buses make 12,500 trips per day, serving 1.3 million passengers. And there are five different types of buses operating in Curitiba including a new 'bi-articulated' bus on the outside high-capacity lanes. Bi-articulated buses – the largest in the world – are three buses attached by two articulations and capable of carrying 270 passengers.

Fourth, there are new *fuel systems* for cars, vans and buses. These emerging new fuels systems include lithium-ion nanobatteries, carbon nanotube batteries and capacitors, hybrid cars powered by petrol/ diesel and batteries (Honda Insight, Toyota Prius) or by gas and steam (BMW), plug-in hybrid electric vehicles, diesel fuel grown from oilseeds, natural gas (Honda GX), ethanol made from corn, sugar or maize, and hydrogen fuel cells (Motavalli 2000: 107; Rifkin 2002: 192–3). Almost all major car companies are developing one or more of these alternative fuel systems while oil companies are also looking to go, as BP expresses this, Beyond Petroleum. MIT's Smart Cities project has developed shareable and stackable individual robot 'cars' (Jha 2005). Other recent post-cars include G-Wiz, TH!NK CITY and Sakura Maranello electric cars, and DaimlerChrysler hydrogen buses and Necar cars. It is thought that 4,000 companies are currently seeking to develop mass production hydrogen cars (Vidal 2002). Rifkin describes the 'world-wide hydrogen energy web' as the next great technological, commercial and social revolution, following on the heels of the 1990 initiation of the internet and the networked society although others are more sceptical (2002: 9, especially ch. 8).

Fifth, there are various *new materials* for constructing 'car' bodies. One model is the ultra-light 'hypercar' made of advanced polymer composite materials (Hawken, Lovins, Lovins 2000). Other technologies include aluminium and nanotechnology which may make possible carbon-based fibres 100 times stronger than steel and one-sixth the weight (US Department of Transportation, 1999: 4–5). A recent example is Lotu's development of a carbon fibre and resin. Such new materials significantly reduce the weight of vehicles and hence the need for powerful engines to move them. Also there may be increasing production of much smaller micro-cars (rather than 4-person family-sized cars) for crowded urban spaces. Current examples of such micro-cars or 'station cars' include the Mercedes Smart Car, the Cabriolet, the Nissan Hypermini, the C1, and PSA's TULIP car as well as Segways and BMW's motor cycle/car hybrid. There also various light transport systems being planned such as ULTra automated taxis at Heathrow activated by a smart card or Taxi2000 prototypes (although note Latour's salutary account of the failure of the pre-digital Aramis: 1996). Some other schemes involve the physical separation of small light micro-cars from large vehicles.

Sixth, there are significant moves to *deprivatize* cars through car-sharing, cooperative car clubs and smart car-hire schemes. Even by 2001 six hundred cities in Europe had developed car-sharing schemes involving 50,000 people (Cervero 2001). Prototype examples developed in La Rochelle (Liselec), in northern California, Berlin, and Japan (Motavalli 2000: 233). In Oxford there is the UK's first hire by the hour car club scheme named Avis CARvenience. Two companies in the United States are Zipcar and Flexcar. In the UK there are various car clubs such as CityCarClub, Car Plus and Carshare. In certain cases this involves smart-card technology to book and pay and also to pay for public transport. These developments reflect the general shift in contemporary economies from what Rifkin terms, ownership to access, as reflected by the delivery of many services on the internet (2000). So we could hypothesize the increasing payment for 'access' to travel/mobility *services* rather than the owning of *vehicles* outright. One important consequence is that if cars are not domestically owned then the coops or corporations providing 'car services' would undertake both the short-term parking and especially the long term disposal of 'dead' vehicles. The former would significantly reduce the scale of car parking needed since vehicles would be more 'on the road', while the latter would radically improve recycling rates (as demonstrated in Hawken, Lovins, Lovins 2000). Overall it is possible to propose the following historic periodization of cars, from luxury or speed vehicles, to family/household vehicles, to cars as owned and driven by individuals, to deprivatized vehicles owned either by cooperatives or corporations and 'leased'.

Seventh and relatedly, there is the development of 'smart-card' *technology* that will transfer information from car to home, to bus, to train, to workplace, to web site, to shop-till, to bank. This connectivity could facilitate a single means of paying for 'travel' whatever the form of transport and simultaneously to deprivatize so-called cars that become more like portals. This is already close to development in Switzerland with the public-private travel card. Vehicles are increasingly hybridized with the technologies of the mobile, personal entertainment system, and laptop computer (as car companies join up with ISPs). Car-drivers and passengers can be personalized with their own communication links (email addresses, phone numbers, web addresses) and entertainment applications (digitally stored music, programmed radio stations). Thus any vehicle is becoming more of a 'smart home' away from home.

Eighth, *communications* are increasingly interconnected with transportation (see Castells, 2001). There is the embedding of information and communication technologies (ICT) into moving objects: mobile phones, palmtop computers, cars, buses, trains, aircraft and so on. Some of this within the car involves smart safety innovations such as AIDE and PReVENT. But more generally as information is digitized and released from location, so cars, roads, and buildings can send and receive digital information ('Intelligent Transport Systems'). This convergence of ICT and ITS will represent an epochal shift as cars are reconstituted as a networked system rather than as separate 'iron cages', as a potentially integrated *nexus* rather than as a parallel *series* (see Foresight 2006). This could produce a shift from the modern divided traffic flow to what Peters terms the organic flow in which all traffic participants are able to survive and co-exist, aided by GPS/ Galileo systems (2006).

So there are eight sets of changes. None is sufficient in itself to tip the car system. But my suggestion is that if certain interdependencies occur in an optimal order then they could provoke a post-car system. A series of small changes could produce a sense of contagion as many changes sweep through various systems. Such a networked system will tame the automobility system that has so far 'driven' out all challenges to its omnipotent taking over the world.

What might this post-car system look like? There will be a mixed flow of slow-moving semi-public micro-cars, bikes, many hybrid vehicles, pedestrians and mass transport integrated into a mobility of physical *and* virtual access. This system, commencing in some societies in the rich 'north', would consist of multiple, dense forms of movement. It would involve small, ultra-light, smart, probably biofuel or hydrogen-based, deprivatized 'vehicles'. Electronic regulators embedded in lampposts and in vehicles will regulate access, organize price and control the vehicle speed. Some such vehicles will be driverless. Smart 'cards' will control and pay for people's access to the various forms of mobility. The movement of vehicles would be electronically and physically integrated with many other forms of mobility. There is electronic co-ordination between motorized and non-motorized transport and between those 'on the move' in many different ways (Hawken, Lovins 2000: 47; see Foresight 2006, on 'good intentions'). Flexibilized travelling will involve access to small, light mobile pods as and when required. And software systems will continuously figure out the best means of doing tasks, meeting up or getting to some place or event. Neighbourhoods will foster 'access by proximity' through denser living patterns and integrated land use. People will live in denser, much more integrated urban areas that will maximize co-presence. Such redesign would 'force' people to bump into each other since their networks will overlap. And this pattern, what Foresight terms 'good intentions', involves carbon allowances as the new currency which will be allocated, monitored and measured. Reduced carbon emissions will constrain personal mobility. This scenario is a more developed version of one interestingly noted in Harvey's *Spaces of Hope* (2000: 270–1; and see Bukatman 1003, on science fiction futures).

Bleak Futures

I have so far suggested that the days of steel and petroleum automobility are numbered. Certainly by 2100 it is inconceivable that individualized mobility will be based upon the nineteenth-century technologies of privately owned one-ton steel bodied cars with petroleum engines. The system of automobility will disappear almost certainly before then but this could be for two different sets of reasons as I analyse below. Moreover, the pattern of nineteenth-century 'public mobility', of the *dominance* of publicly owned, managed and timetabled buses, trains, coaches and ships, will not be re-established. That has been irreversibly lost because of the self-expanding character of the car system that produced and necessitated individualized mobility based upon instantaneous time, fragmentation and coerced flexibility. Whatever the post-car system will be like it will substantially involve *individualized movement* that automobility presupposes and has brought into being during the century of the car. The tipping point towards a post-car nexus is unpredictable. It cannot be read off from linear changes in existing firms, industries, practices and economies. Just as the internet and the mobile phone came from 'nowhere', so the tipping point towards the 'post car' will emerge unpredictably. It will probably arrive from a set of technologies or firms or governments that are currently not a centre of the car industry and culture, as with the Finnish toilet paper maker Nokia and the unexpected origins of the now ubiquitous mobile phone. It will develop in some place and suddenly it will be the fashion. And it will probably emerge in a small society or city-state with very dense informational traffic that can convert into a post car configuration (Iceland perhaps as an interesting prototype which has already announced itself as the first Hydrogen Society).

   Incidentally one further scenario that also needs to be registered here is that of a rather different kind of individualized mobility but also based upon instantaneous time and time–space flexibility. This is 'vertical mobility', with a version of this already present in Sao Paolo based upon helicopter travel that enables rich individuals and corporate warriors to sail above those poor souls trying to get places on the freeway (Cwerner 2006). The development of the helipad as a component of contemporary urban design indicates the potential transformative effects of vertical mobility and a new component of network capital. Also there is a rapid growth of private jets, either owned or more frequently leased, and these take advantage of the empty sky lying underneath the flight paths of military or commercial flights. It is implausible to imagine that vertical systems will be the basis of a mass transit system but if we think automobility induces high levels of inequality then even a modest development of a vertical mobility system will engender, as in Brazil, even higher levels of social inequality. A related version is the development of 'aerial taxis' that are being planned by DayJet and will move people in 5–6 seater planes between US regional airports. Also passenger services to space are being planned by Virgin Galactica to start in 2008. Thirty Virgin pilots are about to be trained as 'space pilots'. I return to vertical mobility below.

I now consider the slightly more mundane scenario of a nexus post car system that is somewhat similar to the 'good intentions' scenario developed within the UK Foresight Programme on how intelligent information systems could deliver safe, sustainable and robust transport futures (Foresight 2006; I was a participant in some scenario building discussions). Many digital transformations provide a golden opportunity to substitute physical mobility with virtual mobility, to enable the traveller to respond with 'intelligence' to choices available and to embed informational systems *within* transport that so far is somewhat non-digital. The Foresight Report also suggests that there are four different scenarios for 2055 and analyses various processes and developments that would have to take place in order that each such scenario could be realized (that is, the method of backcasting; see 2006). My argument here that the two scenarios that are empirically most plausible are 'good intentions' and 'tribal trading' (I rename each below).

With 'tribal trading', oil wars and the escalating impact of global warming mean that there is a substantial breakdown of many of the extensive mobility and communication connections that straddle the world. There is widespread infrastructural collapse and the increasing separation between different regions, or 'tribes'. Systems of repair dissolve and there is increasingly localized recycling of bikes, cars, trucks and phone systems. With tribal trading, what I would call 'regional warlordism', there would be a plummeting standards of living, a relocalization of mobility patterns, an increasing emphasis upon local warlords controlling recycled forms of mobility and weaponry, and relatively weak imperial or national forms of governance. Only the super-rich may travel and they will do so in the air and possibly regularly making tourist-type space trips to escape the hell on earth (to get the ultimate 'tourist gaze'). There is a Hobbesian war of each warlord dominated region against their neighbours especially for access to water, oil and gas. And with extensive flooding, extreme weather events and the break-up of long distance oil and gas pipelines, these resources become exceptionally contested and protected by armed gangs. There have of course already been various oil wars and the heated planet will also usher in water wars. Those who can live in gated encampments will do so. And there are already many foretastes of this scenario but especially contemporary Iraq. There are likely to be many other 'wild zones' where the 'west' is *exiting* as fast as possible if the oil no longer seems to flow, leaving the 'society' to ethnic, tribal or religious warlordism.

So if we had a choice we would surely choose 'good intentions' rather than 'tribal trading' ('regional warlordism'). However, good intentions I now suggest is better characterized as the scenario of the 'digital panopticon'. Why is this? The empirical evidence on climate change suggest that exceptionally rapid major shifts have to take place in order to slow down and to reverse increasing global temperatures. There is only a limited period of time before imperial and national systems will collapse and 'regional warlordism' becomes widespread. There is in Laszlo's terms a 'chaos point' involved here when for a period at least systems may move in one or various directions but this period is limited in duration (2006). A variety of interlocking systems have irreversibly taken the world into uncharted territory. As Stern writes: 'Climate change . . . is the greatest and widest-ranging market failure' (2006: i). The global market has engendered enormous 'external diseconomies' as economists would put it, or untold global risks, as sociologists would say. Either way the adaptive and evolving relationships between enormously powerful systems are like, as Giddens once put via a mobility analogy, a 'juggernaut' careering full pace to the edge of the cliff. And if one was in that juggernaut, even slowing it down slightly would require equally if not more powerful systems than those powering it to its demise.

In the Stern Report the kinds of behavioural changes necessary to mitigate climate change are only weakly described (2006). The Report does not apply systems thinking to 'society' and to the multiple social practices that make up and constitute everyday life. But if we do think such issues through the notion of systems then it is clear that only some exceptionally powerful systems could offset those tendencies moving towards global climate change. It will be necessary to confront the positive feedbacks loops implicated in climate change with a very large and powerful set of novel systems. I will deal here only with mobility systems and especially that of the car but similar points would apply to new kinds of energy production and energy saving. The only way of 'correcting' such a massive market failure and hence taming the dominant car system is by producing a step change in how mobility machines are organized. And this will only come about through converting the 'car' from a series car system to a nexus vehicle system.

But there is no free lunch here. At the level of the globe there will be an integrated earth automatic system of observations and mappings. And at the level of every day a nexus system, as with other elements of the struggle against climate change, presupposes a 'digital panopticon'. The future of human life on the planet thus may well depend upon the extensive *and* intensive 'digitization' of each self. The planet is poised between alternative dystopias because of the irreversibilities that have been established and locked in over the past century or two and with regard to mobility because car tightened its global grasp upon humankind (Latimer, Munro 2006: 35). That long term path dependent pattern of high and increasing carbon consumption through automobility leaves no room for many other alternatives.

This potential nexus system entails a digital panopticon involving satellite tracking; ubiquitous CCTV cameras as part of a smart infrastructure; data mining software; the migration of systems of biometric security into urban areas; the increasing distribution of the 'self' across various databases; more general database-ization that integrate most elements of a person's economic, social and political life; the standardization of space; the embedding of digital processing within the environment; the location of sensors within moving vehicles which increasingly operate smartly; many technologies that continuously can track the position of objects and people with in a couple of decades RFID implants; automated software systems for allocating road space; the development of a smart code space that will come to determine the route, price, access and speed of vehicles; sensors and processors that enable vehicles to self-navigate; and the likely tracking and tracing of each person's carbon allowances and carbon expenditures (Thrift 2004c; Ahas, Mark 2005; Sager 2006:

476–7; Information Commissioner 2006; and generally the journal *Surveillance and Society*). This set of digitizing developments is immense and is not merely a question of so-called civil liberties. Under the sway of a post September 11th 'security-ization' many of these are in rapid development, so much so that in the UK the Information Commissioner himself states that we live in a surveillance society (Information Commissioner 2006: 1). These systems of tracking and tracing surveillance involve step changes that are taking place in the character of life. In order to move around there is a Faustian bargain to be struck, and especially significant is that the car will only be superseded through a massive nexus system that orders, regulates, tracks and soon will drive the each vehicle and each driver/passenger. And this depends upon there being a rich environment full of information and messages that are themselves mobile and which is increasingly sentient. People would be part of sentient, smart and responsive swarming behaviour.

So there are two stark futures. On the one hand, there is 'tribal trading' or 'regional warlordism', a barbarism of unregulated climate change, increased flooding and extreme weather events, the elimination of many existing 'civilizing' practices of economic and social life, and the dramatic collapse of long range mobility and related developments of the past decades, with New Orleans surely the wake up call and an event more iconic of the future of the 'west' than September 11th. Life even in the 'west' here will be nasty, brutish and almost certainly 'shorter', especially at the beach.

But then it might be just possible to avoid this if a whole gamut of transformations takes place now. But this in turn involves a digital Orwell-ization of self and society, with more or less no movement without digital tracing and tracking, with no-one beyond the panopticon. This may tame the car system (and other energy systems) if many other developments take place simultaneously such as the tracking and tracing of each person's carbon allowance which begins to function as the public measure of worth and status. So life goes on and indeed extensive co-presence would be still achievable for many. But only because when the software systems work, everyone and everything is measured and monitored, tracked and traced. The dream of bottom-up self-organized virtual communities turns into the nightmare of the self almost entirely distributed in time–space and only existing through its appearance upon multiple and interdependent databases, including in a foreseeable future a carbon database.

There may be some other scenarios of the future where the flows of many modalities of movement and the joy of effervescent co-presence are secured and ensured in ways which are both sustainable and ensure multiple and roughly equal capabilities. And of course there are multiple unpredictable small but very distributed collective struggles against such systems (see Thrift 2007: ch. 1, especially on banishing nearness as the measure of all things). And unexpected and unpredictable system changes can develop especially through moving across chaos or tipping points. Nothing in the analysis here suggests that all is set in stone and systems are forever (not even the universe itself). But so far mobility futures seem poised between a breakdown of many systems and networks through the multiple feedback loops of global heating *and* a world where the systems and networks work only too well in 'securing' many mobilities and especially the car system, and 'securing' peoples within multiple panoptic environments.

In this book I have elaborated and developed what I term the new mobilities paradigm as a way of recasting the social sciences. It is clear I hope that there are immense benefits for social science of being mobilized in the many ways I have set out and justified here. But the analysis has ended up with the claim that thinking various mobility futures through the lens of this paradigm suggests that global futures are poised between an Orwellian or a Hobbesian future, between the devil and the deep blue sea.

References

Aaltola, M. 2005. 'The international airport: the hub-and-spoke pedagogy of the American Empire', *Global Networks*, 5: 261–78

Abbott, A. 2001. *Time Matters*. Chicago: University of Chicago Press

Abercrombie, N., Longhurst, B. 1998. *Audiences*. London: Sage

Adam, B. 1995. *Timewatch*. Cambridge: Polity

—— 1998. *Timescapes of Modernity*. London: Routledge

Adams, J. 1995. *Risk*. London: UCL Press

—— 1999. *The Social Implications of Hypermobility*. OECD Project on Environmentally Sustainable Transport. Paris: OECD

Adey, P. 2004. 'Secured and sorted mobilities: examples from the airport', *Surveillance and Society*. 1: 500–9

—— 2006a. 'Airports and airmindedness: spacing, timing and using Liverpool Airport, 1929–1939', *Social and Cultural Geography*, 7: 343–63

—— 2006b. 'If mobility is everything then it is nothing: towards a relational politics of (im)mobilities', *Mobilities*, 1: 75–94

Adey, P., Bevan, P. 2006. 'Between the physical and the virtual: connected mobilities', in. Sheller, M., Urry, J. (eds) *Mobile Technologies of the City*. London: Routledge

Adler, J. 1989. 'Origins of sightseeing', *Annals of Tourism Research*, 16: 7–29

Adorno, T. 1974. *Mimima Moralia*. London: Verso

Agamben, G. 1998. *Homo Sacer: Sovereign Power and Bare Life*. Stanford: Stanford University Press

Ahas, R., Mark, Ü. 2005. 'Location based services- new challenges for planning and public administration', *Futures*, 37: 547–61

Ahmed, S. 2000. *Strange Encounters: Embodied Others in Postcoloniality*. London and New York: Routledge

—— 2004. *The Cultural Politics of Emotion*. Edinburgh: University of Edinburgh Press

Albrow, M. 1997. 'Travelling beyond local cultures: socioscapes in a global city', in Eade, J. (ed.) *Living the Global City: Globalization as Local Process.* London: Routledge

Allen, G., Crow, G. 2001. *Families, Households and Society.* London: Palgrave

Amin, A., Cohendet, P. 2004. *Architectures of Knowledge.* Oxford: Oxford University Press

Amin, A., Thrift, N. 2002. *Cities. Reimagining the Urban.* Cambridge: Polity

Anderson, B. 1991. *Imagined Communities: Reflections on the Origin and Spread of Nationalism.* London and New York: Verso

Anderson, S., Tabb, B. (eds) 2002. *Water, Leisure and Culture.* Oxford: Berg

Arellano, A. 2004. 'Bodies, spirits and Incas: performing Machu Picchu', in Sheller, M., Urry, J. (eds) *Tourism Mobilities: Places to Play, Places in Play.* London and New York: Routledge

Aristotle 2002. *Nicomachean Ethics.* Oxford: Oxford University

Arquilla, J., Ronfeldt, D. 2001. *Networks and Netwars.* Santa Monica: Rand

Arthur, B. 1994a. *Increasing Returns and Path Dependence in the Economy.* Ann Arbor: University of Michigan Press

—— 1994b. 'Summary Remarks', in Cowan, G. Pines, D. Meltzer, D. (eds) *Complexity, Metaphors, Models and Reality.* Santa Fe Institute: Studies in the Sciences of Complexity Proceedings, vol. 19

Augé, M. 1995. *Non-Places.* London: Verso

Axelrod, R., Cohen, M. 1999. *Harnessing Complexity.* New York: Free Press

Awdry, W. 2002. *Thomas the Tank Engine: The Classic Library Station Box.* London: Egmont

Axhausen, K. W. 2002. *A Dynamic Understanding of Travel Demand. A Sketch.* Zürich: Institut für Verkehrsplannung und Transportsysteme, ETH, Switzerland

—— 2003. 'Social networks and travel: some hypotheses' *Arbeitsbericht Verkehrs-und Raumplannung 197*, Zürich: Institut für Verkehrsplannung und Transportsysteme, ETH, Switzerland

Bachen, C. 2001. 'The family in the networked society: a summary of research on the American family', *http://sts.scu.edu/nexus/Issue1-1/ Bachen_TheNetworkedFamily.asp* (accessed 31.11.04)

Bachmair, B. 1991. 'From the motor-car to television: cultural-historical arguments on the meaning of mobility for communication', *Media, Culture and Society*, 13: 521–33

Bærenholdt, O., Haldrup, M., Larsen, J., Urry, J. 2004. *Performing Tourist Places.* Aldershot: Ashgate

Bales, K. 1999. *Disposable People. New Slavery in the Global Economy.* Berkeley: University of California Press

Ball, P. 2004. *Critical Mass.* London: Heinemann

Ballard, J. G. [1973] 1995. *Crash.* London: Vintage

Barabási, A-L. 2002. *Linked. The New Science of Networks*. Cambridge, Mass: Perseus

Barrell, J. 1972. *The Idea of Landscape and the Sense of Place. 1730–1840*. Cambridge: Cambridge University Press

Barthes, R. 1972. *Mythologies*. London: Cape

Baskas, H. 2001. *Stuck at the Airport: The Very Best Services, Dining and Unexpected Attractions at 54 Airports*. New York: Simon and Schuster

Batty, M. 2001. 'Cities as small worlds', *Environment and Planning B Planning and Design*, 28: 637–8

Baubock, B. 1994. *Transnational Citizenship*. Aldershot: Edward Elgar

Baudrillard, J. 1988. *America*. London: Verso

Bauman, Z, 1993. *Postmodern Ethics*. London: Routledge

—— *Globalization: The Human Consequences*, Cambridge: Polity Press.

—— *Liquid Modernity*. Cambridge: Polity

—— 'Reconnaissance wars of the planetary frontierland', *Theory, Culture and Society*, 19, 81–90.

—— *Liquid Love*. Cambridge: Polity Press

Baym, K. 1995. 'The emergence of community in computer-mediated communication', in Jones, S. (ed.) *Cybersociety*. London: Sage

Beaverstock, J. 2005. 'Transnational elites in the city: British highly-skilled transferees in New York's financial district', *Journal of Ethnic and Migration Studies* 31: 245–269.

Beck, U. 1999. *Individualization*. London: Sage

—— 2001 'Living your own life in a runaway world: individualization, globalization and politics', in Hutton, W., Giddens, A. (eds) *On the Edge: Living with Global Capitalism*. London: Vintage

Beck, U., Beck-Gernsheim, E. 1995. *The Normal Chaos of Love*. Cambridge: Polity Press.

Beck-Gernsheim, E. 2002. *Reinventing the Family: in Search of New Lifestyles*. London: Blackwell

Beckmann, J. 2001. *Risky Mobility. The Filtering of Automobility's Unintended Consequences*. University of Copenhagen: Dept of Sociology PhD

Beeton, S. 2005. *Film-Induced Tourism*. London: Channel View

Bell, C., Lyall, J. 2002. 'The accelerated sublime: thrill-seeking adventure heroes in the commodified landscape', in Coleman, S., Crang, M. (eds) *Tourism. Between Place and Performance*. New York: Berghahn

Bell, C., Newby, H. 1976. 'Communion, communalism, class and community action: the sources of new urban politics', in Bell, C., Newby, H.,Herbert, D., Johnston, R. (eds) *Social Areas in Cities, Volume 2*. Chichester: Wiley

Benjamin, W. 1992. *Illuminations*. London: Fontana

—— 1999. *The Arcades Project*. Cambridge, Mass: Belknap Press

Berman, M. 1983. *All that is Solid Melts into Air*. London: Verso

Bhabha, H. 1994. *The Location of Culture*. London Routledge

Bijsterveld, K. 2001. 'The diabolical symphony of the mechanical age', *Social Studies of Science,* 31: 37–70

Billig, M. 1995. *Banal Nationalism*. London: Sage

Blackbourn, D. 2002. 'Fashionable spa towns in nineteenth century Europe', in Anderson, S., Tabb, B. (eds) *Water, Leisure and Culture*. Oxford: Berg

Boden, D. 1994. *The Business of Talk*. Cambridge: Polity

—— 2000. 'Worlds in action: information, instantaneity and global futures trading', in Adam, B., Beck, U., B., van Loon, J. (eds) *The Risk Society and Beyond*. London: Sage

Boden, D., Molotch, H. 1994. 'The compulsion to proximity', in Friedland, R., Boden, D. (eds) *Nowhere. Space, Time and Modernity*. Berkeley: University of California Press

Bogard, W. 2000. 'Simmel in cyberspace: strangeness and distance in postmodern communications', *Space and Culture*, 4/5: 23–46

Böhm, S., Jones, C., Land, C., Paterson, M. (eds) 2006. *Against Automobility*. Oxford: Blackwell Sociological Review Monograph

Bondi, L., Smith, M. Davidson, J. (eds) 2005. *Emotional Geographies*. Aldershot: Ashgate

Bourdieu, P. 1984. *Distinction. A Social Critique of the Judgment of Taste*. London: Routledge and Kegan Paul

Brah, A. 1996. *Cartographies of Diaspora: Contesting Identities*. London: Routledge

Braidotti, R. 1994. *Nomadic Subjects: Embodiment and Sexual Difference in Contemporary Feminist Theory*. New York: Columbia University Press

Braudel, F. 1992. *The Mediterranean World in the Age of Philip 11*, London: BCA

Breedveld, K. 1998. 'The double myth of flexibilization: trends in scattered work hours, and differences in time sovereignty', *Time and Society*, 7: 129–143

Breen, R., Rottman, D. 1998. 'Is the national state the appropriate geographical unit for class analysis?', *Sociology*, 32: 1–21

Brendon, P. 1991. *Thomas Cook: 150 Years of Popular Tourism*. London: Secker and Warburg

Brottman, M. (ed.) 2001. *Car Crash Culture*. New York: Palgrave.

Brown, B., Green, N., Harper, R. (eds) 2002. *Wireless World*. London: Springer

Brown, B., O'Hara, K. 2003. 'Place as a practical concern of mobile workers', *Environment and Planning A,* 35: 1565–1587

Brown, J. S., Duguid, P. 2000. *The Social Life of Information*. Boston: Harvard Business School Press

Bryson, N. 1983. *Vision and Painting*. London: Macmillan

Buchanan, M. 2002. *Nexus: Small Worlds and the Groundbreaking Science of Networks*. London: W.W.Norton.

Bull, M. 2000. *Sounding out the City*. Oxford: Berg

—— 2004. 'Automobility and the power of sound', *Theory, Culture and Society*, 21: 243–59

—— 2005. 'No dead air! The iPod and the culture of mobile listening', *Leisure Studies*, 24: 343–55

Bunce, M. 1994. *The Countryside Ideal*. London: Routledge

Burawoy, M. (ed.) 2000. *Global Ethnography*. Berkeley: University of California Press

Burt, R. 1992. *Structural Holes*. Cambridge, Mass.: Harvard University Press

Bukatman, S. 1993. *Terminal Identity*. Durham, US: Duke University Press

Buzard, J. 1993. *The Beaten Track*. Oxford: Clarendon Press

Byrne, D. 1998. *Complexity Theory and the Social Sciences*. London: Routledge

Cairncross, F. 1997. *The Death of Distance*. London: Orion

Cairns, S., Sloman, L., Newson, C., Anable, J., Kirkbridde, A. and Goodwin, P. 2004. *Smarter choices – changing the way we travel*, London: Department for Transport.

Caletrio, J. 2003. *A Ravaging Mediterranean Passion: Tourism and Environmental Change in Europe's Playground*. Unpublished PhD. Lancaster University: Dept. of Sociology

Callon, M., Law, J. 2004. 'Guest editorial', *Environment and Planning D*, 22: 3–11

Callon, M., Law, J., Urry, J. (eds) 2004. *Absent Presence: Localities, Globalities, and Methods*, special issue of *Environment and Planning D: Society and Space*, 22: 3–190

Campbell, C. 1987. *The Romantic Ethic and the Spirit of Modern Consumerism*. Oxford: Basil Blackwell

Capra, F. 1996. *The Web of Life*. London: Harper Collins

—— 2002. *The Hidden Connections. A Science for Sustainable Living*. London: Harper Collins

Carphone Warehouse 2006. *The Mobile Life Report*. London: Carphone Warehouse

Carrabine, E., Longhurst, B. 2002. 'Consuming the car: anticipation, use and meaning in contemporary youth culutre', *Sociological Review*, 50: 181–96

Carson, R. 1961. *The Sea Around Us*. New York: Oxford University Press

Carter, I. 2001. *Railways and Culture in Britain*. Manchester and New York: Manchester University Press

Cass, N., Shove, E., Urry, J. 2003. *Changing Infrastructures. Measuring Socio-Spatial Inclusion/Exclusion*. Report for DfT, Lancaster University: Dept of Sociology

—— 2005. 'Social exclusion, mobility and access', *Sociological* Review, 53: 539–55

Castells, M. 1996. *The Rise of the Network Society*. Oxford: Blackwell

—— 1997. *Power of Identity*. Oxford: Blackwell

—— 2001. *The Internet Galaxy*. Oxford University Press

—— 2004. 'Informationalism, networks, and the network society: a theoretical blueprint', in M.Castells (ed.) *The Network Society*. Cheltenham: Edward Elgar

Casti, J. 1994. *Complexification*. London: Abacus

296 References

Caves, R. 2002. *The Role of Aviation in the UK Socio-Economy*. University of Loughborough: Dept of Civil and Building Engineering

Cerny, P. 1990. *The Changing Architecture of Politics*. London: Sage

Cervero, R. 2001. 'Meeting mobility changes in an increasingly mobile world: an American perspective', Paris: Urban Mobilities Seminar, l'institut pour la ville en mouvement, June

Chamberlain, M. 1995. 'Family narratives and migration dynamics', *Immigrants and Minorities*, 14: 153–69.

Chatterton, P., Hollands, R. 2003. *Urban Nightscapes*. London: Routledge

Chayko, M. 2002. *Connecting. How we form social bonds and communities in the internet age*. New York: State University of New York Press

Chesters, G., Welsh, I. 2005. 'Complexity and social movement(s): process and emergence in planetary action systems, *Theory, Culture and Society*, 22: 187–211

Church, A., Frost, M., Sullivan, K. 2000. 'Transport and social exclusion in London', *Transport Policy*, 7: 195–205

Clark, T. J. 1984. *The Painting of Modern Life. Paris in the Art of Manet and his Followers*. London: Thames and Hudson

Clifford, J. 1997. *Routes: Travel and Translation in the Late Twentieth Century*. Cambridge, Mass: Harvard University Press

Clift, S., Carter, S. (eds) 1999. *Tourism and Sex. Culture, Commerce and Coercion*. London and New York: Pinter

Cloke, P., Milbourne, P., Widdowfield, R. 2003. 'The complex mobilities of homeless people in rural England', *Geoforum*, 34: 21–35

Cohen, R. 1997. *Global Diasporas*. London: UCL Press

—— 2004. 'The free movement of money and people: old arguments, new dangers', paper given to the ESRC/SSRC Colloquium on Money and Migration, Oxford, March

Coleman, S., Crang, M. (eds) 2002. *Tourism Between Place and Performance*. Oxford: Berghahn Books

Coles, T., Timothy, D. (eds) 2004. *Tourism, Diasporas and Space*. London: Routledge

Collis, R. 2000. *The Survivor's Guide to Business Travel*. Dover: Herald International Tribune

Conradson, D., Latham, A. 2005. 'Transnational urbanism: attending to everyday practices and mobilities', *Journal of Ethnic and Migration Studies*, 31: 227–33

Corbin, A. 1986. *The Foul and the Fragrant*. Leamington Spa: Berg

Cornford, J., Pollock, N. 2001. 'Space, place and the Virtual University: the university campus as a "resourceful constraint"', paper given to the Association of American Geographers, February–March

Coveney, P., Highfield, R. 1990. *The Arrow of Time*. London: Flamingo

Cresswell, T. 2001. 'The production of mobilities', *New Formations*, 43: 11–25

—— 2002. 'Introduction: theorizing place', in Verstraete, G., Cresswell, T. (eds) *Mobilizing Place, Placing Mobility*. Amsterdam: Rodopi

—— 2006. *On the Move*. London: Routledge

Crouch, D., Lübbren N. (eds) 2003. *Visual Culture and Tourism.* Oxford: Berg

Cwerner, A. 2006. 'Vertical flight and urban mobilities: the promise and reality of helicopter travel', *Mobilities*, 1: 191–216

Dant, T. 2004. 'The driver-car', *Theory, Culture and Society*, 21: 61–80

Dant, T., Bowles, D. 2003. 'Dealing with dirt: servicing and repairing cars', *Sociological Research Online*, 8: Part 2 unpaged

Davidson, R., Cope, B. 2003. *Business Travel: Conferences, Incentive Travel, Exhibitions, Corporate Hospitality and Corporate Travel.* London: Prentice Hall

Davies, P. 2001. 'Before the Big Bang', *Prospect*, June: 56–9

Davis, M. 2000. *Magical Urbanism.* London: Verso

De Botton, A. 2002. *The Art of Travel.* New York: Pantheon Books

Degen, M. 2004. 'Barcelona's games: the Olympics, urban design, and global tourism', in Sheller, M., Urry, J. (eds) *Tourism Mobilities: Places to Play, Places in Play.* London and New York: Routledge

Delanda, M. 2002. *Intensive Science and Virtual Philosophy.* London: Continuum

Deleuze, G. 1995. 'Postscript on control societies', in G. Deleuze (ed.) *Negotiations, 1972–1990.* New York: Columbia University Press

Deleuze, G., Guattari, F. 1986. *Nomadology.* New York: Semiotext(e)

Demerath, L., Levinger, D. 2003. 'The social qualities of being on foot: a theoretical analysis of pedestrian activity, community, and culture', *City and Community*, 2: 217–37

Derrida, J. 1987. *Positions.* London: Athlone Press

—— 2001. *Cosmopolitanism and Forgiveness.* London: Routledge

DfT 2002. *The Future Development of Air Transport in the UK: North of England. A National Consultation.* London: DfT

Diken, B., Laustsen, C. 2005. *The Culture of Exception. Sociology Facing the Camp.* London: Routledge

Dillon, M. 2003. 'Virtual security: a life science of (dis)order', *Millennium*, 32: 531–58

Dodge, M., Kitchin, R. 2004. 'Flying through code/space: the real virtuality of air travel', *Environment and Planning A*, 36: 195–211

Doyle, J., Nathan, M. 2001. *Wherever Next. Work in a Mobile World.* London: The Industrial Society

DTLR 2001. *Focus on Personal Travel.* London: DTLR/Stationery Office

Du Gay, P., Hall, S., Janes, L., Mackay, H., Negus, K. 1997. *Doing Cultural Studies. The Story of the Sony Walkman.* London: Sage

Dubois, W. 1903. *On the Quest for Golden Fleece.* New York: Bantam

Duffy, R. 2004. 'Ecotourists on the beach', in *Tourism Mobilities: Places to Play, Places in Play.* Sheller, M., Urry, J. (eds), London and New York: Routledge

Durbin, S. 2006. 'Theorising women's networks in the knowledge economy', paper presented to the ESRC Seminar on Gendering the Knowledge Economy, Lancaster, March

298 References

Durkheim, E. 1915. *The Elementary Forms of the Religious Life*. London: George Allen and Unwin

—— [1895] 1964. *Rules of Sociological Method*. New York: Free Press

Durrschmidt, J. 1997. 'The delinking of locale and milieu: on the situatedness of extended milieux in a global environment', in J. Eade (ed.) *Living the Global City: Globalization as Local Process*. London: Routledge

Duval, T. 2004. 'Linking return visits and return migration among Commonwealth Eastern Caribbean migrants in Toronto', *Global Networks*, 4, 51–8.

Edensor, T. 1998. *Tourists at the Taj: Performance and meaning at a symbolic site*. London: Routledge

—— 2001. 'Walking in the countryside', in Macnaghten, P., Urry, J. (eds) *Bodies of Nature*. London: Sage

—— 2002. *National Identities in Popular Culture*. Oxford and New York: Berg

—— 2004. 'Automobility and national identity: representation, geography and driving practice', *Theory, Culture and Society*, 21: 101–20

Edholm, F. 1993. 'The view from below: Paris in the 1880s', in B. Bender (ed.) *Landscape: politics and perspectives*. Oxford: Berg

Edwards, B. 1997. *The Modern Station*. London: Spon

—— 1998. *Modern Terminal: New Approaches to Airport Architecture*. New York: E and FN Spon

Edwards, E. 1999. 'Photographs as objects of memory', in Kwint, M., Breward, C., Aynsley (eds) *Material Memories. Designs and Evocations*. Oxford: Berg

Elias, N. 1978. *The Civilizing Process. The History of Manners*. Oxford: Basil Blackwell

—— 1995. 'Technicization and civilization', *Theory, Culture and Society*, 12: 7–42

Ellegård, K., Vilhelmson, B. 2004. 'Home as a pocket of local order: Everyday activities and the friction of distance', *Geografiska Annaler, Series B*, 86 B: 281–96

Enevold, J. 2000. 'Men and women on the move', *European Journal of Cultural Studies*, 3: 403–20

Evans, P., Wurstler, T. 2000. *Blown to Bits. How the new economics of information transforms strategy*. Boston: Harvard Business School Press

Eyerman, R., Löfgren, O. 1995. 'Romancing the road: road movies and images of mobility', *Theory, Culture and Society*, 12: 53–79

Farmer, P. 1999. *Infections and Inequalities: The Modern Plagues*. Berkeley: University of California Press

Featherstone, M. 2004. 'Automobilities. An introduction', *Theory, Culture and Society*, 21: 1–24

Featherstone, M., Thrift, N., Urry, J. (eds) 2004. *Automobilities*, special double issue of *Theory, Culture and Society*, 21: 1–284

Fennel, G. 1997. 'Local lives – distant ties: researching communities under globalized conditions', in Eade, J. (ed.) *Living the Global City: Globalization as local process*, London: Routledge

Ferguson, H. 2004. *Protecting Children in Time*. Basingstoke: Palgrave

Fevre, R. 1982. *Problems of Unbelief in the Sixteenth Century*. Cambridge, Mass: Harvard University Press

Figueroa, M. 2005. 'Democracy, civil society and automobility: understanding battles against motorways', in Thomsen, T., Nielsen, L., Gudmundsson, H. (eds) *Social Perspectives on Mobility*. London: Ashgate

Finch, J., Mason, J. 1993. *Negotiating Family Responsibilities*. London: Routledge

Flink, J. 1988. *The Automobile Age*. Cambridge, Mass: MIT Press

Florida, R. 2002. *The Rise of the Creative Class*. New York: Basic Books

Flyvbjerg, B., Bruzelius, N., Rothengatter, W. 2003. *Megaprojects and Risk. An Anatomy of Ambition*. Cambridge: Cambridge University Press

Foresight 2006. *Intelligent Information Futures. Project Overview*. London: Dept for Trade and Industry

Forster, E. M. [1910] 1931. *Howard's End*. Harmondsworth: Penguin

—— [1908] 1955. *A Room with a View*. Harmondsworth: Penguin

Fortier, A-M. 2000. *Migrant Belongings: Memory, Space, Identity*. Oxford and New York: Berg

Fortunati, L. 2005. 'Is the body-to-body communication still the prototype?', *The Information Society*, 21: 53–61

Foucault, M. 1976. *The Birth of the Clinic*. London: Tavistock 1991. 'Governmentality', in Burchell, G., Gordon, C., Miller P. (eds) *The Foucault Effect. Studies in Governmentality*. London: Harvester Wheatsheaf

Fox, K. 2001. 'Evolution, alienation and gossip: The role of mobile telecommunications in the 21st century', Oxford: Social Issues Research Centre

Fox Keller, E. 2005. 'Revisiting "scale-free" networks', *BioEssays*, 27: 1060–68

Franklin, S., Lury, C., Stacey, J. 2000. *Global Nature, Global Culture*. London: Routledge

Franz, K. 2005. *Tinkering. Consumers Reinvent the Early Automobile*. Philadelphia: University of Pennsylvania Press

Freund, P. 1993. *The Ecology of the Automobile*. Montreal and New York: Black Rose Books

Frisby, D. 1994. 'The *flâneur* in social theory', in Tester, K. (ed.) *The Flâneur*. London: Routledge

Froud, J., Johal, S., Leaver, A., Williams, K. 2005. 'Different worlds of motoring: choice, constraint and risk in household consumption', *Sociological Review*, 53: 96–128

Fuller, G., Harley, R. 2005. *Aviopolis. A Book about Airports*. London: Black Dog Publishing

Fyfe, N. 1998. 'Introduction: reading the street', in Fyfe, N. (ed.) *Images of the Street*. London: Routledge

Gamst, F. 1993. '"On time" and the railroader – temporal dimensions of work', in Helmers, S. (ed.) *Ethnologie der Arbeitswelt*. Bonn: Holos Verlag

Gans, H. 1962. *The Urban Villagers: Group and Class in the Life of Italian-Americans.* New York: Free Press of Glencoe

Garland, A. 1997. *The Beach.* Harmondsworth: Penguin

Gaskell, E. 1998. *North and South.* New York: Oxford University Press

Gault, R. 1995. 'In and out of time', *Environmental Values*, 4: 149–66

Geffen, C., Dooley, J., Kim, S. 2003. 'Global climate change and the tranportation sector: an update on issues and mitigation options', paper presented to the 9th Diesel Engine Emission Reduction Conference, USA

Gergen, K. 2002. 'The challenge of absent presence', in Katz, J., Aakhus, M. (eds) *Perpetual Contact: Mobile Communication, Private Talk, Public Performance.* Cambridge: Cambridge University Press

Geser, H. 2004. *Towards a Sociological Theory of the Mobile Phone*, Zurich: University of Zurich http://socio.ch/mobile/t_geser1.htm (accessed 10.3.06)

Gibson, J. J. 1986. *The Ecological Approach to Visual Perception.* Boston: Houghton Mifflin

Giddens, A. 1991. *Modernity and Self-Identity.* Cambridge: Polity

—— 1994. 'Living in a post-traditional society', in Beck, B., Giddens, A., Lash, S. (eds) *Reflexive Modernization: politics, tradition and aesthetics in the modern social order.* Cambridge: Polity

Gillespie, A., Richardson, R. 2004. 'Teleworking and the city: myths of workplace transcendence and travel reduction', in Graham, S. (ed.) *The Cybercities Reader*, London: Routledge

Gilroy, P. 1993. *The Black Atlantic: Modernity and Double Consciousness.* London and New York: Verso

—— 2000. 'Driving while black', in Miller, D. (ed.) *Car Cultures.* Oxford: Berg

Gladwell, M. 2000. *Tipping Points. How Little Things can make a Big Difference.* Boston: Little, Brown and Company

Gleick, J. 1999. *Faster. The Acceleration of Just About Everything.* London: Little, Brown and Company

Glennie, P., Thrift, N. 1996. 'Reworking E. P. Thompson's "Time, Work-Discipline and Industrial Capitalism"', *Time and Society*, 5: 275–99

Goffman, E. 1963. *Behaviour in Public Places.* New York: Free Press

—— 1971a. *The Presentation of Self in Everyday Life.* Harmondsworth: Penguin.

—— 1971b. *Relations in Public.* Harmondsworth: Penguin

—— 1972. *Interaction Ritual.* Harmondsworth: Penguin

Golaszewski, R. 2003. 'Network industries in collision: aviation infrastructure capacity, financing and the exposure of traffic declines'. *Journal of Air Transport Management*, 9: 57–65

Goldthorpe, J. H. 1980. *Social Mobility and Class Structure in Modern Britain.* Oxford: Clarendon Press

Gordon, C. 1991. 'Governmental rationality: an introduction', in Burchell, G., Gordon, C., Miller, P. (eds) *The Foucault Effect. Studies in Governmentality.* London: Harvester Wheatsheaf

Gordon, D., Adelman, L., Ashworth, K., Bradshaw, J., Levitas, R., Middleton, S., Pantazis, C., Patsios, D., Payne, S., Townsend, P., Williams, J. 2000. *Poverty and Social Exclusion in Britain*, York: Joseph Rowntree Foundation, York Publishing Services

Gottdiener, M. 2001. *Life in the Air*. Oxford: Rowman and Littlefield

Goulborne, H. 1999 'The transnational character of Caribbean kinship in Britain', in *Changing Britain: Families and Households in the 1990s*, Oxford: Oxford University Press

Grabher, G. 2004. 'Architectures of project-based learning: creating and sedimenting knowledge of project ecologies, *Organizational Studies*, 25: 1491–514

Graham, S. (ed.) 2002. *The Cybercities Reader*. London: Routledge

—— 2004. 'Constructing premium network spaces: reflections on infrastructure networks and contemporary urban development', in Hanley, R. (ed.) *Moving People, Goods, and Information in the Twentieth Century*, London: Routledge

Graham, S., Marvin, S. 2001. *Splintering Urbanism: Network Infrastructures, Technological Mobilities and the Urban Condition*. London: Routledge

Granovetter, M. 1983. 'The strength of weak ties: a network theory revisited', *Sociological Theory*, 1: 203–33

Graves-Brown, P. 1997. 'From highway to superhighway: the sustainability, symbolism and situated practices of car culture', *Social Analysis*, 41: 64–75

Gray, D., Shaw, J., Farrington, J. 2006. 'Community transport, social capital and social exclusion in rural areas', *Area*, 38: 89–98

Green, N. 1990. *The Spectacle of Nature*. Manchester: Manchester University Press

Gregory, D. 1994. *Geographical Imaginations*. Oxford: Basil Blackwell

—— 1999. 'Scripting Egypt: Orientalism and the cultures of travel', in Duncan, J., Gregory, D. (eds) *Writes of Passage*. London: Routledge

Gregory, D., Urry, J. (eds) 1985. *Social Relations and Spatial Structures*. London: Macmillan

Gustafson, P. 2001. 'Retirement migration and transnational lifestyles', *Ageing and Society*, 21: 371–94

Hacking, I. 1998. *Mad Travelers*. Charlottesville and London: University Press of Virginia

Hajer, M., Reijndorp, A. 2002. *In Search of the New Public Domain*. Rotterdam: NAI

Halgreen, T. 2004. 'Tourists in the concrete desert', in Sheller, M., Urry, J. (eds) *Tourism Mobilities: Places to Play, Places in Play*, London and New York: Routledge

Hall, S. 2002. *Haweswater*. London: Faber and Faber

Hamilton, K., Jenkins, L., Hodgson, F., Turner, J. 2005. *Promoting Gender Equality in Transport*. Manchester: Equal Opportunities Commission Working Paper Series no. 34

Hampton, K., Wellman, B. 2001. 'Long distance community in the network society: contact and support beyond Netville', *American Behavioral Scientist*, 45: 477–96

Hanley, R. (ed.) 2004. *Moving People, Goods, and Information*. London and New York: Routledge

Hannam, K. 2004. 'India and the ambivalences of diaspora tourism', in Coles, T., Timothy, D. (eds) *Tourism, Diasporas and Space*. London: Routledge

Hannam, K., Sheller, M., Urry, J. 2006. 'Editorial: mobilities, immobilities and moorings', *Mobilities*, 1: 1–22

Hardt, M., Negri, A. 2000. *Empire*. Cambridge, Mass: Harvard University Press

Harris, P., Lewis, J., Adam, B. 2004. 'Time, Sustainable Transport and the Politics of Speed', *World Transport Policy and Practice* 10: 5–11

Harrison, A., Wheeler, P., Whitehead, C. (eds) 2004. *The Distributed Workplace. Sustainable Work Environments*. London: Spon Press

Harvey, D. 1989. *The Condition of Postmodernity*. Oxford: Blackwell

—— 1996. *Justice, Nature and the Geography of Difference*. Oxford: Blackwells

Harvey, P. 1996. *Hybrids of Modernity*. London: Routledge

Hawken, P., Lovins, A., Lovins, L. 2000. *Natural Capitalism*. London: Earthscan

Hawkins, R. 1986. 'A road not taken: sociology and the neglect of the automobile', *California Sociologist*, 9: 61–79

Hayles, N. K. 1999. *How We Became Posthuman*. Chicago: University of Chicago Press

Heidegger, M. 1962. *Being and Time*. Oxford: Blackwell

—— 1993. *Basic Writings* (ed. by D. Farrell Krell). London: Routledge

Heim, M. 1991. 'The erotic ontology of cyberspace', in Benedikt, M. (ed.) *Cyberspace*. Cambridge, Mass: MIT Press

Heinberg, R. 2005. *The Party's Over: Oil, War and the Fate of Industrial Society*. New York: Clearview Books

Hetherington, K. 1997. 'In place of geometry: the materiality of place', in Hetherington, K., Munro, R. (eds) *Ideas of Difference*. Oxford: Blackwell

Hewison, R. 1993. 'Field of dreams', *Sunday Times*, January 3rd

Hiller, H. H., Tara, M. F. 2004. 'New ties, old ties and lost ties: the use of the internet in diaspora', *New Media and Society*, 6: 731–52

Hine, J., Swan, D., Scott, J., Binnie, D., Sharp, J. 2000. 'Using technology to overcome the tyranny of space: information provision and wayfinding', *Urban Studies*, 37: 1757–70

Hirst, P., Thompson, G. 1999. *Globalisation in Question. Second Edition*. Cambridge: Polity

Hochschild, A. 1983. *The Managed Heart*. Berkeley: University of California Press

Hodgson, F. 2002. 'What's so good about walking anyway?', paper given to ESRC Mobile Network Series, Bristol

Holmes, M. 2004. 'An equal distance? Individualisation, gender and intimacy in distance relationships', *Sociological Review*, 52: 180–200

Horvath, R. 1974. 'Machine space', *The Geographical Review*, 64: 167–88

Hotopp, U. 2002. 'Teleworking in the UK', *Labour Market Trends*, June: 311–18

Høyer, K., Ness, P. 2001. 'Conference tourism: a problem for the environment, as well as for research', *Journal of Sustainable Tourism,* 9: 451–70

Hughes, T. 1983. *Networks of Power: electrification in Western society, 1880–1930.* Baltimore: John Hopkins University Press

Hutnyk, J. 1996. *The Rumour of Calcutta.* London: Zed

Hulme, M., Truch, A. 2005. 'The role of interspace in sustaining identity', in Glotz, P., Bertscht, S., Locke, C. (eds) *Thumb Culture. The Meaning of Mobile Phones for Society.* New Brunswick, USA: Transaction

Huntington, S. 1993. 'The clash of civilizations', *Foreign Affairs,* 76: 28–59

Hutchby, I. 2001. *Conversation and Technology.* Cambridge: Polity

Ihde, D. 1974. 'The experience of technology: human-machine relations', *Cultural Hermeneutics,* 2: 267–79

Information Commissioner, 2006. A *Report on the Surveillance Society.* London: The Surveillance Network

Ingold, T. 1993. 'The temporality of the landscape', *World Archaeology,* 25: 152–74

—— 2000. *The Perception the Environment: Essays on Livelihood, Dwelling and Skill.* London: Routledge

—— 2004. 'Culture on the ground', *Journal of Material Culture,* 9: 315–40

Ito, M., Okabe, D., Matsuda, M. (eds) 2005. *Personal, Portable, Pedestrian. Mobile Phones in Japanese Life.* Cambridge, Mass: MIT Press

Iyer, P. 2000. *The Global Soul.* London: Bloomsbury

—— undated. 'The nowhere man', *Prospect Observer Taster,* 6–8

Jack, I. 2001. *The Crash that Stopped Britain* London: Granta

Jacobs, J. 1961. *The Death and Life of Great American Cities.* New York: Vintage

Jain, J., Lyons, G. 2006. 'The gift of travel time', Bristol: Centre for Transport and Society, University of the West of England

Jain, S. 2002. 'Urban errands', *Journal of Consumer Culture,* 2: 385–404

Jarach, D. 2001. 'The evolution of airport management practices: towards a multi-point, multi-service, marketing driven firm', *Journal of Air Transport Management,* 7: 119–25

Jarvis, 1997. *Romantic Writing and Pedestrian Travel.* London: Macmillan

Jenkins, S., Osberg, L. 2003. 'Nobody to play with? The implications of leisure coordination', Discussion Paper 368, Berlin: German Institute for Economic Research

Jensen, O. 2006. ' "Facework", flow and the city: Simmel, Goffman, and mobility in the contemporary city', *Mobilities,* 1: 143–65

Jha, A. 2005. 'Robot car: streets ahead in cities of the future', the *Guardian,* December 29th

Jokinen, E., Veijola, S. 1997. 'The disoriented tourist: the figuration of the tourist in contemporary cultural critique', in Rojek, C., Urry, J. (eds) *Touring Cultures.* London: Routledge

Jones, K. 1997. *A Passionate Sisterhood: the Sisters, Wives and Daughters of the Lake Poets.* London: Constable

Jones, R., Oyung, R., Pace, L. 2002. 'Meeting virtually – face-to-face meetings may not be a requirement for virtual teams', *ITjournal, HP*: http://www.hp.com/execcomm/itjournal/second_qtr_02/article6b.html, (accessed 15.12.04)

Jones, S. 1995. 'Understanding community in the information age', in Jones, S. (ed.) *Cybersociety*. London: Sage

Jordon, B., Düvell, F. 2002. *Irregular Migration. The Dilemmas of Transnational Mobility*. Cheltenham: Edward Elgar

Joseph, M. 1999. *Nomadic Identities: The Performance of Citizenship*, Minneapolis and London: University of Minnesota Press

Junemo, M. 2004. 'Let's build a "palm island"! Playfulness in complex times', in Sheller, M., Urry, J. (eds) *Tourism Mobilities: Places to Play, Places in Play*. London and New York: Routledge

Kaplan, C. 2006. 'Mobility and war: the "cosmic view" of air power', *Environment and Planning A*, 38: 395–407

Katz, J., Aakhus, M. 2002a. 'Introduction: framing the issues', in Katz, J., Aakhus, M. (eds) *Perpetual Contact: Mobile Communication, Private Talk, Public Performance*, Cambridge: Cambridge University Press

—— (eds) 2002b. *Perpetual Contact*. Cambridge: Cambridge University Press

Kaufmann, V. 2000. 'Modal practices: from the rationales behind car and public transport use to coherent transport policies', *World Transport Policy and Practice*, 6: 8–17.

—— 2002. *Re-thinking Mobility. Contemporary Sociology*. Aldershot: Ashgate

Kaufmann, V., Manfred, M., Joye, D. 2004. 'Motility: mobility as social capital', *International Journal of Urban and Regional Research*, 28, 745–56

Kellerman, A. 2006. *Personal Mobilities*. London: Routledge

Kennedy, P. 2004. 'Making global society: friendship networks among transnational professionals in the building design industry', *Global Networks*, 4: 157–79

Kenworthy, J., Laube, F. 2002. 'Urban transport patterns in a global sample of cities and their linkages to transport infrastructure, land use economics and environment', *World Transport Policy and Practice*, 8: 5–19

Kenyon, S. 2006. 'Reshaping patterns of mobility and exclusion? The impact of virtual mobility upon accessibility, mobility and social exclusion', in Sheller, M., Urry, J. (eds) *Mobile Technologies of the City*. London: Routledge

Kenyon, S., Lyons, G., Rafferty, J. 2002. 'Transport and social exclusion: investigating the possibility of promoting inclusion through virtual mobility', *Journal of Transport Geography*, 10: 207–19

Kesselring, S. 2006a. 'Pioneering mobilities: new patterns of movement and motility in a mobile world', *Environment and Planning A*, 38: 269–79

—— 2006b. 'The social construction of global "airtime–spaces". International airports: global transfer points of the mobile risk industry', paper presented to the Air Time–Spaces Workshop, CeMoRe, Lancaster University, September

Kirn, W. 2001. *Up in the Air*. New York: Doubleday
Kirschenblatt-Gimblett, B. 1998. *Destination Culture: Tourism, Museums and Heritage*. Berkeley: University of Claifornia Press
Klinenberg, E. 2002. *Heatwave. A Social Autopsy of Disaster in Chicago*. Chicago: Chicago University Press
Knorr Cetina, K. 2003. 'How are global markets global? The architecture of a flow world', paper presented to the Economics at Large Conference, New York, November 14–15
—— 2005. 'The rise of a culture of life', *EMBO reports*, 6: S76–S80
Knorr Cetina, K., Bruegger, U. 2002. 'Global microstructures: the virtual societies of financial markets', *American Journal of Sociology*, 107: 905–50.
Kofman, E. 2004. 'Family-related migration: critical review of European studies', *Journal of Ethnic and Migration Studies*, 30: 243–63
Koshar, R. 2002. *Histories of Leisure*. Oxford: Berg
Krugman, P. 1996. *The Self-Organizing Economy*. Cambridge, Mass: Blackwell
Kuhn, A. 1995. *Family Secrets. Acts of Memory and Imagination*. London: Verso
Kuhn, T. 1970. *The Structure of Scientific Revolutions*. Chicago: University of Chicago Press
Kunstler, J. 1994. *The Geography of Nowhere: The Rise and Decline of America's Man-Made Landscape*. New York: Touchstone Books
Laing, R. D. 1962. 'Series and nexus in the family', *New Left Review*, 1: May–June: 7–14
Larsen, J. 2001. 'Tourism mobilities and the travel glance: experiences of being on the move', *Scandinavian Journal of Hospitality and Tourism*, 1: 80–98
—— 2004. '(Dis)Connecting tourism and photography, corporeal travel and imaginative travel', *Journeys*, 5: 20–42
—— 2005. 'Families seen photographing: the performativity of family photography in tourism', *Space and Culture*, 8: 416–34
Larsen, J., Axhausen, K., Urry, J. 2006. 'Geographies of social networks: meetings, travel and communications', *Mobilities*, 1: 261–83
Larsen, J., Urry, J., Axhausen, K. 2006. *Mobilities, Networks, Geographies*. Aldershot: Ashgate
Lasch, C. 1980. *The Culture of Narcissism*. London: Sphere
Lash, S. 2005. '*Lebenssoziologie*: Georg Simmel in the information age', *Theory, Culture and Society*, 22: 1–23
Lash, S., Urry, J. 1987. *The End of Organized Capitalism*. Cambridge: Polity
—— 1994. *Economies of Signs and Space*. London: Sage
Lash, S., Lury, C., Boden, B. 2006. *Global Cultural Industries. The Mediation of Things*. Cambridge: Polity
Laszlo, E. 2006. *The Chaos Point*. London: Piatkus Books
Lassen, C. 2006. 'Rethinking central concepts of work and travel in the "age of aeromobility"', *Environment and Planning A*, 38: 301–12

306 References

Latimer, J., Munro, R. 2006. 'Driving the social', in Böhm, S., Jones, C., Land, C., Paterson, M. (eds) 2006. *Against Automobility*. Oxford: Blackwell Sociological Review Monograph

Latour, B. 1987. *Science in Action: How to Follow Scientists and Engineers through Society*. Milton Keynes: Open University Press

—— 1993. *We Have Never Been Modern*, Hemel Hempstead: Harvester Wheatsheaf

—— 1996. *Aramis or the Love of Technology*. Cambridge, Mass: Harvard University Press

—— 1999. 'On recalling ANT', in Law, J., Hassard J. (eds) *Actor Network Theory and After*. Oxford: Blackwell/Sociological Review

—— 2004. *Politics of Nature*. Cambridge, Mass: Harvard University Press

Laurier, E. 2002. 'The region as a socio-technical accomplishment of mobile workers', in Brown, B., Green, N., Harper, R. (eds) *Wireless World*. London: Springer

—— 2004. 'Doing office work on the motorway', *Theory, Culture and Society*, 21: 261–77

Laurier, E., Buckner, K. 2004. 'Busy meeting grounds: the café, the scene and the business', paper presented to an International Specialist Meeting on ICT, Everyday Life and Urban Change, Utrecht

Laurier, E., Philo, C. 2001. *'Meet you at junction 17': a socio-technical and spatial study of the mobile office*. ESRC Award Final Report (at http://www.geog.gla.ac.uk)

Law, J. 1994. *Organizing Modernity*. Oxford: Basil Blackwell

—— 2006. 'Disaster in agriculture: or foot and mouth mobilities', *Environment and Planning A*, 38: 227–39

Law, J., Hassard, J. (eds) 1999. *Actor Network Theory and After*. Oxford: Blackwell/Sociological Review

Law, J., Hetherington, K. 1999. 'Materialities, spatialities, globalities', Dept of Sociology, Lnacaster University

Law, J., Mol, A. 2001. 'Situating technoscience: an inquiry into spatialities', *Environment and Planning D: Society and Space*, 19: 609–21

Law, J., Urry, J. 2004. 'Enacting the social', *Economy and Society*, 33: 390–410

Layard, R. 2005. *Happiness. Lessons from a New Science*. London: Allen Lane

Leadbetter, C. 1999. *Living on Thin Air*. London: Viking

Lean, G. 1994. 'New green army rises up against roads', *The Observer*, February 20

Lefebvre, H. 1991. *The Production of Space*. Oxford: Blackwell

Lennon, J., Foley, M. 2000. *Dark Tourism. The Attraction of Death and Disaster*. London: Continuum

Leonard, D., Swap, T. 1999. *When Sparks Fly*. Boston: Harvard Business School

Lethbridge, N. 2002. *Attitudes to Air Travel*. London: ONS

Lewis, N. 2001. 'The climbing body, nature and the experience of modernity', in Macnaghten, P., Urry, J. (eds) *Bodies of Nature*. London: Sage

Li, Y., Savage, M., Tampubolon, G., Warde, A., Tomlinson, M. 2002. 'Dynamics of social capital: trends and turnover in associational membership in England and Wales, 1972–1999', *Sociological Research Online*, 7: 1–22

Licoppe, C. 2004. '"Connected" presence: the emergence of a new repertoire for managing social relationships in a changing communication technoscape', *Environment and Planning D: Society and Space*, 22: 135–56

Light, A. 1991. *Forever England: Femininity, Literature and Conservatism Between the Wars*. London: Routledge

Linder, S. 1970. *The Harried Leisure Class*. New York: Columbia University Press

Ling, R. 2004. *The Mobile Connection*. Amsterdam: Elsevier

Ling, R., Yttri, B. 1999 'Nobody sits at home and waits for the telephone to ring: micro and hyper-cordination through the use of the mobile phone', Telenor Forskning of Utvikling, FoU Rapport, 30/99

—— 2002. 'Hyper-coordination via mobile phones in Norway', in Katz, J., Aakhus, M. (eds) *Perpetual Contact: Mobile Communication, Private Talk, Public Performance*. Cambridge: Cambridge University Press

Liniado, M. 1996. *Car Culture and Countryside Change*. Bristol: MSc dissertation, Geography Dept, Bristol University

Little, S. 2006. Twin Towers and Amoy Gardens: mobilities, risks and choices, in Sheller, M. J., Urry, J. (eds) *Mobile Technologies of the City*. London: Routledge

Liu, J., Daily, G., Ehrlich, P., Luck, G. 2003. 'Effects of household dynamics on resource consumption and biodiversity', *Nature*, 421 (Jan): 530–3

Lloyd, J. 2003. 'Dwelltime: airport technology, travel and consumption', *Space and Culture*, 6: 93–109

Lodge, D. 1983. *Small World*. Harmondsworth: Penguin

Löfgren, O. 1999. *On Holiday: A History of Vacationing*. Berkeley: University of California Press

Lovelock, J. 2006. *The Revenge of Gaia*. London: Allen Lane

Lowenthal, D. 1985. *The Past is a Foreign Country*. Cambridge: Cambridge University Press

Lübbren, N. 2001. *Rural Artists' Colonies in Europe 1870–1910*. Manchester: Manchester University Press

Luhmann, N. 1995. *Social Systems*. Stanford: Stanford University Press

Lury, C. 1997. 'The objects of travel', in Rojek, C., Urry, J. (eds) *Touring Cultures: Transformations of Travel and Theory*. London: Routledge

Lynch, M. 1993. *Scientific Practice and Ordinary Action*. Cambridge: Cambridge University Press

Lyons, G., Jain, J., Holley, D. 2007. 'The use of travel time by rail passengers', *Transportation Research A*, 41: 107–20

Lyons, G., Urry, J. 2005. 'Travel time use in the information age', *Transportation Research A*, 39: 257–76

Lyotard, J-F. 1984. *The Postmodern Condition*. Manchester: Manchester University Press

Ma, L., Cartier, C. (ed.) 2003. *The Chinese Diaspora: Space, Place, Mobility and Identity*. New York: Rowman and Littlefields

Macnaghten, P., Urry, J. 1998. *Contested Natures*. London: Sage

—— (eds) 2001. *Bodies of Natures*. London: Sage

Mahoney, J. 2000. 'Path dependence in historical sociology', *Theory and Society*, 29: 507–48

Maier, C. 1994. 'A surfeit of memory? Reflections of history, melancholy and denial', *History and Memory*, 5: 136–52

Majone, G. 1996. *Regulating Europe*. London: Routledge

Makimoto, T., Manners, D. 1997. *Digital Nomad*. Chichester: John Wiley

Mann, T. [1912] 1955. *Death in Venice*. Harmondsworth: Penguin

Marfleet, P. 2006. *Refugees in a Global Era*. Basingstoke: Palgrave Macmillan

Marinetti, F. T. 1909. *The Futurist Manifesto*, no. 4. Paris: Le Figaro

Marples, M. 1959. *Shanks's Pony. A Study of Walking*. London: J. M. Dent

Marsh, P., Collett, P. 1986. *Driving Passion*. London: Jonathan Cape

Marshall, T., Bottomore, T. 1992. *Citizenship and Social Class*. London: Pluto

Marx, K. [1967] 1965. *Capital*, vol. 1. London: Lawrence and Wishart

—— 1973. *Grundrisse*. Harmondsworth: Penguin

Marx, K., Engels, F. [1848] 1952. *The Manifesto of the Communist Party*. Moscow: Foreign Languages

Mason, J. 1999. 'Living away from relatives: kinship and geographical reasoning', in McRae, S. (ed.) *Changing Britain: Families and Households in the 1990s*, Oxford: Oxford University Press

—— 2004. 'Managing kinship over long distances: The significance of "the visit"', *Social Policy and Society*, 3: 421–9

Massey, D. 1994a. Power-geometry and a progressive sense of place, in Robertson, G., Mash, M., Tickner, L., Bird, J., Curtis, B., Putnam, T. (eds) *Travellers' Tales: Narratives of Home and Displacement*. London: Routledge

—— 1994b. *Space, Class and Gender*. Cambridge: Polity

Mauss, M. 1979. *Sociology and Psychology*. London: Routledge and Kegan Paul

May, J., Thrift, N. 2001. 'Introduction', in May, J., Thrift, N. (eds) *Timespace: Geographies of Temporality*. London: Routledge

Maznevski, M., Chudoba, K. 2000. 'Bridging space over time: global virtual team dynamics and effectiveness', *Organisation Science*, 11: 473–92

McCarthy, A. 2001. *Ambient Television*. Durham and London: Duke University Press

McCarthy, H., Miller, P., Skidmore, P. 2004. *Network Logic. Who Governs in an Interconnected World?* London: Demos

McCrone, D. 1998. *The Sociology of Nationalism*. London: Routledge

Meadows, M., Stradling, S. 2000. 'Are women better drivers than men? Tools for measuring driver behaviour', in Hartley, J., Branthwaite, A. (eds) *The Applied Psychologist*. Milton Keynes: Open University Press

Mennell, S. 1985. *All Manners of Food*. Oxford: Basil Blackwell

Meyrowitz, J. 1985. *No Sense of Place*. New York: Oxford University Press

Michael, M. 1996. *Constructing Identities*. London: Sage

—— 1998. 'Co(a)gency and the car: attributing agency in the case of the 'road rage', in Brenna, B., Law, J., Moser, I. (eds) *Machines, Agency and Desire*. Oslo: TMV Skriftserie

—— 2000. *Reconnecting Culture, Technology and Nature*, London: Routledge

—— 2001. 'These boots are made for walking. . . .: mundane technology, the body and human-environment relations', in Macnaghten, P., Urry, J. (eds) *Bodies of Nature*. London: Sage

Miller, D. 1998. *A Theory of Shopping*. Cambridge: Polity

—— (ed.) 2000a. *Car Cultures*. Oxford: Berg

—— 2000b. 'Driven societies', in Miller, D. (ed.) *Car Cultures*. Oxford: Berg

Miller, D., Slater, D. 2000. *The Internet*. Oxford: Berg

Miller, S. 2006. *Conversation. A History of a Declining Art*. New Haven: Yale University Press

Milton, K. 1993. 'Land or landscape: rural planning policy and the symbolic construction of the countryside', in Murray, M., Greer, J. (eds) *Rural Development in Ireland*. Aldershot: Avebury

Mina, E. 2002. *The Business Meetings Sourcebook: A Practical Guide to Better meetings and Shared Decision Making*. London: Amacom

Mische, A., White, H. 1998. 'Between conversation and situation: public switching across network domains', *Social Research*, 65: 695–724

Mishan, E. 1969. *The Costs of Economic Growth*. Harmondsworth: Penguin

Mitleton-Kelly, E. 2003. *Complex Systems and Evolutionary Perspectives of Organisations*. London: Elsevier

Mokhtarian, L., Salomon, I. 2001. 'How derived is the demand for travel? Some conceptual and measurement considerations', *Transportation Research A*, 35: 695–719

Molotch, H. 2003. *Where Stuff Comes From: How Toasters, Toilets, Cars, Computers, and Many Other Things Come To Be As They Are*. New York: Routledge

Molz, J. Germann, 2006. 'Watch us wander: mobile surveillance and the surveillance of mobility', *Environment and Planning A*, 38: 377–93

Morley, D. 2000. *Home Territories: Media, Mobility and Identity*. London: Routledge

Morris, J. 2004. *Locals and Experts: The New Conservation Paradigm in the MANU Biosphere Reserve, Peru and the Yorkshire Dales National Park, England*. Lancaster: Unpublished PhD thesis, Lancaster University

Morris, M. 1988. 'At Henry Parkes Motel', *Cultural Studies*, 2: 1–47

Morrison, S., Winston, C. 1995. *The Evolution of the Airline Industry*. Washington, D.C.: The Brookings Institution

Morse, M. 1998. *Virtualities: Television, Media Art and Cyberculture*. Indiana: Indiana University Press

Motavalli, J. 2000. *Forward Drive*. San Francisco: Sierra Club

Nader, R. 1965. *Unsafe at any Speed. The designed-in dangers of the American automobile.* New York: Grossman

Nandhakumar, J. 1999. 'Virtual teams and lost proximity: consequences of trust relationships', in Jackson, P. (ed.) *Virtual Working: Social and Organisational Dynamics.* London: Routledge

Neumayer, E. 2006. 'Unequal access to foreign spaces: how states use visa restrictions to regulate mobility in a globalized world', *Transactions of the Institute of British Geographers*, NS 31: 72–84

Newmann, M. 2002. 'Making the scene: the poetics and performances of displacement at the Grand Canyon', in Coleman, S., Crang, M. (eds) *Tourism. Between Place and Performance.* New York: Berghahn

Neyland, D. 2005. *Privacy, Surveillance and Public Trust.* London: Macmillan

Nicolis, G. 1995. *Introduction to Non-Linear Science.* Cambridge: Cambridge University Press.

North, D. 1990. *Institutions, Institutional Change and Economic Performance.* Cambridge: Cambridge University Press

Noble, G. 2004. *Bin Laden in the Suburbs: Criminalising the Arab Other.* Sydney: Sydney Institute of Criminology

Nowotny, H. 1994. *Time.* Cambridge: Polity

Nussbaum, M. 2006. *Frontiers of Justice.* Cambridge, Mass: The Belknap Press

Ó Riain, S. 2000. 'Net-working for a living. Irish software developers in the global market place', in Burawoy, M. (ed.) *Global Ethnography.* Berkeley: University of California Press

O'Connell, S. 1998. *The Car in British Society.* Manchester: Manchester University Press

O'Dell, T. 2004. 'Cultural kinesthesis: the energies and tensions of mobility', unpublished paper, Lund: Lund University, Sweden

O'Reilly, K. 2003. 'When is a tourist? The articulation of tourism and migration in Spain's Costa del Sol', *Tourist Studies,* 3: 301–17

Ohnmacht, T. 2005. 'Contrasting time–space paths', paper presented at the New Horizons Project, Social Networks and Future Mobilities, Lancaster, December

Oliver, M. 1996. *Understanding Disability. From Theory to Practice.* Basingstoke: Macmillan

Ong, A. 1999. *Flexible Citizenship: The Cultural Logics of Transnationality.* Durham, US: Duke University Press

Ong, A., Nonini, D. (eds) 1997. *Ungrounded Empires: The Cultural Politics of Modern Chinese Transnationalism.* New York: Routledge

Osborne, P. 2000. *Travelling Light. Photography, Travel and Visual Culture.* Manchester: Manchester University Press

Ousby, I. 1990. *The Englishman's England.* Cambridge: Cambridge University Press

Owen, W. 1987. *Transportation and World Development.* Baltimore and London: Johns Hopkins University Press

Palmer, R. 2000. *Cultures of Darkness*. New York: Monthly Review Press

Papastergiadis, N. 2000. *The Turbulence of Migration: Globalization, Deterritorialization and Hybridity*. Cambridge: Polity Press

Park, R. E. 1970 [1925]. 'The mind of the hobo: reflections upon the relation between mentality and locomotion' in Park, R., Burgess, E., McKenzie, R. (eds) *The City*. Chicago and London: University of Chicago Press

Parker, K. 2002. 'Making connections: travel, technology and global air travel networks', paper presented to Social Change in the 21st Century Conference, Queensland University of Technology, November

Pascoe, D. 2001. *Airspaces*. London: Reaktion

Pearce, L. 2000. 'Driving North/ driving South: reflections upon the spatial/ temporal co-ordinates of "home"', in Pearce, L. (ed.) *Devolving Identities: Feminist Readings in Home and Belonging*. Aldershot: Ashgate

Pemble, J. 1987. *The Mediterranean Passion*. Oxford: Clarendon

Pennycook, F., Barrington-Craggs, R., Smith, D. and Bullock, S. 2001. *Environmental Justice: Mapping transport and social exclusion in Bradford*. London: Friends of the Earth

Perkins, H., Thorns, D. 2001. 'Gazing or performing? – Reflections on Urry's tourist gaze in the context of contemporary experiences in the Antipodes', *International Sociology*, 16: 185–204

Perrow, C. 1999. *Normal Accidents*. Princeton: Princeton University Press

Peters, P. 2006. *Time, Innovation and Mobilities*. London: Routledge

Pinkney, T. 1991. *Raymond Williams*. Bridgend: Seren Books

Pirsig, R. 1974. *Zen and the Art of Motorcycle Maintenance*. London: Corgi

PIU 2002. *Geographic Mobility. A Discussion Paper* (by N. Donovan, T. Pilch, T. Rubenstein). Cabinet Office, London: Performance and Information Unit

Plant, S. (2000), *On the Mobile: The Effects of Mobile Telephones on Social and Individual Life*. http://www.motorola.com/mot/doc/0/234_MotDoc.pdf (accessed 7 March, 2005)

Platt, E. 2000. *Leadville*. London: Picador

Pooley, C., Turnbull, J. and Adams, M. 2005. *A Mobile Century?: Changes in Everyday Mobility in Britain in the Twentieth Century*. Aldershot: Ashgate

Pound, E. 1973. *Selected Prose, 1909–1965*. London: Faber

Pratt, M. 1992. *Imperial Eyes*. London: Routledge

Prigogine, I. 1997. *The End of Certainty*. New York: The Free Press

Putnam, R. 1993. *Making Democracy Work*. Princeton, N.J.: Princeton University Press

—— 2000. *Bowling Alone*. New York: Simon and Schuster

Raje, F. 2004. *Transport Demand management and Social Inclusion: The Need for Ethnic Perspectives*. Aldershot: Ashgate

Ray, L. 2002. 'Crossing borders? Sociology, globalization and immobility', *Sociological Research Online*, 7: 1–18

Reeves, R. 2002. 'Go to work in your pyjamas', the *Guardian*, June

Reich, R. 1991. *The Work of Nations. Preparing Ourselves for 21st Century Capitalism*. New York: Knopf

Relph, E. 1976. *Place and Placelessness*. London: Pion

Resnick, M. 1997. *Turtles, Termites and Traffic Jams*. Cambridge, Mass: MIT Press

Rheingold, L. 1994. *The Virtual Community*. London: Secker and Warburg

Rheingold, H. 2002. *Smart Mobs. The Next Social Revolution*. Cambridge, Mass: Basic Books

Richards, G., Wilson, J. (eds) 2004. *The Global Nomad: Backpacker Travel in Theory and Practice*. Clevedon: Channel View

Richards, J., Mackenzie, J. 1986. *The Railway Station*. Oxford: Oxford University Press

Richardson, T., Jensen, O. 2003. 'Linking discourse and space: towards a cultural sociology of space in analysing spatial policy documents', *Urban Studies*, 40: 7–22

Rifkin, J. 2000. *The Age of Access*. London: Penguin

—— 2002. *The Hydrogen Economy*. New York: Penguin Putnam

Riles, A. 2001. *The Network Inside Out*, Ann Arbor University of Michigan Press

Ring, J. 2000. *How the English Made the Alps*. London: John Murray

Ritzer, G. 1992. *The McDonaldization of Society*. London: Pine Forge

—— 1997. '"McDisneyization"' and "post-tourism": complementary perspectives on contemporary tourism', in Rojek, C., Urry, J. (eds) *Touring Cultures*. London: Routledge

Roche, M. 2000. *Mega-Events and Modernity*. London: Routledge

Rodaway, P. 1994. *Sensuous Geographies: Body, Sense and Place*. London: Routledge

Rojek, C. 1993. *Ways of Escape*. Harmondsworth: Macmillan

—— 1997. 'Indexing, dragging and the social construction of tourist sites', in Rojek, C. and Urry, J. (eds) *Touring Cultures*. London: Routledge

Rojek, C., Urry, J. (eds) 1997. *Touring Cultures*. London: Routledge

Romano, N., Nunamaker, J. 2001. 'Meeting analysis: finding from research and practice' *34th Hawaii International Conference on System Sciences*, Hawaii

Roos, P. J. 2001. 'Postmodernity and mobile communications', *http://www.valt.helsinki.fi.staff/jproos/mobelization.htm* (accessed April 1, 2005)

Root, A. 2000. 'Transport and communications', in Halsey, A., Webb, J. (eds) *Twentieth Century British Social Trends*. London: Macmillan

Rose, N. 1996. 'Refiguring the territory of government', *Economy and Society*, 25: 327–56

Royal Academy of Engineering 2005. *Transport 2050: The Route to Sustainable Wealth Creation*. London: Royal Academy of Engineering

Ryan, L. 2004. 'Family Matters: (e)migration, familial networks and Irish women in Britain', *Sociological Review*, 52: 351–364

Ryave, A., Schenkein, J. 1974. 'Notes on the art of walking', in Turner, R. (ed.) *Ethnomethodology*. Harmondsworth: Penguin

Rycroft, R., Kash, D. 1999. *The Complexity Challenge*. London: Pinter

Sachs, W. 1992. *For Love of the Automobile*. California: University of California Press

Sager, T. 2006. 'Freedom as mobility: implications of the distinction between actual and potential travelling', *Mobilities*, 1: 463–86

Samuel, R. 1994. *Theatres of Memory*. London: Verso

Sardar, Z. 1996. 'alt.civilizations.faq: cyberspace as the darker side of the west', in Sardar, Z., Ravetz, J. (eds) *Cyberfutures*. London: Pluto

Sarker, S., Sahay, S. 2004. 'Implications of space and time for distributed work: an interpretive study of US-Norwegian systems development teams', *European Journal of Informtion Systems*, 13: 3–20

Sassen, S. 2000. *Cities in a World Economy*. London: Pine Forge

—— 2002. 'Locating cities on global circuits', in Sassen, S. (ed.) *Global Networks, Linked Cities*. London: Routledge

Schafer, A., Victor, D. 2000. 'The future mobility of the world population', *Transportation Research A*, 34: 171–205

Scanlan, J. 2004. 'Trafficking', *Space and Culture*, 7: 386–95

Scannell, P. 1996. *Radio, Television and Modern Life*. Oxford: Blackwell

Scharff, V. 1991. *Taking the Wheel: Women and the Coming of the Motor Age*. New York: Free Press

Schivelbusch, W. 1986. *The Railway Journey. Trains and Travel in the Nineteenth Century*. Oxford: Blackwell

Schroeder, J. 2002. *Visual Consumption*. London: Routledge

Schultz, P. 2003. *1000 Places to See Before You Die*. New York: Workman Publishing

Schwartz, B. 2004. *The Paradox of Choice*. New York: HarperCollins

Schwartzman, H. 1989. *The Meeting*. New York and London: Plenum

Scott, J. 1997. *Corporate Business and Capitalist Classes*. Oxford: Oxford University Press

—— 2000. *Social Network Analysis. A Handbook*. London: Sage

Sen, A. 1999. *Development as Freedom*. Oxford: Oxford University Press

Sennett, R. 1977. *The Fall of Public Man*. London and Boston: Faber and Faber

—— 1994. *Flesh and Stone*. New York: Norton

—— 1998. *The Corrosion of Character*. New York: W. W. Norton and Co

Serres, M. 1995. *Angels. A Modern Myth*. Paris and New York: Flammarion

Setright, L. 2003. *Drive On! A Social History of the Motor Car*. London: Granta

SEU 2002. *Making the Connections: Transport and Social Exclusion* www. cabinet-office.gov.uk/seu/publications

Seufert, A., Krogh, A. von, Bach, A. 1999. 'Towards knowledge networking', *Journal of Knowledge Management*, 3: 180–90

Sheller, M. 2003. *Consuming the Caribbean*. London and New York: Routledge

—— 2004a. 'Automotive emotions: feeling the car', *Theory, Culture and Society*, 21: 221–42

314   **References**

—— 2004b. 'Demobilising and remobilising the caribbean', in Sheller, M., Urry, J. (eds) *Tourism Mobilities: Places to Play, Places in Play*. London and New York: Routledge

—— 2006. 'Mobility, freedom and public space', paper presented to the Mobilities in Transit Symposium, Trondheim, June

Sheller, M., Urry, J. 2000. 'The city and the car', *International Journal of Urban and Regional Research*, 24: 737–57

—— 2003. 'Mobile transformations of "public" and "private" life', *Theory, Culture and Society* 20: 107–25

—— (eds) 2004. *Tourism Mobilities: Places to Play, Places in Play*. London: Routledge

—— (eds) 2006a. *Mobile Technologies of the City*. London: Routledge

—— (eds) 2006b. 'The new mobilities paradigm', *Environment and Planning A*, 38: 207–26

Sherry, J., Salvador, T. 2002. 'Running and grimacing: the struggle for balance in mobile work', in Brown, B., Green, N., Harper, R. (eds) *Wireless World*. London: Springer

Shields, R. 1991. *Places on the Margin*. London: Routledge

—— 1997. 'Ethnography in the crowd: the body, sociality and globalization in Seoul', *Focaal*, 30/31: 23–8

Shilling, C. 2005. *The Body in Culture, Technology and Society*. London: Sage

Shove, E. 2002. *Rushing Around: Coordination, Mobility and Inequality*. Lancaster: Department of Sociology, Lancaster University, http://www.comp.lancs.ac.uk/sociology/papers/Shove-Rushing-Around.pdf(02/11), (accessed 18.11.04)

Shove, E., Pantzar, M. 2005. 'Consumers, producers and practices', *Journal of Consumer Culture*, 5: 43–64

Simmel, G. 1990. *The Philosophy of Money*. London: Routledge

—— 1997. *Simmel on Culture*. Frisby, D., Featherstone, M. (eds) London: Sage

Skeggs, B. 2004. *Class, Self, Culture*. London: Routledge

Sklair, L. 1995. *Sociology of the Global System*, 2nd edn. Hemel Hempstead: Harvester

Slater, D. 2001. 'Markets, materiality and the 'new economy', paper given to Geographies of New Economies Seminar, Birmingham, UK, October

Smart, C., Neale, B. 1999. *Family Fragments*. Cambridge: Polity

Smith, A. 1986. 'State-making and nation-building', in Hall, J. (ed.) *States in History*. Oxford: Blackwell

Solnit, R. 2000. *Wanderlust. A History of Walking*. New York: Penguin

Sontag, S. 1979. *On Photography*. Harmondsworth: Penguin

Southerton, D. 2001. 'Squeezing time: allocating practices, co-ordinating networks and scheduling society', *Time and Society*, 12: 5–25

Southerton, D., Shove, E., Warde, A. 2001. *Harried and Hurried: Time Shortage and Coordination of Everyday Life*. Manchester: CRIC Discussion Paper 47, University of Manchester

Soysal, Y. 1994. *Limits of Citizenship*. Chicago: University of Chicago Press

Spillman, L. 1997. *Nation and Commemoration*. Cambridge: Cambridge University Press

Spitulnik, D. 2002. 'Mobile machines and fluid audiences: rethinking reception through Zambian radio culture', in Ginsburg, F., Abu-Lughod, L., Larkin, B. (eds) *Media Worlds: Anthropology on New Terrains*. Berkeley and Los Angeles: University of California Press

Spring, U. 2006. 'The linear city: touring Vienna in the nineteenth century', in Sheller, M., Urry, J. (eds) *Mobile Technologies of the City*. London: Routledge

Standage, T. (2004), 'Virtual meetings – being there', *The Economist* 5/3. http://www.ivci.com/international_videoconferencing_news_051304.html, (accessed January 15, 2005)

Staubmann, H. 1997. 'Self-organization of the economy: a system-theoretical reconsideration of Georg Simmel's *Philosophy of Money*', in Eve, E., Horsfall, S., Lee, M. (eds) *Chaos, Complexity and Sociology*. London: Sage

Stephenson, M. 2006. 'Travel and the "freedom of movement": racialised encounters and experiences among ethnic minority tourists in the EU', *Mobilities*, 1: 285–306

Stern, N. 2006. *Stern Review. The Economics of Climate Change*. (http://www.hm-treasury.gov.uk/independent_reviews/stern_review_economics_climate_change/sternreview_index.cfm accessed 6.11.06)

Stradling, S., Meadows, L., Beatty, S. 2002. 'Behavioural research in road safety: tenth seminar' (accessed on January 4, 2002, DTLR web site)

Sudjic, D. 1999. 'Identity in the city', The Third Megacities Lecture, The Hague (http://www.megacities.nl/lecture_3/lecture.html, accessed 7.3.06)

Sum, N-L. 2004. The paradox of a tourist centre: Hong Kong as a site of play and a place of fear, in Sheller, M., Urry, J. (eds) *Tourism Mobilities: Places to Play, Places in Play*. London: Routledge

Surowiecki, J. 2004. *The Wisdom of Crowds*. New York: Little, Brown

Sutton, R. C. 2004. 'Celebrating ourselves: the family reunion rituals of African Caribbean transnational families', *Global Networks*, 4: 243–58

Switzer, T. 2002. 'Hungarian spas', in Anderson, S., Tabb, B. (eds) *Water, Leisure and Culture*. Oxford: Cowley

Symes, C. 1999. 'Chronicles of labour: A discourse analysis of diaries', *Time and Society*, 8: 357–80

Szerszynski, B. 1997. 'The varieties of ecological piety', *Worldviews: Environment, Culture, Religion*, 1: 37–55

Szerszynski, B., Urry, J. 2006. 'Visuality, mobility and the cosmopolitan: inhabiting the world from afar', *British Journal of Sociology*, 57: 113–32

Taylor, J. 1994. *A Dream of England*. Manchester: Manchester University Press

Tester, K. 1994a. 'Introduction', in Tester, K. (ed.) *The Flâneur*. London: Routledge

316 References

—— (ed.) 1994b. *The Flâneur.* London: Routledge

The Economist 2005. 'Change is in the air', *The Economist*, March 25

Thomas, C. 2002. *Academic Study into the Social Effects of UK Air Travel.* London: Freedom-to-Fly

Thomsen, T., Nielsen, L., Gudmundsson, H. (eds) 2005. *Social Perspectives on Mobility.* London: Ashgate

Thompson, J. 1995. *The Media and Modernity.* Cambridge: Polity

Thrift, N. 1990. 'The making of a capitalist time consciousness', in Hassard, J. (ed.) *The Sociology of Time.* London: Macmillan

—— 1996. *Spatial Formations.* London: Sage

—— 1999. 'The place of complexity', *Theory, Culture and Society*, 16: 31–70

—— 2000. 'Performing cultures in the new economy', *Annals of the Association of American Geographers*, 90: 674–92

—— 2001. 'Still life in nearly present time: the objects of nature', in Macnaghten, P., Urry, J. (eds) *Bodies of Nature.* London: Sage

—— 2004a. '*Driving* in the city', *Theory, Culture and Society*, 21: 41–59

—— 2004b. 'Movement-space: the changing domain of thinking resulting from the development of new kinds of spatial awareness', *Economy and Society*, 33: 582–604

—— 2004c. 'Remembering the technological unconscious', *Environment and Planning D*, 22: 175–90

—— 2004d. 'Intensities of feeling: towards a spatial politics of affect', *Geografiska Annaler Series B*, 86: 57–78

—— 2007. *Non-Representational Theories.* London: Routledge

Thrift, N., French, S. 2002. 'The automatic production of space', *Transactions of the Institute of British Geographers New Series*, 27: 309–35

Toiskallio, K. 2002. 'The impersonal *flâneur*: navigation styles of social agents in urban traffic', *Space and Culture*, 5: 169–84

Torpey, J. 2000. *The Invention of the Passport.* Cambridge: Cambridge University Press

Townsend, A. 2004. *Mobile Communications in the 21st Century City.* http://urban.blogs.com/research/Townsend-TheWirelessWorld-BookChapter.PDF (accessed 30.7.05)

Truch, A., Hulme, M. 2004. 'Exploring the implications for social identity of the new sociology of the mobile phone', paper given to The Global and the Local in Mobile Communication: Places, Images, People, and Connections Conference, Budapest, June 10–11

Tully, C. 2002. 'Youth in motion: communicative and mobile. A perspective from youth sociology', *Young*, 10: 19–43

Turkle, S. 1996. *Life on the Screen.* London: Weidenfeld and Nicolson

Tzanelli, R. 2004. 'Constructing the "cinematic tourist": the "sign industry" of the Lord of the Rings', *Tourist Studies*, 4: 21–42

UDHR 1948. *Universal Declaration of Human Rights.* New York: United Nations

UNDP 2004. *Human Development Report.* New York: UN

Urry, J. 2000. *Sociology Beyond Societies.* London: Routledge

—— 2002a. 'The global complexities of September 11th, *Theory, Culture and Society*, 19: 57–70

—— 2002b. 'Mobility and proximity', *Sociology*, 36: 255–74

—— 2002c. *The Tourist Gaze. Second Edition.* London: Sage

—— 2003a. *Global Complexity.* Cambridge: Polity

—— 2003b. 'Social networks, travel and talk', *British Journal of Sociology*, 54: 155–75

—— 2004a. 'Connections', *Environment and Planning D: Society and Space*, 22: 27–38

—— 2004b. 'Small worlds and the new "social physics"', *Global Networks*, 4: 109–30

—— 2004c. 'The "system" of automobility', *Theory, Culture and Society*, 21: 25–39

—— 2004d. 'Death in Venice', in Sheller, M., Urry, J. (eds) *Tourism Mobilities: Places to Play, Places in Play.* London: Routledge

—— 2005. *Complexity.* Special issue of *Theory, Culture and Society*, 22: 1–274

US Department of Transportation 1999. *Effective Global Transportation in the Twenty First Century: A Vision Document.* US Department of Transportation: 'One Dot' Working Group on Enabling Research

Van der Veer, P. 1995. *Nation and Migration: The Politics of Space in the South Asian Diaspora.* Philadelphia: University of Pennsylvania Press

Van Vree, W. 1999. *Meetings, Manners and Civilization.* London and New York: Leicester University Press

Van Wee, B., Rietveld, P., Meurs, H. 2006. 'Is average daily travel time expenditure constant? In search of explanations for an increase in average travel time', *Journal of Transport Geography*, 14: 109–22

Vaughan, A. 1997. *Railway Men, Politics and Money.* London: John Murray

Verstraete, G. 2002. Railroading American: Towards a material study of the nation', *Theory, Culture and Society*, 19: 145–59

—— 2004. 'Technological frontiers and the politics of mobility in the European Union', in Ahmed, S., Castaneda, C., Fortier, A-M., Sheller, M. (eds) *Uprootings/ Regroundings: Questions of Home and Migration.* New York and London: Berg

Verstraete, G., Cresswell, T. (eds) 2002. *Mobilizing Place, Placing Mobility.* Amsterdam: Rodopi

Vertovec, S. 2004. 'Cheap calls: the social glue of migrant transnationalism', *Global Networks*, 4: 219–24

Vidal, J. 2002. 'Stuttering start for the revolutionary car that some say will save the planet', the *Guardian*, October 17th

Vigar, G. 2002. *The Politics of Mobility.* London: Spon

Vilhelmson, B., Thulin, E. 2001. 'Is regular work at fixed places fading away? The development of ICT-based and travel-based modes of work in Sweden', *Environment and Planning A*, 33: 1015–29

Virilio, P. 1986. *Speed and Politics.* New York: Semiotext(e)

—— 1997. *The Open Sky.* London: Verso

Visconti, L. 1971. *Death in Venice.* Warner Bros Film

318 **References**

Walby, S. 1990. *Theorizing Patriarchy.* Oxford: Blackwell
—— 1997. *Gender Transformations.* London: Routledge
—— 2005. 'Measuring women's progress in a global era', *International Social Science Journal*, 184: 371–87
Walby, S. 2008. *Globalization and Inequalities.* London: Sage
Waldrop, M. 1994. *Complexity.* London: Penguin
Wallace, A. 1993. *Walking, Literature and English Culture.* Oxford: Clarendon Press
Wallerstein, I. 1996. *Open the Social Sciences. Report of the Gulbenkian Commission on the Restructuring of the Social Sciences.* Stanford: Stanford University Press
Walter, T. 1981. 'Family car', *Town and Country Planning*, 50: 56–8
Walters, W. 2006. 'Borders/control', *European Journal of Social Theory*, 9: 187–203
Warde, A., Martens, L. 2000. *Eating Out.* Cambridge: Cambridge University Press
Warhol, A. 1976. *The Philosophy of Andy Warhol. From A to B and Back Again.* New York: Harcourt
Watson, P. 2003. 'Targeting tourists, not terrorists: why airport security is a charade', http://english.pravda.ru/columnists/2003/01/08/41736.html (accessed October 30, 2006)
Watters, E. 2004. *Urban Tribes: Are Friends the New Family*, London: Bloomsbury
Watts, D. 1999. *Small Worlds.* Princeton: Princeton University Press
Watts, D. 2003. *Six Degrees. The Science of a Connected Age.* London: Heinemann
Watts, L. 2006. 'Travel times or "journeys with Ada"', paper presented to Stakeholders Workshop, Department for Transport, London http://www.transport.uwe.ac.uk/research/projects/travel-time-use/papers.htm (accessed 30.10.06)
Weber, K., Chon, K.S. 2003. *Convention Tourism: International Research and Industry Perspectives.* London: Haworth Press, Inc
Weber, M. 1948. *From Max Weber. Essays in Sociology.* London: Routledge and Kegan Paul
Wellman, B. 2001. 'Physical place and cyber place: the rise of networked individualism', *International Journal of Urban and Regional Research*, 25: 227–52
—— 2002. 'Little Boxes, glocalization, and networked individualism', in Tanabe, M., Van den Besselaar, P., Ishida, T. (eds) *Digital Cities II: Computational and Sociological Approaches.* Berlin: Springer
Wellman, B., Haythornthwaite, L. (eds) 2002. *Internet in Everyday Life.* London: Blackwell
Wellman, B., Hogan, B., Berg, K., Boase, J., Carrasco, J-A., Côté, R., Kayahara, J., Kennedy, T., Tran, P. 2005. 'Connected lives: the project', in Purcell, P. (ed.) *Networked Neighourhoods.* Berlin: Springer
Wenger, G. C. 1997. 'Nurturing networks', *Demos Collection*, 12: 28–9

Wenger, W. 1998. *Communities of Practice*. Cambridge: Cambridge University Press

Werbner, P. 1999. 'Global pathways: working class cosmopolitans and the creation of transnational ethnic worlds', *Social Anthropology*, 7: 17–35

West, N. 2000. *Kodak and the Lens of Nostalgia*. Charlottesville: University of Virginia Press

Weston, K. 1991. *Families We Choose: Lesbians, Gays, Kinship*. New York: Columbia University Press

Whatmore, S. 2002. *Hybrid Geographies: Natures, Cultures, Spaces*. London: Sage

Whitelegg, J. 1997. *Critical Mass*. London: Pluto

Whitelegg, J., Haq, G. (eds) 2003. *The Earthscan Reader in World Transport Policy and Practice*. Earthscan, London..

Whitelegg, J., Hultén, S., Flink, T. (eds) 1993. *High Speed Trains*. Hawes, Yorkshire: Leading Edge

WHO 2004. *World Report on Road Traffic Injury Prevention*. Geneva: World Health Organization Publications

Whyte, W. 1988. *City*. New York: Doubleday

Williams, A. 2006. 'Enfolded mobilities: international migration and mobility in the knowledge economy', paper given to Space and Mobility in the Knowledge-based Economy Workshop, Lancaster, September

Williams, R. 1972. 'Ideas of nature', in Benthall, J. (ed.) *Ecology. The Shaping Enquiry*. London: Longman

—— 1988. *Border Country*. London: Hogarth Press

—— 1990. *Notes on the Underground. An Essay on Technology, Society and the Imagination*. Cambridge, Mass: MIT Press

Wilson, A. 1992. *Culture of Nature*. Oxford: Blackwell

Wilson, E. 1995. 'The invisible *flâneur*', in Watson, S., Gibson, K. (eds) *Postmodern Cities and Spaces*. Oxford and Cambridge: Blackwell

Wittel, A. 2001. 'Towards a network sociality', *Theory, Culture and Society*, 18: 31–50

Wolff, J. 1993. 'On the road again: metaphors of travel in cultural criticism', *Cultural Studies*, 7: 224–39

Wong, Y. S. 2006. 'When there are no pagodas on Pagoda Street: language, mapping and navigating ambiguities in colonial Singapore', *Environment and Planning*, 38: 325–40

Wood, D., Graham, S. 2006. 'Permeable boundaries in the software-sorted society: surveillance and the differentiation of mobility', in Sheller M., Urry, J. (eds) *Mobile Technologies of the City*. London: Routledge

Wordsworth, W. 1876. *The Prose Works*, vol. 2. London: E. Moxon

—— [1844] 1984. *The Illustrated Wordsworth's Guide to the Lakes*. London: Book Club Associates

World Travel and Tourism Council 2006. *Media and Resources Centre* http://www.wttc.org/2004tsa/frameset2a.htm (accessed 7.3.06)

320 **References**

Young, M., Willmott, P. 1962. *Family and Kinship in East London.* Harmondsworth: Penguin

Zerubavel, E. 1982. 'The standardisation of time: a socio-historical perspective', *American Journal of Sociology*, 88: 1–23

Zimmerman, M. 1990. *Heidegger's Confrontation with Modernity.* Bloomington: Indiana University Press

Zohar, D., Marshall, I. 1994. *The Quantum Society.* New York: William Morrow

Zukin, S. 2003. 'Home-shopping in the global marketplace', paper presented to 'Les sens du mouvement' colloquium, Cerisy-la-Salle, Normandy, June

Index